Richard Strauss's Orchestral Music
and the German
Intellectual Tradition

Richard Strauss's Orchestral Music and the German Intellectual Tradition

THE PHILOSOPHICAL ROOTS
OF MUSICAL MODERNISM

Charles Youmans

Indiana University Press

Bloomington and Indianapolis

This book is a publication of

Indiana University Press
601 North Morton Street
Bloomington, IN 47404-3797 USA

http://iupress.indiana.edu

Telephone orders 800-842-6796
Fax orders 812-855-7931
Orders by e-mail iuporder@indiana.edu

The paper used in this publication meets
the minimum requirements of American
National Standard for Information
Sciences—Permanence of Paper for
Printed Library Materials, ANSI Z39.48-1984.

Manufactured in the United States of America

Library of Congress Cataloging-in-
Publication Data

Youmans, Charles Dowell, date
Richard Strauss's orchestral music and the
German intellectual tradition :
the philosophical roots of musical modernism / Charles Youmans.
    p. cm.
Includes bibliographical references (p.) and index.
ISBN 0-253-34573-1 (cloth : alk. paper)
1. Strauss, Richard, 1864–1949.   Orchestra music.
2. Orchestral music—History and criticism.
3. Music—Germany—20th century—Philosophy
and aesthetics.   I. Title.
ML410.S93Y68 2005
784.2'184'092—dc22

                                    2004023224

1   2   3   4   5   10   09   08   07   06   05

56617228

For Frances and Hannah

Contents

Acknowledgments

This book could not have been written without the generous assistance of Richard and Gabriele Strauss, who kindly made available the resources of the Richard-Strauss-Archiv and granted permission to quote from these materials. They have my deepest gratitude. Christian Wolf, director of the splendid Richard-Strauss-Institut, and his associate Jürgen May also provided invaluable support during my archival work. As always, Bryan Gilliam has been my principal scholarly influence, through his deep understanding of the composer and his insightful responses to my work. At an early stage, I gained immeasurably from conversations with Reinhold and Roswitha Schlötterer, whose grasp of the humanistic tradition continues to inspire me. Further thanks go to the friendly and efficient staff of the Bayerische Staatsbibliothek, especially Sabine Kurth, and to Günter Brosche of the Österreichische Nationalbibliothek. Over the years I have benefited greatly from contact with other scholars working on Strauss, among them Walter Frisch, James Hepokoski, Timothy L. Jackson, Morten Kristiansen, Suzanne Lodato, Graham Phipps, Mark-Daniel Schmid, R. Larry Todd, and Scott Warfield. My colleagues at Penn State—especially Michael Broyles, Maureen Carr, Taylor Greer, Jay Hook, Eric McKee, and Marica Tacconi—comprise a scholarly community as stimulating as it is friendly. Richard Green, Director of the Penn State School of Music, has been a constant source of encouragement. My research and writing have been funded by grants from two institutions at Penn State: the College of Arts and Architecture and the Institute for the Arts and Humanities; I would particularly like to acknowledge the assistance of Edward V. Williams and Laura Knoppers. For permission to quote from previously published work I would like to thank the editors of *Nineteenth-Century Music*, *The Musical Quarterly*, and the *Journal of Musicology*. At Indiana University Press, Gayle Sherwood has been a model of efficiency and sound editorial judgment. My thanks go also to Jane Lyle, Linda Oblack, Betsy Garman, and Jimmée Greco for their able assistance with the publication process, and to Jason Fick for preparing the musical examples. Finally, heartfelt appreciation and a well-earned *Glückwunsch* to Nancy, Frances, and Hannah, my beautiful family, who survived a few German adventures and more than a few informal lectures on Strauss, all the while managing to keep me healthy and happy.

Richard Strauss's Orchestral Music

and the German Intellectual Tradition

Prologue

Intellectual History and Artistic Production
The Case of Richard Strauss

Music's Philosophical Status in Late-Nineteenth-Century Germany

Arnold Schoenberg, the dominant figure of Austro-German musical modernism, once declared that "*the only revolutionary* in our time was Strauss."[1] To the extent that this remark had anything to do with Strauss—its main purpose was of course to shape perception of Schoenberg himself—it was obviously not meant as a compliment.[2] Yet that rhetorical consideration does not mean that the idea had no basis in fact. We know that listeners around 1900 counted Strauss's music, in particular his orchestral music, among the most important documents of the rising movement known as "die Moderne."[3] Carl Dahlhaus has sketched the outlines of "early modernism," a first wave of post-romanticism that began around 1890, peaked with the mature orchestral works of Strauss and Mahler, and then subsided even as Schoenberg made the atonal experiments that gave rise to his New Music.[4] The staggering impact of that more radical phase of modernism obliterated, for scholars and for listeners, the first period's avant-garde edge. A reinvestigation is in order, then, for as Schoenberg's provocative comment implies, neither repertory can be properly understood until we grasp what defined a "revolutionary" in that cultural context.

One reason that the specific character of early modernism became

increasingly difficult to perceive during the twentieth century is that beginning with Schoenberg, modernism was ever more closely associated
with musical technique as opposed to aesthetics. From this standpoint—
which equated the new with increased dissonance, avoidance of a tonal
center, unconventional melodic and rhythmic structures, and so on—
Strauss stood as an important precursor, at least until *Elektra* (1908) gave
way to *Der Rosenkavalier* (1910). But those features were never central to
Strauss's own brand of modernism, and they had nothing to do with
Schoenberg's judgment of him as a musical firebrand. Strauss's revolution
targeted something different: a widespread and generally accepted
nineteenth-century aesthetic that survived the otherwise jarring transition from the era of Wagner and Brahms to that of Schoenberg. This
defining musical preconception, so all-pervading that Strauss represented
his culture's only significant dissenting voice, was the conviction that
music had unique transcendental powers.[5]

There is no question that critics in the 1890s and early 1900s recognized Strauss as a fundamentally different kind of composer than his
immediate forebears and indeed than his contemporaries. Likewise,
Strauss clearly made the most of that reception, cultivating an image of
notoriety and consciously using scandal to publicize his compositions.
But the substance of the matter—the reasons he was considered different
and the ways in which he tried to be different—were not strictly musical.
To an informed listener it was perfectly obvious that the harmonic, melodic, and orchestrational techniques used by Strauss in his tone poems
came mostly from Wagner, and the formal procedures from Liszt, Wagner, and Beethoven.[6] Certainly the works had a personal stamp, but if
we want to know how listeners could hear in Strauss an "end of music"
as they knew it, we must look outside the purely musical.[7] Only after
Strauss was well established as a modernist did his music begin to show
features anticipating Schoenberg's expressionist idiom—the very features
that now earn him a place in books on twentieth-century music.[8]

The basic novelty embodied by Strauss consisted of a new way of
relating music to extramusical realms of experience. Although he composed for an audience that prized orchestral music as a metaphysical art,
a unique avenue to the ideal, Strauss reveled in superficiality, choosing,
in Adorno's words, "to abandon himself to unmitigated exteriority."[9]
Rather than using his music to preach redemption or apotheosis, Strauss
brought it to bear on the everyday, the physical, the world of experience.
For critics such as Ernst Otto Nodnagel, this new aesthetic orientation
represented a terrible danger; the greatest living talent had turned his

back on spirituality and now sought to bring about the "dissolution" (*Auflösung*) of the art.[10] Mahler, to Nodnagel a musician in the true sense, remained faithful to the aesthetic and spiritual aims of Wagner. But Strauss pushed music into the world of "fashion" (*Mode*), a world thoroughly disconnected from the higher planes of existence. Adorno made the same point in his lesser-known 1924 essay on Strauss, writing that "in Strauss the reality of forms has vanished for good; it continues to exist only as appearance."[11] From a philosophical standpoint, of course, "reality" is synonymous with metaphysics.

This desacralization of music (so described by James Hepokoski) was emphatically not a part of Schoenberg's modernist agenda.[12] Although he did not couch his argument in specifically Wagnerian terms, Schoenberg too sought to protect the status quo. His explicit claim to have personally gathered together and extended the technical traditions of the leading nineteenth-century composers is well known.[13] Less understood is his corresponding position in the field of aesthetics. With his turn away from programmatic music to "absolute" genres (chamber symphony, string quartet, *Klavierstück*), Schoenberg embraced the cause of musical autonomy, a view that was rapidly becoming the dominant force in musical aesthetics precisely because it could support metaphysical expectations that seemed hopelessly outdated in the context of programmatic music or opera. If the technical practices of Brahms and Wagner found a synthesis in the music of Schoenberg and his followers, so too did a particular set of aesthetic pretensions, explicit or implicit, that in the years around 1900 were so pervasive that no composer save one would think of challenging them.

This situation too was described by Carl Dahlhaus, who pointed out that composers representing an apparent variety of aesthetic viewpoints in the late nineteenth century actually shared a fundamentally Schopenhauerian conception of music.[14] A range of opinions did exist as to how music might realize its philosophical promise, but the fact of that promise and the elementary features of its character were beyond debate. Dahlhaus would have done well to emphasize that demonstrating the currency of this view does not require razor-sharp historical acuity or the perspective of intervening decades, but simply a fair reading of the principal aesthetic texts of the period. It was a commonplace, but to this day it is not understood as such, which explains the continued belief of many modern scholars that the period was defined by a conflict between the advocates of programmatic music and those of absolute music. Anette Unger, for example, rightly highlights the formalism/programmaticism debate as a context for interpreting Strauss's music but ignores the crucial fact that underneath it all, the two sides were fighting for the same prize: credibility on the metaphysical level of musical signification.[15]

That said, I would like to introduce this book's central argument by considering in some detail an early source that lays out these ideas as a lived reality rather than a detached historical discovery. The underlying homogeneity of late-nineteenth-century musical aesthetics was described thoroughly, systematically, and noncontroversially at least as early as 1929, in Felix M. Gatz's *Musik-Ästhetik in ihren Hauptrichtungen* (Musical Aesthetics in Its Principal Currents).[16] Not the least noteworthy feature of this book is that it is a collection of source readings, a Strunkian compendium bringing together excerpts ranging chronologically from Kant to Pfitzner and representing every prominent approach to the subject. In its overt avoidance of a polemical or tendentious tone it is a model textbook. Likewise, the number of selections is not strongly weighted in one direction or the other—toward or against "formalism," for example—but strikes a balance that gives a strong overall impression of carefully planned diversity. The excerpts are presented not in chronological order, however, but within a scheme of categories situated entirely and unequivocally beyond the debate concerning programmatic and absolute music. Gatz does not ignore that debate, but he consciously deemphasizes it in order to sharpen our sense of an overall unity at the end of the century. Thus in the final section Hanslick and Zimmermann stand side by side with Wagner and the early Nietzsche, under the heading of "Music as an Autonomous Art." Also included in that section, as one of the latest excerpts in the collection, is Schoenberg's 1914 essay "The Relationship to the Text."

Gatz's substantial introduction offers a wealth of insight into the assumptions of musical aesthetics during this period.[17] His approach to the field is Hegelian, tracing an intellectual-historical progression toward increasingly precise and compelling (in his view) accounts of the nature of music.[18] The fundamental problem confronted by nineteenth-century aesthetic thought in this reading was the form/content dichotomy. Thus the two principal categories in which Gatz organized his sources were the "heteronomy-aesthetic" (*Heteronomieästhetik*) and the "autonomy-aesthetic" (*Autonomieästhetik*), the former a relic of the tradition of mimesis and tending toward a "subordination" (*Unterordnung*) of the art, the latter rejecting any point of view that did not treat music as an end in itself.[19] This account did not lead to anything recognizable as "formalism" in the conventional sense, however, but to an ever-increasing metaphysical prestige for the art. Historical progress had steadily narrowed the focus of musical aesthetics onto the art itself, as the philosophical substance that once belonged to an extramusical "content" was transplanted or sublimated into music.

Gatz supported his claims historically, by demonstrating that virtually all nineteenth-century writers on aesthetics had reached a common conclusion by the end of the century. That conclusion had not emerged suddenly, as an epiphany marking the instantaneous origin of the autonomy-aesthetic, but through a gradual process, the roots of which were already present in the "content-aesthetic" (*Inhaltsästhetik*), the most primitive form of the heteronomous perspective. Wagner's analysis of Beethoven's Ninth, for example, belonged in Gatz's view to the content-aesthetic by virtue of its basic acceptance of the form/content dichotomy (implicit in the claim that Beethoven's music needed a text in order to clarify the content of the work). But Wagner's rejection of the possibility that music could communicate rather than merely intensify an extramusical content already pointed beyond the content-aesthetic, according to Gatz; it suggested that music's own meaning lay outside of a precisely defined content. Yet at the same time, Gatz identified as a content-aesthetic the species of formalism that claimed music had no content, because it too used the dichotomy to frame the argument. Its interest for the historian lay in its demonstration of the need for a more advanced theory explaining the nature of music without reference to that dichotomy.[20]

The first aesthetic to answer that need was the "incarnation-aesthetic" (*Incarnationsästhetik*), which Gatz classified under the rubric of heteronomy but identified as a more advanced conception than any content-aesthetic. Here the terms "form" and "content" gave way to another pair, "reality" (*Wesen*) and "appearance" (*Erscheinung*), in which the explicit separation of the components was eliminated. Music in the incarnation-aesthetic was not a "reflection" (*Abbild*) but an "embodiment" (*Ebenbild*); it was the actual physical manifestation of the underlying idea rather than a representation of it or a vessel in which it was contained.[21] Gatz conveyed this view most effectively when using the image of body and soul, a metaphor that preserves, appropriately, the underlying tension between a deep unity and a still-perceptible duality. Thus if the incarnation-aesthetic was not the final stage of musical understanding for Gatz, it nevertheless made a breakthrough by framing a new species of problem.

The quintessential advocate of the incarnation-aesthetic for Gatz was

Schopenhauer. Liszt too subscribed to this view, in a manner more fo-cused on emotion than on metaphysics, but it was Schopenhauer who most clearly isolated the distinction between the content-aesthetic and the incarnation-aesthetic, in his description of music's uniquely direct relationship with the will. The differentiation between "representation" (*Darstellung*) and "being" (*Sein*) at the center of Schopenhauer's system was for Gatz the root of every incarnation-aesthetic, including those of Hartmann, Moos, Vischer, and even Hegel.[22] Whatever the distinctions, these philosophers all shared the claim, according to Gatz, that music was a mode or mechanism through which the absolute could become, as opposed to represent, reality.

At the same time, Gatz found that these philosophers also shared a fundamental belief, however hazily articulated, that the reality made physical in music was extramusical at its pre-objectified level. Notwith-standing the underlying unity of reality and appearance, then, these the-ories all retained the assumption of heteronomy, because they all claimed that music's significance (*Bedeutung*) resided in the fact that at a deeper level of reality it was not music at all. This problem—and it was indeed a problem, for musicians of every stripe—was answered by the autonomy-aesthetic. The autonomy-aesthetic did not grow from the incarnation-aesthetic, Gatz held, but alongside it; the latter was subor-dinate to the former not because one gave rise to the other, but because one described more authentically than the other the actual character of music's fundamental essence.[23]

The most striking feature of Gatz's account emerges with his descrip-tion of the ultimate nature of autonomous music. The founding principle of the autonomy-aesthetic, Gatz argued, was that music had an indepen-dent, positive existence outside "space, time, nature, soul, [and] cos-mos."[24] Music was neither a representation nor an incarnation of metaphysical reality; it actually *was* metaphysical reality, now made per-ceptible. The autonomy-aesthetic stood according to Gatz at the furthest conceivable remove from conventional "formalism," for rather than sep-arating music from an external reality, autonomy obliterated the distinc-tion between the two. This outlook brought about a kind of apotheosis of musical metaphysics, culminating in a remarkable repositioning of mu-sic as a meta-metaphysics: music now became an essence compared to which all other forms or manifestations of reality had to be regarded as somehow imperfect, partial, or false. "It has no content that it must trans-late into tones, but it is itself the untranslated and untranslatable original language [*Ursprache*]."[25]

Gatz believed that the difficulty of grasping and accounting for music's ultimate nature (or nature's ultimate musicality) explained the breathtakingly diverse range of aesthetic theories available at the end of the nineteenth century, all of which sprang from the same basic presumption. Moreover, these important contemporary theories of the late nineteenth century were characterized by Gatz as having sprung from older sources in which the truth about music was implied but not clearly or thoroughly formulated. Hanslick's central insights, for example, which Gatz found deeply opposed to those of the "form-aesthetic" (*Formäs-thetik*), were already present in the writings of Wackenroder, Tieck, E. T. A. Hoffmann, Schumann, and even the early Wagner. The later Wagner, on the other hand, particularly in the essay "Beethoven," arrived at the autonomy-aesthetic from the other side, using a critical evaluation of Schopenhauer's ideas as a means by which to reach independently the metaphysical conclusions of the autonomy-aesthetic. For Hanslick, as for Wagner, the decisive step was the realization that an adequate musical aesthetic required a new conception not of music but of reality.[26]

The greatest weakness of Gatz's argument, the distance from which he regards his aesthetic sources, is also its greatest strength. From a philosophical perspective his account can seem crude, simplistic, and lacking in detail. The richness of nuance so characteristic of German aesthetic writing at the time does not always find a place in his brief survey. Yet his streamlining of the issues is not significantly different from the kind of distillation that a practicing musician of the time would have applied in forming personal conclusions about matters that could neither be ignored nor mastered with academic precision. For someone not predisposed to split hairs, Gatz's theorizing of an underlying unity would have seemed not only plausible but perhaps even obvious. This presumption makes sense even with regard to the widest conceivable extremes, Friedrich von Hausegger and Eduard Hanslick, the leaders of ostensibly opposing camps. Like his contemporaries, Strauss knew the work of both writers; Alexander Ritter, his hyper-Wagnerian mentor, had taught him to conceive of contemporaneous musical aesthetics as a pitched battle between these two well-defined antagonistic camps.[27] But Hausegger and Hanslick also shared important common ground—a basic idealistic conception of music—and it is not difficult to imagine that a young composer with a sharp mind and catholic interests could have seen through to that important level of agreement.

Although Hausegger's theory was ostensibly concerned with "expression," the terms in which he framed it are those of Gatz's autonomy.[28]

In constructing a definition of music's essential nature, Hausegger methodically traced a path from physical qualities to metaphysical ones. The building blocks of the art—sounds—are physical. Composers manipulate these sounds, placing them in "relationships determined by certain laws," and these interactions in turn are apprehended as sensations ("effects produced in our ears by sound-producing causes").[29] Only after these sensations are processed by the brain and nervous system does music begin to transcend its physical basis—that is, only then does it become what Hausegger believes it is. The "expression" that defines authentic musical experience occurs through "sympathetic contact with human sensibility"; timbre, in particular, plays a crucial role in facilitating the moment of effective communication. But the result extends far beyond human perception, in that a connection is formed between perception and the otherwise imperceptible underlying reality of the world: "nature discloses her soul to us in music," giving us an adequate experience of the metaphysical substance underlying the physical world and showing us that reality at its core is somehow musical.

The scientific trappings of Hausegger's aesthetic and his difficult academic-philosophical prose style should not obscure the basic fact that his argument leads to both a metaphysical conception of music and a musical conception of metaphysics. "Plumbing the depths" of music yields the realization that music is the quintessential means by which nature "can reveal herself to us in the very process of becoming into existence." Music achieves its peculiar philosophical effect by "decomposing what we were accustomed to know as our world" and by "drawing us into a life-world of vital truth by the side of which the external world appears as no more than a phantom." This capacity, and an instinctive human awareness of it, established for Hausegger the high esteem in which music is held; only through music are we able to "know," in an idealistic sense. Differing levels of compositional accomplishment and differing degrees of awareness and understanding on the part of listeners dictate that the extent to which this kind of communication succeeds in given situations will vary widely. Yet the theoretical possibility exists, and in certain exceptional cases (e.g., Wagner) it is realized.

On the surface, Eduard Hanslick would seem unlikely to have sympathized with Hausegger's conclusion that "artists are mankind's priests, for true art is true religion." Hausegger's book was in fact a direct, antagonistic response to Hanslick (albeit a relatively late one; *Die Musik als Ausdruck* was published in 1885, while the first edition of *Vom Musikalisch-Schönen* appeared in 1854). Yet with regard to the claim that music held within it a metaphysical level of significance or some unique potential for apprehending truth, there was no disagreement. This dimension of Hanslick's aesthetic is often overlooked, despite the immense success of *Vom Musikalisch-Schönen* (ten editions by 1902) and the subsequent widespread popularity of "formalism" (however crudely conceived).[30] Popular opinion aside, Hanslick did not rule out a broader metaphysical reading of music's autonomous nature, any more than he rejected the idea that music could express emotions. But although he excluded emotional content from the discussion of the musically beautiful, on the grounds that only specifically musical traits could be beautiful in this particular way, Hanslick placed his metaphysical claims at the center of his theory of musical beauty.

Hanslick's rejection of feeling stems from the fundamentally human character of emotions. As part of the human realm, emotions belong to the *diesseits*, and so they inhibit our experience of metaphysics. The explicit goal of the treatise, to understand music "as objectively as possible," required that Hanslick limit the human (i.e., subjective) elements of the equation to those necessary for perceiving music.[31] In seeking objectivity, however, Hanslick was seeking not just scientific precision—music as it could be described by the music theorist or the systematic musicologist—but objectivity as fundamental reality, conceived philosophically and indeed spiritually. Beauty for Hanslick could only be conceived as a spiritual quality; in the chapter devoted to describing the "musically beautiful," he stated unequivocally that "we recognize no beauty devoid of spirit [*Geist* (a word that Hanslick used in this section interchangeably with *Seele*)]."[32] The fact that this spiritual content could only be found in "the musical structures themselves" was less a comment on music than on that content itself, which Hanslick conceived as inherently musical.

The very purpose of musical aesthetics, then, was in Hanslick's view to apprehend the spiritual content embodied by musical structures. By rejecting a "general metaphysical concept of beauty" (i.e., one applying to all arts) he did not dispose of metaphysics entirely, but limited its apprehension and indeed its very nature to the musical sphere.[33] The unique position of music among the arts lay in the inseparability of form and content. By no means did Hanslick intend to suggest that music had one but not the other: just as "no independent content exists" in a given musical work, so "[music] has no form apart from its content."[34] Hanslick's readers have always recognized that music for him had no independent content, but few have understood that by the same token music had no independent form. And it was precisely in this basic indivisibility that music showed its unique connection to the level of reality that was otherwise unavailable to human faculties.

A strong, youthful belief in this special capacity (he wrote the book at age twenty-eight) motivated Hanslick's sole foray into aesthetics. Thus in the first edition he did not try to hide his polemical aspirations but openly described his mission as a "vindication of the spiritual substance [Gehalt] of music."[35] But from what did music need to be vindicated? From programmatic music, which obscured and jeopardized music's spiritual aims. "Only by unequivocally denying every other sort of 'content' [Inhalt] can we rescue music's 'substance' [Gehalt]."[36] The rejection of programmatic music, and likewise of Wagnerian opera, was done explicitly in order to protect the unique metaphysical position of the art. At times Hanslick's writing can sound—perhaps not by accident—positively Schopenhauerian, as with the suggestion that for a good listener "music works not merely and exclusively through its own beauty, but at the same time as a sounding representation [tönende Abbild] of the great movement of the cosmos."[37] In fact, the relationship between these thinkers is not at all distant; the public appropriation of Schopenhauer by Wagner and his followers should not rule out the possibility that in Hanslick, the philosopher may have found his most effective advocate.

Dahlhaus pointed out that the paragraph in which that final sentence appeared was removed from the second and subsequent editions in response to critique by Robert Zimmermann. The discussion of music's "spiritual substance" remained intact, however, and there is little doubt of its central position in both the development and the final form of Hanslick's aesthetic. The belief that he represented an empty "formalism," a contentless physicality, was largely the product of attacks from the opposing camp (Zimmermann's critique having been a friendly amendment). An early example here was August Wilhelm Ambros, who in 1855 unfairly characterized Hanslick as an empiricist rather than accepting the more difficult challenge of confronting and responding to an alternative musical metaphysics.[38] Hanslick was vulnerable to the charge that he had reduced music to a "mere play of forms" and that he hoped to turn aesthetics into a second-rate science; his text is easily misinterpreted, because it is short, wide ranging, and primarily directed against the view that the feelings expressed by music are its aesthetic content. That Hanslick declined to respond with a formal philosophical elaboration should not be interpreted as tacit agreement, however, for he may well have decided that the autonomy aesthetic would eventually win out on its own. Ambros too, and indeed Wagner himself, had maintained that a program would be superfluous if the music connected with it was expressively and structurally effective. If Hanslick did believe, then, that autonomy no longer needed "rescuing," the subsequent history of musical aesthetics in the nineteenth and early twentieth centuries bore out that conviction: while programmatic music struggled unsuccessfully to rid itself of suspicion and continued to fall back on claims that ultimately the music in programmatic works was self-sufficient, the autonomy aesthetic found a renewed credibility without which the Second Viennese phenomenon would have been unimaginable.

The artistic development of Strauss's greatest contemporary illuminates this issue from the side of creation rather than reception. Although Mahler renounced programmaticism, or at least the public dissemination of programs, his determination to use music for contemplating the metaphysical only intensified.[39] This choice, as much as any specifically musical tendencies, strengthened his credibility with the next generation of Austro-German composers. Mahler was no formalist, but by restricting his utterances to the strictly musical he rendered his exalted philosophical aspirations believable. What is more, his familiar remark that he and Strauss were miners digging from opposite sides of a mountain indicates that he knew what he was doing.[40] The goal toward which Mahler felt they were both digging was the same goal toward which composers in the Austro-German tradition had strived since E. T. A. Hoffmann: the noumenal, infinity, *das Unendliche.* Strauss worked as a program musician, Mahler as an autonomist-come-lately, but they hoped for the same result (or so Mahler believed in 1896), just as the ostensibly antagonistic camps of late-nineteenth-century aesthetics held the same underlying aspirations. This reading of Strauss is of course profoundly mistaken but forgivably so, because Mahler did not have enough information at the time to recognize that fact (Strauss's most celebrated work at that time being *Tod und Verklärung*). Nevertheless the metaphor is brilliant in its recognition of the fundamental common ground shared by outwardly antagonistic forces in the musical culture of his time.

Hanslick's means of reaching the goal won out largely because a rigorous theory of musical autonomy became the most effective method of enshrining music's philosophical prestige, by insulating it from discussion. This point can be effectively illustrated by counterexamples from the works of lesser-known composers who attempted to follow in Wagner's footsteps with operatic plots drawing explicitly on philosophical issues. Inevitably these attempts degenerated into self-parody. Karl Goldmark's *Merlin* (1886), composed to a libretto by Siegfried Lipiner (whose

intellectual influence on Mahler is well documented), attempted to trans-
fer Wagner's well-worn spiritual-dramatic apparatus of redemption (*Erlösung*), ideal love, and musical salvation to the world of King Arthur.
The result was unintentional comedy; after Merlin succumbs, Amfortas-
like, to an impure attraction, he loses both his power as wizard and his
ability to play the harp, regaining them only through the redemptive
self-sacrifice of the woman he loves. Hans Pfitzner's early operatic attempts, *Der arme Heinrich* (1893) and *Die Rose vom Liebesgarten* (1901),
likewise drove overt Wagnerian philosophizing to absurdity, on a superficial level with characters who bear philosophically conceived concept-
names (Siegnot, Minneleide), but more substantially by placing simple,
uninteresting Christian conversion themes at the center of the plot. (In
Heinrich, the protagonist is converted from marauding knight to Christian penitent through the actions of a virgin would-be martyr.) This
brand of crude, direct spiritualization of music had no hope of succeeding
with audiences who nevertheless proved themselves eager to accept a
more subtle treatment of music as a form of religion. Most spectacular
in this misguided vein was the unfinished trilogy *Die Erlösung* by Felix
Weingartner, who hoped to bring his explicitly stated conviction that
"music is metaphysical" to fruition through a series of "mystery plays"
to be performed at a specially constructed *Festspielhaus*. Weingartner
showed himself a more nuanced Wagnerian by presenting a philosophical
justification of the trilogy, constructing his argument by weaving together Wagnerian, Schopenhauerian, and Buddhist elements. The bizarre, overblown spirituality of the work proved unworkable, however,
even to a composer whose spiritual commitment was second to none.[41]

German opera collapsed between *Parsifal* and *Salome* largely because
it attempted a direct, explicit engagement with philosophical and religious issues. The results were highfalutin to the point of silliness, and
no composer with good sense, ambition, and a survival instinct would
have followed that road for long. Even Wagner seems to have recognized
(by repeatedly expressing a desire to return to the symphony) that the
future of musical metaphysics lay with autonomy.[42] (One would hope
that he felt some remorse over the crude manipulations of Schopenhauer's philosophy he had perpetrated while justifying his desire to compose operas.)[43] With these developments in mind, the time has come to
ask why Strauss, the greatest composer of the era, chose to continue
writing programmatic music, and why his programmaticism became ever
more physical and superficial. Parody too became a central and self-
conscious feature of his music—a disconcerting, elliptical sort of parody

that often left listeners wondering whether this or that passage by Strauss was meant seriously or ironically. Here the words of Schoenberg begin to have an important meaning that belies their apparent nonchalance. If Strauss had seen himself as leader of the next generation of *Zukunfts-musiker*—as providing updated, refined examples of Liszt's symphonic poems—he would not have been revolutionary. If, on the other hand, he meant to use programmaticism to expose the weakness of the goal toward which both programmatic and autonomous music were currently striving, then he was utterly on his own. Perhaps, then, Schoenberg was right. Perhaps Strauss recognized (to put it more critically than Schoenberg would have done) that the absurdity typical of explicitly philosophical music had infected all serious music in that cultural context, with the principal aesthetic difference between works being the degree to which strange pretensions were kept under wraps—heard, felt, believed, but never discussed.

But did Strauss have the breadth of vision to recognize an underlying unity in the aesthetics of programmaticism and autonomy? Did he have sufficient education and experience to grasp the relevant issues? And did he have a compelling personal interest in this debate? In spite of a vast body of primary sources and dozens of biographies, these questions remain open. For every indication of contemplative sensitivity there is an anecdote betraying greed or bad taste; for every sign of boorishness, a sneaking suspicion that the public persona was a ruse. The documentary evidence, however, when considered on its own and not in conjunction with rumor and disinformation, leaves little doubt that Strauss had the ability and the motivation to reflect seriously on the aesthetic status of his art. The following section presents a survey of that evidence, in advance of the later chapters' more-detailed studies of specific issues.

The Role of Aesthetics in Strauss's Creative Life

The public image of Strauss as detached celebrity-craftsman, an image that he himself did much to create, would seem to raise doubts that he could have penetrated the aesthetic debates of his time to any significant extent, if indeed they interested him at all.[44] Moreover, our assumptions about the composer have been powerfully shaped by the seeming parallelism between the nonchalance of his personality and the technical command so obvious in his music.[45] The sheer ease of his technique, despite its forbidding complexity, has led many to accept uncritically Strauss's own implicit suggestion of an underlying intellectual laziness.

The surviving documentary evidence, however, tells a different story. Whatever airs he put on in public, the closest thing that the private Strauss had to a religion was *Arbeit:* constant labor, not only in musical composition but in his approach to daily life as a mature, *gebildet* human being (skat notwithstanding).[46] That feature of his personality was just as apparent in his early years, when the Mendelssohnian schoolboy distinguished himself both in the classroom and in his already-chosen professional field, as it was at the end, when as an octogenarian he divided his "retirement" between rereading Goethe and producing new masterpieces.

The process of musical creation was to Strauss an intensely private activity, to be pursued diligently, quietly, and alone, in the *Werkstatt.*[47] Even more personal was the literary, historical, cultural, and philosophical study that became an indispensable precondition for his artistic creativity, especially during his period of maturation. If we leave aside for a moment the well-worn assumptions about his personality, it is not difficult to imagine that a young composer in his position would have wanted to conceptualize his art in a larger cultural context. In his late teens and early twenties, Strauss regularly came into contact with major figures in German music: Hans von Bülow, Johannes Brahms, Cosima Wagner, Hermann Levi, Clara Schumann, Hans Richter, and a host of others. Each of these artists held fervent beliefs about the larger cultural and philosophical significance of music, which they shared with him, sometimes quite aggressively, in hopes of steering the energies of a rising star. This experience encouraged him to approach his art from both the musical and extramusical sides of the equation, even as it revealed the professionally dangerous necessity of choosing allies. It is natural, then, that the intellectual dimension of his life should have become ever more private as it developed. For the historian, it is the most difficult dimension to reconstruct, but if we are to gain a clearer understanding of how Strauss "became himself" (to paraphrase Nietzsche), it may also be the most important.

The thesis of the present book is that Strauss's coming of age was an intellectual as well as a musical process, with the intellectual side of things directly affecting, in specific and sophisticated ways, all of his major works for orchestra. Given the profusion of biographical writing on Strauss, it is strange that such a project could still be possible or that it could yield an original, far-reaching theory of his maturation. Two misguided traditions in Strauss scholarship account for this possibility: a simplistic conception of the effect of Alexander Ritter on Strauss's development (complicated by the misunderstanding or devaluation of other influences) and a failure to appreciate the extent and the depth of Strauss's intellectual activity during the 1880s and the 1890s. In what remains of this chapter, I offer a preliminary description of the problematic nature of these traditions, in order to demonstrate the need for the detailed alternative account of Strauss's maturation presented in the subsequent chapters.

If our present understanding of Strauss's musical maturation is an oversimplification, that problem is rooted in the composer's own writings. The account that Strauss shared with the public tells that after a highly conservative upbringing controlled by his father, he came under the influence of Alexander Ritter, crossed over to the New German camp, and pursued the implications of that shift at least until his first successful operas (even after a dispute over Strauss's first opera, *Guntram* [1893], brought about an estrangement between student and mentor).[48] The historical record, on the other hand—Strauss's music, correspondence, sketches, diaries, and other evidence—belies the notion of a clean break between a period of conservatism and one of radical experimentation. Strauss had known the music of Wagner and Liszt well before meeting Ritter, and his interest in composers outside the New German orbit continued, although it manifested itself in more-complicated ways for several years. From 1885 until at least 1888, Strauss worked actively on both sides of the fence, producing several important works (the *Burleske* [1886], the Violin Sonata [1887]) that juxtapose antithetical styles without celebrating one at the expense of the other. Creatively, his immediate response to Ritter was thus to examine with greater intensity than before the heterogeneity of musical life in late-nineteenth-century Germany.

Strauss's desire to survey the options and to reflect on them critically points not to Ritter but to Hans von Bülow, whose impact on the young composer has always been underestimated. The profound respect that Strauss had for this difficult man never waned; he considered Bülow the greatest performing musician he ever knew, and he devoted an entire essay to his influence, whereas Ritter found only a place in the above-mentioned general memoir of "youth and apprenticeship." Even during the period of Ritter's greatest influence, the spring of 1886, Strauss called Bülow the finest source of "maturity of artistic understanding" (*Reife künstlerischer Erkenntnis*) to be found in Europe.[49] Bülow was fiercely independent, but that infamous quality sprang from a profound awareness of the full range of musical styles and viewpoints. He knew the music of Brahms and of Wagner as deeply as any of his contemporaries, and he had unique qualifications for comparative analysis, having enjoyed (if that is the right word) intimate relationships with both composers.[50] At the time when Strauss knew him, Bülow was by no means unwilling to discuss Wagner or indeed to perform his music, and Strauss clearly learned much in this regard (for example, Bülow's interpretation of the *Tristan* Prelude, which Strauss and many others regarded as definitive).[51] Moreover, just as important as Bülow's knowledge of the two leaders was his enthusiasm for other composers. Already while in Meiningen Strauss found himself surprisingly affected by a private evening of Johann Strauss waltzes.[52] Bülow's Frankfurt master classes, which Strauss audited in 1885, encompassed Bach, Mozart, and Beethoven as well as Mendelssohn, Chopin, Liszt, and Brahms.[53] The crucial feature of the musical excellence embodied by Bülow was catholicity, peppered liberally with critical commentary that did not prevent him from gleaning everything of value from any music with which he came into contact.

If any single character trait was decisive in Strauss's development, it was that like Bülow, he had a limitless musical curiosity matched by a knack for pulling the best out of his influences. Whatever the level of accomplishment in a musician who interested him, Strauss separated the wheat from the chaff and then incorporated the positive qualities into his personal style in a productive way. This talent is illustrated best by his relationship with Ritter, who was regarded by many, despite his connections (his wife was Wagner's niece), as an out-and-out crackpot.[54] No one who knew him would have imagined that he could provide an indispensable ingredient to the formation of genius, if the genius himself had not confirmed it. Similarly, Friedrich Wilhelm Meyer, a conductor, composer, and teacher whose creative talent was modest at best, nonetheless bore much of the responsibility for the staggeringly solid grounding in form, harmony, and counterpoint that was to characterize even Strauss's most adventurous music.[55] Meyer would have been taken aback and perhaps even appalled had he lived to hear the uses to which his teaching would be put, just as Franz Strauss would find no consolation in his son's fastidious attention to tempo and phrasing or his lifelong appreciation of Mozart, all legacies of the conservative indoctrination that in other respects misfired so badly. One might say the same thing of Hermann Levi, Hans Richter, Hans von Bronsart, Cosima Wagner, and a host of other important figures whom Strauss the pupil dissected in his ruthless drive to self-formation.

Strauss took seriously anyone who had a significant knowledge of music, and he did so throughout his career. Just as he held no biases, however, he accepted no one's ideas wholesale. Every influence, no matter its source, was subject to a kind of editing and personalization that would enable it to become part of Strauss's artistic personality for the long term. Taking into account this feature of his personality is never more important than when considering the influence of Ritter. The idea that Strauss would have turned his back on his previous learning at the moment of a "conversion" is fundamentally inimical to his conception of the art. He was far too advanced as an artist by 1885 to have subordinated himself in the manner and to the extent that has been assumed. This fact would be more widely recognized if the sophistication of his "absolute" works of the 1880s were more widely appreciated. Not only were the major efforts of this group mature—important in a national sense and recognized as such by peers—they contain remarkable hints of Strauss's future. The Violin Sonata, with its collage-like treatment of Brahms, Liszt, Beethoven, and Schubert, is in spite of its traditional title every bit as striking, new, and one might even say "modernist" as *Aus Italien*. In the *Burleske*, an orchestral counterpart of the Violin Sonata, Strauss attacked both of these styles, with tongue in cheek but with an incisiveness far more explicit and even crass than he would have dared in a piece of chamber music. By 1886, Strauss firmly believed that the mantle of Wagner was just as available to him as that of Brahms. He chose neither, motivated by a growing realization that the distinction was no longer worth preserving.

This fact rules out the possibility that Strauss's wide-ranging musical interests during the 1880s grew from simple careerism. Yes, he clearly recognized that making a career as a composer was a political project as well as an artistic one, and he may well have wanted to establish connections in every possible direction, in order to hedge his bets. And it is true that just a few years later, in negotiations over the publications of his first tone poems, he showed himself to be a hard-nosed advocate of his own interests, even when the publisher was a family friend who did not anticipate making significant royalties.[56] If careerism were the only factor, however, then we would have to call him rather an inept politician, for on the artistic level the young Strauss alienated virtually every important person with whom he came into contact—not always immediately, but inevitably and openly.

However important those political considerations, Strauss also cast a wide net for cultural reasons, which were not solely musical. The Munich in which he grew up was also the Munich of Ibsen, a city of literary progressivism where avant-garde developments brought artists into frighteningly real conflicts with civil authorities.[57] The concerns of these writers bore little or no resemblance to the issues about which musicians argued so passionately, and one can easily imagine that the debates then taking place within music must have looked rather small to someone not religiously attached to this or that musical philosophy. Certainly an awareness of the censors, and of what they could and could not control, hovered in the back of Strauss's mind when he contemplated the graphic musical possibilities inherent in a program based on Don Juan.[58] If there is reason to expect that he would have applied the intellectual experiences available to him to his creative activity, the context in which he grew up would have given him plenty of material to consider. The case for that tendency in his personality is largely circumstantial but nonetheless very strong.

The education that Franz Strauss forced on a gifted youngster obsessed with music became in the end something that the mature artist could not have lived without. Strauss was not a potential academic or even a natural systematic thinker, but he read voraciously throughout his life, even in periods when his productivity as conductor and composer seems impossibly enormous. His close friends always admired this quality. Mahler delighted in their conversations about history and literature, as we learn from Alma—certainly not a source inclined to exaggerate Strauss's intellect.[59] The pith typical of the correspondence with Hofmannsthal would not have been possible without Strauss's encyclopedic familiarity with literature, especially Goethe, Schiller, and the classics, and European history, a field in which Hofmannsthal obviously considered Strauss his equal.[60] As he became older, Strauss rarely encountered conversation partners who could keep up with him; Karl Böhm found it impossible and confessed to being completely overwhelmed.[61]

For his part, Strauss always made it a practice to assess the cultural literacy of important people with whom he came into contact, and those judgments played a role in the formation of his opinions, particularly about composers. This habit had formed already in 1885, when after spending some evenings alone with Brahms in a pub he concluded that the elder man was "well read but without any particular signs of genius."[62] The absence of a spark was probably an unspoken comparison to Bülow, who delivered literary allusions in spades and with razor-sharp wit. The young Strauss regarded such broad learning as more than superficially important; for at least the next two decades it was rare for him to form a serious artistic relationship with anyone not deeply cultivated in areas outside of music. Besides Bülow, Ritter, and Mahler one thinks particularly of Cosima Wagner, Arthur Seidl, and Friedrich Rösch—three individuals whose musical expertise could not possibly measure up to Strauss's but who nevertheless became his most important influences in the 1890s, the crucial period in the final formation of his creative personality.

Strauss took his personal education much more seriously than is widely admitted. Looking back on his life at age eighty-one, he regarded his training in the gymnasium, "the benevolent guardian of European culture," as the determining formative experience of his life, one without which he could not have produced his life's work.[63] What is more, Strauss believed that later generations, if deprived of that same opportunity, would lack the wherewithal to appreciate either German music or the larger context of European humanism from which it grew—a scenario in which the culture itself would wither.[64] In a passionate plea on behalf of the "humanist gymnasium," Strauss called himself a "German Greek, even to this day" and identified the Greek spirit, tempered by the "moderating influence of the central European climate . . . and landscape," as the source of European cultural achievement from "Michelangelo, Raphael, Grünewald, Shakespeare, Kant, Schopenhauer, and Schiller" to "the greatest of them all, Goethe."[65] Unless the gifted members of the society were systematically trained in that tradition, the tradition would come to an end, and German musical culture, which in Wagner had completed a "cultural development of two thousand years," would lose its audience, its relevance, and its ability to sustain itself.

All indications are that when Strauss passed his matriculation examination, at age eighteen, he had formed lifelong habits that could not be strengthened by further formal education. It was in recognition of this fact that in 1883 he left the University of Munich (where he had taken courses in philosophy, aesthetics, cultural history, and Shakespeare) after one semester; looking back on that decision he recalled making a determination that he could pursue the same program of learning on his own, and more effectively: "I soon opted for the acquisition of that kind of knowledge through reading and making my own choice of teachers!"[66] His intellectual self-confidence grew further thanks to a network of relationships with gifted peers whose scholarly inclinations at least matched his own. Chief among these were Seidl, who took his PhD at the University of Leipzig in 1887 with a dissertation on aesthetics and would later serve as an editor of the first complete edition of Nietzsche's works; Rösch, who was recognized as a bona fide academic genius while a schoolboy in Munich, then made a career in law while also conducting professionally and writing on musical aesthetics; and Max Steinitzer, another budding academic, whose biography of Strauss is uniquely authoritative because of the closeness of his relationship with the composer during the 1880s. Abandoning the hope of earning a degree did cost him some suffering, however, as is shown by his unvarying practice of signing his name as "Dr. Richard Strauss" after being awarded an honorary doctorate from the University of Heidelberg in 1903.

Seidl and Steinitzer both provided important evidence of the centrality of intellectual activity to Strauss's creative life. More than any other biographer, Steinitzer emphasized the parallelism between Strauss's compositional apprenticeship and his intellectual one, claiming that Strauss was not a finished artist until he had worked out for himself an idea of music's position in the intellectual and cultural spectrum. Steinitzer's observations are particularly helpful regarding the first half of the 1880s, after Strauss's formal education had been completed but before the engagement at Meiningen. His account of the interaction among a mixed population of student thinkers and composers establishes the presence in Munich of the kind of dialogue in which Mahler and Siegfried Lipiner participated in Vienna at about the same time.[67] For the Munich group, however, a crucial difference existed: these young thinkers concentrated not on Nietzsche's *Die Geburt der Tragödie* and its recasting of Wagner's own tendentious reading of Schopenhauer, but instead on Schopenhauer's texts themselves, which they read and discussed without a mediating influence. This practice of going directly to the philosophical texts, bypassing not only Wagner's readings but the readings of any secondary authority, would remain a crucial distinguishing feature of Strauss's working method as a philosophically concerned composer.

Seidl went even further in emphasizing the intellectual component of Strauss's early creative life. In his 1896 "Richard Strauss: Eine Charakter-Skizze," the earliest biography of the composer and one based predominantly, according to the author, on personal experience, the developmental milestones are not musical but intellectual: the gymnasium, the introduction to various readings of Schopenhauer, and the encounter with Nietzsche's works.[68] This approach was not just a young PhD's predilection for intellectualizing or an enthusiastic *Straussianer's* attempt to find a promotional angle. In fact, it simply recounted personal experience. When Strauss and Seidl both lived in Weimar (1889–93) they collaborated on a revival of the local Wagner Society, organizing lecture-demonstrations in which specific examples of music were placed in a larger intellectual context for the benefit of the lay audience. Seidl's letters to Strauss from the early 1890s likewise pursue the intellectual side of Strauss's art, occasionally betraying frustration that the composer would not open up to him concerning a mode of musical thought that he knew was ongoing in Strauss's work.[69] This frustration bothered him intensely, because he believed, as he would later state in a review of Strauss's *Also sprach Zarathustra,* that one could not understand Strauss's art fully without gaining admittance into the *"geistige Werkstatt,"* that is, without understanding his inner intellectual and spiritual life.[70]

We know from personal sources—diaries, sketches, and marginalia, which presumably were accessible only to Strauss himself—that that inner life was even more extensive and complicated than Seidl suspected. By far the most important source of this kind is a notebook in which Strauss wrote, over a period of about two decades, many of his most personal observations about his reading, his ongoing creative projects, and personal encounters that struck him as significant.[71] This source has been known to scholars since Schuh, who mentioned a number of the items in his 1976 biography, but as yet no one has made use of the contents in a critical study of Strauss's music (or indeed in any study whatsoever).[72] The types of entry in this source vary widely. Some are personal anecdotes, for example, a conversation between Strauss and Bülow in which the former advocates Ritter's Hauseggerian aesthetic of expression against Bülow's suggestion that Brahms's Violin Sonata in D Minor, op. 108 (dedicated to Bülow), was "new." Other entries deal with possible creative projects, among them an opera on Don Juan (conceived after the completion of the tone poem) in which some characters are obviously modeled on members of Strauss's inner circle of friends. The majority of the entries, however, are notes taken from historical and philosophical reading material and personal responses to that reading. The work that accounts for the most extensive set of notes is Schopenhauer's *Die Welt als Wille und Vorstellung;* his notes deal with all four books in the first volume of the text, and in many instances Strauss cited page numbers (of the Brockhaus edition of 1888). A slightly later set of notes obviously reflects the influence of Nietzsche, though the particular works that Strauss read are not mentioned. Other notes have to do with Wagner's *Oper und Drama,* Max Stirner's *Der Einzige und sein Eigentum* (1844), a number of historical volumes (among them Alwin Schultz, *Das höfische Leben zur Zeit der Minnesänger;* Felix Dahn, *Die Könige der Ger-*

manen; and Wilhelm Arnold, *Deutsche Urzeit*), and Rudolf Louis's *Der Widerspruch in der Musik* (1893).

Willi Schuh observed that this notebook was the only source of its kind to survive.[73] Whether it was the only source of its kind to have existed is another question; this notebook had special value to Strauss (because it also documented his trip to Egypt, Greece, and Italy in 1892–93), but other such records would likely have been discarded. Strauss often gave away his musical sketches, thinking that they were of no use once the composition had been finished, and working materials of a nonmusical nature certainly had even less value for him. (At the end of his life, Alice Strauss is known to have removed autograph documents from wastebaskets around the house.) But in any case, more important than the question of how many such sources may have existed is the fact that this one documents both serious reading and a sustained effort to process the information so that it could be useful for creative purposes. The source shows without question that Strauss had specific reactions to particular passages in these texts, that he worked through particular questions or problems that concerned him, and that he did this completely on his own, without any expectation that the activity would become public knowledge. Like the musical sketches that do survive, this source provides us with a glimpse of a modus operandi, not in the working-out of musical material but in the treatment of ideas that ultimately grounded those creative choices.

In the correspondence it is really only the letters to Strauss from Friedrich Rösch, Seidl, and Cosima Wagner—people who were at once intimate friends and somehow removed from his life—that show any evidence of this side of the composer.[74] (The correspondence with Ritter, which is lost, would of course shed light as well.) Strauss was laconic and even uncommunicative regarding his creative process in correspondence; although hints can be found in correspondence with Ludwig Thuille and his parents, the exchanges with Rösch, Seidl, and Cosima are the only ones that show the urgency and even desperation with which he grappled with extramusical issues. More than once there is the clear indication in the correspondence with Rösch that Strauss's creative work cannot proceed without a satisfactory resolution of the topic at hand; clearly, in these cases creative progress could not take place without satisfactory resolution of nonmusical problems that actually determined the composer's creative direction. This is a Strauss that few people would recognize, but it is one who is documented, one who left underlining and marginalia in philosophical texts that many have believed he never opened. He did open them, and we shall see that the observations he made on those occasions are equally striking for their intellectual perception as for the direct ways in which they affected his compositional practice.

The latter part of the period of intense philosophical activity documented by the surviving notebook also marked the beginning of a new assertion of control in Strauss's dealings with the public. From the mid-1890s (that is, around the time of the premieres of *Guntram* [1894] and *Till Eulenspiegel* [1895]), Strauss attempted to shape the public perception of the intellectual content of his works through a carefully delimited and controlled release of information about the works.[75] Information was communicated in only two ways. One was through published guidebooks, in which professional writers presented simplified, easy-to-grasp interpretive schemata designed to appeal to a large audience of listeners eager to satisfy a dilettantish thirst for intellectual content but loathe to wrestle with difficult musico-philosophical questions. By sanctioning such publications, Strauss forestalled the possibility of rejections such as those Mahler had experienced due to the ostensible incomprehensibility of his programs. Yet by hiring ghostwriters, Strauss preserved deniability should misunderstandings arise, and more important he could assert his authority while maintaining distance from a process of explanation that he found either distasteful or too difficult to be worth pursuing publicly.

Strauss's other method of communicating the extramusical content of his works did involve direct contact with the public, but it was much more cryptic and indeed seems to have been designed less to share information than to create confusion and thus interest. Even as Strauss struggled privately with fine points of philosophy, and even as he released simplistic guidebooks that would encourage the average listener to believe that he or she could successfully unravel a massive and convoluted musico-philosophical argument, he also baited the public with tidbits dropped to newspaper gossip columns—utterances reliably attributed to him in which he flirtatiously, quasi-ironically painted himself as a composer who in his heart of hearts had no patience for sustained contemplation and might be invoking this level of creativity only for the notoriety that it might bring. After the *Guntram* experience it is not difficult to understand why Strauss would have given up sincere public philosophizing. He might just as easily have given up philosophical programmaticism altogether, however, and the fact that he continued to promote belief in that level of significance in his music, even as he seemed to deny it, placed Strauss in control by undermining the audience's decision-

making power. If a listener found the programmatic content unsophis-
ticated, Strauss could say that he never intended to engage in a meaningful synthesis but only wanted to provide a musician's free response to
an idea that he had never professed to understand fully. If Strauss were
criticized for excessive seriousness, he could respond that the listener was
finding meaning in the work that Strauss had not put there. And if someone found in Strauss's music an effective representation or commentary
on some extramusical idea—well, there would be no need for any response at all.

This last approach to reading Strauss's music has been little used,
though attempts become more serious the further back one goes in the
historical record. There is substantial evidence that this approach can
yield important results: not "the meaning" but perhaps a meaning, even
a sophisticated one that the composer himself could have conceived.
Strauss had the disposition for that kind of approach, and he is known
to have concerned himself with such matters in the course of creative
work. Moreover, by denying it or remaining silent about it, he could
allow it to work on its own without burdening it with the personal weight
that a Mahlerian confession of intentions would have added. Those who
had ears to hear would be able to piece together the argument on their
own. Those who did not were free, and indeed encouraged, to listen to
the music in the manner that the public Strauss identified as the only
correct way. It is only because of the success of that latter mode of
listening that the topic of this book remains to be addressed at this late
date.

I. The Private Intellectual Context of Strauss's Early Career

1

The "Conversion"
Strauss and Wagnerism

*F*or historians, as for music theorists, contemplating Strauss means contemplating Wagner. Musically, dramatically, spiritually, and intellectually, Strauss came to maturity by responding to his greatest and nearest forebear. What started as a learning process became a way of life; from the 1870s, when he discovered the operatic repertoire in standing-room at the Munich Court Opera, through his conquest of the principal orchestral and stage genres (a feat not achieved since Mozart), to the magnificent resignation of the *Four Last Songs*, Strauss's personality evolved by means of dialogue with a model he could not ignore. Bland imitation was never the goal, even in the 1890s, when one Munich critic diagnosed in Strauss a terminal Wagnerian "imitation-bacillus."[1] Rather, Strauss's creative personality took shape through critical reception: by manipulating his heritage, he found an identity. Paradoxically, then, it may be his encounters with Wagner that show us most clearly what makes Strauss unique.

Despite its importance for his creative development, Wagnerian influence on Strauss has aroused relatively little scholarly interest. The composer himself bears some responsibility here, for while he openly acknowledged the artistic debts in his music, he saw no reason to discuss them. Others have followed his lead, so that the very power of Wagner's presence has discouraged research, leaving basic questions unaddressed. As late as 1990, a non-German could write an avowedly preliminary study of the Wagnerian roots of Strauss's leitmotivic technique, producing original and useful observations.[2] Musical allusions to Wagner fill Strauss's tone poems and operas, but the cataloging and description of these cases has only begun and barely scratches the surface.[3] The resurgence of scholarly interest in Strauss owes some of its momentum to the recognition that his methods of borrowing anticipate techniques used by canonical twentieth-century modernists (or postmodernists).[4] Thus until we have a broad and reasonably comprehensive knowledge of what Strauss borrowed from other composers—particularly from his favorite source—our knowledge of his own style and character will be severely limited.

Even more neglected than the musical details of the relationship has been Strauss's reception of Wagnerian ideology: the complex of social theory, philosophy, and aesthetics that formed the interpretive context of the works. Strauss's own account of his metamorphosis into a *Wagnerianer* emphasized the philosophical dimension over the musical; absorption of Wagner's compositional style was to him a separate issue and by no means the decisive one.[5] Likewise, when Strauss backed away from his initial self-characterization as a devoted servant of the "cause," his reasons were intellectual, not musical.[6] If the principal achievement of Strauss's early maturity was, as Bryan Gilliam has maintained, his use of Wagner's "sacred" musical language "to demythologize the philosophy that gave us that very language," then his understanding of that philosophy deserves careful explanation, as does the process by which he came to that understanding.[7]

Such an undertaking must begin with the observation that there was no single, authentic Wagnerian philosophy available to Strauss in the mid-1880s, but a range of philosophies, each struggling for survival and bent on distinguishing itself from the pretenders. Scholarly accounts of Wagnerism as a cultural phenomenon have increasingly focused on the movement's multiplicity, even in narrowly circumscribed historical contexts.[8] Bayreuth itself housed a range of Wagnerian ideologies during the late nineteenth century, though none of them, no matter how submissive, could persuade Wagner that his legacy was safe.[9] Berlin too was a hotbed of Wagnerian debate, as were Vienna, Frankfurt, Dresden, and Strauss's hometown of Munich. In German-speaking countries (the only countries that Strauss knew at this stage of his career), one could find almost as many readings of Wagner as there were sophisticated musicians. For someone who learned by example and who had regular access to many of the greatest practitioners of his art, developing a personal Wagnerian philosophy would have been anything but simple.

The complex nature of Wagnerism in late-nineteenth-century Germany raises questions about Strauss's supposed "conversion," an idea that seems to have originated in Max Steinitzer's 1911 biography.[10] If Strauss did experience a revelatory moment on the road to Damascus, to what was he converted? As someone who pored over the *Gesammelte Schriften* on a daily basis, he would have been equipped to distinguish, where necessary, Wagner's own worldview from the "Wagnerian" ideas of his disciples, as well as to disentangle the views of rival disciples. Moreover, given his philosophical bent he would surely have taken an interest in the dialectical confrontations in Wagner's own thought, such as the pre- and post-Schopenhauer positions on the relationship between music and poetry. All too often the mere fact that Strauss "became a Wagnerian" has preempted analysis of these questions, in favor of a reliance on unsupportable assumptions about the stability of ostensibly Wagnerian ideas. This practice is especially questionable in view of the sources of Strauss's knowledge: he had no direct experience with Wagner, but virtually all of his important mentors and contacts did know Wagner personally. Thus the bulk of his information, much of it contradictory, was both secondhand and authoritative.

In what follows, I seek to overturn the two most common assumptions about Strauss's encounter with Wagnerism: that he perceived the movement as coherent and consistent, and that he accepted it at a particular moment in his career. In its place I supply an account both more complicated and more faithful to the reality of the experience. The first section of the chapter presents a survey of the kinds of Wagnerism that Strauss encountered, from his earliest experiences until about 1895. Each of these had some discernible effect on him, but more important than those isolated examples of influence was, I would hold, the cumulative effect of Wagnerian pluralism. Of the substantial number of serious musicians whom Strauss came to know during these years, most were positively disposed toward Wagner, and each had a private, distinct brand of Wagnerism. At opposite ends of this spectrum were Alexander Ritter and Cosima Wagner, who represented (respectively) extravagant metaphysical speculation and extreme practical fastidiousness. From those individuals, who are treated separately in the chapter's final two sections, Strauss learned just how far one might go in turning the Wagnerian legacy to one's own ends. Separately they offered Strauss compelling, if contrasting, examples of orthodoxy; taken in conjunction they suggested that the only limits on Wagnerism were one's imagination.

Perhaps it was out of reluctance to publicize that freedom that Strauss settled for potted versions of this episode in his career. Whatever his reasons, he has not been alone; neither his supporters nor his antagonists have seen any advantage in contradicting Steinitzer's description of the shift as immediate, overwhelming, instinctive, and essentially inexplicable. But when scrutinized, that account becomes problematic in virtually every respect, right down to the familiar claim that Strauss experienced a youthful period of pure antagonism toward Wagner. The truth is that he always saw something of interest in Wagner's music, and he always regarded it with a critical eye. The grounding of these judgments became more solid each time Strauss learned a new approach to Wagner, but his attitude became less reductive, not more, as time passed. In this respect his thought reflected the diverse character of German Wagner reception as a whole—a feature taken as a matter of course by thoughtful musicians of the time (such as Hans von Bülow, whose attitudes toward Wagner were nothing if not conflicted) but which Strauss was to exploit in uniquely radical fashion.

Pluralism in Strauss's Early Exposure to Wagner

It is fitting that Strauss's earliest encounter with the music of Wagner was also his first experience on a public stage. At the age of five he performed as a Messenger of Peace in a scene from *Rienzi* presented at a children's festival in the Munich Odeon. It was a decidedly positive experience, in which Strauss served as choir leader and "got lots of applause" (as he wrote to a cousin). A year later he returned as a Minnesänger in *Tannhäuser*.[11] We cannot know what effect these occasions had on the mature Strauss's views of Wagner; perhaps none. More interesting is what they say about the position of Wagner's music in Munich. If knee-jerk reactionism or partisan fist-shaking were the only available responses to Wagner, one could hardly expect a lighthearted children's parody to have become a tradition. In fact as early as 1870 his music enjoyed, even in Munich, a level of noncontroversial, everyday acceptance in which even the son of Wagner's Bavarian nemesis could participate.

Much has been made of the antagonism felt toward Wagner by Franz Strauss, the "Joachim of the horn" (according to Bülow) whose vitriol was tolerated by Wagner for the sake of his beautiful playing.[12] Strauss did hear plenty of diatribes in the family household. As a teenager he even borrowed his father's better lines, such as "in ten years no one will know who Richard Wagner is."[13] Yet Strauss did not, as has been suggested, defy his father in order to get to know Wagner's music. This myth has been sustained by misleading anecdotes, above all that of the famous row that followed Franz's discovery of his son sneaking pianissimo through the orchestral score of *Tristan*.[14] The authenticity of that story is unquestionable, but no more so than Franz's complicity in his son's rapidly growing awareness of Wagner during the 1870s.

By the time Strauss was sixteen he had heard all the major works of Wagner from *Tannhäuser* to *Götterdämmerung* at least once. He gained this experience with the consent of his father, who allowed him to attend the Court Opera in standing-room places reserved for relatives of orchestra members. The implications of this permission should not be taken for granted; Franz was no unwitting facilitator. When he traveled to Bayreuth in 1882 to take part in the premiere of *Parsifal* (as a favor to Hermann Levi, who had conducted Strauss's First Symphony), Franz took his son along, allowing the musical significance of the event to override whatever personal distaste it held for him.[15] What these acts of tolerance tell us is that however odious Franz found Wagner's music, he did not wish to limit his son's awareness of it. He found the process exasperating, to be sure, but he chose not to hinder it in any practical respect. History has paid more attention to his complaints than to his actions.

The same might be said of Strauss's letters to Ludwig Thuille, the cheekiness of which later became a source of embarrassment. These documents must be read between the lines. From *Siegfried*, which Strauss found "so boring you could die," he nevertheless gleaned enough information to fill several pages of commentary, including a half-dozen musical examples and a discussion of motivic connections with *Das Rheingold*.[16] Similar analyses followed his attendance of the other *Ring* operas and *Lohengrin*; each time a thin veneer of sarcasm concealed densely packed observations, microscopic in precision. If we remember who Ludwig Thuille was in the late 1870s—the only teenage musician whom Strauss admired, a future distinguished theorist, and an abject conservative whose beliefs were already grounded in considerable musical learning—these reviews read ambiguously, their halfhearted conservative piling-on more than countered by growing interest.[17] In fact, his frequent ironic announcements of support—"I have become a Wagnerian"—say less about himself than about Thuille, who would have been appalled by the slightest hint of an honestly positive reaction. In any case, Strauss's blow-by-blow descriptions betray at least a significant fascination, which was carried through in future developments.

The inner conflict that Strauss felt concerning Wagner mirrored the broader context of reception that he encountered as an aspiring professional musician. Particularly after 1883, pro and con were by no means easy to distinguish. Wagner's death set off a mad scramble among his followers, pitting one-time allies against one another in disputes unsurpassed in bitterness. As it happened, Munich figured centrally in the developing crisis. In the spring of 1883, the leaders of the Münchner Wagnerverein, concerned that the festivals might not survive the crisis of Wagner's death, founded the Allgemeine Richard Wagner-Verein, a society devoted explicitly to securing the festivals "for all time" and financially supporting performances at least every third year. The unspoken agenda of this new society was to take advantage of the power vacuum that existed in the months between Wagner's death and the 1883 festival. With the help of the *Wiener* Akademische Wagner-Verein, the new society got off the ground immediately, establishing at a conference in Nuremberg in May 1883 a central leadership and branches in most major German cities. The *Bayreuther Blätter* was taken over as the society's principal organ, with Hans von Wolzogen remaining as editor. The suddenness of these moves and the threat they represented to continued Wagner family control of the Bayreuth enterprise played a significant role in stimulating Cosima Wagner's resolve when she emerged, unexpectedly to some, as Bayreuth's controlling authority.[18]

Strauss followed this chain of events through his boyhood friend Arthur Seidl, a musician, scholar, and critic who would become one of his most influential confidantes.[19] Seidl was a member of the Münchner Wagnerverein and the Allgemeine Richard Wagner-Verein and deeply concerned with the future of Bayreuth.[20] At stake, in his view, was not merely control of the festivals, but the question of whose interpretation of Wagner would emerge as the dominant force in German musical life. The legal dispute between Munich and Bayreuth over the performing rights to all of Wagner's works after *Rienzi* (which had been ceded to Ludwig II, and on his death passed to the Bavarian government) was also a conflict over style: staging, costumes, acting, and musical interpretation.[21] Strauss would become directly involved in that conflict during his first term as a conductor in Munich (1886–89). But for the time being he remained a bystander, bewildered by the conflicting currents of Wagnerian partisanship.

More than a few such currents swirled in the person of Hans von Bülow, who in 1885 offered Strauss his first professional post as conductor. Universally regarded as one of the foremost authorities on performing Wagner's music (alongside Liszt, Richter, and Levi), Bülow kept aloof from most discussions of the composer. In no way, however, can he be considered an out-and-out antagonist. Bülow continued to perform Wagner's orchestral music (with the understandable exception of the *Siegfried-Idyll*) from the time of his split with Cosima until the end of his career; it was the conducting of opera, not of Wagner, that he loathed.[22] In the 1880s, his performances of the overtures, particularly *Tristan,* moved Strauss to call him the greatest performing musician of the day.[23] That view was shared by Cosima, who in the aftermath of Wagner's death hoped, in all seriousness, that Bülow would take over as principal conductor at Bayreuth.[24] His refusal was a function of personal, not musical, distaste, and that ability to separate the art from the artist wore off on Strauss, who sat awestruck in rehearsals at Meiningen with score in hand while Bülow conducted from memory. Strauss's appraisals of that experience suggest that it may have been the most profound Wagnerian influence of all, on musical grounds alone.

Bülow's influence was not limited to musical technique. His favorite critical appreciation of Wagner had long been Nietzsche's *Die Geburt der Tragödie,* a book produced after the breakup of Bülow's marriage to Cosima.[25] It was likely in this positive Wagnerian context that Strauss first heard of Nietzsche, whose subsequent turn from Wagner—still working itself out in 1885—would ultimately ground Strauss's own critique. Nietzsche's complicated attitude toward Wagner, especially the respect implied by the virulence of his attack, mirrored what Strauss saw in Bülow, at least in terms of its complexity. By the mid-1880s, then, Strauss had encountered a model of mature Wagner reception, one involving ambivalence, contradiction, and conflict. Sophisticated interpretation, given the unique profundity of this art, consisted more in separating the glorious from the odious than in wholesale acceptance or rejection.

In that respect Alexander Ritter provided something of a negative model.[26] Despite the idiosyncrasy of his claims for the philosophical import of Wagner's achievement, he retained a merciless partisan disposition that allowed no questioning of the Master's wisdom, whatever the subject matter. Not surprisingly, Ritter's pantheon of heroes coincided with Nietzsche's enemies: Plato, Jesus, Schopenhauer, Wagner. But where Nietzsche found complicated interpretive challenges, Ritter saw black and white. At first his rock-solid convictions and his frighteningly clear vision of right and wrong appealed to Strauss, as much for their lack of equivocation as for what they taught him about Wagner (though the idea of music as purveyor of metaphysical truths held a novel attraction). The traditional contention, however, that Ritter became the single most important influence in Strauss's artistic career—a contention first made by Strauss himself—rings hollow unless we conclude that Ritter's principal contribution was to convince his young friend to confront Wagnerism head-on. Strauss did just that, beginning with Ritter's own ideas, which he reduced to rubble by the time of the completion of *Guntram* (1893). It was for initiating that critical process that Strauss always remained in Ritter's debt; no one else could have provided so large a target.

Professionally, in the immediate context of Strauss's new position at the Munich Court Opera in 1886, Ritter's influence exacerbated difficulties already present. At that time the leadership (the intendant of the Court Opera, Carl Freiherr von Perfall, the intendant of the Court Theater, Ernst von Possart, and the *Hofkapellmeister*, Hermann Levi) wished to assert their institution artistically as the leading force in Wagnerian performance—an intention that, as Cosima recognized, threatened the very existence of the festivals. Strauss was a wild card in all of this and could easily have joined up permanently with the Munich establishment; indeed he should have, given his position. In 1886, however, it remained all too easy for Perfall and Levi to underestimate the future clout of a twenty-two-year-old third conductor with less than a year of professional experience, and they ignored him. In the meantime, with Ritter whispering in his ear, Strauss looked with idealistic fervor toward Bayreuth and nursed budding resentments against his "incompetent" superiors. (Among his loudest complaints was having to give up the production of *Die Feen* to his immediate superior, Franz Fischer, after having conducted the rehearsals himself; never mind that Fischer was less than five years removed from conducting *Parsifal* at the Festspielhaus.)[27] Effectively locked out of Wagnerian practice in Munich, then, Strauss retreated to the Weinstube Leibenstock with Ritter and other powerless intellectuals, biding his time until the opportunity came to join the Bayreuth cause.

Idle theorizing was to Strauss a fate worse than death; thus the invitation from Cosima Wagner to serve as a rehearsal pianist at the 1889 festival came not a moment too soon. In Cosima, Strauss encountered a most palatable kind of Wagnerism, one devoted solely and tirelessly to the practical issues of mounting productions of the works. If these productions bordered on unintentional parody—by aiming to make time stand still, in skewed, simplified "models" based on the authority of a single person's memory—Strauss could overlook that shortcoming. Her interests and resources mattered more to him, for the time being, than her ability. What he wanted above all was guidance, for within a month of the festival he took up a new position in Weimar, a relatively provincial theater in which he would have full responsibility for producing *Rienzi, Tannhäuser, Lohengrin,* and *Tristan.*[28] At last, then, active Wagnerism on the conducting podium was within his grasp.

At the same time Strauss encountered at Bayreuth other kinds of devotion that expanded his awareness of the range of Wagnerian cultural philosophizing. First among these was the racist idealism of Hans von Wolzogen, the *weltfremd* sycophant whose estranged brother, Ernst, an enthusiastic Wagner-detractor nauseated by personal experience in Wahnfried, would become Strauss's librettist for *Feuersnot.*[29] Wolzogen became a Schopenhauerian before he became a Wagnerian and thus credited his interest in Wagner to the essay "Beethoven."[30] This philosophical orientation left him too far removed from the music for Strauss, who attempted only once to play the role of Wolzogenite, in a conductor's appreciation of the 1891 production of *Tannhäuser* published in the *Bayreuther Blätter.*[31] He also got to know the proto-fascist Houston Stewart Chamberlain, whom he soon recognized as a "literary lackey," endlessly occupied with nuances of interpretation that had little or nothing to do with music.[32] Henry Thode, who defined the true Bayreuthian by a commitment to "absolute idealism" (musical understanding having little relevance), made a similar impression.[33] That Thode was to some extent a rival of Chamberlain must have been apparent to Strauss, but the fact of their proximity to Cosima does not seem to have swayed him from concluding that they were more or less pale imitations of Ritter.[34]

The overriding importance of the Bayreuth experience, then, was for questions of practice. At Weimar, Strauss seems for a time to have been genuinely interested in applying Cosima's recommendations. This determination brought him glory at Wahnfried but conflict with the Weimar intendant, Hans Bronsart von Schellendorf, a genuine artist once closely associated with Liszt. Bronsart had profound doubts about Cosima's qualifications, calling her "unmusical, though certainly clever [*geistvoll*]" and claiming that any trained musician who had spent time with Wagner could give a more reliable account of his intentions than she.[35] With his technical expertise, broad experience, and complex mind, Bronsart may have been Strauss's most sensible advisor on Wagnerian matters. Beyond pointing out that current Bayreuth tempi in some cases contradicted Wagner's known intentions, Bronsart reminded him that Wagner himself was known to change his mind; "preservation" was tantamount to oversimplification. And even as early as 1890 Bronsart recognized that Wagnerian partisanship was fading, as friends and enemies alike acquired a new "objectivity" that rendered any kind of extremism anachronistic. The choice facing Strauss was to join the mainstream or wreck his career by preaching "ultraradical" absurdities.[36] Although Strauss rarely acknowledged Bronsart's wisdom at the time, as he matured he steered himself ever more in the direction represented by Bülow and Bronsart: practical appreciation of Wagner based on good musicianship, with a considered indifference to questions of philosophy and ideology.

This dephilosophized attitude toward Wagner is the one that controlled Strauss's outlook when he assumed the position of *Kapellmeister* at the Munich *Hofoper* in 1894. It was, of course, an attitude that disgusted Ritter, but one that Strauss had worked out in detail in his first opera, *Guntram*. That Strauss's 1894 debut as conductor at Bayreuth (in *Tannhäuser*) was also his swan song suggests that others may have gotten wind of his newly materialist perspective. Yet Strauss's open participation in the development of Munich's own "model performances" probably also played a role in his alienation from Bayreuth, particularly where Cosima was concerned. In any case, what is most fascinating about this period of Strauss's career is the range of Wagnerian perspectives from which he had by then distanced himself. Franz Strauss, Thuille, Seidl, Ritter, Cosima, Bülow, Bronsart, Levi, Wolzogen—all represented distinct outlooks on Wagner, and all believed that Strauss had somehow or other committed treason. Most interestingly, those who considered themselves pro-Wagner inevitably concluded that Strauss was rejecting Wagnerian art itself.

It is not surprising, then, that the central artistic project of this period of Strauss's life—the problematically epigonic *Guntram* (1893)—should have scandalized critics of every stripe. Particularly in Munich, where the work received a single performance some eighteen months after its Weimar premiere, it met with shrill resistance from all sides. As expected, critics generally at odds with Wagnerian harmonic and orchestrational complexity found the opera disastrously elaborate. The length of the title role, supposedly greater than that of *Tristan*, came in for special attention, as did the size of the orchestra, the difficulty of the parts, and the overall demands made on singers, players, and audience. In the words of the anonymous critic of the *Neue Musik-Zeitung:* "In this opera Richard Strauss has written a score which in complexity, polyphony, tormented and tearing harmonies, nerve-whipping dissonances, new orchestrational effects, disturbing rhythm, and finally physical and spiritual demands on the endurance of singers' throats, leaves *Tristan* far behind!"[37] For the conservatives, then, Strauss had "out-Wagnered Wagner"—no easy feat.[38]

Yet critics positively disposed toward Wagner did not accept *Guntram* any more readily. These writers offered a different, more-nuanced criticism, faulting Strauss less for technical extravagance than for a failure to grasp the spiritual level of Wagnerian art. Indeed the opera's technical mastery became a liability, given the absence of a compelling spiritual dimension: "It cannot be denied that the Wagnerian school, if one can speak of such a thing at all, has exercised the greatest influence on this undoubtedly quite talented musician. Unfortunately this influence reveals itself only through certain external manifestations, not through the composer's spirit and inner being."[39] Besides explicitly recognizing the deeply varied nature of Wagnerism as a movement, this critic voiced a concern on the minds of many Wagnerians whom Strauss knew personally. As he approached maturity, his interest in Wagner was becoming ever more confined to technical issues. This trend affected not only his compositions—though it manifested itself first and most strongly in this area—but also his activities as conductor and prominent musical personality. After 1893, Strauss curtailed his participation in the public discussion of Wagner. He withdrew from the Allgemeine Richard Wagner-Verein, after having revived (along with Seidl) the Weimar chapter, and he became a quiet bystander at Bayreuth. Instead of deepening his awareness and advocacy of the extramusical parameters of Wagner's art, he lost interest in them. And, as in his compositions he began to treat Wagner's music as a compendium of musical devices that he could deploy in his own exciting and personal way, so in his conducting work he used effective performance of Wagner as a means of advertising his skills as a practicing musician.

With respect to Wagnerism, then, the arrival of Strauss's maturity is defined by a critical purgation, whereby the varied extramusical perspectives on this art were jettisoned as a group. Doubtless his contempt for dreamers and dilettantes played a major role in this process. But just as important were his own philosophical inquiries, whose roots lay in the mid-1880s but whose impact would be felt for the remainder of his career.

Alexander Ritter and Metaphysical Wagnerism

If the contexts of Wagnerism swirling in Strauss's young mind were forbiddingly complex, his explanations of their effects on him could be shockingly simple. In memoirs and in private correspondence, his account of the Wagnerian experience always returned to a single figure, the shadowy and eccentric Alexander Ritter. If we take Strauss at his word, nearly every significant development in his conception of music had something to do with Ritter. At one time or another, both early and late in life, he credited Ritter with explaining to him the music-historical significance of Wagner and Liszt; curing him of prejudices against those composers; introducing him to the writings of Wagner and Schopenhauer, and to Hausegger's concept of *Ausdruck;* demonstrating how a poetic idea could generate a musical structure transcending depleted formal archetypes; and turning him into a *Zukunftsmusiker.* In 1889, Strauss went so far as to declare to Dora Wihan, perhaps his closest confidante at the time, that only through Ritter had he found "a solid view of life and art."[40]

Strauss's numerous appreciations of Ritter leave no doubt that this relationship stimulated his artistic development in unique ways. And though they include no mention of a "conversion," they do suggest that the friendship produced some sort of definitive transformation. The character of that transformation, however, has not been fully understood. Strauss's writings leave a misleading impression by dealing obliquely with the fundamental fact of the Strauss-Ritter association: that during the composition of *Guntram* the two became deeply and irrevocably estranged. From 1893 until Ritter's death in April 1896, they remained hopelessly divided on the questions that had formed the basis of their friendship—this in spite of the continuing cordiality of their relations and Strauss's faithful advocacy of Ritter's works (particularly the one-act operas *Der faule Hans* [1885] and *Wem die Krone* [1890]). The very fact of that advocacy, which Strauss maintained in utter isolation well into the twentieth century, speaks to a lingering sense of guilt, as does Strauss's choice of "Alexander" as the middle name of his only child. (The child's first name, "Franz," can be interpreted similarly.) As Strauss well knew, Ritter considered his protégé's unequivocal rejection of his aesthetic views the most bitter disappointment of his life.

By 1893, Ritter had made frustration and failure a way of life. As violinist, conductor, composer, and writer he had set high goals for himself and fallen short of every one. Sadly, his early years had shown great promise, if no signs of genius. Born in Russia in 1833 to a successful German businessman, he grew up in Dresden, where his mother moved the family after her husband's early death. Julie Ritter, a native of Hamburg and a person of marked literary inclinations, was to become one of Wagner's principal patrons during his Swiss exile. She was not, however, the most enthusiastic Wagnerian in her household, at least during the 1840s. Alexander, his older brother, Carl, and their school-friend Hans von Bülow outstripped all competition. In addition to the Dresden premieres of *Rienzi* (1842) and *Der fliegende Holländer* (1843), they attended all nineteen performances of *Tannhäuser* given in 1845–46, standing in the hallway when they could not get a seat. Through Alexander's violin teacher, the second concertmaster at the Hofkapelle (one Franz Schubert), the brothers wrangled an introduction to Wagner, who by 1849 could be found in the Ritter home listening to a quartet by Carl and explaining his need for financial freedom to Julie. For her part, Frau Ritter soon considered support of Wagner her "sacred duty," and when he was forced into exile she even considered accepting his invitation to move her family to Switzerland.[41]

In the meantime, Alexander found his own ways to involve himself in the cause of new music. After completing his work at the Dresden gymnasium and spending two years studying violin in Berlin under Ferdinand David, Ritter married Wagner's niece Franziska (son of Albert Wagner) and moved to Weimar. There he took up a position (thanks to Bülow's recommendation) in the Weimar Hoforchester. At twenty-one, then, Ritter found himself a member of the Wagner family, living in a New German Elysium, enjoying personal contact with Liszt himself (who pronounced him "a remarkable human being," as Ritter proudly reported to his wife), and practicing his art for the good of the cause. Two years later he received an offer of the dual position of concertmaster and music director at Stettin, and in 1856 he set out to assume a position of independent leadership in the German musical world, eager to disseminate knowledge gained from the masters themselves.

Stettin was the beginning of the end. Appalled by the laziness of musicians wedded to routine, Ritter treated as enemies those who displeased him and succeeded only in clarifying the battle lines. What is more, his determination to introduce Liszt's symphonic poems into the repertoire alienated the local press. After a poorly received performance of *Tasso* he responded in what would become typical fashion, lecturing his antagonists in a rebuttal dripping with sarcasm. Thus 1858 brought a return to Dresden, where he turned to composition while awaiting another offer. In 1860 he and Franziska both received offers at Schwerin; she took hers, but he continued to devote himself to composition, producing mainly violin works (for the time being). Three years later, though, the Ritters once again took up dual positions, this time at Würzburg. Here they stayed for the next nineteen years, with Ritter pursuing a wide array of musical activities (including the composition of numerous collections of lieder) that never quite convinced the public of his importance. His most successful moments came as first violinist of a quartet that toured regionally in the 1860s; as a composer he could develop only at the deliberate pace his talent would allow, and as a conductor he became wildly frustrated, finally giving it up in order to open a music store, which too failed.

As Ritter neared fifty he once again faced the necessity of looking for work, and the ever-faithful Bülow came through, this time with an offer aimed at his friend's relative strength: a position as violinist in the Meiningen Hoforchester. Though a former *Musikdirektor* could only look on a regular performing position as a demotion, associating with this remarkable orchestra offered Ritter the highest level of artistic collaboration and achievement of his life. And most significantly (as far as he was concerned), he made the acquaintance of Strauss, in whom he saw an opportunity to make good all his years of struggle. For Ritter this friendship represented a sort of last chance, and a most unexpected one. If he could turn Strauss's talent to his own ends, if he could convince him of the truth, Ritter believed he could at last make a significant practical impact on behalf of the New German cause.

Incredibly, Ritter seemed to achieve his goal. The two were inseparable, and when Strauss left Meiningen within six months, to fulfill his apparent destiny by joining the staff of the Munich *Hofoper*, Ritter followed and joined the orchestra. That he had sunk now to the second violins did not concern him, for he had determined to achieve his goals through Strauss. For the next three years they lived as mentor and protégé, spending days in rehearsal, evenings in the Weinstube Leibenstock on Promenadeplatz, and sharing many a supper at the home of Strauss's parents or in the modest Ritter apartment. In patient conversation Ritter laid out his view of music and life, ever more encouraged by Strauss's willingness to listen and learn, never suspecting that the intimacy of their discussions would in the end ground a thorough and merciless critique.

The content of Ritter's specific discussions with Strauss is not well documented, and the surviving correspondence is scanty, though some crucial items do survive. Still, the basics of what Ritter imparted can be reconstructed in some detail. In 1890, after moving to Weimar, Strauss wrote out several pages of notes for an unfinished article about Ritter that he intended to publish in a local newspaper; this document gives a good basic introduction to his mentor's worldview.[42] First and foremost, Ritter considered music a means of expression, roughly in Hausegger's sense. Form and content might relate to one another in varying ways— old means might be used to express new ideas, new means to express old ideas, or new means for new ideas ("the highest Beethoven, Wagner and Liszt!"). Music that disavowed any sort of expressive content, on the other hand, was "worthless." Ritter himself published his thoughts on this topic in a humorous parody of Hanslick's *Vom Musikalisch-Schönen*, entitled "Vom Spanisch-Schönen." This brief essay describes the author's discovery of a Spanish manuscript in which words are arranged not according to their meaning but following principles of symmetry and visual beauty. Complex formal arrangements abound, but sense remains entirely absent. As a theorist of this strange art explains, "in many places this amusement has become a kind of formal pastime. Of course, only people who don't understand Spanish enjoy it."[43]

The central tenet of Ritter's philosophy, then, and the contention that Strauss had to accept in order to proceed with his indoctrination, was that music served a higher extramusical purpose. Embracing this belief must have been difficult for the nuts-and-bolts musician in Strauss. The side of his personality that had reveled in his humanistic education at the Ludwigs-Gymnasium, however, stood ready to consider the possibility that his calling might have a deeper intellectual significance. Ritter's primary virtue, as Strauss planned to argue in his article, consisted in his clear awareness of the thesis of Wagner's *Opera and Drama*: that (as Strauss reminded himself) "the means of expression (music) had been made the goal, and the goal of expression (drama) had been made the means." The distinction between form and content soon became a kind of litmus test for Strauss. Adjacent to the notes for the Ritter article but apparently not intended for inclusion, he recalled a meeting with Bülow in which the elder man asked whether Strauss did not find a particular passage in the scherzo of a Brahms violin sonata "new." "In music with no poetic content," Strauss responded impatiently, "I can find nothing new." Clearly the content that Strauss expected was emotional expression, but his characterizations of it at this stage are not precise and altogether lack the abstruse philosophizing of Hausegger's writings.

While these principles hardly seem sophisticated enough to distinguish Ritter from any other composer who could recite the basic assertions of *Opera and Drama*, Ritter did bring a personal stamp to the matter with his focus on the spiritual power of Wagner's art. Though Ritter has rightly been characterized as an anti-Semite and a virulent German nationalist, his brand of Wagnerism was far more embedded in metaphysical concerns than in these (to his mind) essentially political issues.[44] As Strauss told it, even the production of new works in the Wagnerian style served primarily to protect the spiritual efficacy of Wagner's own music dramas. The absolute necessity of founding a Wagnerian school of composition—one that would sustain the public's attention—stemmed from the need to maintain the proper performance style, without which Wagner's works could not possibly achieve their proper effect. "Even the smallest talent" had something to contribute here, if exercised in an authentically Wagnerian manner, since a full repertory of such works would ensure the survival of the preconditions for effective performance of the Master's "monumental works." The occasion for which Strauss intended his article, the first Weimar performance of Ritter's two operas, indicates that it was in this light that Ritter saw himself as a contemporary German composer.

Alongside the Wagnerian issues raised in this article stood Ritter's concomitant devotion to Liszt. Here substantive information is more difficult to come by. Clearly it was Ritter's influence that stimulated the production of *Aus Italien* (1886) and the series of *Tondichtungen* that followed immediately afterward: *Macbeth* (1888, rev. 1891), *Don Juan* (1888), and *Tod und Verklärung* (1889). In these pursuits Strauss proceeded from the belief that Liszt represented the only reasonable continuation of Beethoven's legacy (a point he made explicitly in correspondence with Thuille).[45] Strauss used Beethoven alone, however, to justify his new symphonic direction to Hans von Bülow, famously citing Beethoven's own (ostensible) willingness to adjust musical form in his works to the "musical-poetic content" that he wished to express.[46] And in later years he would carefully distinguish his own "tone poems" from Liszt's "symphonic poems," though without clearly articulating his reasons. Ritter seems not to have been able to make a complete Lisztian of Strauss, then, though he did convince him that the only way open to him lay in programmatic composition in a more or less Lisztian spirit.

At the level of aesthetic content, distinctions between Wagner and Liszt mattered little to Ritter, and this was the level that appealed most strongly to Strauss—at least for now. Here Ritter advanced a form of neo-romanticism unsurpassed in its exaggerated spiritual claims. Liszt and Wagner revealed to the world the same content that had been offered by other great idealists—principally Plato, Jesus, and Schopenhauer—but now it became available in a uniquely apprehensible form, the language of late-nineteenth-century German music. The grandeur of such a view, the Wagnerian bravado with which it placed this art at the summit of the entire Western intellectual tradition, obviously attracted a young composer proud of his own relatively limited brashness. It was only a matter of time, though, before Strauss came to his senses. When he did, he happened to be in Egypt, to which circumstance we owe the existence of the most significant documentary source of Ritter's world-view: a pathetic fifteen-page letter from Ritter to Strauss that marked the end of their meaningful artistic relationship.

The proximate cause of the crisis was a revision that Strauss had carried out on the final act of his first opera, *Guntram*. This work, conceived as the first great tragedy of the post-Wagnerian era (and as the coronation of Wagner's successor), had occupied the two men since 1887, when Strauss had begun writing the libretto. Its plot concerned a young member of the "Streiter der Liebe" (Champions of Love), a brotherhood of minstrel-priests who used music to disseminate spiritual truths. On his first mission Guntram sins by killing an evil duke in self-defense; shortly thereafter his Gurnemanz-like mentor arrives to return him to the brotherhood for judgment. In the first version of the opera Guntram was to atone for his transgression in accordance with the brotherhood's decree. In the revision, however, he rejects his mentor's demands and flings his lyre to the ground, announcing that music can play no meaningful role in spiritual *Erlösung*. The implications were not lost on Ritter, notwithstanding Guntram's decision to retire to the woods to live a life of asceticism "in imitation of the Saviour." Strauss had turned his opera into a vehicle for the message that music was an unspiritual art.

Shortly after the 1894 premiere, Arthur Seidl wrote a review in the *Neue Deutsche Rundschau* suggesting that with this opera Strauss had rejected the "Bayreuth Grail-Brotherhood."[47] In fact what Strauss had rejected was Ritter's specific version of Wagnerism. Ritter became aware of this revision almost immediately after it was made, in December 1892. But at that time he was still in Munich, while Strauss had only recently set out on what was to be journey of some eight months. (Its purpose was to clear up a recurring lung ailment.) Sensing that he would be unable to change Strauss's mind, Ritter nevertheless summed up the basis of their endangered artistic relationship, in a last-ditch effort to recapture the devoted wonder with which Strauss had originally received his teaching. He recalled his own awakening to the significance of Wagner, in whom he had recognized "the artistically revealed summit of philosophical and religious culture." He relived his fears that after Wagner's death no one would be found to take up the cause, and his joy at discovering in Strauss "a gift that would enable you to build upon Wagner's achievement *in his sense*." And finally, he evoked the memory of the early days of their relationship, "when the understanding of the Wagnerian *works* grew in you more and more, as more and more you penetrated Wagner's worldview—which is based solely on Schopenhauer's epistemology and ideal-Christian *religiosity*—and made it your own." But now Strauss apparently had no use for anything but Wagner's musical technique: "What alone of Wagner has survived in you? The mechanics of his art."[48]

Strauss could not help but see the fairness of these charges, and he stood prepared to respond. Citing Schopenhauer, who was to become his principal weapon against spiritual interpretations of music, he attempted to explain himself in a carefully worded rebuttal.[49] (The Schopenhauerian issues in this exchange are discussed in chapter 2.) It was pointless, however, as he knew it would be; Strauss had rejected the very essence of Ritter's artistic philosophy, and the two were never reconciled. In hindsight, perhaps the most remarkable fact of all is that they had formed a relationship in the first place, given the idealistic substance of Ritter's views. That there *was* a relationship, and that it was no passing fancy, is as certain as the impossibility that Strauss could have remained a Ritter disciple permanently.

Strauss's claims that Ritter influenced him more profoundly than anyone else tell us that in his own view the crucial challenge of his maturation process was to come to terms with musical idealism. An atheist from his teens, Strauss would become a musical atheist as well—a composer utterly without interest in or patience with romantic (and neoromantic) beliefs regarding music's extramusical capacities. Still, he was no thoughtless iconoclast. His distaste for metaphysical mumbo jumbo may have been a natural predisposition, but his mature conclusions in that regard came as a consequence of direct experience and a sincere attempt at belief. Ritter had exercised influence by providing the most cogent, nuanced, passionate argument of music's metaphysical significance that Strauss ever encountered. In dealing critically with this particular theory Strauss dealt with what it represented, a principal vein of German musical romanticism.

In the end, Ritter considered Strauss's failure primarily moral and secondarily a function of ignorance and intellectual dilettantism. In the letter on *Guntram*, he suggested that Nietzsche lay behind the revision, a judgment that ignores Guntram's ostentatiously Christian declarations in his final monologue. This lapse and others like it point out Ritter's own dilettantism, at least regarding writers with whom he suspected he would not agree. More troubling to Ritter than Strauss's interest in Nietzsche, though, was his intention to separate the ethical and musical spheres. In one of the two major articles that he contributed to the *Bayreuther Blätter*, "Three Chapters: On Franz Liszt, on 'Die heilige Elizabeth' in Karlsruhe, and on Our Ethical Defect" (1890), Ritter argued for the essentially moral nature of aesthetic choices.[50] All Bayreuthians, if they were true believers, traced their faith back to a moment of epiphany (*Erkenntnis*) in which they realized that music existed to convey eternal truths. But pitifully few, according to Ritter, had the moral strength to retain the sacred memory of that moment and to remain devoted to it in practical ways, on a daily basis, in their professional lives. As a Wagnerian for nearly fifty years, Ritter believed he was one. In Felix Mottl, the rising star at Bayreuth whose performance of *Die heilige Elizabeth* took Ritter back to his idyllic Dresden days, he recognized another. Few others remained. And the distressing failure of two prominent unnamed professionals to keep the faith offered little hope for the future. (One of these traitorous musical leaders was obviously Bülow, whose continuing avoidance of Bayreuth Ritter resented, even though Bülow had kept Ritter afloat professionally for three decades.)

That Ritter would issue a plea for Wagnerian faithfulness in the *Bayreuth Blätter*, of all places, demonstrates a remarkable degree of enthusiasm but also a change in his conception of the enemy. In the old days, as Ritter recalled them, there was a recognizable distinction between the "Semitic view" of music, which saw it as an art of "sounding forms" (*tönende Formen*) perceived by the understanding alone, and the "Aryan view," which "recognized in music a language bestowed upon us through metaphysical influences, called upon to express the highest ideals that the inner eye of humanity can perceive."[51] But no longer could one assume that Jews were Jews and Aryans were Aryans. As Ritter explained in his other full article for the *Blätter*, "What Does the 1891 Festival Teach Us?," the time when the opposition was concentrated in a "confessionless consortium" ended with the first Bayreuth festival. Beginning in 1876 it had "rained Wagnerians," so that by 1891 the principal enemies of Wagnerism were no longer to be found among the avowed antagonists. Now the greatest danger was posed by those who had come late to the movement and lacked a thorough knowledge of the philosophical underpinnings of Wagner's art. Young Wagnerians in particular stood in grave danger of remaining perpetually superficial, learning Wagner's works but never grasping the spiritual content they were designed to express. The role of all mature Wagnerians, whose numbers were dwindling, was to stop the progress of this development before it was too late.[52]

On the surface it may seem odd that the *Bayreuther Blätter* would have run two substantial articles in three years by a little-known fanatic rebuking the readership for moral weakness and insufficient understanding of Wagner's overall artistic project. Given the tenuous situation of the festivals, however, even in the early 1890s, the choice makes some sense. The survival of this enterprise was by no means guaranteed at this time, and it would not be guaranteed until all unless German theaters, large and small, could be convinced that Bayreuth represented a uniquely authoritative source that it was their duty to emulate. Ritter contributed to this project by pointing out common "errors," irritatedly and with the histrionic impatience of one long in the know.

Still, Ritter's preoccupation with spirituality, his genuine conviction that music and the music dramas themselves were only a means, marked him as an extremist among extremists and could not long sustain serious attention. Even in Wahnfried he found no resounding agreement; as Strauss became a center of attention (beginning in the summer of 1889), Ritter faded into the crowd. In Bayreuth, as in those outposts in the wilderness, the branches of the Wagner Society, a work-centered theory of Wagnerism predominated. When Strauss revived the Weimar branch of the society in 1891, two years after assuming the position of *Kapell-meister*, meetings were devoted mostly to piano-vocal performance. The first four gatherings of this group included readings of scenes from *Die Walküre, Das Rheingold, Lohengrin, Götterdämmerung, Parsifal*, and *Sieg-fried*, as well as the *Siegfried-Idyll* and Liszt's *Héroïde funèbre*. Discussion of ideas, on the other hand, took place in sporadic, sparsely attended "Leseabende" such as that on 16 February 1891, at which Arthur Seidl read from the *Wagner-Lexikon* and "a small circle of members" reflected on the concepts of "revolution, reformation, and regeneration."[53] The focus on performance was typical and was a conscious choice of Strauss; whatever influence Ritter still had on his views, Strauss's interest in Wagner seems to have remained primarily artistic. In that fact we can see both the continuing force of his earliest attitudes about Wagner and the newly prominent role of Bayreuth's leader, Cosima Wagner.

Practical Wagnerism at Cosima Wagner's Bayreuth

With Cosima Wagner's invitation to join the staff of the 1889 festival, Strauss the Wagnerian stepped out from the shadows. At last he could put theory into practice, an opportunity that had eluded him for three years in Munich. And the stature of the invitation's source strengthened his belief in his potential as a conductor. Despite a clear understanding of his artistic abilities, Strauss seems not to have realized until 1889 just how high he could ascend in the world of conducting and how rapid that ascent could be. In Bayreuth, working side-by-side with artists whom he viewed as the leaders of European music and forming relationships with the Master's earthly representatives, his ego took root in fertile ground. That summer brought some of his most cherished successes to date, even though he achieved them as a rehearsal pianist ("I am the only one besides Levi and Mottl who plays in the piano rehearsals," he reported to his father) and preparer of the *Parsifal* choirs.[54] Equally thrilling were the visits to Wahnfried, at first for soirees and larger gatherings, then in casual, private affairs alone with the family. Soon Strauss felt thoroughly at home in the company of these great ones; by the time he left for Weimar, to begin a job whose principal attraction was a Wagner-friendly atmosphere, he believed he was destined for a position of leadership in German music.

However close her relationship to Wagner, and however deep her understanding of the works, Cosima interested Strauss primarily because she held the keys to the castle. Three years of stagnation had taught him that earning a professional reputation could be tedious; Bayreuth success would clear away many obstacles. Even Ritter was thinking along these lines. During the rehearsal period (in the month prior to the festival's opening) he became particularly anxious, asking Strauss in late July 1889 for "further reports; particularly, how your relationship with Frau Wagner is taking shape. You know what hopes for the future I am building on that."[55] Franz Strauss, on the other hand, had his doubts about the ultimate benefits of Wahnfried sycophancy, and in this case his son heeded the warnings (or at least claimed to), "reassuring" him of his "caution" in expressing opinions about what he saw and heard.[56] Though circumspection was not one of Strauss's strong suits, in this case he found hidden reserve and muzzled his normally forthright judgment for the sake of future gain.

Talent, prudence, and idolatry proved an irresistible combination to Cosima. Shortly she began to spread the word among the inner circle, for example to Chamberlain, to whom she described Strauss as "our rising star," a talent nearly the equal of the ill-fated Heinrich von Stein.[57] (So comprehensively positive was her impression that at one time Cosima envisioned Strauss as a prospective husband of Eva Wagner.)[58] It is not known who initially brought him to her attention. As early as 1887 Strauss had visited Wahnfried as a dinner guest, but the invitation to participate professionally was probably mediated by Cosima's advisors. Adolf von Gross would have known of Strauss's dissatisfaction with his Munich duties; as to musical qualifications, any number of Bayreuth's musical associates could have vouched for him. Of little consequence in the decision-making process was Strauss's music. Cosima only came to know *Don Juan* after the 1889 festival, and in any case she was no more interested in his compositions than in those of Felix Mottl or Hans von Bülow. What mattered to her was aptitude and loyalty, and here the scouts (Ritter among them) gave her nothing to fear.

Strauss's principal demonstration of loyalty came after he left Bayreuth that summer, when he took up his duties in Weimar. The experience of the 1889 festival taught him that the way out of his essentially probationary status at Bayreuth was to become a "loyal soldier of the cause" and to play the role as ostentatiously as possible. This meant, first of all, implementing Cosima's controversial performance-practice dicta to the letter and reporting the fact to her in great detail. Strauss understood perfectly well the challenge facing the Meister's widow: though Bayreuth was Wagner's own theater, he had died and taken his credibility with him; his absence left serious doubts about the home of Wagnerian authenticity. Levi and Richter certainly had reasonable claims, but so did many less-friendly individuals. Cosima's nightmare was for Bayreuth to become one good Wagner theater among several or, worse yet, a second-tier venue. To safeguard against this possibility and to preserve Bayreuth's unique status, she needed to publicize, as widely and regularly as possible, the existence of a performance style realizable only at Bayreuth. Provincial theaters could play a crucial role in helping her meet that challenge. Attempts to reproduce the Bayreuth style at theaters like Weimar would whet audiences' appetites, while the very inadequacy of the results would confirm that authenticity resided only on the Green Hill. Obviously the larger theaters would not fall into line, but she did not want them to, for with their larger resources they could have posed a genuine challenge. The presence of recognizable distinctions between productions at Bayreuth and those at, for example, Munich served her purpose; thus her distress when Munich mounted its own "historically authentic" production of *Lohengrin* hard on the heels of the Bayreuth production of 1894.[59]

Strauss did not let her down. Although Bronsart, the Weimar intendant, had a New German pedigree nearly as impressive as Ritter's (having studied piano with Liszt and served as Bülow's intendant in Hannover), Strauss arrived ready to make radical improvements. From his first Wagnerian production, *Lohengrin*, on 6 October 1889, the new *Kapellmeister* (not *Hofkapellmeister*, a title held by the rapidly aging Eduard Lassen) set to work bringing local practice into line with Cosima's wishes. He had made this intention clear to Bronsart during negotiations for the position, explaining that his study of Wagner's writings and dramas had shown him the need for fundamental reform in all areas of operatic performance, including conducting style and musical execution, but extending to vocal delivery, enunciation of text, acting, and set design. After a summer at Bayreuth, he had specific requirements in each of these areas, endorsed by the "highest authority." In rehearsals for *Lohengrin*, Strauss took "unprecedented steps" (as he informed Cosima), including two five-hour orchestral rehearsals, a blocking rehearsal that he himself supervised, and a series of piano rehearsals *"in Szene"* for soloists and choir. That the performance failed (in his view), particularly with regard to the stage presentation, only strengthened his resolve. He informed Bronsart that given the many "abuses, in the disregarding of the Meister's stage directions," the Weimar productions of Wagner would have to be rebuilt from the ground up. This declaration indicated what Bronsart could expect from his new employee for the remainder of their professional relationship (which lasted through the spring of 1894).

However much Strauss annoyed his intendant, the enthusiasm that he brought to the productions and his insistence that everyone perform at their highest level energized performers and audiences alike. His particular concern, and particular strength, was the integration of drama and music. On the conducting front he had much advice to offer regarding orchestral execution—particularly concerning tempi—though he remained severely limited by the tiny orchestra. Strauss had no intention of remaining in the pit, however, and pulled no punches in criticizing the "errors and stupidities" perpetrated by the stage director. He did not have the last word in this regard (strictly speaking he did not have the last word in any regard, but the force of his personality exhausted the opposition), yet he solicited extensive advice from Cosima anyway, because he wanted to be fully armed when conflict arose, and because he believed that decisions about musical interpretation had to be made with the pace and appearance of the stage action in mind. At times his questions to her seem comical in their pedantry:

[In act 1, scene 2, of *Tannhäuser*, mm. 4–8] should Tannhäuser close his eyes once more while Venus flatteringly draws him back?

After Venus's words "Reut es dich so sehr ein Gott zu sein?," during the rising sixteenth-note figure, may Tannhäuser make a slight movement of refusal, or should he remain still during Venus's entire speech?

Is it well that at the words "Fern von hier, in weiten, weiten Landen, dichtes Vergessen hat zwischen heut[e] und gestern sich gesenkt," Tannhäuser looks earnestly at Elizabeth's face, and first turns away at "all mein Erinnern," and that he makes no movement whatsoever up until "Euch zu begrüßen," where perhaps a small, humble, adoring gesture is not out of place?[60]

These queries speak volumes about Cosima's artistic leadership at Bayreuth, which preserved her minutely detailed memories in rigid perpetuity as though they were Wagner's final intentions. Of course, Cosima did not have any memories of a production of *Tannhäuser* under Wagner's direction, because she had not attended one, but that detail does not seem to have mattered to Strauss, or at least he did not mention it.[61]

One might reasonably ask whether Strauss's consultations with Cosima in this first year at Weimar were primarily for her benefit—that is, whether he actually considered and implemented her lengthy responses to his questions. (And she never failed to respond to his questions with clear, detailed directions.) All evidence indicates that he followed her advice religiously, right down to demonstrating for the ballet-master how the dancers should move in the Venusberg scene. That he did act on her suggestions leaves open the matter of whether he agreed with them, however. What they do show is that he was preparing for an event that would clinch his future at Bayreuth: a visit from Cosima during which she could see his work for herself, by attending a Wagnerian performance under his direction. Whatever else Strauss took from the 1889 festival, it is clear that he believed he could win a conducting assignment in 1891, if he played his cards right. (The year 1890 was to be an off-year, in preparation for the new production of *Tannhäuser*.) From there, a position as *Hofkapellmeister* at a major theater was only a step away, or so he believed. As far as Strauss and his career were concerned, his principal mission at Weimar was to impress Cosima.

It mattered little to Strauss that in the meantime he was burning his bridges to Bronsart and Lassen. Lassen he considered tired, if not lazy, and only marginally competent. Bronsart took him to task for his attitude toward those above him in rank, but otherwise he treated Strauss with remarkable understanding and a touching fatherly concern by no means to be expected of an intendant in this period. His reward was ever-increasing conflict with a twenty-five-year-old whose talent was surpassed only by his stubbornness, and whose thoughts were never far from the Festspielhaus podium. Indeed, if Strauss had not become gravely ill with a lung infection in May of 1891, he would have achieved his goal. Even in June of that year an agreement stood that he would conduct three performances of *Parsifal* and several of *Tannhäuser*. But as his convalescence extended he realized that he would have to wait another year.

The circumstances of the 1891 festival brought the first signs of a breach in the relationship between Strauss and Cosima. Though he arrived in Bayreuth in time for the start of rehearsals and pronounced himself ready to conduct, Cosima refused to consider it. At first he seems to have been flattered, or at least to have taken it as a sign of her long-term interest in him. He described the situation to his father: "Although I feel very well and healthy, Frau W. absolutely will not let me conduct his year. She says she would be terribly anxious and could not listen without agitation to a single note that I conducted."[62] By the following spring, however, he could not control his frustration, and a full-fledged controversy erupted over the tentative assignments for the 1892 festival. In January, Strauss had mounted his fourth Wagnerian production at Weimar, *Tristan* (in an ingenious *Nuancierung* that made the work playable by an orchestra with six first violins). Then in mid-March he believed he had reached an understanding with Cosima that he would be given full responsibility for one of the four works to be performed that year: *Parsifal, Tristan, Die Meistersinger,* or *Tannhäuser.* By 28 March, however, he had learned that his only responsibilities that season were to be the rehearsals of *Meistersinger* and the last two performances, with the dress rehearsal and first performances led by Hans Richter.

After the 1888 *Die Feen* episode in Munich, Strauss could not stomach the idea of doing the same thing at Bayreuth, even for Richter. He immediately fired off an angry response to Cosima, in a tone she rarely heard from friendly quarters: "if it is not possible for you to assign one of the four works to me alone, then I must ask you today to give up my participation in the festivals altogether, for I am of no use whatsoever in the role of a rehearsal-loafer as it is played by the unmusical assistants."[63] Of course he was bluffing; in his next letter (31 March) he accused a demon of guiding his pen and announced himself ready to serve Bayreuth by filling the lamps with oil if necessary. But his patience was running out; the timetable was already a year behind, and further delay had to be avoided at all costs. In the end, illness once again scrapped his debut, and the next opportunity came not until 1894, by which time Strauss was an altogether different person.

Given that by the mid-1890s Strauss had succeeded in alienating, or at least disappointing, all his other mentors (principally Ritter, Bülow, and his father), it is not surprising that his relationship with Cosima likewise came to a difficult end. The principal cause seems not to have been related to the conducting assignments at Bayreuth, however. The two patched up their differences by late summer 1892, when Strauss left for Greece, Egypt, and Italy to attempt a final cure of his lungs. Cosima resumed addressing him as "Expression" (*Ausdruck*), and all seemed well. But by the time Strauss did finally make his Bayreuth debut, in the 1894 production of *Tannhäuser*, other differences had surfaced, this time firmly artistic in nature and thus more serious. Since early in their correspondence, Strauss and Cosima had engaged in significant discussions of issues in contemporary musical aesthetics. Initially, these involved little more than commiserating about the sorry state of German musical taste, which could applaud works such as *Cavelleria rusticana* or Gounod's *Faust* while greeting Wagnerian masterpieces with indifference. These exchanges did much to sustain Strauss as he confronted what he viewed as Weimar's ignorant public and misguided, overly rigid artistic establishment. At the same time, however, they pointed up areas of seemingly benign disagreement that eventually turned into something more.

Curiously enough, the root cause of their eventual estrangement was Strauss's compositions. Cosima made it clear from the beginning that she considered new music a secondary activity for those in the Bayreuth circle, and Strauss did not press her, though he kept her apprised of his latest creative activity and asked for advice on fundamental aesthetic questions. The first opportunity Cosima found to hear Strauss's music came when she visited Weimar for a purpose more central to their relationship, to attend a performance of *Lohengrin* in February 1890. While there she allowed him to play *Don Juan* for her at the piano. Apparently she reserved judgment during the visit, for her first letter to him on her return to Wahnfried contains what is obviously a first response. By no means was it unequivocally positive. Gently but firmly, she admonished him "to listen closely to your heart, and here and there command your intelligence, which is always at the ready, to be quiet."[64] Her principal fear seems to have been that if left to his own devices he would become another Berlioz; indeed, within a month she responded to a remark Strauss had made about Berlioz's Requiem (he had found it "the most significant piece of church music outside the *Missa solemnis* and the *Graner Festmasse*") by declaring the work a "monstrosity" that "truly horrified" her.[65]

She had good reason to worry, for even at this early stage of their relationship Strauss stood ready to defend his ground. With a startling degree of confidence in the validity of his own position, he dared to contradict her, claiming that circumspection was unnecessary with regard to intelligence in an artist whose heart was properly motivated: "It is my belief (speaking generally) that in the case of a broad and generously disposed artistic nature the unconscious and the instincts, which together form the fundamental basis of every true and intensive creative urge, whether in the creative or the interpretive artist, will always be more powerful than the intellect, however highly developed the latter may be."[66] As was to be expected, he received (within three days) a detailed elaboration of the distinction between the intellectual and emotional sides of artistic creation. This time she sounded not unlike Franz Strauss, claiming that the most important lesson to be learned from Wagner's compositions was "simplicity." In contrast to Franz, however, Cosima defined simplicity (*Einfachheit*) in extramusical terms, as a function of the poetic material of the work. The problem of *Don Juan* lay in Strauss's concentration on the protagonist's actions rather than on the essential, universal idea of which that protagonist gave concrete expression: "It seemed to me, in your *Don Juan*, as if the behavior of your characters interested you more than the way those characters had spoken to you. I call that the play of the intelligence against the emotions." For an extramusical subject to generate the substance of a musical work, however, it had to be purged of its narrative aspects, reduced to a concentrated idea whose "universal" emotional content could then find expression through music. The program should not be used as a plot to be represented pictorially, but as a source of a particular, basic emotional "motive" that only music could adequately communicate. In the case of *Don Juan*, Strauss's brilliant representation of the plot had undermined the emotional efficacy of the music, rendering it impotent on the level of expression.[67]

Here, as Strauss must have realized, Cosima appealed to the authority of Wagner's essay "On Franz Liszt's Symphonic Poems" (1857). In this relatively brief essay, one of his most lucid explanations of his concept of "poetic intent," Wagner described the composer's responsibility to reduce the content of his poetic program to "a thoroughly compact ideal form" that could then be used to generate the musical form or "thread" of the work. Stimulated by an appropriately prepared (i.e., concentrated) poetic subject, the composer could use music to communicate that subject's emotional essence with unrivaled depth.[68] Berlioz formed a negative example; his preoccupation with pictorial effects in *Romeo and Juliet* had rendered the work emotionally sterile, just as, according to Cosima, Strauss's similar preoccupation had doomed his *Don Juan*. According to both Wagners, then, narrative effects had little or no value in the work of a "tone poet"; the program's primary function was to provide the kernel of poetic meaning that in turn gave rise to a unique, self-sufficient musical form.

In his next letter, Strauss returned to his standard deferential tone and promised that his next tone poem, *Tod und Verklärung*, would serve as proof that he had understood her. As one might imagine, the musical depictions of sighs, heartbeats, spasms, ticking clocks, and (once again) the moment of death failed to reassure her. Rather, she heard the work as an even bolder step away from Wagner, and after attending a performance of it in Berlin in February 1891 she warned him not to allow the "jumble of modernity" to derail his artistic development. Once again her advice fell on deaf ears, as we learn from her comment immediately after his Bayreuth debut: "so modern, and yet he conducts *Tannhäuser* so well."[69]

This quip served as Strauss's Bayreuth epitaph. By the next festival, the 1896 new production of the *Ring* honoring its twentieth anniversary, Strauss's place on the roster had been taken, for better or worse, by Siegfried Wagner himself. More to the point, reports of *Guntram* had made their way to Wahnfried, to ears better able than most to discern the fundamentally anti-Wagnerian tone of its philosophical conclusions.[70] And worst of all, Strauss had returned to Munich, where his position as designated successor to Levi put him in charge of Bayreuth's principal competition in Wagnerian performance. Strauss did attend the 1896 festival and was received with politeness at Wahnfried. His letters home to Pauline, however, show that he had seen through the illusion of Bayreuth authenticity. Siegfried's incompetence was just another symptom of Bayreuth's general artistic sterility, a condition unlikely to subside as long as fidelity stood higher as a Wagnerian value than competence and artistic sensitivity.

To that extent Ritter and Cosima shared a common philosophy as Bayreuthians. For both of them, when push came to shove, a moral sense of faithfulness to Wagner controlled all artistic decisions. Ritter would have reorganized the entire German operatic establishment in accordance with his view that the highest responsibility of opera houses nationwide was to preserve and teach an appropriate performance style for Wagner's works. Cosima cherished similar goals but allowed them to be implemented only by individuals willing to submit absolutely to her authority. (Thus her choice in 1886 of Felix Mottl as musical director, over Richter or Anton Seidl.) That authority had at best an unsteady foundation in artistic judgment. However intimately she had known Wagner,

Cosima's *Fachkenntnis* hovered equidistant from dilettantism and genius. In this respect she possessed no greater ability than Ritter, only greater power, for where he had nothing but pipe dreams, at least she could see her peculiar visions realized. In both cases, the driving force was a desire to live in the past; they had known Him, and now that he was gone the future promised only greater or lesser degrees of corruption.

Strauss, on the other hand, lived for the future. It was precisely at the time of his breakup with Cosima that he began to identify his new works explicitly as belonging to the twentieth century. The critical side of this impulse surfaced in the published score of the 1895 song "Wenn," which begins in E-flat major but ends in E major. At the change in signature Strauss placed an asterisk and recommended that "singers who intend to perform this song in the nineteenth century take this passage a half-step lower and thereby end the work in the key with which it began."[71] Yet looking forward was also a positive, productive, "optimistic" attitude for Strauss, with serious implications. The dedication of *Also sprach Zarathustra*—"to the twentieth century"—was by no means simply a joke; *Zarathustra* is the only one of Strauss's tone poems without a real dedicatee and the first not presented to one of the major influences on his creative life. (The earlier tone poems were offered to Ritter [*Macbeth*], Thuille [*Don Juan*], Friedrich Rösch [*Tod und Verklärung*], and Arthur Seidl [*Till Eulenspiegel*]). Perhaps the work was in fact dedicated to himself, to his own future. Certainly he guided his career down a path much more his own after his appearance at Bayreuth in 1894 and his marriage later that fall.

Strauss was not unsympathetic with the desire to preserve appropriate performance standards for Wagner's works. He did not believe, however, that his highest artistic mission was to protect an idealized past, and this un-Bayreuthian determination compelled him to demonstrate in some specific way that what had come before had either fallen short or lost its relevance. That project would be primarily creative—a project for a composer. Moreover, composing meaningfully in the 1890s necessitated distancing oneself from Wagner; otherwise one would produce either cheap imitations or training exercises. It is worth noting that Strauss's compositional activity came to a virtual standstill during his period of intense Wagnerism. In the years 1890–94 he composed a small set of incidental pieces (for *tableaux vivants* at a Weimar court gathering), a fanfare for A. W. Iffland's play *Der Jäger*, six lieder, and two pieces for piano quartet. Only the lieder were published (the last four as op. 27). That lull, a striking exception in Strauss's long life, can be explained only by the fact that serious Wagnerism precluded creative activity or obviated the need for it. But a critique, a suggestion that music had a future, would demand new music, music that could justify its own existence.

Engagement with Wagner fostered the development of Strauss's creative personality because it allowed him to proceed, at his own pace, from imitation to reaction and finally to assimilation. Pedagogically this was a technique he had practiced throughout his life, and it did not change now. Indeed, in this instance it had its most important results, leading him forcefully to an independent, mature personality. Although this process brought unfortunate consequences for his personal relationships and temporary professional setbacks, in the long run it helped him in every respect. Experience taught Strauss that offending people, even powerful people, could be good for one's career. Well before he reached the pinnacle of his profession, Strauss had a lengthy list of those who liked him less than they once had; as Hofmmansthal would later remind him, "you have not looked for many friends, and have not had many."[72] But the longer the list of enemies, the greater his fame, and at no point in his life was that rule more important than in his dealings with the Wagnerians. Strauss understood that for him success depended on "musical secession" (as Cosima put it in 1896, one year before the Viennese secession)—on establishment and control of a non-Wagnerian space, a space that could be inhabited by someone devoted to the music of a new century.[73] Without the unique breadth of his experience of Wagnerism, that recognition might never have come.

2

Music and the "Denial of the Will"
Schopenhauer in Strauss's Life and Work

*I*t is widely known that Strauss had a significant encounter with the philosophy of Schopenhauer during the 1880s and early 1890s. The intellectual substance of that encounter, however, has received little attention.[1] Strauss's own account would seem to make further investigation unnecessary; it states simply but directly that Ritter introduced him to the philosophy, with decisive implications for his creative work.[2] Yet that claim is a gross oversimplification, notwithstanding its source. During the decade-long period in which Strauss occupied himself intensely (if sporadically) with the details of Schopenhauer's philosophy, he had access to a variety of readings, and his own views evolved through several markedly different phases. There was much more to this process than simply becoming aware of Schopenhauer and reacting musically. As with his experience of Wagnerism, Strauss faced the imposing challenge of deciding among conflicting interpretations, and he engaged in what can fairly be described as a passionate struggle to develop personal conclusions about an important and confusing set of issues. In the introduction to this chapter I will sketch the history of that struggle, before considering in the subsequent sections the three most important concerns in Strauss's reception of Schopenhauer.

By limiting his public recollection of the matter to Ritter, Strauss diverted attention (deliberately or otherwise) from the fact that he studied Schopenhauer both before he met Ritter and after their relationship had cooled. Those activities too were of decisive importance. As I will demonstrate, when Strauss rejected Ritter's interpretation (during the winter of 1892–93), he did so on Schopenhauerian grounds, believing that his own reading was more fair and more faithful to the philosophical text. Finding that way out would have been more difficult, and perhaps impossible, had Strauss not entered into the relationship equipped with knowledge supplied by prior experience. The break with Ritter was ultimately a disagreement about how freely one should manipulate canonical texts and indeed how fully one ought to understand those texts before turning them to one's own purposes. Strauss's views on this subject were much more conservative than those of Ritter—or Wagner, for that matter. His stubborn fidelity to Schopenhauer's ideas and his command of them were unusual among composers of that era, and they provide compelling evidence of a pragmatic kind of intellectual profundity.

That a nonacademic would have busied himself with Schopenhauer should not be surprising. The philosopher's enormous influence at the end of the nineteenth century was strongest outside of academe; one thinks not only of Nietzsche and Wagner but of Freud, Burckhardt, Tolstoy, and a host of others.[3] Strauss's educational background gave him a means of entry just as effective as what these others would have had in their late teens. At the gymnasium he gained not only an appreciation for careful thought but also a context and a methodology for approaching philosophical texts. Modern philosophy was of course not covered in the gymnasial curriculum, but the classics, in the original languages, were a mainstay.[4] The study of Plato and Aristotle provided him with a framework within which to conceptualize later philosophical approaches—a sense of long-term vision that was also central to Nietzsche's thought and indeed to any German thinker of the era. (Strauss would easily have recognized, for example, that Kant had a place in an idealist tradition leading back ultimately to Plato.) At this educational level the developments of the modern era (scholasticism, humanism, rationalism, the Enlightenment, and so on) would not have been considered from a strictly philosophical perspective, but they would inevitably have figured in the study of history, which was Strauss's favorite subject and remained a passion throughout his life.[5] The subject of history in the overtly humanist institution of the gymnasium meant intellectual history as much as political and social history, especially in more recent periods. On the completion of his *Absolutorium*, then, Strauss did have a basic intellectual context into which to fold specialized philosophical knowledge, and he had at least a basic conception of intellectual rigor.

During his study at the University of Munich (1882–83), Strauss's teachers included several prominent neo-Kantians, including the "objective idealist" Carl Prantl and the positivists Alois Riehl and Friedrich Jodl, as well as the older figure Moriz Carrière (who was famously vilified by Nietzsche in *Schopenhauer as Educator*).[6] Hegel's influence notwithstanding, German academic philosophy since mid-century had lost its reputation as queen of the sciences, and it now counted as a "learned discipline beside others," largely mired in narrow technical debates.[7] Understandably, Strauss had little patience for this pursuit. The well-attended lectures on Schopenhauer by the young *Privatdozent* Jodl, however, offered "more stimulation" according to Steinitzer, and they became the subject of regular discussions with Rösch and Seidl.[8] Jodl's principal scholarly concern was the history of ethics, within which he identified Schopenhauer as a stage in the passage toward a morality fully divested of metaphysics as well as religion. Eventually Jodl would found a movement, "Ethische Kultur," devoted to nonreligious moral education and a form of antimetaphysical monism.[9] These ideas resonated with the intuitive atheism of the young Strauss, who belonged to the first generation of European society in which, as Bryan Magee has noted, "large numbers of intelligent and well-educated people were open about not believing in God."[10] More important, whatever the extent to which Strauss accepted Jodl's claims, to understand them he had to be conversant with the fundamentals of Schopenhauerian philosophy: the "will" as the basic metaphysical force of the universe; perceptible reality as an objectification of that will; and the moral imperative of "denial of the will" (*Willensverneinung*), by temporary or permanent means (art and ascesis, respectively). We cannot know how deeply he delved into these matters at this stage of his life, but even this basic level of understanding establishes that at the time of the encounter with Ritter, Strauss was something more than the philosophical novice that he is thought to have been.

If in 1885 Strauss did not need Ritter to explain the nuts and bolts of Schopenhauer's philosophy any more than he needed him for an introduction to Wagner's music dramas, how did Ritter so profoundly alter Strauss's world? The answer is that he related the two, with a complex theory of the mutual dependence between Schopenhauer's philosophy and Wagner's musico-dramatic method. Ritter convinced Strauss, at least briefly, that Wagner's musical technique was uniquely suited to accomplish the philosophical redemption described by Schopenhauer. In providing this link, Ritter brought together concerns whose practical relationship Strauss had never seriously considered, thereby revolutionizing the young composer/conductor's beliefs about his mission as an artist. This new theory came at an opportune time, just as Bülow was initiating Strauss into a revelatory style of musical interpretation, one that would leave an impression even longer-lasting than Ritter's. It is no surprise that in the company of such authoritative and passionate figures, this particular view of Schopenhauer eclipsed all other possibilities, at least for the time being.

On the other hand, Ritter's mastery of the details of Schopenhauer's philosophy is questionable, and indeed it has been questioned, at least generally, by two early writers. Max Steinitzer, who belonged to Strauss's circle of friends in the early 1880s, acknowledged Ritter's impact, but on balance he emphasized Strauss's university work and his private studies, clearly believing that Ritter had provided a novel way of construing a philosophy with which Strauss was already familiar.[11] Similarly, Erich Urban found it difficult to believe that Strauss could have been profoundly affected by such "a confused thinker, an unclear head"; Urban looked instead to Bülow as the main source of Strauss's aesthetic reorientation.[12] Ritter obviously did exert influence, but not through a comprehensive and unassailable mastery of the philosophical subject matter, and that shortcoming allowed it to work in ways that he did not intend.

For example, rather than introducing Strauss to Schopenhauer, Ritter stimulated a return to the text for further study. By Christmas 1889 Strauss owned an edition of Schopenhauer's complete works, a gift from his parents.[13] That they gave him the complete five-volume set suggests the seriousness of the enthusiasm; by far the more common approach to Schopenhauer at this time was through the one-volume *Aphorismen zur Lebensweisheit (Aphorisms on the Wisdom of Life)*, the "Bible of the educated bourgeoisie."[14] Over the next several years, particularly during his Weimar period (beginning in 1889), Strauss continued to work his way through the text—not constantly, it would seem (his professional and artistic activities would have precluded it), but with a regularity that demonstrates a sort of nagging compulsion. By June 1892, he wrote to his sister that he longed for a "reasonable discussion," even with Thuille about hunting dogs, "just so that for once I can get Schopenhauer, who is already totally spoiled for me, out of my head."[15] The cause of that distaste would gradually emerge during the next ten months: after an extended apprenticeship with Ritter, and after years of personal study designed to facilitate the transition from apprentice to mature advocate, Strauss found himself unable to reconcile the aesthetics he had received from Ritter with the philosophical conclusions that he gleaned from Schopenhauer's text. Diaries and letters written during his trip to Greece, Egypt, and Italy (1892–93) show Strauss first turning Schopenhauer's philosophy against Ritter's aesthetics, then attempting to use parts of Schopenhauer's text to undermine that very philosophy (see below). In other words, there exists a documented private critique of Schopenhauer by Strauss, which until now has received virtually no attention. Ultimately that critique forced Strauss either to abandon Schopenhauer or abandon his art. The choice was not as easy as we might imagine, and it motivated his turn to a new source: Friedrich Nietzsche.

In the following sections, I describe the three main issues in Strauss's early involvement with Schopenhauer: Ritter's interpretation of Schopenhauer; the impact of Ritter's and Strauss's divergent readings of Schopenhauer on *Guntram*; and Strauss's final, systematic critical rejection of the philosopher. This evidence shows that Strauss recognized and rejected the distortive aspects of Ritter's interpretation after formulating his own painstaking, scrupulous reading of the text. He then incorporated what he considered a faithful distillation of Schopenhauer into his revision of the plot of *Guntram*, the composition that he considered the crowning achievement of his early career. That he did so provides compelling evidence of the seriousness with which he regarded the implications of philosophical study for his artistic activity. Ironically, it was his very respect for the dignity of Schopenhauer's thought that led Strauss to disavow that philosophy altogether.

Schopenhauer as Interpreted by Ritter

The attraction of Schopenhauer's philosophy to Ritter was its integration of the metaphysical and the ethical, with art serving as a means to bring that relationship to light and allow it to work in the lives of ordinary humans. Because the interdependence of metaphysics, ethics, and art has been insufficiently considered in the sparse literature on Ritter, the specifics of his debt to Schopenhauer have yet to be illuminated. Strauss's own assessment of Ritter did stress the breadth of his accomplishments (as composer, performer, and *literatus*), but with insufficient depth to explain fully the project's integrative thrust—the belief that art existed to communicate a metaphysically based moral code. Siegmund von Hausegger, Ritter's son-in-law and the author of his only biography, described the impetus of his creative work, especially the two one-act operas *Der faule Hans* (1885) and *Wem die Krone?* (1890), as moral in the tradition of Schiller.[16] Yet here too the details of that orientation are lost amid a wash of sentimental protest against Ritter's own conclusion that the modesty of his creative gifts bore some responsibility for his failure to win more converts.

Like Schopenhauer, Ritter suffered for many years in the belief that he had discovered a great truth that the world chose to ignore. In order to rectify this situation, he sought to win over someone with genuine talent, who might serve as a more effective advocate. The history of this last desperate attempt at communication, which is told in the lengthy letter of 17 January 1893 that Ritter wrote during the breakdown of their relationship, places great emphasis on Schopenhauer and thus gives important evidence of that dimension of Ritter's worldview.[17] Indeed, when reading it one might easily imagine the atmosphere of the Ritter *Tafelrunde*, where more than one important member of turn-of-the-century German musical culture heard of the vital importance the philosophy of pessimism held for their artistic pursuits.[18]

First and foremost, Ritter appropriated the Schopenhauerian concept of *Willensverneinung* (denial of the will) as the "only demonstrable goal" of the lives of cultural leaders, whose mission was to assist the rest of humanity in achieving that same goal. Ritter added a nuance to Schopenhauer here with the claim that artists had a special responsibility to communicate on a broad scale what Schopenhauer himself identified as the main accomplishments of the *Die Welt als Wille und Vorstellung*: the revelation of the true inner nature of the universe (as will) and the identification of an appropriate human response (denial of the will).[19] The connection of the metaphysical to the ethical was already demonstrated by Schopenhauer himself; indeed, the nature of the metaphysical demanded an ethical response. Likewise, Schopenhauer's book 3 described the capacity of art to provide moments of "will-less knowing." Ritter simply added the claim that artists, and above all musical dramatists, were called upon to evangelize, as it were, so that widespread implementation could become a reality.

That Ritter considered the idiom of the Wagner-Liszt school (as Ritter characterized it) the most effective means of accomplishing this task is not at all surprising. That he treated *Willensverneinung* as a serious goal of life, on the other hand, may seem bizarre. One must remember, however, that Schopenhauer's fame and influence, which had only begun to emerge in the last years of the philosopher's life, reached enormous proportions in the 1880s. If in university philosophy departments he never quite overtook Hegel, in the rest of European culture he enjoyed a reputation as one of the greatest thinkers in the Western tradition. Bryan Magee has argued that this phenomenon was driven by the bourgeois culture of which Strauss and Ritter were so thoroughly a part, rather than by Schopenhauer's remarkable influence on the period's greatest geniuses. For a great many ordinary educated Germans at the end of the century, skepticism about God did not rule out simultaneous misgivings about the ability of science to answer all of life's questions. Schopenhauer filled this gap, with a blind, unconscious force that seemed all the more credible for the contrast its pessimistic associations provided with the optimism institutionalized by religion, science, liberalism, socialism, and nationalism. Furthermore, Schopenhauer identified a response that, if not obviously practical, at least offered a focus for spiritual contemplation.[20]

According to Ritter, all of the great spiritual thinkers of the past had shared the common objective of *Willensverneinung*. This idea too was drawn directly from Schopenhauer, who found prototypical "saints" among Christian, Hindu, and Buddhist traditions.[21] But unlike Schopenhauer, an avowed atheist (and therefore a nearly unique phenomenon among Western philosophers up to that time), Ritter theorized that Christianity was the only appropriate modern religious framework for authentic denial.[22] This choice, which flew in the face of Schopenhauer's explicit dismissal of Christianity, reflected Ritter's passionate Catholic faith, but it also allowed him to argue that the musico-dramatic technique of Wagner (as composer of *Parsifal*) offered the only true of hope for members of society at large to rise to this higher spiritual level. "Bayreuthians"—the brotherhood into which Ritter had initiated Strauss—served the world by preaching and bringing about this Christianized form of *Willensverneinung*.[23] If they gave up that holy mission, humanity would be lost.

In attempting to recall Strauss to this cause, Ritter reminisced about the joy he felt during the gratifying days in Meiningen "when I saw how the understanding of the Wagnerian *works* heightened in you more and more, as more and more you penetrated Wagner's worldview—which is based solely on Schopenhauer's epistemology and ideal-Christian *religiosity*—and made it your own."[24] Ritter's joy during this period came not from anticipation of the practical advantages of having Strauss in the camp (which would be many), but from seeing that Strauss had grasped the spiritual content of Wagner's works. Regardless of one's musical abilities, the Master's dramas would remain an empty shell, no better than a Brahms symphony, until one had learned to interpret them as conduits for truths far more momentous than anything specifically musical. At bottom, Wagner thus had a purely practical importance for Ritter, as the creator of a means better suited than any other to communicate Schopenhauerian/Christian truths. The music drama was not the end but the phenomenal embodiment of the end, and unless that fact were understood the works were doomed to misfire.

In Ritter's view, the Wagnerian project had been misfiring a good bit since the death of its founder. Now it faced an uncertain future, precisely because no single individual could be discovered who possessed both a musical technique adequate to the demands of the music dramas and a profound understanding of "Schopenhauer's epistemology and ideal-Christian religiosity." This absence left German culture without a conductor who could bring these works to the stage in a spiritually authentic manner, and without a composer who could build on Wagner's accomplishment. But the arrival of Strauss had appeared to change all that, in answer to Ritter's lifelong wish:

> My friendship for you was based on the foundation of a confident hope. In Wagner's works I had recognized the artistically revealed summit of philosophical and religious culture. Who would be qualified to build upon this summit? For long years I remained on the lookout for such a person, yearning, but in vain. Should Wagner's achievement really become a dead end, because in the entire German nation no a single person competent to the task could be found? This question tormented me with agonizing worry and deep pain. Until finally I recognized in *you*, dear friend, a gift of which I believed it possible to suppose, that it would enable you to build upon Wagner's achievement in *his sense*.[25]

Strauss's unusual strength, according to Ritter, lay in his rare combination of prodigious musical skill and profound philosophical understanding. Given Strauss's already pronounced distaste for religion, it was probably overly optimistic for Ritter to hope that his protégé would concern himself in any detailed way with the Christian side of things. But Ritter did not dwell at length or in isolation on Christianity—which points to the centrality of Schopenhauer in his thought, as well as to Strauss's good command of the philosophical issues. What mattered above all was that Strauss conceived of Wagnerian art as an epistemological mechanism directed toward denial of the will, and that he wielded it with that goal in mind.

The proximate cause of this letter was of course the eleventh-hour revision of *Guntram*, the work that Ritter had always believed would revitalize Wagnerian art and catalyze a widespread consummation of

Schopenhauer's redemptive vision.[26] None of that would be possible, Ritter believed, if the opera did not have an appropriate denouement. Ritter fully approved of the crisis in Strauss's plot—Guntram's sense of guilt over having killed the evil duke while having fallen in love, unconsciously, with the duchess. The crux of the matter was the crisis's resolution, however. Guntram had to find redemption through atonement for both the outward sin and the inner sin. In this necessity Ritter saw an opportunity to demonstrate the moral power of Schopenhauerian self-denial, which was to be taught to Guntram after he submitted himself to the brotherhood's judgment at the behest of his mentor, Friedhold. *Willensverneinung*, when played out in this quasi-mythical dramatic context, would be modeled for the masses; at Guntram's side they would receive instruction in the appropriate response to sin and would feel, thanks to the music, the spiritual power of redemptive renunciation.

Alas, Strauss had other ideas. In December 1892, while hundreds of miles south of Munich and thus out of Ritter's reach, he decided that Guntram would determine his own redemption, by leaving behind both the duchess and his mentor in order to seek atonement as an ascetic. Ritter's negative response to this choice is well known, but the specific Schopenhauerian grounds for his complaints have not yet been explained. The revision was to him "eminently unmoral" precisely because it eliminated Guntram's "self-overcoming" (*Selbstüberwindung*): a conscious act of self-denial undertaken by the hero in accordance with higher spiritual laws in spite of the personal consequences. In other words, the revision had, in Ritter's view, eliminated the crucial Schopenhauerian feature of the plot. The oath to the brotherhood was necessary because it symbolized commitment to something outside of the self; honoring that commitment in the context of a prosecution would make concrete the idea of self-denial. Guntram's determination of his own punishment thus amounted to a self-affirmation, something Ritter could not reconcile with Schopenhauer.

Ritter also complained about this revision on Christian grounds, but that criticism must be read in light of Ritter's belief that Jesus himself was one of history's great models of denial of the will. Anachronism did not stand in the way here; Schopenhauer had merely given a name and an explanation to a spiritual state already known through example. For this reason, the character of Guntram (said Ritter) was to be conceived in the drama as Christian: "Guntram's character has developed from an upbringing that was directed exclusively in the sprit of a Christian worldview. He has learned to observe the world in *this* spirit. In addition he

has learned his art and: how it is to serve this spirit." The interchange-
ability of Christian and Schopenhauerian worldviews for Ritter is shown
by his conclusions about what this revision would do to Strauss's ability
to compose in the Wagnerian style. Just as Guntram's abandonment of
the brotherhood's Christian worldview would destroy him as an artist—
because his art was meant "to serve this spirit"—Strauss himself would
bring about the destruction of all that Wagner had achieved by abandoning its philosophical underpinning: "nothing of Wagner's worldview
remains in you. What alone of Wagner has survived in you? The mechanics of his art. But to use this art for the glorification of a worldview
that directly contradicts the Wagnerian is not *to build upon* Wagner's
achievement, but: *to undermine it.*"[27] In the drama and in real life, the
interdependency among religious, philosophical, and musical components was absolute. Any attempts to modify the complex could only result
in a mockery of the whole. Strauss's apparent rejection of Schopenhauer
amounted to a rejection of Wagner, even though Ritter offered no specific musical evidence to support that conclusion.

Guntram as a Schopenhauerian Opera

Like Ritter's critique of the *Guntram* revision, Strauss's subsequent estrangement from Ritter has been widely acknowledged but only dimly
understood. The elder man's disappointment had a subtler motivation
than that Strauss had refused to throw the new third act "into the fire."
After receiving Ritter's plea, Strauss responded by sending to him, and
also to Thuille (who was at the time still meeting regularly with Ritter
at the Leibenfrost), a carefully reasoned Schopenhauerian justification for
the new plot.[28] In light of Schopenhauer's own statements about the
means of achieving *Willensverneinung*, this alternative reading of Schopenhauer is not only reasonable but nearly unavoidable. And the new
third act, when interpreted from this standpoint, comes off as a remarkably well-informed piece of philosophical drama—one might even call it
a dramatization of Schopenhauer's ultimate conclusions about the power
of music. To Ritter's dismay, however, this justification also exposed either the tendentious features of his reading of Schopenhauer or perhaps,
and worse, his ignorance.

In defending himself to Ritter, Strauss first reminded Ritter that the
idea of a fraternal order "that has taken upon itself the task of uniting
art and religion" was the first stimulus of *Guntram*.[29] (Strauss began draft-
ing the plot after encountering an article on medieval artistic-religious

orders in the *Neue freie Presse* in the summer of 1887.)[30] But to Ritter's horror, Strauss now claimed that the central artistic task of *Guntram* was to demonstrate the implausibility of the brotherhood's goals. The belief that music could be used to help an individual achieve *Willensverneinung* or to promote widespread awareness of the need for *Willensverneinung* Strauss called "utopian." And he did so not on his own authority but on that of "our friend Schopenhauer, [who] also takes this view in Volume 3 of *Die Welt als Wille und Vorstellung*."[31] Strauss appealed here to a passage at the end of the third book that serves as a segue to the fourth book by concluding that art does not have the power to bring about a permanent, comprehensive stilling of the will. In Schopenhauer's view, this unavoidable conclusion definitively marginalized art vis-à-vis the dilemma at the core of his philosophy, for in the end the best that can be expected from art is a brief glimpse of what might be brought about more effectively by other means:

> That pure, true, and profound knowledge of the inner nature of the world [provided by art] now becomes for him [the artist] an end in itself; at it he stops. Therefore it does not become for him a quieter of the will, as we shall see in the following book in the case of the saint who has attained resignation; it does not deliver him from life for ever, but only for a few moments. For him it is not the way out of life, but only an occasional consolation in it, until his power, enhanced by this contemplation, finally becomes tired of the spectacle, and seizes the serious side of things. The St. Cecilia of Raphael can be regarded as a symbol of this transition. Therefore we will now in the following book turn to the serious side.[32]

This was likely the first and only time that Ritter found himself accused of a lack of philosophical seriousness. Nevertheless, in view of this major turning point in Schopenhauer's own text, Ritter could not avoid admitting that for the philosopher himself, art had strict limits. The artist as artist succeeds in perceiving the will and in giving objective form to this knowledge, but he cannot proceed to the all-important next step of using this knowledge effectively on the metaphysical plane. Instead he finds himself trapped, endlessly perceiving and representing the will but never actually quieting it for more than a few instants. An artist hoping to move beyond perception into action would have to undergo a transformation, giving up the promising but ultimately ineffectual means (art) for a different approach outlined by Schopenhauer in his fourth book.

With this new understanding of the practical relationship between art and spirituality in Schopenhauer's philosophy, Strauss took his decisive step away from Ritter. Following *Guntram's* example, Strauss determined to treat art as a self-contained sphere of activity, one that could achieve only its own ends, not those of religion, philosophy, or ethics. He considered *Parsifal* the exception that proved the rule:

> According to Schopenhauer the artistic contemplation and representation of ideas are independent in themselves of all ethics; and even though Wagner succeeded in the case of *Parsifal*, that does not mean to say that every other artistic undertaking which intends too strong an ethical tendency from the first does not already, insofar as it is art, (Schopenhauer, vol. 1, pp. 294ff.), contain the seeds of death in itself. [The parenthetical reference to Schopenhauer is Strauss's.]

The nuances of Strauss's reading of Schopenhauer are important here. He did not mean to argue for aesthetic formalism but to restrict art to its proper activity of "representing" the metaphysical state of affairs, preventing it from extending beyond representation into acts or attempted acts that Schopenhauer himself had declared must fail.

The passage to which Strauss referred deals with tragedy and how this highest form of poetry achieves its effect. The purpose of tragedy, according to Schopenhauer, was "the representation [*Darstellung*] of the terrible side of life." By giving humans an indication of "the unspeakable pain, the wretchedness and misery of mankind, the triumph of wickedness, the scornful mastery of chance, and the irretrievable fall of the just and the innocent," tragedy communicated "the nature of the world and of existence."[33] That act or representation did not on its own bring about any response, however; it merely allowed the people witnessing the tragedy to perceive the situation accurately. The question of how to respond lay outside the purview of drama and indeed outside the purview of art.

Strauss understood this distinction, and he used it, in the letter to Thuille, to justify his new third act. Declaring that "it's precisely on the subject of 'artisthood' and pure perception [*reine Anschauung*] that I've found some wonderful ideas in Schopenhauer," Strauss pointed out that the philosopher's own writings ruled out art as a means of achieving *Willensverneinung*. As Strauss construed Schopenhauer, it was not the place of the artist to affirm or deny the will: "*he simply represents it.* That's all—but that's also—'*all!*' It's what Goethe did, it's what Wagner did, and we little chaps should follow their example and not *preach* a moral sermon."[34] Here Strauss cited the greatest figures known to him as proof that the artist's sole mission was to use his "pure perception" and to give external form to that knowledge. No further moral, religious, or philosophical duty existed, because none was possible. Attempts to use art to effect a particular response to the situation—attempts that were the founding mission of Guntram's brotherhood and Ritter's Bayreuth—exceeded the mission and capacity of artisthood.

In the letter to Ritter, Strauss likewise made it crystal clear that he did not believe that art could serve to implement a metaphysically based ethics: "In an artist whose works have this strong ethical or religious tendency the religious emotion always outweighs the artistic emotion. So it is with my brotherhood: the men who had those ambitions were better Christians than artists. Perhaps you will object that the two cannot be separated; but I believe that they are separate, in principle!" There is a strong suggestion here that although the principle was firmly grounded in Schopenhauer's philosophy, if it had not been, Strauss would have subscribed to it anyway. Some two months later Friedrich Rösch would agree that Schopenhauer was dangerous to genuine artists and had been a danger to Wagner himself; Wagner had overcome the philosopher only because he was "an unbelievably full-blooded, *deeply feeling* artist" and thus had "never let Schopenhauer's 'pure, will-less knowing' pass for *art*."[35] Yet this was not Strauss's only reason for abandoning Ritter's reading of Schopenhauer, and he cited to Thuille and to his father the "evidence" (*Belege*) drawn from Schopenhauer, in hopes that they might be able to explain in person what he feared he could not communicate in writing.[36] In the end, Ritter had no way around the embarrassing fact that Strauss had a more solid footing in Schopenhauer than he. The long-awaited protégé, who possessed the creative gifts to realize a theory decades in the making, had instead dismantled the theory and left his mentor with the unpleasant realization that his life's work had been grounded in error.

Perhaps the strongest evidence that Strauss's revision of the third act was Schopenhauerian rather than anti-Schopenhauerian comes through a comparison of the philosophical text and the libretto of *Guntram*. One does not have to dig deeply in *Die Welt als Wille und Vorstellung* to justify this view. Taking into account the main points of the text, particularly in the last two books, the plot can easily be read as a kind of dramatization of Schopenhauer's ideas—which may well account for the poor reception that the opera received. This exercise also lends further support to Strauss's claim that his reading of the philosopher was more plausible than Ritter's. And, on a more basic level, it demonstrates once again that Strauss actually did read and understand the text, absorbing at least as much as we might expect of an educated nonspecialist.

The basic outlines of *Guntram*'s plot indicate that it was intended as a Schopenhauerian opera from the beginning, as would be expected given the centrality of this philosophy, or some version of it, in his worldview even in 1887. According to Schopenhauer the goal of drama was to reveal mankind as representation (*Vorstellung*) of the will, by "true and profound presentation of significant characters" and by "the invention of pregnant situations in which they disclose themselves."[37] These two recommendations effectively summarize the entire plot of *Guntram*, an opera that in spite of its length has little or no action (a similarity with *Tristan* that critics did not fail to notice). At bottom, the dramatic action of *Guntram* consists merely of the introduction of the protagonist, the killing of Duke Robert, and Guntram's attainment of higher self-knowledge through reflection on his feelings for Freihild. If any complaint was to be made with respect to Schopenhauer's formula, then, it was that Strauss had followed it too closely, by focusing completely on the crisis-motivated transformation of Guntram's character and omitting the kind of subplots, secondary characters, and other trappings necessary to sustain a large-scale drama.

For Schopenhauer, tragedy as a species of drama had its purpose in communicating "the nature of the world and of existence" through individuals who objectify the will's endless striving. Embodying the "antagonism of the will with itself" in a well-developed dramatic character had the effect of bringing the will into a "fearful prominence." The audience witnessing this individual's struggle with his own nature as manifestation of the will could then apprehend the hopeless predicament of existence, the inescapable fate of every individual to reenact in endless particular manifestations the striving of the will. And for a brief time, the isolated acts of this character would allow those observers to see beyond the individual to the basic force motivating him and all other humans.[38]

In Strauss's revision, Guntram makes this function of his character all too plain, by spelling out for Freihild his reasons for rejecting the brotherhood. The "gruesome curse of life," he says with striking pessimism, is that while individuals may feel themselves called to higher good, all humans are "bound to the earth with a thousand chains of miserable weakness." Whatever positive impulses he finds in himself are "forfeit to the curse of sinful humanity," so that he finds himself, like all his fellow humans, in the grasp of larger powers that act through him in spite of his own wishes. In Schopenhauerian terms, what Guntram describes here is his first glimpse through the *principium individuationis*, the delusion that prevents human individuals from sensing their nature as manifestations of a larger force. And as Schopenhauer found in such circumstances, when the principle is recognized, "the egoism resting on this [principle] expires with it": "The *motives* that were previously so powerful now lose their force, and instead of them, the complete knowledge of the real nature of the world, acting as a *quieter* of the will, produces resignation, the giving up not merely of life, but of the whole will to life itself."[39] Guntram rejects the brotherhood and leaves Freihild because he recognizes individuation as an illusion. Relationships between people can only perpetuate that illusion and certainly can offer no positive assistance in combating the universal driving force.

After his revelation, Guntram knows that his authentic spiritual mission is to seek to make that experience permanent. His solution, which was the root cause of Ritter's distress, is a textbook duplication of Schopenhauer's recommendations: Guntram determines to expiate his guilt through renunciation of human relationships and of his art, and through a permanent retreat into isolated asceticism. The nobility of the tragic hero in Schopenhauer's system grew from the decision to "renounce for ever all the pleasure of life and the aims till then pursued so keenly"; only that renunciation could promise an end of subjection to the will.[40] In Guntram's case, renunciation is a painfully explicit step-by-step process, involving love, education, and finally music. That he breaks his lyre is certainly the most powerful symbolic act of the opera: in accordance with Schopenhauer's explicit determination that music can only provide momentary relief from the striving of the will, Guntram rejects the brotherhood's central premise, that music is the most powerful means of bringing about spiritual redemption. The significance of this act cannot have been lost on Ritter, who now had to endure the destruction of his worldview, at the hands of his prized pupil, by means of the very philosophy underlying it all.

From Strauss's perspective as well as Schopenhauer's, what happens to Guntram is nothing more than spiritual evolution. After his transformation, Guntram adopts the perspective of Schopenhauer's fourth book: all life is suffering, all human pleasure affirms individuation, and only the passive negation of existence (as opposed to suicide) can lead to salvation. Guntram's retreat thus owes something to what Schopenhauer saw as the sublime effects of solitude in nature, which acts as a "summons to seriousness, to contemplation, with complete emancipation from all will and its cravings."[41] Experience of nature in its totality inevitably causes us to "lose ourselves in contemplation of the infinite greatness of the universe in space and time," so that "we feel ourselves as individuals, as living bodies, as transient phenomena of will."[42] But the crucial component of asceticism, the defining trait of the life that Guntram embraces, is the "mortification of one's own will" through a "free denial of itself" that comes about after "the complete knowledge of its own inner being has become for it the quieter of all willing."[43] Once he recognizes that human existence is simply a series of particularized manifestations of a larger negative force, there is no longer any need for him to maintain any connection to other humans. His only goal is to negate his own existence, because "for him who ends thus, the world has at the same time ended."[44]

Strauss's Misgivings about Schopenhauer

When Ritter complained that Strauss had ruined the character of Guntram by having him "philosophize," he was the first of many to make that charge. He also correctly described what the character was doing, in the sense that Guntram's lines in the third act had become a kind of exegesis. The real problem for Ritter, though, was not simply that Guntram philosophized, but that he preached a philosophy not sanctioned by Ritter himself; musical philosophizing, was, after all, the very mission of Ritter's life. Strauss refused to budge on the Schopenhauerian validity of Guntram's philosophical conclusions, but he did feel empathy for Ritter, which moved him to attempt a kind of reassurance with the claim that "*I* am not giving up art, and I'm not Guntram either!"[45] It is doubtful that Ritter worried either that Strauss would give up composition or that he would devote himself to *Willensverneinung* as an ascetic. Just those obvious realities, however, told him also that for Strauss the possibility of a Schopenhauerian form of musical composition had come to an end.

Seidl was close enough to this debate to recognize what was going on, and he continued to maintain, in print, that with Guntram's dismissal of Friedhold and the brotherhood, Strauss was rejecting Ritter and the Bayreuth school (or at least Ritter's conception of the Bayreuth cause).[46] Strauss's subsequent denial of that suggestion should not be taken seriously; irritated by public discussion of a private matter, he punished Seidl in a way that he knew would inflict real pain on a journalist—by denying in public what he confirmed in private—and Seidl told him frankly that he considered the denial disingenuous.[47] Yet Strauss must also have known that opening this debate to the public would have had wider implications for Wagnerism in general. He had made the awkward discovery that Ritter, a regular contributor to the *Bayreuther Blätter* and a not-too-distant relation of Wagner, had been manipulating Schopenhauer in a free, almost grotesque fashion for rhetorical purposes. By this time Strauss knew enough of Wagner's prose to sense that what he had found in one authoritative Wagnerian source might well repeat itself in the Master's own writings. The last thing he wanted, as he nursed his young career, was to be identified as the person who indicted Wagner and his followers for their cavalier or simplistic interpretations of canonical philosophical texts. For all public purposes, then, he washed his hands of the issue.

In private, on the other hand, he could not rid himself of the matter so easily. Here we find additional compelling evidence that for Strauss, working through philosophical issues, particularly Schopenhauerian ones, was of central importance to his own creative life. We might expect that in the aftermath of the *Guntram* revision Strauss would have put Schopenhauer behind him once and for all and moved directly to some sort of post-Schopenhauerian art-centered aesthetic. That step did come, but not immediately. Instead, the months following the completion of the *Guntram* libretto (on 24 November 1892) saw renewed study of Schopenhauer and indeed the most activity yet, as Strauss attempted to work through what can reasonably called a crisis. This story is documented once again not only in his own diaries but in correspondence, with Thuille, Rösch, and now also with Cosima Wagner. In the end, this episode was just as important as the *Guntram* debate for determining Strauss's future course as an artist.

The first outward sign of an emerging critique of Schopenhauer came in the letter to Thuille of 13 February 1893, in which Strauss reported not only that he had found support for his third act in *Die Welt als Wille und Vorstellung*, but that he now had a few "modest reservations."[48] Thuille received only cryptic hints about the nature of these reservations: a loaded observation that Schopenhauer was an artist rather than a philosopher ("despite his solemn protestations") and the strange claim that Schopenhauer himself had not recommended either affirmation or denial of the will, but had merely represented them. No further mention of this matter appears in the Thuille correspondence, perhaps because Thuille seems to have had less patience with such debates than others among Strauss's friends. But it would soon emerge in correspondence with Cosima that Strauss hoped to undermine the conclusions of the fourth book, specifically the claim that *Willensverneinung* could be a practical goal in modern society. His initial reasons for this continuing preoccupation are not clear. One may have been guilt-feelings vis-à-vis Ritter; perhaps he thought that by discrediting the fourth book but leaving the third book intact, he could undo the damage he had done to Ritter's worldview. That sort of selective reading of Schopenhauer is not unknown among philosophers; a decade and a half later Hans Vaihinger would enthusiastically retain Schopenhauer's pessimism and irrationalism but reject his metaphysics, "because since I had studied Kant the impossibility of all metaphysics had seemed to me obvious."[49] Or, Strauss's own responsibilities with regard to the will may have been on his mind; his clear-eyed reading of the fourth book had brought him to a crossroads, and we will see in the exchange with Rösch that neither Strauss nor Rösch was willing simply to dismiss Schopenhauer out of hand. Whatever the early motivation of this critique, however, it led Strauss to the same choice faced by Guntram—the choice between music and metaphysics—and in the end he consciously and determinedly took the opposite path as his protagonist.

With Cosima, Strauss went into a fair amount of detail. Presumably he raised the subject because he considered her a genuine authority; after all, she had been present during the writing of Wagner's *Beethoven*.[50] He would be disappointed in this respect, for she told him immediately that she had not studied Schopenhauer herself, so that all she knew of Schopenhauer was contained in that essay.[51] (It is interesting here that she did not say that everything any composer would ever need to know of Schopenhauer was contained in *Beethoven*.) Nevertheless, he did try out some aggressively critical ideas on her, in a level of detail that he was apparently not ready to share with his circle in Munich.

He began by reviving a thread from the letter to Thuille, with the assertion that *Die Welt als Wille und Vorstellung* was not in fact a philosophical text but an "artwork." This time, however, he provided a justification: "I call it an artwork, because in knowledge of the true being of the world it rises far above all 'science,' and in its beautiful form and wonderful symphonic construction arouses truly the highest aesthetic pleasure."[52] This sentence is loaded with Schopenhauerian code, with which Strauss obviously hoped to impress Cosima and demonstrate that the bolder aspects of his subsequent commentary had a legitimate, informed grounding. She did not understand any of it, unfortunately, but if she had, she would have been more convinced than ever of the sophistication of Strauss's philosophical knowledge. What Strauss attempted here was to praise Schopenhauer within the philosopher's own technical language. Specifically, Strauss evoked the distinction between scientific and aesthetic knowledge as a framework through which to present a positive critical assessment of Schopenhauer's text. For Schopenhauer, scientific knowledge was intimately bound up with the "principle of sufficient reason," which underlay concepts such as necessity and causality and formed the basis of the humans' belief in their ability to know. Aesthetic knowledge, on the other hand, circumvented the principle of sufficient reason and reached directly to the "ideas," the first-level objectifications that served as the objects of imitation for all nonmusical arts.[53] Precisely this kind of knowledge characterized the genius, whose unusually strong aesthetic sense rendered him (or her) better suited than others for contact with the ideas. In the larger scheme of Schopenhauer's metaphysics, aesthetic knowledge thus took a higher place than scientific knowledge, because it offered the subject a moment of "will-less" perception.[54]

Strauss understood well that in the Schopenhauerian view, the strength of art as a human endeavor resided in the metaphysical implications of the aesthetic mode of perception (*Erkenntnisweise*). Perhaps out of a sense of gratitude for the broader philosophical dignity that this theory lent to his own pursuits as composer, but certainly and more importantly for ulterior motives as well, he proceeded to analyze the text itself in these terms. By calling *Die Welt als Will und Vorstellung* an artwork, by commending its superior insight into the "true being of the world" (relative to science), and by citing the "aesthetic satisfaction" to be gained from it, Strauss granted it a higher Schopenhauerian status than it claimed. Not only had Schopenhauer explained the relation of art to the metaphysical sphere; he had demonstrated it practically with a stimulating and effective artistic creation. (The beauty of Schopenhauer's prose makes this argument at least understandable, if not compelling.)

Cosima made no comment on the technical sophistication of this discussion or on the crucial implicit accusation that this final section of Schopenhauer's text betrayed the remainder of the work and thus should be disregarded. If she had known the full extent of the crisis, perhaps she would have made a greater effort. Obviously the fourth book came as a great disappointment to the composer in Strauss, who had been won over to this way of thinking about music in the first place by the claim that his art had a unique, unsurpassed philosophical power. The end of the third book, with its abrupt dismissal of art as a permanent means of quieting the will, undermined everything that Ritter had taught him and told him that he would have to start anew in the development of a musical aesthetic. Moreover, Schopenhauer's shift from the aesthetic to the ascetic would, if taken seriously, force Strauss to give up Schopenhauer altogether, for as he told both Cosima and Rösch, his own personal limitations would never allow him to follow the path of Schopenhauerian saintliness. ("I cannot help myself. The halo will never be my lot.")[55] "Predestination" was a factor here, he claimed, referring obliquely to Schopenhauer's demolition of the concept of free will. But Strauss also argued for the validity of his own understanding of the text and for his experience as artist, both of which told him that Schopenhauer's ultimate conclusions need not be considered the last word.

The underlying strategy of his response was to discredit the fourth book by accusing Schopenhauer of making an unjustified about-face. Citing the "one-sided" qualities of the conclusions in book 4, Strauss argued that the "individual [i.e., individualist] Schopenhauer" contradicted himself in order to place a nonartistic state of being at the apex of his philosophy: "[Schopenhauer] draws conclusions that do not stand wholly in accord with the wonderful objective attitude of the first books. Here I am thinking especially of the somewhat one-sided representation of the 'sufferings of the world' and the glorification of the modification of the will in the life of the saints."[56] Calling Schopenhauer an artist allowed Strauss to argue that the philosopher should not have contradicted his third book in order to place philosophy at the forefront of his system, for he really was no philosopher at all. If this argument seems a bit far-fetched, Strauss nevertheless believed that he could support it, above all through personal experience that had been confirmed by what he read in book 3. "The joy of pure, will-less knowing," he remarked to Cosima, could be fully appreciated only by "he who has experienced it." Indeed, the defining quality of the "life of the Genius"—a life that he believed, not without reason, he was now living—was the life of the "pure, will-less subject of knowledge."[57]

These lines are little more than out-and-out parroting of book 3, where passages supporting this view of the artistic genius are easily found. For example: "Now, according to our explanation, genius consists in the ability to know, independently of the principle of sufficient reason, not individual things which have their existence only in the relation, but the Ideas of such things, and in the ability to be, in face of these, the correlative of the Idea, and hence no longer individual, but pure subject of knowing."[58] Strauss's purpose at this stage was not uncritical appropriation, however, but the turning of Schopenhauer against himself. In a passage in book 4 in which Schopenhauer called satisfaction of any kind a delusion, "always *negative only*, and never positive," Strauss wrote in the margin "all of this does not apply to artistic production"—and he did so not based on his own opinions, but on what he had read about art in book 3, before Schopenhauer's decidedly abrupt turning-away from art.[59]

Along with praise of some of the ideas on art in Schopenhauer's third book, Strauss attacked passages from the fourth book as "utopian" (the word he had used in discussing these questions with Ritter), frankly disavowing the view that stilling of will in an individual could have any effect on the will at large: "Thus far the only recognizable *goal of the will* is: that in the individual it has become *conscious* of itself as willing, that it *recognizes*, regardless of whether it *wants* to affirm or deny (strength of predestination in the particular individual)—I believe that our intellect, bound as it is to time and space, can go no further without becoming utopian."[60] The highest goal for humans, in this view, was mere awareness of the will's existence, brought about through the moments of will-less perception facilitated by art. To Rösch, Strauss even claimed that denial of the will was not possible—"up until now progress in the denial of the will against the affirmation of the same is nowhere to be found"—a position that Rösch found absurd: "It is truly a great naïveté to impute to poor Schopenhauer that he has completely overlooked the simple truth (i.e., strictly speaking, the simple tautology) that the will always 'wills,' i.e., always affirms itself, and never wills to be redeemed."[61] Rösch was of the opinion that "millions" had already achieved denial of the will in India—a belief shared by many intellectuals of his time, strange as it may seem today.[62] Strauss's attack on Schopenhauer thus seems to have upset him as much as it did Ritter, though in a different way. In any case, there was no question of naïveté on Strauss's part, only an ever stronger willingness to manipulate Schopenhauer for his own purposes.

Cosima was more sympathetic, telling Strauss that he should content himself to worry with the status of the genius, because born artists "cannot fully experience the serenity [*Heiterkeit*] of the saint."[63] She seems not to have understood, or cared to understand, the substance of his philosophical critique, however, and neither she nor Rösch (who for his part knew Schopenhauer through and through) offered any assistance in finding a meaningful response to Schopenhauer's undeniable rejection of music as a redemptive force. If there was a way for composers who both understood and believed in Schopenhauer to remain composers in good conscience, they could not show it to him. Strauss apparently suspected that this would be the outcome, for his diary shows in the first two months of 1893 an already quite developed and even more radical set of critical remarks about Schopenhauer.[64] This material carries none of the conciliatory flattery that comes through in the letter to Cosima. Instead, it prepares a wholesale rejection, a last resort that he may have believed he could avoid with guidance from someone not aligned with Ritter but equally invested in the debate. In the absence of such help, the material in the diary became the way of the future.

The central principle of this critique was "affirmation of the will," an idea that Strauss found in *Die Welt als Wille und Vorstellung* and adopted in direct contradiction to Schopenhauer, who considered it an avoidance of one's moral responsibilities and indeed the very opposite of *Willens-verneinung*. The justification of this new affirmative worldview involved some bizarre speculation on the power of sexual experience; one alternative form of redemption that Strauss suggested, for example, was to be found in the "condition of the receiving woman." There is more here than reflection on adolescent sexual encounters, however. Adjacent to his comments on the redemptive capacity of sex, Strauss paraphrased arguments from *Die Welt als Wille und Vorstellung* (found in section 60 [book 4] and in "The Metaphysics of Sexual Love"), so as to juxtapose that position with his own and thereby to bring the differences clearly into focus. Where Schopenhauer found "delusion" (*Wahn*), Strauss saw the "way to the redemption of the will." Where Schopenhauer lamented the will perpetuating itself, Strauss celebrated the liberating energy of physicality: the "affirmation of the body" and the "'*consciousness*' of affirmation." For the new, anti-Schopenhauerian Strauss, the answer to the will was to be found not by resisting or denying the will, but by reaching harmony with it.

Though many of the comments in this section of the diary have to do with the body, there are other important instances of Strauss using Schopenhauer's own statements as the basis of a critique. The right of self-determination, which so many authors have cited as evidence of the influence on Strauss of Max Stirner, is already asserted by Schopenhauer, in a passage underscored by Strauss in his edition of *Die Welt als Wille und Vorstellung:* "Imitating the qualities and idiosyncrasies of others is much more outrageous than wearing others' clothes, for it is the judgement we ourselves pronounce on our own worthlessness. Knowledge of our own mind and of our capabilities of every kind, and of their unalterable limits, is in this respect the surest way to the attainment of the greatest possible contentment with ourselves."[65] Strauss used similar language in rebellious declarations to Ritter ("In the last resort each one of us is the only person who knows *what* he is. But what he does with himself after he has recognized himself is his business!") and to his father ("in the end there is no one who can forbid me to look at the world through my own eyes from time to time, even if they do not always see straight. In the end it is only what one has seen *oneself* that has any real significance.").[66] Yet this independent streak had a Schopenhauerian basis, bearing out Strauss's claim to his father, made in the same letter as the above quote, that he was "reading only Wagner, Schopenhauer, and Goethe."

The belief that he could use Schopenhauer against himself was apparently also influenced by a burgeoning interest in Nietzsche. Another of the passages flagged in Strauss's copy of *Die Welt als Wille und Vorstellung* describes the situation of a person who had mastered the details of Schopenhauerian philosophy "but had not come to know, through his own experience or through a deeper insight, that constant suffering is essential to all life," and "who found satisfaction in life and took perfect delight in it." Such a person, who would be in a situation very much like the one Strauss found himself in now, would wish "that the course of his life as he had hitherto experienced it should be of endless duration or of constant recurrence."[67] We shall see in the discussion of the tone poem *Also sprach Zarathustra* that Strauss had a high degree of sensitivity to literary connections between the major figures in the German tradition. Here what he found was a neat overlapping of Goethe's Faust and Nietzsche's *Übermensch;* Schopenhauer himself had been a prophet of the philosopher who was about to become Strauss's new hero. For someone on the lookout for a way around Schopenhauer, there can hardly have been a more compelling piece of evidence.

The repeated and varied ways in which Strauss attempted to suggest during this period that Schopenhauer's system was flawed tell us a great deal about Strauss's personality as a thinker. They demonstrate first that Strauss felt unqualified to criticize Schopenhauer's philosophy without reading and learning it himself. Secondhand reports would not do, even if they came from Wagner. The critique also indicates that Strauss understood Schopenhauer in a more detailed way than most of his acquaintances during this period, only one of whom actively engaged Strauss in debate. Finally, we can infer from all of this information that Strauss considered Schopenhauer himself an authority figure, and indeed one of greater intellectual and artistic importance than any of the composer's living mentors. The questions with which he wrestled at this time were of crucial significance for his artistic career—otherwise the ruthlessly efficient Strauss would not have entertained them for any length of time. Whatever else one gathers from this material, then, it is apparent that Strauss felt the need to come to some kind of reasoned closure with respect to Schopenhauer. The course of much of the rest of his career—up until the last few years of his life—shows that he largely succeeded.

3

Strauss's Nietzsche

$\mathcal{N}$o musician since Wagner has been more widely associated with Nietzsche than Richard Strauss. In the popular imagination, as among scholars, Strauss has long stood as the paradigmatic Nietzschean composer, notwithstanding works by Mahler, Delius, Schoenberg, Webern, Boulez, and numerous others who have engaged with the philosopher in one way or another (usually through his poetic magnum opus, *Also sprach Zarathustra* [1883–85]). Even Theodor Adorno, a thinker as profoundly influenced by Nietzsche as he was appalled by Strauss, called the philosopher Strauss's "mentor."[1] For better or worse, our conception of Nietzsche's impact on the European musical world has been defined largely by his perceived impact on Strauss.

Ironically, scholars during the last hundred years have concluded with equal readiness that Strauss understood Nietzsche on a low intellectual level, if at all. Even the recent wave of new studies, many of them among the best scholarly treatments of the composer to date, holds largely to this tradition. In a prominent reading of the tone poem *Also sprach Zarathustra* (1896), the late John Daverio labeled Strauss's interpretation of Nietzsche "wrongheaded," flatly asserting that Strauss misunderstood his programmatic source.[2] John Williamson, whose book on the same work lays out a range of possible connections between text and music, nevertheless has questioned whether Strauss could have controlled Nietzschean ideas in any systematic way, observing that "nothing that Strauss wrote in letters, sketches and programmes actually spelled out a coherent system of thought dependent upon Nietzsche."[3] And comparing Strauss to Mahler, Stephen Hefling has expressed similar concerns about his ability to think philosophically at all—with good reason, it would seem, for Hefling cites no less an authority than Willi Schuh, Strauss's tireless and faithful defender, who concluded that the composer "did not possess what it would have taken to get thoroughly and comprehensively to grips with Schopenhauer."[4] With remarkable consistency, writers chronologically situated to survey the entirety of Strauss's career have determined that philosophy in his music is only skin deep.

On the other hand, the early critics of *Zarathustra* took a different view, whatever their allegiances. The Berlin critic Max Marschalk, a decided antagonist, rejected claims by the authors of the first guidebooks (*Erläuterungen*), Arthur Hahn and Heinrich Reimann, that Strauss had construed Nietzsche's work as poetry rather than philosophy.[5] Marschalk found the work not merely sensationalist but decidedly philosophical, and therein, he believed, lay its danger.[6] Ferdinand Pfohl, reviewing the Berlin premiere, wondered half-seriously when Strauss would get around to Kant's *Critique of Pure Reason*.[7] Such criticism was common, indeed so much so that Strauss took the unusual step of personally entering the discussion, releasing a *Briefstelle* in which he warned that those expecting "philosophy translated directly into tones" would be disappointed.[8]

Vague though they are, the assumptions of these early writers are supported by the same kind of evidence that documents Strauss's struggles with Schopenhauer: diaries, correspondence, musical sketches, and marginalia in personal copies of philosophical texts. This material shows that while Strauss may not have mastered "thoroughly and comprehensively" any particular philosophical system, he did reflect considerably on the central issues of Nietzschean philosophy, particularly as they pertain to the aesthetics of Schopenhauer. Though Strauss eagerly took professional advantage of the Nietzsche fad of the mid-1890s, his reading of the philosopher was actually motivated by the "reservations" (*Vorbehalten*) and "doubts" (*Zweifel*) that he felt about Schopenhauer.[9] But because the depth of Strauss's investigation of *Die Welt als Wille und Vorstellung* has been overlooked—in spite of Schopenhauer's central position in the specific brand of Wagnerism to which Strauss was introduced by Alexander Ritter, and in spite of the fact that over the course of more than a decade Strauss repeatedly studied this text—the background necessary for understanding his attraction to Nietzsche has not been available. In so far as Strauss's compositional apprenticeship involved intellectual as well as musical development, that apprenticeship ended with his considered rejection of Schopenhauer's musical aesthetics. And it was this rejection that brought Strauss into the Nietzschean fold.

Strauss's public stance concerning Nietzsche placed equivocation in the foreground—starting with the famously cryptic subtitle of *Zarathustra*, "frei nach Nietzsche"—and thus it reinforced the assumption of his ignorance. In this light, the evidence from his private materials implies a conscious determination to keep his philosophical speculations out of the public forum. But if the composer's published claims contradict the documentary evidence, by discounting philosophical contemplation or downplaying it as a mere artistic stimulus, his completed artworks confirm that Nietzsche's vision of a post-Schopenhauerian artistic landscape figured centrally in Strauss's musical coming-of-age. Indeed, all of the orchestral works from *Till Eulenspiegel* (1895) to *Eine Alpensinfonie* (1915) bear witness to an intensifying Nietzschean outlook.

Nietzsche and *Guntram*

The work that first suggested to early critics that Strauss's worldview was shifting in the direction of Nietzsche was not *Also sprach Zarathustra* but *Guntram*. Arthur Seidl, one of the most philosophically aware critics of his generation, saw the opera as transitional for Strauss, who now had one foot in Schopenhauer and the other in Nietzsche.[10] Most other writers, however, took it as a declaration of a new faith. Hermann Bischoff held that to describe the content of the third act accurately required the Nietzschean "jargon of the 'modern spirit'": Guntram started out as a "collectivist" but ended as an "individualist."[11] Gustav Brecher, like Bischoff a personal acquaintance of the composer, asserted that "in the dramatic-psychological transformation [*Wandlung*] of Guntram we must recognize Strauss's own spiritual transformation [*geistige Umwandlung*] . . . from the democratic principle to the aristocratic!"[12] This loaded vocabulary also found its way into Ernst Otto Nodnagel's account of a "development from socialist to individualist, or indeed anarchist."[13] Very few writers, on the other hand, shared the view expressed by Otto Lessmann that *Guntram* relied too heavily on Schopenhauer, and even in Lessmann's case that conclusion may have reflected a simple impatience with the hackneyed themes of *Erlösung* and *Entsagung* rather than a studied philosophical opinion.[14]

The belief that Guntram served as spokesman for a revolution in Strauss's own worldview rested solely on the character's decision to leave the brotherhood. That decision likely would not have made so powerful an impact if it were not couched in language borrowed from the "anarchist individualist" Max Stirner, culminating in the infamous declaration, "Mein Leben bestimmt meines Geistes Gesetz; / mein Gott spricht durch mich selbst nur zu mir" (The law of my spirit determines my life; / my god speaks through me only to me). These tortured lines are standard fare in Stirner's *Der Einzige und sein Eigentum* (*The Ego and His Own*) (1845), a book that Strauss had indeed been reading, though he told Eugen Lindner in 1892 that his interest in Stirner's "philosophy of egoism" was only as a "curiosity" (*Kuriosium*).[15] In any case, by the early 1890s Stirner was valued less in his own right than as a forerunner of Nietzsche, with Stirneresque vocabulary and affirmations of self-determination readily accepted as signs of a Nietzschean outlook, even when that latter's name was not mentioned.

In his letter decrying the revision, Ritter interpreted Guntram's outburst in precisely this manner, complaining fiercely about the influence of both Stirner and Nietzsche. Wondering how Guntram could have learned to speak in this strange way, Ritter asked, "has the jester perhaps sneaked in a copy of Stirner to Guntram overnight [that is, during Guntram's imprisonment in act 3]? Or Nietzsche's 'Beyond Good and Evil'?"[16] Thus again the language proved decisive, in spite of the content. The effect of Stirner on the poetry is easy enough to comprehend, but a reader as sensitive as Ritter should have recognized that any ostensible individualism on Guntram's part was undermined by the fact that his withdrawal was designed to expiate his guilt, "in imitation of the Saviour" (as Guntram declares). Neither Stirner nor Nietzsche had anything to do with that denouement, as Strauss would point out in his response. Rösch, unlike Ritter, correctly perceived the moral orientation of the new plot, but he complained about it while criticizing Guntram's new dialect: "I find it entirely wrong for Guntram's characterization that after he has already decided, firmly and definitively, to become his own judge, he returns once again to a sphere of thought [*Ideenkreis*] in which he moved earlier . . . as 'Champion of Love,' as 'member of the brotherhood,' which is to say as 'dogmatist.'"[17] Strauss's response to this letter does not survive, but the next letter from Rösch mentions that Strauss had received this criticism with impatience, and we can well imagine what had annoyed him: the goal of the work was not to attack the moral law represented by the brotherhood but to consider how best to live up to it.[18]

On this basis, but for many additional reasons as well, the notion of

Guntram as a Nietzschean work is unsustainable. There is no question, for example, of this opera repudiating the "Schopenhauerian-Christian moral orientation," as Ritter charged. Stirner had indeed made an extended attack on Christianity, and Nietzsche had conflated Christianity and Schopenhauer's philosophy, but Guntram obviously did not assume this viewpoint. Whereas Nietzsche looked to the day when people would become "lawgivers," making their own morals, Guntram merely tried to implement Christian morality in a different and more effective way. He did so out of faith in an absolute good, a naive conviction that Nietzsche called the "will to truth."[19] And his surrender to this will rendered his individualism an illusion, in the Nietzschean view, which held that "the terms 'autonomous' and 'moral' are mutually exclusive."[20] Abandonment of Freihild and the brotherhood provided the trappings of autonomy, but in fact all it accomplished was to remove the elements of his life that interfered with his perception of "truth."

The defining personal qualities of Guntram likewise flout Nietzschean dicta. After he kills the evil duke, the driving force of his personality is a bad conscience—as Nietzsche would say, he is "not equal to his deed" but lapses into "sighing about inner depravity."[21] He also explicitly disparages and forsakes sensuality, again taking a position that for Nietzsche had its background in both Christianity (as hostility to life) and Schopenhauer (as a "philosopher's resentment").[22] With his subsequent dismissal of Freihild, Guntram completes his embodiment of what Nietzsche called the "religious neurosis," the components of which were solitude, fasting, and sexual abstinence.[23] (On this particular issue Strauss agreed strongly with Nietzsche and even chastised Ritter for his "extraordinary little private hatred of sexual love.")[24] Most damaging of all from the Nietzschean perspective was Guntram's devotion to ascesis, an insidious lifestyle that "governed all philosophy" because it was the natural outcome of any search for truth.[25] With his symbolic rejection of art (with the destruction of his lyre), Guntram does uphold the Nietzschean view that art and ascesis are opposites.[26] Yet he obviously lacks nobility (as opposed to the duke, who seems conceived as a personification of Nietzsche's "blonde beast"), and he makes sure to clarify during his farewell that he does not disavow *Mitleid* (which is to be the future purpose of Freihild's life) but only his own ability to use it for the greater good.[27]

If Strauss had consciously set out to create a comprehensively anti-Nietzschean character, he could not have improved substantially on Guntram. The possibility that he intended to promote a Nietzschean world-view but simply did not understand it very well thus seems remote. What we do have here, however, is strong evidence that Strauss was already conversant with Nietzsche's ideas during the composition of *Guntram;* that character can hardly have been so thoroughly, fastidiously anti-Nietzschean by chance alone. That Ritter and the other critics missed this level of meaning is only to be explained by their own limited understanding of Nietzsche. Among the critics only Seidl did not miss it, or at least did not miss it completely, and it is not surprising that his writings offer some of the most important clues for a reconstruction of Strauss's early reading of Nietzsche. They also begin to show how Nietzsche did become, gradually, a productive force in Strauss's creative activity.

Toward a Nietzschean Worldview

Of all Strauss's contemporaries in the 1890s, none was better equipped to perceive the obscure Schopenhauerian legitimacy of *Guntram* than Arthur Seidl (1863–1928), one of the few critics of the day whose devotion to a progressive (i.e., post-Schopenhauerian) aesthetics of music matched Strauss's.[28] Seidl had been a friend of the composer from the early 1880s (during Strauss's brief attendance at the University of Munich), and he had participated with some regularity in the informal discussions that Ritter led in Munich *Weinstuben* beginning in 1886. When Strauss chose in 1889 to leave Munich for Weimar in order to exercise his abilities more effectively on behalf of Wagnerism, he looked forward to a reunion with Seidl, who had moved to Weimar the previous year. Once Strauss was settled they worked closely together to revive the local chapter of the Wagner Society, Strauss organizing the performances and Seidl giving the lectures.[29] In the long run, though, the Wagnerian cause had no more lasting effect on Seidl than on Strauss, and he underwent an intellectual transformation much like Strauss's, at virtually the same time.

During his early career Seidl was a passionate and formidable Wagnerian. His 1887 dissertation in philosophy at the University of Leipzig, "On the Musically Sublime" (Vom Musikalisch-Erhabenen), traced the metaphysics of music back to Kant with the goal of shoring up Wagner's philosophical grounding. He maintained close ties to Bayreuth at least until 1892, publishing regularly in the *Bayreuther Blätter* and advocating a kind of "moral rebirth" (*sittliche Wiedergeburt*) clearly related to, if not derived from, the ideas of Ritter.[30] But shortly thereafter he began to distance himself from Wagnerism, largely because of a growing impatience with the metaphysical preoccupations of "Philosophie-Kapellmeistern" and "Festspiel- und Erlösungskomponisten."[31] Seidl believed that without a definite, determined move away from Wagnerian philosophizing, the musical future of Germany would remain caught in the "vicious circle" (*circulus vitiosus*) of pessimism and Christianity preached by "the Romantic Schopenhauer." To avoid this fate, contemporary music needed to pursue "Nietzsche's modern artisthood and anti-Christianity" ("[das] moderne Artisten- und Antichristentum Nietzsche's"). If music were to participate meaningfully in twentieth-century culture, composers would have to abandon "this old Wagner-spasm of hyperidealistic 'redemptions'" ("diesen alten Wagner-Krampf hyperidealistischer 'Erlösungen'"), that is, divorce it from the Platonic-Christian-Schopenhauerian philosophical tradition against which Nietzsche polemicized.[32]

Seidl's theorizing of a post-metaphysical but philosophically aware aesthetics set him apart from virtually all of his peers in German-language music criticism, whether they championed *Weltanschauungsmusik* or Hanslickian formalism. Likewise, his serious scholarly interest in Nietzsche (he would later work for several years at the Nietzsche Archive in Weimar) kept him at a remove from the controversy-mongering (pro and con) of contemporaneous Nietzsche reception.[33] Seidl operated outside of the mainstream precisely because he invoked Nietzsche as a solution to a specific artistic problem. And one might easily say the same of Strauss: though he was intellectually responsible—that is, he worked out solutions to his aesthetic dilemmas through careful reading of philosophical texts—he did not attempt to formulate a comprehensive philosophical system, because he sought only an authoritative response to a particular difficulty. Thus when Strauss returned from Egypt in 1893, carrying the newly completed *Guntram* and ready to resume his post at the Weimar *Hofoper* (for what would be the final year), the critical results of that journey came immediately into focus for his theoretically minded friend.

What sets Seidl apart as an observer of this period of Strauss's life is the complexity and subtlety of his thought. Unlike his peers (and virtually all subsequent scholars), who played down the difficulties associated with the transition, Seidl recognized that it caused profound inner conflict. Seidl's verdict on *Guntram*—that the work suffered artistically because it was a mishmash of Schopenhauer and Nietzsche—described with unique precision the impossibly awkward position in which Strauss found himself as he contemplated his next step as a composer.[34] Even more telling is the account given by Seidl of the scene in Strauss's apartment just before the premiere of *Guntram* (10 May 1894). As Strauss prepared himself for the extraordinary moment when he would force Wagnerism to expose the fatal defect of its philosophical premises, he spent the afternoon reading a novel by the Stirner disciple John Henry Mackay, a choice that Seidl interpreted as an extension of his Nietzsche study.[35] Seidl related that some months before, on the occasion of the critic's departure from Weimar, the two had discussed Nietzsche; now he was pleased to find that Strauss had extended this line of thought into the creative realm, with two settings of Mackay that would ultimately become part of op. 27 (*Heimliche Aufforderung* and *Morgen;* the collection was given to Pauline as a wedding present in 1894). Seidl did not bother to explain the relationship between the choice of Mackay and the occasion of the premiere, but clearly this was Strauss's point of no return: after *Guntram* the secret about Schopenhauer would be out, musical metaphysics would be hopelessly undermined, and German music would have to find a new direction. For a critic, reasoned destruction of the aesthetic foundation of nineteenth-century music might have been enough. But for a creator, the moment of destruction would present a new and greater problem: how to ground this future in an art all its own.

Unfortunately Seidl did not name the specific books by Nietzsche involved in their discussion, only saying that Strauss read and commented on passages from the "main works" (*Hauptwerke*). Other evidence, however, allows the establishment of at least a preliminary chronology of Strauss's reading of Nietzsche. We know that Strauss read *Jenseits von Gut und Böse* (*Beyond Good and Evil*) no later than April 1893, when he reported his impressions of the book to (of all people) Cosima Wagner (see below). (His denial to Ritter in February that he had ever read the book can be discounted; Ritter obviously knew that Strauss had taken it with him, and the claim that he had not bothered to open it is not credible.)[36] In 1896 Seidl provided circumstantial evidence that Strauss had read *Menschliches, Allzumenschliches* (*Human, All Too Human*). In describing the content of the as-yet incomplete tone poem *Also sprach Zarathustra*, Seidl said that it would carry the title of "Also sprach Zarathustra" but its "subject" (*Gegenstand*) would be *Menschliches, Allzumenschliches.*[37] Given Strauss's distancing process from Wagnerian aesthetics (or Ritter's version of it) in 1892–93, it is likely that *Human, All Too Human* would have been of great interest to him, for it documented precisely the moment in Nietzsche's career at which the break occurred, and perhaps more important, it laid out a vision of post-Wagnerian art.

Establishing that Strauss read Nietzsche before November 1892 (when he left for Greece) is more difficult. Two drafts for a Don Juan opera from March 1892 show Strauss immersed in Stirner, particularly the latter's explicitly antimetaphysical view of sexual love (which would have contrasted with Ritter's opinions).[38] On a trip to Berlin in early April 1892 Strauss had the opportunity to meet Mackay, whom he described to his father as "the most significant antagonist of Schopenhauer and Christianity."[39] During that same trip Strauss attended Bülow's final performance with the Berlin Philharmonic (5 April), which closed with a speech by the conductor exalting the ideas of Stirner, a one-time personal acquaintance. Strauss seems, then, to have been caught up in the "Stirner Renaissance" then underway in Berlin.[40] The principal antagonist in the Don Juan sketch, however, a character identified only as "A." but clearly a philosophical stand-in for Ritter, is described as a "'pessimist' (Schopenhauer, Christ)"—a terminological constellation drawn from Nietzsche, whose own rising fame was just then beginning to overwhelm Stirner's. If the protagonist was characterized in Stirneresque terms as a "proponent of absolute egoism," the basis of the critique is nevertheless fundamentally Nietzschean.

A speculative case might also be made that Strauss came to know *The Birth of Tragedy* while in Meiningen. Bülow's opinion of Nietzsche's music notwithstanding, he admired this text greatly, and he surely would have recommended it to a bright, literate young composer/conductor experiencing a new enthusiasm for Wagner. For that matter Ritter too must have known it, though his continuing close relationship with the Wagner family put him in a better position than Bülow to understand in the mid-1880s (before the publication of the latter's most important anti-Wagnerian works) the severity of Wagner's break with Nietzsche. But if Strauss did read this work, he did not tell Rösch, who believed in 1893 that Strauss had read only *Beyond Good and Evil*.[41] Indeed, Rösch clearly felt that he was offering a revelation to Strauss with the information that "earlier he [Nietzsche] was even a Wagnerian!"[42] Likewise, Seidl's writings indicate that his first awareness that Strauss was interested in Nietzsche came in 1893; given his close involvement with the Nietzschean project around the turn of the century and his prolific career as a writer, he likely would have remarked on earlier evidence had he known of any.

One thing that is clear about Strauss's interest in Nietzsche in the 1890s is that it was limited to the late anti-Wagnerian works. Whatever other reasons he may have had for this enthusiasm, Strauss obviously hoped to find a ready-made philosophical underpinning for his rejection of Schopenhauer. The ambiguity that Seidl would later sense in *Guntram* (between Schopenhauerian and Nietzschean perspectives) was the result of a full-blown personal crisis, documented in letters to Cosima Wagner and Friedrich Rösch. Once he had discovered that Schopenhauer did not consider music an avenue to lasting denial of the will, Strauss determined, logically, that he would have to choose between Schopenhauerian philosophy and music. For a brief time, that necessity posed a painful dilemma, for strangely enough, Schopenhauerian denial remained a serious concept in 1890s Germany; Rösch went so far as to claim that in India "millions" had already achieved it.[43] When Strauss, immediately after the revision of *Guntram*, sought assistance from Rösch in discrediting Schopenhauer, or rather seeking approval of a radical critique, he undoubtedly was seeking, at the same time, those very things on his own in Nietzsche.

According to Rösch, who summarized Strauss's requests before responding to them, Strauss needed philosophical support for four specific assertions, all of which aimed to demonstrate that Schopenhauer could no longer be taken seriously. The most important of these was his need for justification of a positive, affirmative conception of physicality—construed not only sexually, but in a broader antimetaphysical sense. Related to this issue was his need for a compelling argument for the special status of the artist, a status that would allow unique philosophical privileges but would not rely on a metaphysical foundation. In order to explain his own irresistible urge to attack Schopenhauer, he wanted to discover, in a source other than *Die Welt als Wille und Vorstellung*, a thoughtful claim that free will (as individual freedom of choice) did not exist; where his own personality was concerned, Strauss believed that "predestination" was the controlling factor. And finally, he hoped to find evidence (i.e., an authoritative assertion) that the will was an affirmative force.[44] As with his study of Schopenhauer, Strauss approached Nietzsche with specifics in mind, having worked through other philosophical problems until he arrived at an impasse. He would find them, and this time the results would be more productive for his creative life.

A similar but less focused laying-out of his problems can be extracted from the crucial letter to Cosima on *Die Welt als Wille und Vorstellung* (see pp. 76–79), here focused on the problem of free will.[45] Unfortunately, neither she nor Rösch seemed particularly interested. Rösch responded impatiently that such ideas "could only slip out from one in a desert" (Strauss was writing from Egypt), while Cosima simply seemed bored. This double dead-end left Strauss with no choice but to delve more deeply into Nietzsche himself, which is precisely what he did, as his subsequent letters to Rösch and Cosima demonstrate.

The ideas for which Strauss searched are readily available in *Beyond Good and Evil*, the one text by Nietzsche that we know he did have with him. Indeed, the answers to his specific questions are so prominent that one wonders whether Strauss had found them before framing the 15 March letter to Rösch and had used them to focus his thoughts. A critique of the enemies of physicality, for example, is one of the book's central themes: religion and idealist philosophy had dominated European culture for so long because they had been able to "reverse the whole love of the earthly and of dominion over the earth into hatred of the earth and the earthly."[46] Strauss told Rösch that he admired this redirection of philosophy toward objectivity, despite recognizing its dangers, which had caused the "first pathbreaker" Nietzsche's insanity.[47] We shall see (below, p. 194–195) that in the tone poem *Also sprach Zarathustra* Strauss's protagonist experiences a breakdown as a result of attempting to emulate the objective physicality of the sun; at precisely this moment in the particell Strauss inscribed the famously derisive words of the Earth-Spirit to Goethe's Faust: "you resemble the spirit whom you imagine, not me" ("du gleichst dem Geist den du begreifst, nicht mir").[48] Living out a worldview based on physicality, purged of metaphysics, would not be easy, but intellectual honesty allowed no other alternative in the modern historical moment, with the approach of the twentieth century.

Nietzsche's antimetaphysical agenda penetrated every area of his thought—artistic, social, and political—in conceptual leaps that Strauss seems to have been able to follow. To Cosima the composer praised the book's overarching antidemocratic tendency, which he called "highly congenial" (*höchst sympathisch*).[49] Strauss held strong views against democracy throughout his life, as is well known. But the philosophical basis of those views has not yet been recognized. In *Beyond Good and Evil*, Nietzsche identified democracy specifically as a Schopenhauerian phenomenon: the "herd," which out of weakness of character sought refuge from real life in an imagined noumenal realm, now sought to gain political control.[50] The very same impulse that had produced Platonic philosophy and Christian spirituality underlay the democratic movement, thereby interfering with the efforts of the most talented human individuals and enacting in the social sphere a corrupt philosophy, a diseased illusion.

The implications of this new worldview for artisthood likely had much to do with Strauss's sense, expressed to Cosima, that Nietzsche

marked the dawn of the "philosophy of the future."[51] Although he called
Nietzsche's remarks on the south in music "comical," he clearly had some
sympathy for the contrast between Mendelssohn's "lighter, purer, hap-
pier" style and the "magnificent, overladen, heavy, and late art" of the
Meistersinger prelude; the dichotomy would be more than palpable in *Also
sprach Zarathustra*.[52] Strauss often complained to Cosima about the negative influence of ordinary Germans on music, so he undoubtedly would
have found something attractive in the idea of a "supra-German" music.
Yet even more to the point would have been a supra-metaphysical music,
which Strauss was actively seeking and which Nietzsche described explicitly: "I could imagine a music whose rarest magic would consist in
this, that it no longer knew anything of good and evil . . . an art that
would see fleeing towards it from a great distance the colors of a declin-
ing, now almost incomprehensible *moral* world, and would be hospitable
and deep enough to receive such late fugitives."[53] The vision of an art
big enough to move outside of metaphysical questions—still able to raise
them, but without danger of being suffocated—offered Strauss precisely
what he sought: a reasoned circumvention of Schopenhauer.

None of this meant, on the other hand, that Strauss saw himself as
having voluntarily assumed the duties and power of an artist. He considered the fact that he was an artist a matter of "predestination," something
that he could not control any more than he could decide whether to
follow or disavow the Schopenhauerian redemptive path.[54] *Beyond Good
and Evil* provided support for this view, through Nietzsche's characterization of free will as a delusion a "hundred times refuted." In this context,
Strauss's experience of musical inspiration (*Einfall*) closely matches
Nietzsche's description of the human process of thinking: "a thought
comes when 'it' wants, not when 'I want.'"[55] And Nietzsche himself found
a similar connection between artistic creation and the absence of free
will, pointing out that every artist "obeys thousandfold laws" that he or
she could not possibly account for or even perceive.[56]

Perhaps the most important assistance that Strauss found in Nietzsche
at this moment in his career was a complex, problematized engagement
with the term "will." At a time when he very much wanted to argue for
an "affirmation" of the Schopenhauerian will, Strauss found that Nietzsche had introduced another kind of will, a "will to power," that corresponded roughly to the kind of immersion in oneself that the composer
now hoped to pursue. At this early stage in the formation of Nietzsche's
concept, the will to power meant an individual's proud, self-conscious
assertion of the unchangeable facts of his character: "a living thing desires

above all to vent its strength," physically, emotionally, intellectually, and spiritually, without the hindrance of ethical and philosophical responsibilities grounded in something outside of life. This will had something very different to offer than the hope of nonexistence; this will came into being through self-affirmation.

It is tempting to conclude that in relating his impressions of Nietzsche to Rösch and Cosima, Strauss saw an advantage in painting himself as a bumbler. He confessed to Cosima that his overall impression was one of "confusion," an admission that presumably allowed her to overlook his characterization of Nietzsche's observations on women as "sharp-witted" (*scharfsinnig*).[57] With Rösch he clearly assumed a subordinate position, asking for assistance without ever fully disclosing the extent of his own work. But the diary entries, when read from a Nietzschean standpoint, suggest something different. We have seen that in these private materials Strauss took a much harder line toward Schopenhauer than he revealed to Cosima and Rösch. The vocabulary of these comments makes it clear that Nietzsche was supplying the ammunition. The explicit devotion to "the '*consciousness*' of affirmation," as opposed to denial; the conception of spiritual life as a process of "never-ending *becoming*"; the central role of the body ("affirmation of the will must properly be called affirmation of the body"); and the rejection of Schopenhauer's "*Pessimismus*" all clearly come from Nietzsche.[58]

Strauss's personal copy of *Also sprach Zarathustra*, in the edition published in Leipzig by C. G. Naumann in 1893, contains markings helpful in establishing where he got these ideas. To my knowledge this source has not been previously studied, although it has resided (at least in the recent past) in a display case at the Garmisch villa. Most of the markings are simple lines drawn in the margin to indicate passages that Strauss considered significant. Also included, however, are eleven separate references to pages in the autograph score of the tone poem, and in one case Strauss added an indication of a key ("Asdur"). These latter connections to the tone poem are discussed below; here I would draw attention to a network of correspondences between Strauss's Nietzschean reflections in the diary and certain passages that he flagged in the text. Of the twenty-four marked passages, most are small, only four exceeding fifteen lines of text. (The total amount of text concerned is just under three thousand words.) Moreover, the Nietzschean entries in the diary point strongly toward a single chapter, "On the Blissful Islands" from book 1. Figure 3.1 presents a comparison of sentences from the diary with passages that Strauss marked in the text. In these cases, the corre-

Passages in Strauss's Diary	Passages Marked in Strauss's Copy of *Also sprach Zarathustra*
"Artistic contemplation, artistic production (and philosophy) outweighs all suffering tenfold in its joy."	"Creation—that is the great redemption from suffering[. . .]" (Book Two, "On the Blissful Islands")
["Künstlerische Anschauung, künstlerische Produktion, (auch die Philosophie) wiegt in ihrer Freude all Leiden zehnfach auf."]	["Schaffen—das ist die grosse Erlösung vom Leiden(. . .)] (Book Two, "Auf den glückseligen Inseln")
****	****
"*Consciousness* of the affirmation of the will is our ultimate goal—so far. What is to come, who knows! I affirm *consciously*, that is my happiness."	"[. . .]my *willing* always comes to me as my liberator and bringer of joy[. . .]" ("On the Blissful Islands")
["Das *Bewußtsein* der Bejahung des Willens ist unser letztes Ziel—bis jetzt. Was noch kommen soll, wer weiß es! Ich bejahe *bewußt*, dies ist mein Glück!"]	["(. . .)mein *Wollen* kommt mir stets als mein Befreier und Freudebringer(. . .)"] ("Auf den glückseligen Inseln")

Figure 3.1. Comparison of passages in Strauss's diary with passages marked in his copy of *Also sprach Zarathustra*.

spondence is closer to paraphrase than mere resonance, establishing definitively what one might otherwise have reasonably assumed—that Strauss was using particular Nietzschean ideas as a critical weapon and as a foundation of a new worldview.

The marginalia in Strauss's copy of *Die Welt als Wille und Vorstellung* also confirm the Nietzschean basis of the criticism. It is not surprising that most of Strauss's annotations come in the fourth book; the problem was posed not by Schopenhauer's aesthetics (the topic of the third book), but by the mechanism of permanent *Erlösung*. Three of the four issues

Passages in Strauss's Diary	Passages Marked in Strauss's Copy of *Also sprach Zarathustra*
"The consciousness of *eternal being* in the eternally new, never-ending *becoming*[...]"	"[...]the best images and parables should speak of time and becoming[...]" ("On the Blissful Islands")
["Das Bewußtsein des *Ewigseins* in ewig neuem, nie endenden *Werden*(...)"]	["(...)von Zeit und Werden sollen die besten Gleichnisse reden(...)"] ("Auf den glückseligen Inseln")
	"[...]in knowing and understanding, too, I feel only my will's delight in begetting and becoming[...]" ("On the Blissful Islands")
	["Auch im Erkennen fühle ich nur meines Willens Zeuge- und Werde-Lust(...)"]("Auf den glückseligen Inseln")
****	****
"Will is desire: the desire for eternal being in continual renewal."	"Willing liberates: that is the true doctrine of will and freedom[...]" ("On the Blissful Islands")
["Wille ist Wollen: Aus Wollen des Ewigseins in fortwährender Erneuerung."]	["Wollen befreit: das ist die wahre Lehre von Wille und Freiheit(...)"] ("Auf den glückseligen Inseln")

Figure 3.1 (cont.).

for which Strauss hoped to find support in Nietzsche, according to the letter to Rösch—the special experience of the artist, affirmation, and predestination—came about as reactions to specific passages in *Die Welt als Wille und Vorstellung*.[59] At a passage in section 58 in which Schopenhauer held that all pleasure is merely the satisfaction of a want and

Passages in Strauss's Diary	Passages Marked in Strauss's Copy of *Also sprach Zarathustra*
"Affirmation of the will must properly be called affirmation of the body"[. . .]	"Listen rather, my brothers, to the voice of the healthy body" (Book One, "Of the Afterworldsmen")
["Bejahung des Willens muß ganz richtig Bejahung des Leibes heißen(. . .)"]	["Hört mir lieber, meine Brüder, auf die Stimme des gesunden Leibes(. . .)"] (Book One, "Von den Hinterweltlern")
	"[. . .]to the discerning man all instincts are holy[. . .]" (Book One, "Of the Bestowing Virtue"
	["(. . .)dem Erkennenden heiligen sich alle Triebe(. . .)"] ("Von der schenkenden Tugend")

Figure 3.1 (cont.).

therefore disappears when the want disappears, Strauss wrote, "this does not hold true for artistic production!" ("trifft alles auf künstlerisches Produktion nicht zu!"). In section 60, where Schopenhauer examined the affirmation of the will, Strauss recognized an issue over which he would have to break with Schopenhauer, writing that "certainly affirmation and denial of the will would be a fundamental contradiction!" ("gewiss wäre Bejahen u. Verneinen des Wollens ein Widerspruch an sich!"). (It was also from this section that Strauss drew the comparison of affirmation of the will and affirmation of the body.) And extensive underlining in section 55, which deals with inflexibility of character, indicates an early stage in his evolving concern with predestination.

Strauss also took notice of two passages that famously anticipate the "eternal recurrence," one comparing the absurdity of the fear of death with the idea that the sun would fear on setting that it would never again rise, and another (described in chapter 2) that praises the fearless character of a hypothetical man "who desired, in spite of calm deliberation, that the course of his life as he had hitherto experienced it should be of endless duration or of constant recurrence."[60] That he noticed this second passage strongly suggests that Strauss heard its Nietzschean resonance. In the first example, he left more-explicit confirmation; adjacent to Schopenhauer's comparison of the permanence of the will and the impermanence of its objectifications, Strauss wrote, "being in becoming/ the final goal of this eternal becoming is consciousness of it!"[61] By interjecting a bit of Nietzschean commentary at this moment in the text, Strauss sought to justify his contention that Schopenhauer had contradicted himself; Schopenhauer had anticipated Nietzsche's ideas but had failed to pursue them.

In these sources an emerging, deliberately Nietzschean side of Strauss's personality came forward, one not ready to reveal itself in public or indeed even to his most intimate friends. At first blush that reluctance seems to reveal insecurity about his intellectual abilities, but the subsequent course of Strauss's career—the resumption of orchestral composition after the completion of *Guntram*—offers another explanation. Though Strauss would have liked simply to cut the ties between his compositional style and the Schopenhauerian philosophy from which it emerged, though he wanted to move to a new Nietzschean stage of his career marked by optimism and lightness, he did not find himself immediately able to do so. And it was through this inability that he demonstrated most clearly the depth with which he had understood Nietzsche.

Nietzschean Concerns in the Tone Poems

That Strauss's post-*Guntram* tone poems tend toward the autobiographical is easy enough to discern; two of them, *Ein Heldenleben* and *Symphonia domestica*, are more or less explicitly so, and the other four at least flirt with the idea. The connection between artistic content and personal experience is hardly more clear today, however, than it was in 1900, when Seidl noted that important biographical issues in Strauss's works had been overlooked because of an insufficient awareness of the composer's inner development. "I'll tell you a secret," wrote Seidl. "*Strauss* too greeted the *rising* sun as a 'solitary human'" (as had Zarathustra in Nietzsche's prologue, which Strauss placed at the head of the tone poem).[62]

Although Seidl knew from personal experience that Strauss's Nietzsche reception was significant and sophisticated, even he had difficulty gaining access to the details of that reading. Strauss's reluctance to show his cards stemmed in part from mistrust; he considered Seidl's 1895 article on the autobiographical nature of *Guntram* a minor betrayal, half-jokingly telling his friend that he was "one of the most indiscreet people of this century."[63] When Seidl received a prepublication copy of the score of *Also sprach Zarathustra* in late 1896, he implored Strauss to confirm his already "very precise" (*sehr bestimmt*) impressions of the work's intellectual content with a description of the "personal and ideal meaning [*Deutung*] of the work." Even at this early stage, Seidl noted, confusion over the program threatened to harm the initial reception, but that problem could be overcome if Strauss would give him "at least the essential points for the correct understanding of your intentions." He also took Strauss to task for making "ironic, and therefore ambiguous" public statements about the work.[64] Apparently Strauss's answer did not satisfy him, for some three months later he sent a "detailed questionnaire" (now lost), following up on his request in December to know why Strauss had appended Nietzsche's prologue to the score.[65] By this time the stakes were higher than ever, for Seidl was calling the new work a "landmark, for the modern spirit, for post-Wagnerian music at the end of the century, *and* for a new spirit of musical aesthetics."

We do not know the extent of Strauss's response to these pleas or whether he accepted Seidl's promise that this time he would not publish anything without first getting the composer's approval.[66] But one way or another Seidl gleaned enough information for "Also sang Zarathustra" (1900), an underappreciated essay that is of profound significance not just for this tone poem but for all of Strauss's orchestral music after *Guntram*. The thesis of this essay is that Strauss's philosophical shift in *Guntram* from Wagner/Schopenhauer to Nietzsche required a "convalescence" (*Genesung*), the evidence of which was found in the tone poem. Seidl suggested a parallel between Strauss's rejection of metaphysics and Zarathustra's (and, by extension, Nietzsche's), with the same network of concepts at issue and the same personal struggles. What Seidl was not in a position to know in 1900 was that he had identified a programmatic thread running through all six programmatic orchestral works that would follow *Guntram*.

The post-*Guntram* tone poems are unified by engagement with Nietzschean issues that fall into two main categories. The first is the recurring existential angst that plagues Zarathustra, a character who, despite being confused with the *Übermensch* in much of the critical literature, actually serves only as a "prophet" of the *Übermensch*. Though Zarathustra recognizes metaphysical "longing" (*Sehnsucht*) as the definitive human flaw and prophesies a time when this longing will have been overcome, he himself remains susceptible to moments of weakness. Nietzsche's distribution of these struggles throughout the work, rather than at the beginning, highlights the cyclical (eternally recurring) nature of Zarathustra's philosophical *Lebensgang* (a feature not without its own autobiographical relevance). The second category represents the other end of the cycle: the positive, optimistic, post-metaphysical, post-Wagnerian joy that will ultimately define *übermenschlich* existence, the existence of one who has overcome metaphysics. As Zarathustra's life wavers between these opposed but interrelated states of mind, so does Strauss's music respond alternately to one or the other, and so too did Strauss's private worldview fluctuate with troubling but productive regularity.

As we have seen, Strauss's public comments imply that little is to be learned about Nietzsche from the tone poem *Also sprach Zarathustra* (1896). He apparently regarded public acceptance of this contention as crucial, for he worked harder to control the initial reception of this piece than he did for any other tone poem. An officially sanctioned *Erläuterung*, which Strauss described as written "exactly according to my intentions," was released; that it contained his own private reading of the piece, however, rather than the reading that he wanted his audiences to follow is certainly doubtful.[67] Dissociation from the details of Nietzsche's philosophy, whether through Hahn's account of an evolutionary program or Strauss's own claim that the work could be listened to as a C-major symphony in four movements, reassured potential ticket-buyers that advance philosophical knowledge was not required or even helpful. Elsewhere, though, he admitted that he had indeed hidden (*hineingeheimnisst*) certain connections to Nietzsche in the work, and in any case Strauss had long maintained that programmatic works could be understood on different levels without falsifying their meaning.[68]

In fact, the program of *Zarathustra* is designed to highlight a central argument of Nietzsche's book: the tragic realization that metaphysical longing, the flaw separating the human from the superhuman, cannot be permanently defeated but must be overcome again and again, in eternally recurring cycles. Strauss's tone poem lays out, in a kind of outline, an individual's process of coming to that conclusion. Like Nietzsche's prologue, it begins with the goal: a glorious sunrise as a symbol of pure physicality, separate from and antithetical to metaphysics. This defining moment is followed by a series of attempts by a human protagonist to "become like" nature (in the words of Nietzsche's prologue), and then three further stages: a crisis precipitated by the realization that the process of overcoming must be repeated eternally; a "convalescence" (*Genesung*); and an ending that captures the never-ending oscillation between optimism and despair by juxtaposing the key of nature (C major) with the key of metaphysical hope (*Tristanesque* B major).

The framework of this plan is suggested by the passages that Strauss marked, with page numbers from the score, in his copy of Nietzsche's text. These are given in figure 3.2, in the order of the musical passages to which they refer. When placed in the proper sequence, they lay out a fairly straightforward programmatic narrative. In the prologue, Zarathustra expresses his admiration for the sun—his desire to approximate its symbolic state. To that end he determines "to be human again," to replay an earlier cycle of his development. In the sections from "Von den Hinterweltlern," we learn that his youth and his quality of being human were characterized by the "dream and fiction of a God," a "colored vapor" that he finally rejected as "human work and madness." Responding to this enlightenment he turned to the physical, the "voice of the healthy body," and consigned metaphysical hopes to the "graves of his youth." But soon he found that abandoning his preoccupation with the afterworld would not be so simple. "Disgust" overcame him, he "fell down like a dead man," and he was forced to look for a new and more sophisticated solution. He found his solution in a new kind of music, born of "chaos" and directed against "purple melancholy" (cf. "colored vapor"). The victory represented by this music is distinguished in a crucial way, however, from Zarathustra's state just prior to his collapse. What this new music expresses is not freedom from metaphysics but the longing for freedom from metaphysics. The state envisioned by Zarathustra can never be fully attained; the cycle of disgust and liberation will continue eternally.

Given this evidence as a basis for interpretation, one can make reasonable inferences about the personal relevance of this philosophy and about Strauss's reasons for choosing the sections headings that he placed in the score. By situating "Der Genesende" at the center of his tone poem, Strauss highlighted that portion of Nietzsche's book most directly relevant to his own dilemma, in the process demonstrating a remarkable sensitivity to Nietzsche's argument. Robert Gooding-Williams has pointed out that already at the end of the prologue, Zarathustra "no longer takes for granted the success of his enterprise."[69] This nagging sense of self-doubt boils over in "Der Genesende," in a crisis that Strauss

"S[eite]. 1" appears in the margin of "Zarathustra's Prologue," section 1. [Because passage was printed in the published score, I have not included it here.]

"S. 3" (m. 23ff.) appears in the margin of "Von den Hinterweltlern," paragraphs 1-2.

"Einst warf auch Zarathustra seinen Wahn jenseits des Menschen, gleich allen Hinterweltlern. Eines leidenden und zerquälten Gottes Werk schien mir da die Welt.

Traum schien mir da die Welt und Dichtung eines Gottes; farbiger Rauch vor den Augen eines göttlich Unzufriednen."

[Once Zarathustra too cast his deluded fancy beyond mankind, like all afterworldsmen. Then the world seemed to me the work of a suffering and tormented God.

Then the world seemed to me the dream and fiction of a God; colored vapor before the eyes of a discontented God.]

"S. 4 etc." (mm. 35ff.) appears in the margin of "Von den Hinterweltlern," paragraphs 5-6.

"Diese Welt, die ewig unvollkommene, eines ewigen Widerspruches Abbild und unvollkommnes Abbild—eine trunkne Lust ihrem unvollkommnen Schöpfer:—also dünkte mich einst die Welt.

Also warf auch ich einst meinen Wahn jenseits des Menschen, gleich allen Hinterweltlern. Jenseits des Menschen in Wahrheit?"

[This world, the eternally imperfect, the eternal and imperfect image of a contradiction—an intoxicating joy to its imperfect creator—that is what I once thought the world.

Thus I too once cast my deluded fancy beyond mankind, like all afterworldsmen. Beyond mankind in reality?]

Figure 3.2. Passages from Strauss's personal copy of Nietzsche, *Also sprach Zarathustra* (Leipzig: C. G. Naumann, 1893) marked with page references to the autograph full score. In each case the annotation of a page number appears adjacent to a vertical line drawn in the margin and encompassing the given passage from Nietzsche. Translations are by R. J. Hollingdale (London: Penguin, 1969).

chose to highlight for important personal reasons. The desperation of his pleas to Rösch for help in discrediting Schopenhauer ("you should help me, not *lecture* me on things I already know") betrays apprehension that Schopenhauer might have been right, and the content of this tone poem confirms that in 1896 he still had not rid himself of it completely.[70] "Der Genesende" represents the moment at which Zarathustra realizes that he must "return eternally to this identical and self-same life, in the

"S. 9" (mm. 82ff.) appears in the margin of "Von den Hinterweltlern," paragraphs 7-9.

"Ach, ihr Brüder, dieser Gott, den ich schuf, war Menschen-Werk und -Wahnsinn, gleich allen Göttern!

Mensch war er, und nur ein armes Stück Mensch und Ich: aus der eigenen Asche und Gluth kam es mir, dieses Gespenst, und wahrlich! Nicht kam es mir von Jenseits!

Was geschah, meine Brüder? Ich überwand mich, den Leiden-den, ich trug meine eigne Asche zu Berge, eine hellere Flamme erfand ich mir. Und siehe! Da *wich* das Gespenst von mir!"

[Ah, brothers, this God which I created was human work and human madness, like all gods!

He was human, and only a poor piece of man and Ego: this phantom came to me from my own fire and ashes, that is the truth! It did not come to be from the 'beyond'!

What happened, my brothers? I, the sufferer, overcame myself, I carried my own ashes to the mountains, I made for myself a brighter flame. And behold! the phantom *fled* from me!]

"S. 10-12" (mm. 98ff.) appears in the margin of "Von den Hinterwel-tlern," at the antepenultimate paragraph.

"Hört mir lieber, meine Brüder, auf die Stimme des gesunden Leibes: eine redlichere und reinere Stimme ist diess."

[Listen rather, my brothers, to the voice of the healthy body: this is a purer voice and a more honest one.]

"S. 22" (mm. 164ff.) appears in the margin of "Das Grablied," para-graphs 1-4.

"Dort ist die Gräberinsel, die schweigsame; dort sind auch die Gräber meiner Jugend. Dahin will ich einen immergrünen Kranz des Lebens tragen.

Also im Herzen beschliessend fuhr ich über das Meer.—

Oh ihr, meiner Jugend Gesichte und Erscheinungen! Oh, ihr Blicke der Liebe alle, ihr göttlichen Augenblicke! Wie starbt ihr mir so schnell! Ich gedenke eurer heute wie meiner Todten.

Von euch her, meinen liebsten Todten, kommt mir ein süsser Geruch, ein herz- und thränenlösender. Wahrlich, er erschüttert und löst das Herz dem einsam Schiffenden."

[Yonder is the grave-island, the silent island; yonder too are the graves of my youth. I will bear thither an evergreen wreath of life.

Resolving thus in my heart I fared over the sea.

O, you sights and visions of my youth! O, all you glances of love, you divine momentary glances! How soon you perished! To-day I think of you as my dead ones.

A sweet odor comes to me from you, my dearest dead ones, a heart-easing odor that banishes tears. Truly, it moves and eases the solitary seafarer's heart.]

Figure 3.2 (cont.).

"S. 36 bis 44" (mm. 263-320) appears in the margin of "Der Gene-sende," at the last 2 paragraphs of section 1.

"Heil mir! Du kommst—ich höre dich! Mein Abgrund *redet*, meine letzte Tiefe habe ich an's Licht gestülpt!

Heil mir! Heran! Gieb die Hand——ha! lass! Haha!——Ekel, Ekel, Ekel——wehe mir!"

[Ah! you are coming—I hear you! My abyss *speaks*, I have turned my ultimate depth into the light!

Ah! Come here! Give me your hand—ha! don't! Ha, ha!—Disgust, disgust, disgust—woe is me!]

"S. 45" (mm. 321ff.) appears in the margin of "Der Genesende," at the first 5 lines of section 2.

"Kaum aber hatte Zarathustra diese Worte gesprochen, da stürzte er nieder gleich einem Todten und blieb lange wie ein Todter. Als er aber wieder zu sich kam, da war er bleich und zitterte und blieb liegen und wollte lange nicht essen noch trinken."

[Hardly had Zarathustra spoken these words, however, when he fell down like a dead man and remained like a dead man for a long time. But when he again came to himself, he was pale and trembling and remained lying down and for a long time would neither eat nor drink.]

"S. 47ff." (mm. 338ff.) appears in the margin of "Zarathustra's Pro-logue," section 5, paragraph 10.

"Ich sage euch: man muss noch Chaos in sich haben, um einen tanzenden Stern gebären zu können. Ich sage euch: ihr habt noch Chaos in euch."

[I tell you: one must have chaos in one, to give birth to a dancing star. I tell you: you still have chaos in you.]

"zu Seite 78. Asdur" (mm. 561ff.) appears in the margin of "Das Nacht-lied," paragraph 2.

"Nacht ist es: nun erst erwachen alle Lieder der Liebenden. Und auch meine Seele ist das Lied eines Liebenden."

[It is night: only now do all songs of lovers awaken. And my soul too is the song of a lover.]

"zu Seite 87" (mm. 669ff.) appears in the margin of "Von der großen Sehnsucht," at the ninth and tenth paragraphs from the end.

"Aber willst du nicht weinen, nicht ausweinen deine purpurne Schwermuth, so wirst du *singen* müssen, oh meine Seele!—Siehe, ich lächle selber, der ich dir solches vorhersage:

—singen, mit brausendem Gesange, bis alle Meere still werden, dass sie deiner Sehnsucht zuhorchen,—"

[But if you will not weep nor alleviate in weeping your purple melancholy, you will have to *sing*, O my soul! Behold, I smile myself, who foretold you this:

to sing with an impetuous song, until all seas grow still to listen to your longing.]

Figure 3.2 (cont.).

greatest things and the smallest": he will again confront in himself the human lust for cruelty, which disguises itself as "pity" (*Mitleid*), and he will again have to overcome the instinctive desire to find psychological refuge in an "afterworld" (*Hinterwelt*).[71] Zarathustra's "disgust" (*Ekel*) is a response to the realization that this process will never end. Human existence, no matter how enlightened, is always susceptible to the paralyzing "doubt" (*Zweifel*) that gave rise to the consoling idea of metaphysics in the first place.

The centrality of these concepts in the genesis of Strauss's program for *Zarathustra* is clear; they already figure in the first programmatic sketches, which reproduce the important landmarks in Nietzsche's developing argument.[72] The first ideas were little more than words: "worship/doubt" (*anbeten-zweifeln*) and "recognition/despair" (*erkennen-verzweifeln*) in one source, and "beholding/worship, experience/doubt, recognition/despair" (*Schauen-Anbeten, Erleben-Zweifeln, Erkennen-Verzweifeln*) in another. As unfocused as these reflections may seem, they do point toward a cyclical pattern of experience in which periods of doubt alternate with optimistic phases—just the sort of oscillation that one hears in the first six sections of the tone poem. Both sketches also imply an intensification of the process, in which doubt becomes despair (the relationship being more obvious in German than in English). However optimistic this tone poem may be—and Strauss trumpeted that quality on the title page, with the designation "symphonic optimism"—the inevitable periodic return of pessimism figures decisively in the program, the form, and the succession of moods.

The disposition of chapter headings in the score strongly implies that Strauss read "Der Genesende" as both a distillation of the book's main ideas and a replaying of events always already in the past and the future. This approach to the text is both insightful and exegetically effective. In the oration "Von den Hinterweltlern," the first heading that Strauss included in the published score (it also appears early in the book, at part 1, section 3), Zarathustra identifies himself as "the convalescent," to whom "it would be suffering and torment to believe in . . . phantoms." That observation returns in "Der Genesende," but this time with the clarification that such suffering is inescapable; indeed, as Zarathustra explains to his animals, accepting the necessity of its recurrence is the very heart of convalescence. By pulling these two sections out of the text and placing them at the beginning and the climax of a simplified musico-dramatic narrative, Strauss demonstrated his own recognition that "Der Genesende" answered and commented upon the earlier section but was also presupposed by it, in a way that undermines the text's linearity. And the relationship between "Der Genesende" and "Von den Hinterweltlern" is not unusual in the text, as we can see from examining the other sections chosen by Strauss, each one of which refers in some way to the moment of collapse and recovery.

Reading these sections in light of their relationship to "Der Genesende" allows one to see that these connections comprise a survey of Zarathustra's most important conclusions, as though Strauss intended to provide a concise compendium. Each of them also refers directly to Zarathustra's (and Nietzsche's) circular conception of history. The discourse against "pity" (*Mitleid*) in "Der Genesende" reopens a discussion seemingly concluded in "Von den Freuden- und Leidenschaften," where Zarathustra pronounces man "something that must be overcome." But in the later section we find the new realization that any "overcoming" simply begins the process anew. In "Von der Wissenschaft," Zarathustra describes the prehistory of man as a period of courage and the arrival of man as the onset of an era of fear. This section comes after "Der Genesende," however, in which we have already learned to think of history in circular terms, that is, terms that render linearity meaningless. "Das andere Tanzlied" also follows "Der Genesende" in the text, and its purpose is to make concrete the earlier description of music and dance as the means of grasping and living out the doctrine of eternal recurrence. From a large-scale formal perspective, this "Tanzlied" answers a need introduced in "Von der grossen Sehnsucht"—it resolves a structural dissonance, so to speak, so that a specific example of longing and arrival that is described on a small scale in "Der Genesende" actually plays out on a large scale across the text, into which the components of the miniature version are embedded. Yet another such example involves "Das Grablied." Here the declaration that "only where there are graves are there resurrections" cannot make sense until the arrival in "Der Genesende" of the moment powerful enough "to make even the graves listen," that is, the moment when the meaning of the eternal recurrence becomes clear. And that meaning finds poetic expression in the "Nachtwandlerlied," which Strauss placed at the end of his tone poem, completing the progress toward the doctrine of eternal recurrence in the same manner as "Der Genesende" completes the "down-going" begun in the prologue.

What all of these relationships demonstrate is that Strauss did have a rationale for choosing the headings that he chose; he did not intend simply to use interesting titles, although one can certainly listen to the work in that way as well. Whether or not he meant for anyone else to reflect on the concerns that were at issue for him in the work, he himself had a personal stake in coming to terms with Nietzsche's large and complicated constellation of ideas. The act of creating a tone poem allowed him to grasp them intellectually and to use that process as a stimulus of musical creativity, regardless of whether any listener could go back and reconstruct the process. In this sense, his approach to programmaticism was very much like Mahler's, for whom the program served as scaffolding that could be discarded once the work was completed. The difference is that for Strauss the application of that method did not rule out the simultaneous construction of a program to be used by the listener—one that might have had little or nothing to do with the process of creation. In any case, on the level of creation, it is of crucial importance to find Strauss engaging with a set of specific Nietzschean issues, for he by no means limited his artistic treatment of them to his sole outwardly Nietzschean tone poem. It is this fact that establishes a biographical significance for this line of thought. In one way or another, the dilemma that found its way from Nietzsche's *Zarathustra* to Strauss's *Zarathustra* resurfaces in every tone poem that Strauss composed after rejecting Schopenhauer.

Though early critics of *Ein Heldenleben* certainly noticed its outwardly autobiographical characteristics, they could not comment on the inward or personal features of the work, because once again Strauss kept them to himself. The crucial bit of evidence is a programmatic sketch that includes among the hero's antagonists "inner enemies: doubt, disgust" ("innere Feinde: Zweifel, Ekel").[73] Not coincidentally did Strauss revive the language Nietzsche had used to characterize Zarathustra's struggle against the unavoidable human preoccupation with metaphysics. The original title of *Heldenleben*, "Held und Welt," recalls the confrontation between nature and human that opens the earlier tone poem; in the short score of *Zarathustra* Strauss had described this beginning as an encounter between "Individuum" and "Welt."[74] Whatever the outward conflicts in *Heldenleben*, at its core this tone poem traces an individual's coming-to-terms with subjectivity. The real enemies, one's own human weaknesses, can never be fully vanquished but only held in check, through love, artistic creation, and a kind of wise resignation. The end of *Heldenleben* is thus not at all a victory but rather an adjustment, an acceptance, identical in kind to the concluding disagreement of *Zarathustra:* the highest experience of life available to humankind is clear-eyed acceptance of the inevitable periodic return of doubt.

The constant battle against vain metaphysical hopes figured significantly in Strauss's lifelong appreciation of nature. One could easily write off that interest as a typically German love of the outdoors and *Wanderung*, but for Strauss that enthusiasm assumed, after the Nietzsche experience, a specific philosophical connotation that neither faded nor required frequent reiteration. The deep-seated association of nature and philosophy is demonstrated by the complicated evolution of the program of *Eine Alpensinfonie*, which Strauss for a time considered calling "Der Antichrist." This work's musical connection to *Zarathustra* has always been clear, due not least to the majestic unfolding of the C–G–C "nature" motive when the climber reaches the summit. Little attempt has been made to account for that allusion, however, and just as the musical relationship is far more nuanced than commentators have noticed (see chapter 7), the association on the intellectual and programmatic level is likewise deep and multifaceted.

Strauss gave specific reasons for wanting to appropriate Nietzsche's title: the new work contained "moral purification through one's own strength, freedom through work, [and] worship of eternal glorious nature."[75] The relationship of those specific ideas to Nietzsche's *Der Antichrist* is not immediately clear, and the date of the statement, 19 May 1911 (the day after Mahler's death), raises the possibility that Strauss was belatedly imposing a Nietzschean interpretation on a composition already twelve years in the making. (Although *Eine Alpensinfonie* was completed in 1915, the first sketches date from 1899.) But from the first, this tone poem, which started out with an entirely different programmatic conception altogether, incorporated the language of Strauss's private understanding of Nietzsche. The earliest version of the program, variously titled "Künstlers Liebes- und Lebenstragödie," "Künstlertragödie," and "Liebestragödie eines Künstlers," traces the mental collapse of the artist Karl Stauffer (1857–91). Strauss conceived of Stauffer as a "consciously *working*, joyfully creating artist" (bewußt *arbeitenden* u. schaffensfreudigen Künstler)—that is, he described him with the same vocabulary that he had used to characterize his own post-Schopenhauerian worldview during the first months of 1893. Stauffer loses his grip on reality, however, not only because of a broken relationship with a woman, but under the sinister influence of "doubt" (*Zweifel*), which undermines his self-confidence as an artist. The defining Zarathustrian weakness, which hovers menacingly at the end of the *Zarathustra* tone poem and also stands as the principal foe in *Heldenleben*, here goes out of control and brings the protagonist to precisely the fate met by Nietzsche himself. Walter Werbeck has pointed out that the combination of "Zweifel" and a prominent "Freundin" makes this first program a kind of hybrid of *Zarathustra* and *Heldenleben*.[76] These are not superficial details, however, or tried-and-true props, but concepts that lie at the very center of Strauss's reception of Nietzsche, concepts that had profound implications for a composer who was obviously unsure of his ability to live out a Nietzschean view of the world.

When he shifted from one programmatic conception to the other, Strauss jettisoned the Stauffer plot entirely, with the exception of one detail: the opening sunrise. Optimism returned as "Künstlertragödie" became "Alpensinfonie," and the worldview that for Stauffer had been destroyed by "Zweifel" took over the culminating position in the work. At this stage Strauss planned a four-movement work beginning with a *Bergsteigerung* and ending with a movement devoted to spiritual "freedom," one sketch referring to the last movement as "freedom through work" ("Befreiung durch die Arbeit"), the other calling it "freedom in nature" ("Befreiung in der Natur"). The relationship between "work" and "nature" is confirmed by Strauss's comment on the death of Mahler; they were two sides of the same coin, two equally important facets of a healthy Nietzschean worldview. Moreover, these were concepts that Strauss had consistently developed during the compositional gestation of *Zarathustra*, *Heldenleben*, and the *Alpensinfonie*, for the purpose of addressing his own "doubts." He ultimately rejected the idea of incorporating them into music and instead settled for a single movement dealing with the climb up the mountain, but that choice demonstrates above all that the ideas no longer needed artistic working-out—they had been assimilated into his personality. Similarly, his ultimate decision not to use Nietzsche's title seems to mark a rejection of what might have become dangerously explicit musical philosophizing. Werbeck reads the specific wording of Strauss's "Antichrist" comment—"Ich *will* meine Alpensinfonie: den Antichrist nennen" (italics mine)—as a sign that the idea was new in 1911. But one might more precisely consider it a kind of passionate outburst. Disgusted with the tragic fate of Mahler, who in his own way became a victim of the "Jewish-Christian metaphysics," Strauss decided in a moment of anger to make his anti-metaphysical views explicit—to declare war, in words as well as in music, on the continuing destructive force of idealism. After a while that anger passed, but what remained—another confrontation between an individual and objectivity, this time culminating in a gesture of momentary conquest on the mountain peak—confirmed that Strauss had found a philosophy that would take him down a healthier path.

Till Eulenspiegel, Don Quixote, and *Symphonia domestica* seem at first glance too lighthearted to be involved in these metaphysical quagmires, even if their playfulness is construed as a species of Nietzschean optimism. Nevertheless, in each of these works we find an individual confronting recurrent doubts related to the "afterworld." *Till* places the issue most clearly in the foreground, anticipating the ironic idiom of *Zarathustra*'s "backworldsmen" during the scene where "disguised as a parson, [Till] oozes unction and morality," but shortly thereafter reaching a moment in which Till "because of his mockery of religion . . . feels a sudden horror at his end" (m. 196).[77] The experience actually pushes him onto a six-four harmony in A-flat (m. 206)—the defining tonal sign of the "backworldsmen"—but the approach of "pretty girls" distracts him. The trumpets here recall Mahler, who in 1895 was soon to turn strongly against Nietzsche with the appropriation/critique of the "Midnight Song" in the fourth movement of the Third Symphony. (In this light Tim Ashley's characterization of *Eine Alpensinfonie* as an homage to Mahler is particularly compelling.)[78] Also relevant here is the obvious critical treatment of Wagner, from the Tristan chord as raspberries (first at m. 47) to the quotation of the *Siegfried-Idyll* in the epilogue. Whatever else this enigmatic final gesture might accomplish, it signals a reactivation of Till's metaphysical uncertainty. After an A-flat arpeggio emerges (at m. 642) from the F-major quotation, a brief return to F leads eight measures later to another A-flat chord under a fermata—the same ending as the previous such episode. This time, however, Till snaps out of it on his own, so that the work's final moment of cheek, which points explicitly to Wagner and to the worldview with which Strauss associated him, comes as a conscious choice made by the individual at the center of it all.

Not the least appealing of Till's qualities to Strauss must have been his vacillation. Just as Till's bravado could give way in an instant to deep fear, so did Strauss find it difficult to put aside once and for all the questions that he thought he had answered in *Guntram. Don Quixote,* the third or fourth tone poem to be conceived since *Guntram* (it is not possible to know which), again lies strikingly close to personal experience. The tale of a pathetic aging idealist who spends his life railing against phantom enemies before dying a quiet and lonely death is one that Strauss had witnessed in real life. The fact that the character and Strauss's mentor were each a "Ritter" is perhaps misleadingly suggestive; still, Strauss's first diary entry mentioning the piece (16 April 1897) came four days after the first anniversary of Ritter's death, and four days after the birth of Strauss's only son, Franz Alexander (namesake of Franz Strauss and Ritter). The time was right, apparently, to compose a fable about the tragic consequences of idealism. By now certain ingredients seem to have become de rigueur—the difficult encounter with a group of religious figures (in this case penitents), for example. More interesting is the connection to *Faust* through a thinly veiled quotation of the main theme of the first movement of Liszt's *Faust Symphony* (Allegro agitato ed appassionato), just at the moment when the don loses his mind contemplating "[das] ritterliche Ideal" (m. 63). What distinguishes this tone poem from the previous two, and indeed from the following three, is the protagonist's eager acceptance of idealism. Don Quixote is a negative example (not unlike Guntram), a vision of the fate of those who lacked the strength of character to abandon metaphysical Wagnerism.

By comparison, the *Symphonia domestica* seems as down-to-earth as a work could be. For Strauss, though, the mundane details of family life played a decisive role in combating the "enemies" described in the *Heldenleben* sketch. From this standpoint, *Domestica* can be read as a compositional extension of *Heldenleben*'s idyllic/domestic ending, which in fact shows clear signs that the enemies have not been vanquished. Strauss's first ideas for this "symphony" draw a connection between family life, work, and the sun (Strauss's favorite Nietzschean symbol), such that the first two are construed as a means of achieving the state of the last.[79] The visual imagery and the musical technique by which they are achieved thus serve a purpose in the ongoing critical project, diverting attention away from the nonphysical. The work's only moment of serious difficulty comes during a section marked privately as "Schaffen und Schauen," where the composer becomes hopelessly mired in hyper-expressive developmental chromaticism.[80] The way out is found in the famously graphic love scene, the purpose of which recalls the diary passages on female sexual experience (see p. 80).[81]

The issue of tone painting provides another example of Nietzschean oscillation in Strauss's music, this time of a strikingly broad sort having to do with musico-programmatic extremes in Strauss's last six tone poems. While certain works show pronounced and sustained pictorial tendencies, others eschew that kind of writing almost entirely (or at least to a striking extent, given Strauss's reputation). *Ein Heldenleben* and *Don Quixote*, for example, stand at opposite ends of the spectrum; *Don Quixote* revels in the smallest physical details, from Sancho's smell to the sounds of livestock, while *Heldenleben* keeps mainly to the realm of ideas (notwithstanding the carping of the critics). That the works were conceived together, *Don Quixote* acting as a "Satyrspiel" to its more elevated partner, supports the possibility of a deliberate philosophical complementarity.[82] *Till Eulenspiegel* and *Zarathustra* share a similar relationship, with *Till* illustrating a long series of recognizable physical events, and *Zarathustra*, after its spectacular sunrise, renouncing that kind of thing altogether. With the final pair, *Domestica* and *Alpensinfonie*, this cycle was finally broken; yet while both "symphonies" consistently resort to pictorialism, they also add a new complementary relationship: family life and nature, which in Strauss's worldview were two sides of the same coin.

The broader implications of tone painting in these works will be explored in chapters 5 through 7. At this stage, however, it is useful simply to note that the tendency of Strauss's last six tone poems to cycle between alternate varieties is emblematic of the fundamentally Nietzschean outlook that binds them together. If radical tone painting operated for Strauss as an anti-metaphysical mode of composition—and it certainly did have an anti-Wagnerian flair that went beyond the merely playful—then we might look on Strauss's output from *Guntram* to the *Alpensinfonie* as a Zarathustrian nonchronological fluctuation between doubt and optimism. Of course, though individual works lean one way or another, both the problem and the solution figure into each work, as both seem to have inhabited Strauss's own personality. By the time he reached *Domestica* and the *Alpensinfonie*, though, he had found a solution he could live with. And as the philosophical dilemma faded, so did his interest in orchestral composition. With the help of the quintessential nineteenth-century genre, he managed to put the nineteenth century behind him, musically and philosophically, in a manner healthier than Nietzsche's, but one that the philosopher might have recognized.

4

Goethe and the Development of Strauss's Mature Worldview

$\mathscr{I}$n the autumn of 1944, as the eighty-year-old Richard Strauss endured his country's self-destruction and his body's slow collapse, he set out to reread the complete works of Goethe. An optimist even in the deepest depression of his life—the Propyläen edition that he owned is some three feet long—Strauss turned to the past for new perspective, on himself and on the strange era into which he had managed to survive. "I will be young again with Goethe and then once again old with him—in his way, with his eyes."[1]

One can hardly blame Strauss for wanting to escape himself. The regime he had served from 1933 to 1935 was obliterating centuries of German culture and endangering the survival of his artistic legacy. That threat now touched his family, with the very real possibility that the Nazis would remove his beloved Jewish-born daughter-in-law, Alice Strauss, along with his two "non-Aryan" grandsons.[2] Musical creativity offered him little solace; according to his own testimony, his career had officially ended in 1941 with his final opera, *Capriccio* (1941), the subsequent works serving only to prevent his wrist from becoming stiff.[3] How different an end must Strauss have anticipated over the course of a career spanning six decades. How different this end would be from that of Goethe, who died content, renowned, and at the height of his powers, or from that of Faust, who found with his last breath the moment that he wished would last forever.

Perhaps, though, with Goethe's help some sense might be made of this debacle—or so Strauss reasoned. How would Goethe have handled such a predicament? How might the past be used to reinterpret the present? Those were the questions at the root of this grand reading project. I offer that view as an alternative to the traditional scholarly conclusion that Strauss's turn to Goethe was a retreat to an idealized past, a failure of nerve akin to his 1910 abandonment of the proto-expressionist experiments of *Salome* and *Elektra* for the luxurious tonality of *Der Rosenkavalier*.[4] Yes, Strauss was known to avoid discomfort; this was a composer, after all, who responded to hyperinflation in post–World War I Vienna with a ballet called "Whipped Cream." Scholars now recognize, however, that *Der Rosenkavalier* was not a retreat from modernism but a reinvention of it, an approach from a different angle. It is modernist not in spite of its "outdated" musical material but because of it; when the old is made new, the new is itself revitalized.[5] In the same way, when Strauss's final years slipped ever deeper into depression and unproductivity, he sought another vantage point, hoping that by surveying his existence through the eyes of another he could lend it a new meaning.

Intellectually, Strauss had no more constant companion throughout his life than Goethe. From his blissful teenage years until the pampered agony of his postwar retirement, as Strauss strove to maintain his humanistic values in an ever more modern world, he regarded Goethe as his principal model.[6] The artistic debt is obvious in the area of lieder; Goethe was the only poet Strauss set in every decade of his life from the 1870s to the 1940s. But the novels, plays, and longer poems interested him as well, to the extent that (according to his elder grandson) the only work that he read but a single time was the *Farbenlehre* (1810).[7] When Strauss reached adulthood and assumed the responsibilities of a professional career, any period of free time was sure to bring renewed engagement with Goethe. During a year spent convalescing in Greece and Egypt (1892–93) the first item on his reading list was *Wilhelm Meisters Wanderjahre* (1829). (His travel diary begins with the declaration "1892, the wander-years begin!")[8] When a tour with the Vienna Philharmonic took him to Rio de Janeiro in 1920, he brought along Goethe's literary essays.[9] Thoughts of Goethe were always in dialogue with ongoing creative projects, no matter how powerful the directly related artistic figures (see the discussion of the genesis of *Also sprach Zarathustra* in chapter 3). In Hofmannsthal's view, a "Goethean atmosphere" of "purification" stood as the central unifying feature of their three post-*Elektra* masterpieces, *Der Rosenkavalier* (1910), *Ariadne auf Naxos* (1912; rev. 1916), and *Die Frau ohne Schatten* (1917).[10] And for his final instrumental masterpiece, the *Metamorphosen* (1945), Strauss returned to Goethe for inspiration, closing out his career by confirming an undying enthusiasm.[11]

This sustained interest in Goethe has been generally recognized by scholars, if not particularly well studied. Completely ignored, on the other hand, has been the regularity with which Strauss turned to Goethe in moments of personal difficulty. Therapeutic Goethe-reading, such as Strauss attempted in 1944, was a method of crisis resolution that he used many times, indeed during every major upheaval in his career. The principal obstacle to scholarly understanding here has been a simple lack of interest in the music Strauss composed to Goethean texts—a forgivable lack, perhaps, given that the body of work in question is actually quite small. All told, these compositions include about a dozen lieder, a setting for chorus and orchestra of the ode *Wandrers Sturmlied* (1885), the unfinished singspiel *Lila* (1895–96), and the "study for strings" *Metamorphosen* (1945), which began as a setting of the poem "Niemand wird sich selber kennen" (No one can know himself). This output is hardly impressive for someone who wrote nearly two hundred lieder, twelve large-scale orchestral works, and more operas than Wagner. Yet when placed in the context of his career, those compositions take on a disproportionate significance, owing to their placement at junctures of creative transformation and to their deep engagement with the issues motivating those shifts.

The first section of this chapter considers the role of Goethe in four important moments of transition in Strauss's creative life. The first two of these moments produced the mature Strauss: the absorption of Ritter's philosophy in the 1880s and the self-directed move through Schopenhauer to Nietzsche in the 1890s. It was through these experiences that Strauss evolved an intellectual justification for appropriating Wagner's musical style while rejecting the underlying aesthetic assumptions. Those two nineteenth-century transformations were matched by a pair in the twentieth century. The first took place around the end of World War I, when, faced with an array of rising modernisms and profoundly disinclined to join any of them, Strauss rededicated himself to an artistic solitude that had served him well but now seemed unlikely to bring him either critical or popular success. This choice effectively solidified a development begun with *Der Rosenkavalier,* as Strauss searched for a means of distancing himself from the nineteenth century without consigning music to a future of highfalutin ugliness. This latest phase of iconoclasm lasted for most of the rest of his career, but ultimately was broken off by the Indian Summer, a period of beautiful music stimulated by a nostalgia bordering on despondence. In the ostensibly post-career compositions yielded by this final crisis, Strauss came face-to-face with the chilling results of his own critique of musical idealism, and he wondered, right to the end, whether he had made a mistake.

In the chapter's second section, I consider Goethean influence in Strauss's life and career from a broader vantage point. The remarkable biographical parallels between these two great figures, which range from amusing coincidence to out-and-out modeling, bespeak a profound impact on Strauss, one that could manifest itself in unconscious but momentous ways. A survey of these areas of correspondence has never been made, and it yields striking and valuable results, indicating that on some experiential level, subconscious or otherwise, a deep knowledge of Goethe always shaped Strauss's thoughts and actions.

Goethe and the Transitional Moments in Strauss's Career

Each of the four most dramatic moments of transition in Strauss's career elicited from him a composition involving Goethe. With one exception, these are unheralded and relatively modest works: *Wandrers Sturmlied, Lila*, three settings (op. 67, nos. 4–6) from the *West-östlicher Divan* (1918), and the masterpiece *Metamorphosen*. Whatever their impact on listeners, however, in Strauss's creative life these pieces had profound significance, for in every case, the issue treated in Goethe's text was the issue motivating the shift. Irrespective of their success as artworks, then, their value as lenses through which to study Strauss's artistic dilemmas is immense.

Wandrers Sturmlied, a Brahmsian setting for chorus and orchestra of Goethe's rowdy, youthful Pindaric ode, was completed in May 1885, some five months before Strauss met Ritter in Meiningen. The work is a product of Strauss's "Brahmsschärmerei," a period of intense influence that seems to have come on rapidly some time during 1884.[12] This influence lasted well beyond the formation of the friendship with Ritter, a fact that has not been widely acknowledged, perhaps because scholars have deemed the personal relationship between Strauss and Brahms insignificant. But it is worth remembering that in the fall of 1885, at the very time when he was coming to know Ritter, Strauss also spent a great deal of time with Brahms, who was in Meiningen to observe Bülow's preparations for the premiere of the Fourth Symphony.[13] While there Brahms attended a performance of the now two-year-old Second Symphony in F Minor, a work that betrayed his own impact (cf. Brahms's Third) as well as that of Schumann and which he famously pronounced "ganz hübsch."[14] In the course of daily meetings at Weimar's Sächsische Hof he was undoubtedly made aware of the existence of the *Sturmlied,* the Cello Sonata (1883), and the recently completed Piano Quartet in C Minor (1885). Strauss also traveled along with Brahms, Bülow, and several others to Weimar, where they toured Goethe's home (courtesy of Erich Schmidt, curator of the Goethe Archive) and examined Goethe's manuscripts, letters, and diaries.[15] That the irascible Brahms, who could be cruelly impatient with young composers (witness the tragic story of Hans Rott), regularly spent time with Strauss obviously flattered the younger composer; whereas to others Brahms was "very cool and frightfully malicious," to Strauss he was "always quite amiable" (*liebenswürdig*).[16] It is not surprising, then, that notwithstanding Strauss's rapidly growing interest in *Zukunftsmusik* in the mid 1880s, the impact of Brahms can be felt as strongly as ever in two important works composed after that autumn: the *Burleske* (1886) and the Violin Sonata (1887). The latter work was produced simultaneously with Strauss's first genuine tone poem, *Macbeth.* Ritter disciple or not, Strauss retained a strong interest in artistic engagement with Brahms for several years after arriving in Meiningen.

What is new about the Brahmsian influence in these later works is that now, instead of acting alone or along with the related influence of Schumann, it confronts influences from the New German camp—influences that, for their part, are easily perceived but by no means predominant. Whereas this tension between Brahms and Wagner creates humor in the *Burleske,* in the sonata it creates problems, complicating the style and thus suggesting a kind of aesthetic struggle. Because Strauss learned to compose by imitating past masters, his early works are naturally derivative.[17] By 1886, however, he was perfectly capable of wiping his music clean of allusions if he wished. But at just the moment in his development when one would expect him to have made the leap to originality, he reinforced the citational element of his music, composing "music about music," allusion highlighted as allusion.[18] And he did so, it would seem, because of a persistent inner conflict concerning the two great musical figures of his time.

The significance of *Wandrers Sturmlied,* a work thoroughly neglected by Strauss's biographers, is that it shows the same heterogeneity of influence, deployed with manipulative control and to confrontational effect, a full year before the meeting with Ritter. Superficially the work is modeled on Brahms's *Gesang der Parzen*, a Goethe setting for chorus and orchestra that Strauss had recently heard in Berlin. Hanslick recognized the debt at once, in the D-minor opening, with its "einschneidenden Akkorden über grollenden Bässen und Paukenwirbeln!"[19] Another possible Brahms model is a choral setting of Schiller's *Nänie*, which as R. Larry Todd has noted seems in some respects a closer match.[20] Either way—and both of these works had their effect—one can see why commentators taking only a passing glance at the work have failed to detect more than the work's outwardly Brahmsian layer.

Nevertheless, along with the nod to Brahms, this music bears more than a trace of Wagner, in echoes qualitatively equivalent to those that would become a hallmark, for better or worse, of the tone poems. The fortissimo D-minor orchestral din, with the upper voice falling chromatically from the dominant, would easily have evoked for the late-nineteenth-century German ear the opening of *Der fliegenden Holländer* (ex. 4.1). The repeated building toward authentic cadences that are thwarted by all manner of deceptive resolution is likewise a Wagnerian specialty, particularly in the guise found at m. 17, where a deceptive cadence on the flat submediant is decorated with an appoggiatura a tritone above the bass (ex. 4.2). (Precisely the same gesture occurs in the Prelude to *Tristan und Isolde*, at m. 17, as Strauss no doubt knew.) More generally, the heavy-handed use of the half-diminished seventh chord to

Example 4.1a. *Wandrers Sturmlied*, mm. 19–23

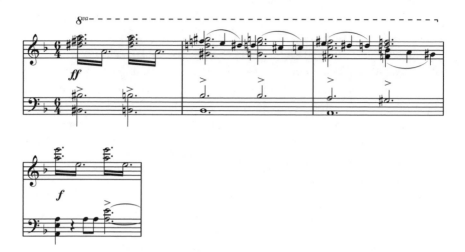

Example 4.1b. *Der fliegende Holländer*, Overture, mm. 21–24

Example 4.2a. *Wandrers Sturmlied*, mm. 15–17

Example 4.2b. *Tristan und Isolde*, act 1, Prelude, mm. 16–17

preserve instability and steer the music in unexpected directions represents another of Wagner's favorite techniques.[21]

It would be easy to write off these influences as mere imitation (conscious or unconscious), such as one can hear throughout Strauss's student compositions. But to do so in this case, where he juxtaposed not simply two influences but the two poles of contemporary German musical life, would be naive, given the central role that witting allusion would play in Strauss's future career, not just in *Guntram* and the tone poems of the 1890s, but in the operas (one thinks first of *Der Rosenkavalier* and *Ariadne auf Naxos*, although examples could be cited from virtually any work).[22] Strauss was far from an apprentice in 1884. The recently completed Second Symphony would soon gain him national fame, and within two years he would produce an orchestral work that remains in the standard repertory (*Aus Italien*). As he stood on the threshold of a major career, he recognized that to guarantee his success he would have to make a place for himself between Brahms and Wagner—no easy task, as so many of his colleagues were then learning.[23] The obvious approach would have been to choose one path or the other, and of course most biographers have seen him as having proceeded in this way. But the *Sturmlied* indicates that quite early in his maturity he experimented with another possibility, which we might regard either as integration or a kind of staged confrontation designed to open up a new way forward.

If *Wandrers Sturmlied* seems not quite able to choose between fusion and mutual destruction, that lack of focus stemmed from an understandable preliminary difficulty: how to muster up the self-confidence to manhandle two of the greatest figures of the Austro-German musical canon. The solution to that problem was supplied by Goethe, whose poem provided a source of hope. By putting his faith in Genius, the artist could accomplish any task, no matter how forbidding: he could withstand any storm, rise above any "Schlammpfad," gain the strength of Apollo, attract the muses, and soar above water and earth, "göttergleich."[24] Ego would pull him through—and as we have seen, ego meant a great deal to Strauss in the 1890s, when he made it a grounding principle of his aesthetics. In 1884, when the price of critical acclaim seemed to be epigonism, a bolder path, one of individualism and even iconoclasm, offered a better hope of achieving the higher kind of success he envisioned.

This is a context in which the relationship between Goethe's poem and a Brahmsian/Wagnerian pastiche can make sense. The musical implications of the work are immediately apparent when one compares the formal approach of the Second Symphony with that of *Wandrers Sturm-lied*. The Symphony is thoroughly traditional in every respect; the movements follow typical forms almost too closely, and the few cases of apparent innovation, such as the recollection of each movement's principal themes at the end of the finale, have clear precedents in Brahms or Schumann. The *Sturmlied*, on the other hand, presents the first example in Strauss's oeuvre of a formal practice common in his tone poems: in outlines the work is in sonata form, but each section after the first subject becomes formally ambiguous through the displacement of one of its formal functions to another section (see diagram 4.1).[25] The second subject, for example, is gesturally recognizable, but its attempts to modulate ultimately fall back onto the tonic key. The development is harmonically normal—it modulates widely and rapidly—but it introduces new thematic material rather than working out previously introduced themes. A clear recapitulatory gesture in the tonic marks the end of the development, yet the remainder of that section functions as a developmental transition to the D-major setting of stanzas five and six. The fundamentally different poetic character of these final two stanzas justifies the change of mode (the poet has arrived and no longer calls out to Genius). On the musical level, however, the function of that section hovers between recapitulation and coda. (There is a strong relationship, by the way, between this work and Schoenberg's *Verklärte Nacht*.)

As James Hepokoski has explained, the challenge in confronting a form like this is to make sense of the ambiguities without explaining them away. Strauss wants us not to decide one way or another, but to reflect on the relationship between the music and the poetic content.[26] This same challenge is made in all the tone poems. Here, where it is presented for the first time, it has perhaps the most direct autobiographical significance in any work by Strauss (which is saying a great deal). Poetically,

m. 1	23	53	88	92	162	208	222	279
Introduction	P	S		"Development" (new thematic material)	"Recapitulation" (double return, then thematic development)		Coda/Tonal Recapitulation (Apotheosis)	
Dm: i	i	move to III thwarted	Dm: PAC	modulatory	Dm, then modulatory	Dm: V	DM	PAC
	stanza 1			stanza 2	stanzas 3 and 4		stanza 5	stanza 6

Diagram 4.1. The Form of *Wandrers Sturmlied*.

musically, and biographically, this work tells us that meaningful development and self-realization require daring, fearlessness in the face of uncertainty, profound knowledge of artistic tradition, and an aggressive willingness to shape that tradition to one's own ends.

In a letter to Engelbert Humperdinck in early 1885, Strauss remarked that composing *Wandrers Sturmlied* had been difficult for him because the music had to be "in form and content as deep and philosophical as possible."[27] That concern for intellectual profundity grew significantly over the next decade, first as he responded positively to the Wagnerian idealism espoused by Ritter, then as he gathered the philosophical evidence to dismantle it. As Strauss's private philosophical study intensified, his compositional activity diminished, to the extent that from 1889–93 his only creative project was the ill-fated *Guntram*, an opera that began as the work of Wagner's successor but metamorphosed into a musical parody of the discarded idol, or in the words of an early critic, "a monstrous fantasy on Wagner's complete works."[28] Once again Strauss changed paths, then, but this time more decisively, for he was now thirty and fully mature as an artist. The best-known manifestation of this new freedom is *Till Eulenspiegels lustige Streiche* (1895), an instant classic with the public despite its use of the Tristan chord for tongue-flapping raspberries (or because of it, as the case may be). In the same year, Strauss once again set to work on a Goethean project, the little-known singspiel *Lila*, through which he reconsidered the genre of opera and its relationship to musical aesthetics.

Lila is a modest part of Goethe's output, even a trifle, which probably explains why the teenage Strauss felt equal to setting it and why he put it aside incomplete.[29] His return to it in adulthood would be difficult to grasp had he not supplied, in a letter to Cosima Wagner, three reasons for his renewed interest.[30] First, he liked that it was not a full-fledged opera. "Nothing about the piece should be at all operatic," he wrote; instead it would be "discreet." Second, he was interested in the contrast between spoken dialogue and song, and particularly in the problem of writing transitions between the two. He wanted to approach this challenge with feigned innocence, "as though 'the works' [of Wagner] had never been written." Finally, Strauss saw in *Lila* another opportunity to juxtapose conflicting musical styles. "What attracts me to the work is that the two kinds of music which exist today are brought together in it in a highly drastic confrontation . . . music as the expression of the psyche . . . and music as the play of notes." What is most striking about this plan, and most telling about Strauss's current attitudes concerning music, is that the play's verdict on those two types of music undercuts the basic premise of Wagnerian musical aesthetics. Music does act as a redeeming force in *Lila*; salvation comes from "music as the play of notes," not "music as expression," and the art's power is shown to be a function of its superficiality.

The plot of *Lila* concerns a kind of temporary insanity.[31] The protagonist, a young noblewoman with a melancholic temperament, frets over the safety of her traveling husband, then is plunged into depression when word arrives that he has been wounded. Her family members do what they can to calm her, so that the large house, normally filled with music, dancing, and revelry, becomes quiet and morose. Still, she grows worse, finally receiving an erroneous report that her husband has died. At this news she loses all grip on reality, leaves home, and wanders the hills, gazing at the moon by night and sleeping by day in a ramshackle hut.

When her husband returns, she does not recognize him and remains in the grip of elaborate delusions involving fairies, ogres, and a "Dämon." Finally an itinerant doctor proposes a cure: the family should play along, gradually steering her toward reality. Most important, they should resume the normal, gay, music-filled life of their aristocratic existence. It has been a mistake, he says, to think that she would be helped by suppressing the family's usual carefree lifestyle and its music in particular; in fact, that approach has made the problem worse. His plan works, although Goethe does not show us exactly how, for he leaves the final act, in which the cure takes place, largely up to "the taste of the performers."

We do not know precisely how Strauss would have handled that act, because he gave up the project for another after a few months. Still, it is not difficult to imagine which parts of the drama would have required which kind of music. If music in the New German style were necessary, it would be on the moonlit hills, the land of the deranged, which Goethe describes at the opening of act 2 as a "Romantische Gegend." This scene demanded music that could make self-destruction attractive. The real world, on the other hand, the lucid world, would be distinguished by music that was deliberately mundane. Lila can only rejoin the community of the sane when she is cured of her romantic delusions—a cure brought about by music proclaiming stylistically its emptiness of spiritual content. What Lila needs most of all is a grounding in physical reality; as her worried husband observes just after his return, "her thoughts were always too little on the earth."

In the aftermath of *Guntram*, Strauss concluded that his creative efforts needed the same kind of redirection as Lila's fragile mind. Here, as in *Wandrers Sturmlied*, Goethe gave him what he needed to face the challenge: not just courage, but a reasonable artistic justification for the path that he was about to take. In the post-*Guntram* tone poems, the first of which was *Till Eulenspiegel*, Strauss began to address with more directness the psychologically pernicious effects of the Wagnerian musical aesthetic. As his confidence in that decision grew, his interest in composing a work that made the point explicit waned. Ironically, Cosima was more disappointed than anyone; she had taken great interest in the work, being either too obtuse or too self-confident to recognize its connection to Strauss's slow withdrawal from Bayreuth.[32] For his part, Strauss was ready to burn that bridge once and for all. Faced with regular inquiries about his progress, he finally announced that he was now "working on a symphonic poem, the title of which will actually be *Also sprach Zarathustra:* it takes up so much of my energies that for the time being I have to put *Lila* on one side, without giving it up altogether."[33] Few of Strauss's contemporaries would have had the nerve to tell Cosima Wagner that he did not have time for a collaboration because he was working on a composition inspired by Nietzsche. Even Strauss might not have done so in such blunt fashion had he not been writing on 12 April 1896, the very day of Alexander Ritter's death. Before telling her of his plans for *Zarathustra*, Strauss wrote that he had "just now said a final farewell to the body of my dear friend."[34] After taking leave of the person who had shown him the meaning of musical idealism, Strauss also laid to rest his relationship with that philosophy's public standard-bearer, thereby obligating himself further to maintain the difficult path of aesthetic revolution.

The openly anti-Wagnerian Strauss, the composer who turned Wagner's musical technique against the philosophy that produced it, was widely acknowledged during the twenty years after *Zarathustra* as Europe's greatest living musician. This period saw the production of his last five tone poems as well as his five greatest operas: the self-consciously scandalous *Salome*, the even noisier *Elektra*, and beginning in 1910 three works that combined a return to tonality with radical musico-dramatic experimentation. Despite their innovative features, however, and despite their success among future audiences, *Der Rosenkavalier* (1910), *Ariadne auf Naxos* (1912; rev. 1916), and *Die Frau ohne Schatten* (1917) traced a steady decline in Strauss's reputation as fashionable iconoclast. Though the latter work was conceived as an "epitaph to post-Romanticism," its cool reception signaled a lack of public confidence that Strauss would know what to do next.[35] Indeed, to many the end of World War I coincided with the end of Strauss's career as a leader of musical composition.

Strauss himself did not share that opinion: eight of his fifteen operas were composed after 1920. But notwithstanding that irrepressible productivity, he did recognize his growing artistic isolation. He knew as well as anyone, for example, that the current climate demanded an explicit disengagement from the nineteenth century, yet none of the responses that were to gain public and/or critical acclaim—and they ranged widely, from Schoenberg, Webern, and Berg to Weill and Hindemith—held any genuine interest for him. Berlin, where the latter two composers would rise to fame, likewise lost its appeal, and not only because of the administrative chaos accompanying governmental transition.[36] Vienna, to Strauss the city of Hofmannsthal rather than of Schoenberg, held an attraction primarily because the job of codirector of the Vienna State Opera offered some of the freedom (with a five-month commitment per year) that he was to have gained from his evaporated fortune (confiscated by the British government at the outbreak of World War I). The crucial challenge of Strauss's life at this stage was, as at other such moments, to find the intellectual justification for a solitary aesthetic path that in technical terms would work itself out through compositions not yet produced (the first major work in this vein being *Intermezzo*).[37]

Although going it alone was old hat for Strauss, who had alienated three different mentors before he was thirty and watched his fame increase the more he mocked his greatest predecessors, this time things would be different. No longer the representative of youth, and no longer technically radical or uniquely down to earth, he would have to distinguish himself through a kind of counterrevolution. His credibility as an antiestablishment figure was obviously gone, but paradoxically his future work would be measured by the standards of an emergent modernist orthodoxy defined by younger figures whose music he found uncongenial at best. By refusing to participate, he reaffirmed his nonconformism, regardless of his position in the political world of music. Conformity was no more attractive to Strauss when associated with novelty than in any other context. Thus, even when rebellion seemed, for once, more likely to hurt his reputation than to enhance it, he rebelled anyway.

A concise, personal expression of this me-against-the-world situation comes in three settings from Goethe's *West-östlicher Divan*, composed in

1918. The poems are drawn from the "Buch des Unmuts" (Book of Displeasure), a choice that reflects in the first place Strauss's displeasure with the publisher Bote und Bock, to whom he was compelled to offer the songs in the settlement of a legal dispute.[38] That cartoonish dimension of the songs has been widely reported, but in poetic content and musical treatment these compositions have a much deeper meaning.[39] Each of the poems deals with a kind of opposition, in keeping with the basic themes of Goethe's cycle—West versus East, German versus non-German, the individual versus a foreign culture. The poet's recommendation in each case is to defuse the tension in a typically Eastern manner, through resignation, acceptance, and withdrawal. Also mixed into the solution, however, is independence, even hubris.[40] These poems thus capture the strange cocky hermeticism that Strauss had cultivated since the mid-1890s, even as they reflect a keen sense of the advance of old age. This mixture defines the attitude that he would now have to assume toward his musical environment in order to remain productive and true to his own artistic vision.

The second song, "Hab ich euch denn je geraten" (Have I then ever advised you), is the most direct challenge in the set to those who would disparage the poet's creative choices.[41] The poem throws down the gauntlet to critics—"Nun, so fördert eure Sachen!" (All right then, look after yourself!)—while also asserting the artist's authority of self-determination, on the basis of experience, natural ability, and, ultimately, because "so wollt er's machen" (that's the way he wanted it). Such was Strauss's attitude, now and always, toward conflict about his own music. He maintained that disposition now, perhaps for his own benefit, perhaps for others', but in any case because he could sense perfectly well that the circumstances of his reception were changing. Stylistically the setting leaves no doubt about where his own musical interests lay; struggle and antagonism are couched in violent, disjunct declamation and tonal instability, while the passages in the first person are set with luxuriant tonal lyricism, intensified here and there (notably in the penultimate measure) by colorful but unproblematic borrowed harmonies.[42] His own tastes would guide his creative activity, without apology and without regard for criticism.

A stronger but subtler connection to Strauss's predicament comes in "Wer wird von der Welt verlangen" (Who shall from the world demand), which touches on a theme that Strauss identified at the end of his life as the principal topic of his oeuvre: the basic separation of the individual from the collective. Although Adorno took Strauss to task for commodifying this breach, in fact the composer believed he had thematized it in obvious, audible ways throughout his career, and in his last written reflections he wondered how so many people could have missed that dimension of his work.[43] His rejection of Wagner's musical idealism, for example, had been based on the very notion that one could not expect to wring from nature, even with the help of music, the kind of knowledge that even nature "selbst vermisst und träumet" (itself lacks and dreams of). In a more immediate sense, Strauss the artist could not have hoped in 1918 to bridge the gap between his own attitudes and those of the larger musical world. Attempts to ignore this reality could only become detours, leading to further dilemmas or to changes in perspective no more settled than what had existed before. In his setting, Strauss found a straightforward musical analogue for this kind of vain striving: chords that resolve in unexpected ways. Although the harmonies of the prologue can be explained as chromatic alterations of a fairly simple progression, the immediate effect of the harmonic motion is to suggest a series of musical demands that are not satisfied in the anticipated manner. Similarly, moments of harmonic arrival, in particular the F-major arpeggios in mm. 4–5 and 10–11, are approached nontraditionally; what is demanded earlier in the music arrives later, of its own accord, on its own terms—"und was du vor Jahren brauchtest, möchte sie dir heute geben" (and what you needed years ago [or measures ago] it is ready to give you today).

The third song, "Wanderers Gemütsruhe" (Wanderer's peace of mind), concerns base or mean forces, the likes of which Strauss felt were surrounding him and darkening Europe's musical landscape. For the setting he returned to the C-minor-to-C-major trajectory that he had used in *Death and Transfiguration*—another work about an individual struggling against a sinister foe—which itself recalled the musical and psychological progression of Beethoven's Fifth Symphony.[44] In the song, that tonal and psychological development is harassed by fourth-based chords unusual in Strauss's output but familiar in Schoenberg's songs from the early 1900s, just when the younger composer's admiration for Strauss turned into animosity. As always, Strauss and his music battled very specific foes. But rather than confronting them, as he had done twenty years before in *Ein Heldenleben*, Strauss now hoped to let them "drehn und stäuben" (spin and crumble). Inborn optimism and a long, charmed career taught him to trust in his future and to be patient. The slow decline of the next decades would stretch even that patience beyond the breaking point, however, and by the Second World War would it

cost him his faith. The stoicism that he found in Goethe in 1918 ultimately gave way to a different view, an unprecedented pessimism, this
too drawn from the poet closest to his heart.

The *Metamorphosen*, written in 1945, was Strauss's last great orchestral work. It was also his first great orchestral work in nearly thirty years,
and as Bryan Gilliam has noted, the first serious one, in a certain sense,
since *Tod und Verklärung*.[45] That hiatus, which lasted roughly as long as
Mahler's entire adult life, was brought to an end by a public descent into
pessimism, something entirely new in Strauss's orchestral music. Before
the *Metamorphosen*, Strauss had avoided dark endings (*Don Juan* closes
with justice), even in *Macbeth*, the original version of which concluded
with the triumphant entrance of Macduff.[46] But in what he certainly knew
would be his final statement in the genre, he ended with a funeral march,
establishing that, as Timothy L. Jackson has argued, this metamorphosis
had a negative direction, leading to something frightful, even sinister.[47]

For a model Strauss took not just any funeral march, but the *locus
classicus*, the second movement of Beethoven's *Eroica*. What starts as allusion—thinly veiled, though Strauss claimed not to have been aware of
it initially—becomes in the final measures a despondent quotation.[48] On
a different level the work refers to another model, also by Beethoven:
the same C-minor-to-C-major trajectory found in "Wanderer's peace of
mind," now in reverse, but serving as the defining tonal feature and
therefore the decisive fact in interpreting the piece. Reversing the modal
trajectory of *Death and Transfiguration* called into question not only that
work's spiritual assumptions but those of the Fifth Symphony. In 1888,
Strauss updated Beethoven while providing a New German alternative
to the First Symphony of Brahms. In 1945, he offered a tragic new perspective on his own previous belief, and on Beethoven's.

Strauss never announced a program for the *Metamorphosen*, and he
never described any explicit connection to Goethe. Jackson's study of the
sketches established that connection definitively, while at the same time
leaving open the question of why Strauss would have deprived the work
of its text and recast it for string orchestra. The poem, "No one can
know himself," is overtly philosophical, but it also considers the practical
implications of self-reflection—in other words, it is a kind of poem that
Strauss had set for chorus before, not only in the *Deutsche Motette* (1913)
but in *Wandrers Sturmlied*.[49] But by shifting the work to orchestra and
giving it a programmatic title, he brought it to his preferred medium for
music with private philosophical significance, as though to place, belat-

edly, a capstone on that part of his oeuvre. That step obviously took a heavy emotional toll; what is most poignant about Paul Sacher's account of the dress rehearsal—which Strauss asked to conduct himself, because he could not bear to attend the premiere—is that if he wanted to hear his final orchestral work, and thereby say a proper farewell to the genre that had created both the public and the private Strauss, he had to do it in the presence of at least a few other human beings, the musicians themselves.[50] They did not know what they were witnessing, and Strauss had no reason to tell them or anyone else.

Although the premiere was successful, controversy erupted some days later when a Dutch critic claimed that Strauss had written an elegy for Hitler.[51] The composer's denial interested no one, for both sides had already made up their minds, and that lack of discussion continues to be a problem. To this day no one has observed, for example, that this music could very well have dealt with Hitler without being an elegy. All things considered, it would be remarkable if Strauss had not been thinking of Hitler. He certainly recognized that in the *Eroica*, the greatest German composer of that era contemplated Europe's most influential leader. Strauss, the greatest German composer of his own era, reengaged with that historically marked composition from amid the smoldering ruins to which his country had been reduced by the twentieth century's version of Napoleon. He can hardly have done so without reflecting on his own relationship with that leader—not necessarily to mourn Hitler or to pay homage to him, but simply to meditate on what had occurred.

From the early 1930s until 1945, Strauss's attitude toward Hitler changed significantly. Initially believing that the new government provided an unprecedented opportunity for improving the administrative, educational, and general public position of music in Germany, Strauss eventually saw his most cherished artistic institutions go up in flames.[52] This debacle concluded a slow, inexorable process; a full ten years earlier he had learned, with his 1935 dismissal as president of the Reichsmusikkammer, that his control over even his own fate was relatively limited. During this period he also became ever more conscious of his approaching death. The end of his life paralleled the approaching demise of a nation that had allowed its cultural legacy and its cultural integrity to be hijacked. In Strauss's bruised psyche, a once almost belligerent optimism now finally gave way to pessimism, as he concluded that he was "an insignificant man . . . with only a few unimportant words to utter in the last act of a drama."[53] His atheistic worldview allowed no room for a personal future, and that expected end now also seemed to await the art in which he had placed his hopes for a kind of immortality. From the late Strauss's vantage point, change—psychological, physical, artistic, political—produced negative results.

Ruminating on metamorphosis while returning to a genre that belonged to his youth, Strauss cannot have helped but reflect on the transformations that defined his artistic coming-of-age: imitator of Haydn and Mozart, conservative follower of Brahms, minion of Bayreuth, anti-Wagnerian modernist, defender of tonality, incipient postmodernist. As these changes multiplied, they pointed ever more clearly toward a kind of relativism that spelled doom for the tradition of German art music. As a young man, Strauss embraced this prospect. He was an optimistic nihilist, and he wanted music—or at least his music—to be nihilist as well: without ethical responsibility, without metaphysical substance, without a connection to anything larger than itself. He succeeded, which is a credit to his energy and determined independence. Seen from 1945, however, that success had unforeseen, tragic implications.

The suppressed text of the *Metamorphosen* is a poem about identity and responsibility. "No one can know himself, detach himself from his Self-I [*Selbst-Ich*]," wrote Goethe:

> Yet he tries to do it every day,
> That which is clearly from the outside,
> What he is and what he was
> What he can and what he wants to do.[54]

The loss of objectivity, the absence of a grounding sense of reality, imposed an inescapable fluidity on one's own sense of self, even (or particularly) if one were an artist. But that fact did not absolve one of the responsibility of striving to find the reality that could not be held fast or of believing in the truth that could not exist. The idea of perspectivist truth, here articulated poetically rather than philosophically, had enabled the young Strauss to let music just be music. His blindingly fast changes of direction, his disconcerting incongruities, grew from a desire to celebrate the obsolescence of philosophical mooring. But the old Strauss, equally devastated by Germany's cultural collapse and his own impending death, discovered that liberation from metaphysics produced nihilism. This realization was horrific and inescapably real to him. Worst of all, he cannot have failed to see that Ritter had predicted this outcome, at least in a general sense, some fifty years before. The crux of Ritter's argument against the mature Straussian aesthetic was that once music lost its ethical dimension, disaster would follow. In the words of Wagner, music was a means—not simply to the communication of dramatic content, but to the sustenance of a nation's moral spirit.

Somehow, the bizarre spirituality of that strange man had produced an accurate forecast. Of course he would not have identified anti-Semitism as a root cause of Germany's moral undoing. But in his view the retreat of German music from an overt philosophical responsibility was a harbinger of national disintegration. Strauss's increasingly celebratory flouting of that responsibility crushed him, even though he did not live to hear anything beyond *Till Eulenspiegel.* Had he known the remaining five tone poems, one can only imagine his ire. The *Metamorphosen,* however, which was finished on 12 April 1945—precisely forty-nine years after Ritter's death and forty-nine years after Strauss's letter to Cosima about *Zarathustra*—might have reassured him that although it was too late, Strauss had, with Goethe's help, finally understood.

Goethe in Strauss's Life and Worldview

In perhaps the most interesting of his famously provocative self-appraisals, Strauss once called himself "the last mountain of a large mountain range."[55] Not the least telling detail of this metaphor is its lack of self-deprecation; here, for once, he abandoned the nonchalant fatalism of a "first-class second-rate composer" and granted himself a position of cultural significance. The later Strauss did see himself as an important figure, and he believed he was part of a great tradition, a heritage that was monumental in its historical consequence, unsurpassed in its cultural achievement and never to be repeated.

Music figured centrally in that tradition, but not, in Strauss's view, as a romantically conceived distillation of all that was good in the other arts or as a new and more effective metaphysics. Instead, music was one component among the many that comprised the German humanistic legacy. Self-styled as Germany's last musician, Strauss staked his claim to historical significance on works that refuted overblown nineteenth-century notions of music's importance. Though he always championed Wagner's music, through performance and appropriation, Strauss refused to allow that music's aesthetic underpinning to overwhelm German culture entirely. That he was the first German musician to take that position—the only important one of his generation—reflects above all his broad, one might say European, perspective on the German artistic landscape. On the level of cultural history, the real Strauss was the one who wandered for hours in art museums, who read history voraciously, whose conversation brimmed with literary allusions, who believed (in the words of his grandson) that "a cultivated European must know Latin and Greek, or else he's not a fully qualified human being."[56] Every bit the Renaissance man—as much as any contemporaneous literary figure—he knew as well as anyone that the mountain range was not only bigger than any one artist, it was bigger than any one art. If as a musician, then, Strauss extended a line from Bach through Beethoven to Wagner, as a German artist he delivered the culture as a whole from the unseemly encroachment of his own art upon the others.

At the root of this determination was Strauss's admiration for Goethe. However powerful the influence of Wagner, it was Goethe who for Strauss stood at the center of the German intellectual and artistic tradition. Goethe, not Wagner, was the *Vollendete*, the finished human being who commanded the full range of knowledge required for self-realization. Goethe, not Wagner, embodied the coolheaded wisdom that, combined with encyclopedic learning, characterized maturity. Espousing this view of Goethe would not have distinguished Strauss from most other German artists around 1900. But living it, putting it into practice as though he were implementing Goethe's approach to life in a new historical context, set Strauss apart. The suggestion that Strauss, consciously or unconsciously, lived a life that was in many respects Goethean would have seemed perfectly natural to him, and thus it is perhaps not surprising that to a remarkable extent the biographies of Strauss and Goethe can be told side by side. Their intellectual backgrounds, their goals, their early creative successes, their responses to contemporaneous aesthetic movements, their relationships to avant-garde and conservative peers, the role of their personal lives in their art—these attitudes and experiences parallel one another with a remarkable consistency that bespeaks a deeper kind of influence than the heated encounters the young Strauss experienced with Wagner, Schopenhauer, and Nietzsche. When Strauss expressed hope at the end of his life that he would find the same kind of posthumous fame enjoyed by Goethe ("when he died, Goethe was never so alive and renowned as he is today"), he found support in the awareness that their paths had long overlapped.[57] The effect of that awareness is difficult to gauge, but the fact of its existence tells us much about Strauss's inner life.

Strauss was placed on a Goethean path early on, indeed, long before he had any say in the matter. The guiding principle of Strauss's upbringing was not the acquisition of musical skill but the development of cultural awareness, broadly construed. His parents insisted on a thorough, first-rate education not because they were reluctant to have their son pursue a musical career or because they felt that he might end up as a civil servant, but because they considered *Bildung* essential to his success as a composer—every bit as important as solid musical technique. To become a great musician, Strauss would have to be a mature humanist, or so they believed. Goethe was not the sole father of this humanistic outlook or even the principal one (that honor belonged to Humboldt), but he stood unrivaled as an example of the fulfilling existence to be had by those willing to devote themselves consistently to learning and self-examination. More than any other modern figure, Goethe showed that life could be improved through regular, diligent acquisition of knowledge.

The daily activities of the mature Strauss were very much like those of the mature Goethe.[58] The academic subjects of his schoolboy days—languages, history, ancient and modern literature, visual art—became the interests that occupied his adult life. Skat was the exception that proved the rule. When he was not conducting, Strauss was learning, with a relentless curiosity that did not distinguish between activities with a creative goal and activities that were their own goal. Even Adorno admitted that "he amassed a wide range of knowledge and information outside his field, collected assiduously."[59] His inexhaustible energy for composition was thus merely the most evident (and most professionally developed) sign of an abiding devotion to productive effort. Too often Strauss's relaxed public manner overshadows the reality that his reason for living was *Arbeit*, construed broadly as exertion for the sake of personal betterment. Financial concerns were not about money for its own sake but about time, without which he could not pursue the mutually reinforcing projects of creation and learning that sustained him. Goethe himself faced much the same dilemma through most of his life, relying on his court salary much as Strauss depended on his conducting positions, and always mildly resenting the interference of everyday matters in his routine of private study. In both cases, that jealous protection of time and energy for work was hardened by a life-threatening illness during early adulthood, the principal torment of which was boredom, not fear of death.

Strauss and Goethe both lived into their eighties, through periods extraordinarily varied, even given the amount of time involved. Their lives spanned world-altering political changes that were accompanied and inspired by revolutionary shifts in the conception and perception of art. For both figures, responding to the bewildering flux in their environment necessitated an artistic attempt to embrace that stupefying totality without advocating a simplistic consistency. This imperative became all the more acute when they each found that they had in a sense outlived themselves, becoming historical before they had died. Friedrich Sengle has described the late Goethe as a kind of living historical record, in which successive eras were brought into a simultaneous relationship.[60] No single fact can explain an urge to create that persists undiminished through more than eight decades; habit may have been as important as anything. But of crucial importance in both of these cases is a common and obvious determination to engage at once with the full spectrum of possibilities, from abstruse erudition to earthy simplicity, from groundbreaking novelty to arch-conservatism. *Faust*, which occupied Goethe's career for over fifty years, encompasses an enormous breadth in tone, style, and character, but it is no wider than what we find by surveying Strauss's output in any given decade from the 1880s on. This need for sweeping variety confused and even angered younger contemporaries, who criticized it without always acknowledging their own debts to this or that part of the whole.

Strauss and Goethe both gained their first artistic success and their first notoriety through a youthful engagement with romanticism (or in Strauss's case, neo-romanticism).[61] Both likewise concluded, while still young and notwithstanding the explosive popularity of *Werther*, *Don Juan*, and *Tod und Verklärung*, that romanticism was a dead end. (Thomas Mann remarked that the later Goethe regarded *Werther* with "affectionate horror.")[62] What followed was not abandonment, however, but critical engagement, as we see for example in the characters of Mignon and the Harper—quintessentially romantic figures, fully recognizable as such but nonetheless profoundly out of place in the world of Wilhelm Meister and thus the objects of a critical consideration at a remove.[63] That same distance would mark Strauss's handling of Wagnerian style after the break with Ritter. It was through this reaction against romanticism that Strauss as well as Goethe developed the defining features of a post-romantic artistic personality. The need to highlight the separation between themselves and their creations and the determination to undermine any sense that their art was intended to communicate in an uncomplicated way some sort of stable truth created an aesthetic in which older artistic material—"classic" or otherwise—could be turned to new purposes. Thus Goethe and Strauss remained marked by their early experience of romanticism, even as they moved on toward apparently retrospective styles that actually sprang from a post-romantic orientation. Meanwhile, the movements that they left behind clearly owed a debt to the abandoning pioneers. Goethe inspired the romantics just as much as they annoyed him, and Schoenberg's free atonal music draws on the Strauss of *Don Juan* and *Salome* as well as on Wagner and Brahms.[64]

The tendency to iconoclasm developed early in both Strauss and Goethe, as a reaction against a father attempting to control the son's career and through a precocious agnosticism acquired during the teenage years as an innocent consequence of taking schoolwork seriously. For both of them, the reckless daring that caused trouble in youth produced fame in early adulthood; the daring coarseness of *Götz von Berlichingen* bore significant responsibility for its early impact, no less than the frighteningly graphic qualities of Strauss's early tone poems.[65] A willingness to flirt with the banal remained constant, no matter the seriousness of the subject (as Monika Lemmel has observed, for example, with regard to the *West-östlicher Divan*).[66] But part and parcel of this earthy streak was a belief in the value of indulging the senses. That impulse gained considerable strength through experience with Italy, experience the principal manifestation of which was an intensified fascination with the visual— Goethe producing voluminous sketches, Strauss turning mountain ranges into melodies.[67] The conviction that art was tied to physical experience never weakened, even though the fame connected with the early creative products of that conviction became a burden.

Eventually the necessity of relating to a public with its own set of expectations led both of these artists to create a persona for public consumption. That Strauss chose the skat-playing Bürger, as opposed to Goethe's stiff minister, matters less than that they both shared their true views only sporadically, in fragments, and liberally mixed with disinformation. Many who knew them detected a coolness, an indifference rooted in egoism. Karl Otto Conrady has said that Goethe's contemporaries "always had difficulties making sense of Goethe's character"; they called him a "riddle," a "chameleon," who particularly in old age "remained indistinguishable as though behind changing masks."[68] Certainly the control of emotions was calculated, even narcissistic; on the day of his wife's death, Goethe noted in his diary (which of course he knew would become public record) that he had continued the normal activities of his life, performing color experiments and sending off engravings.[69] Strauss too could make a show of not caring about the vitally important (for example, by calculating royalties during the premiere of

Salome or presenting the *Four Last Songs* to Alice Strauss with the words "here are the songs your husband ordered"), but as with Goethe, the choreographed nonchalance asks for a deeper reading.[70]

Paradoxically, this self-centered, self-conscious disengagement lay behind Strauss's and Goethe's tendency to autobiography. The presentation of artificial selves, part fact and part fiction, proved to be the surest way to keep audiences guessing. Thus although the mature Goethe was determined to "take his life and feelings to the public," in Nicholas Boyle's words, each such work "contains a secret, something left unspoken."[71] The tendency was thus not gratuitous in either case but served a basic aesthetic function. *Faust*, perhaps the quintessential magnum opus in Western culture, revolves around a character whose limitless thirst for knowledge was modeled on Goethe's own, but whose other qualities bear at best an uncertain relationship with the author's. In a more focused historical and cultural setting, *Wilhelm Meister* replayed important strands of Goethe's intellectual and emotional development, but (especially in the *Wanderjahre*) in what Stefan Blessin has called a proto-modernist "fragmentary and fissured [*lückenhaft*]" manner that highlights the incompleteness of the reader's knowledge.[72] *Werther* too had an obvious autobiographical dimension, even as Goethe attempted to erase himself as author through the epistolary format and by actually leaving his name off the first edition.[73] For Strauss the overtly autobiographical elements of works such as *Heldenleben* and *Symphonia domestica* overshadowed a subtler but more thoroughgoing tendency to use the tone poems as laboratories, through which he could gain perspective on artistic dilemmas that for whatever reason demanded private resolution. Biography is not separable from art in Goethe or in Strauss, but neither side of the equation is a simple key to the understanding of the other.

Other propensities seem likewise to have accomplished the goal of rendering their art somehow opaque. For example, Strauss and Goethe both frequently indulged in sudden changes of style—instantaneous shifts apparently designed to shatter the possibility that a listener or reader could perceive an overarching consistency of artistic vision. The most obvious cases of incommensurate adjacent works are well-known: for Strauss, *Elektra* and *Der Rosenkavalier*, *Salome* and *Symphonia domestica*, *Macbeth* and the Violin Sonata; for Goethe, the *Römische Elegien* and *Hermann und Dorothea*, *Faust* and *Wilhelm Meister*.[74] Perhaps even more aesthetically significant are the examples found within works. Erich Heller has written that for Goethe the problem of explaining "a world that has lost its unity" is a theme in many of Goethe's works before *Faust* part 1, but with *Faust* Goethe for the first time approached it through an artwork that itself had lost, or disavowed, its own unity.[75] *Wilhelm Meisters Wanderjahre* takes fragmentation as a principle of form, leaving the reader no choice but to accept massive gaps and wild lurches, while *Faust* part 2 pushes both historical sweep and intertextuality to an unprecedented level of virtuosity. Although Strauss's breadth of vision is not always quite so great, a heterogeneous, mercurial handling of style is a defining feature of virtually all of his major works beginning with *Guntram*, and (as we have seen) it is foreshadowed in several earlier compositions. Heterogeneity within a single work established that this was not a matter of rapid artistic evolution but of a new conception of style, one that made incompatible modes of creation simultaneously available but equally disconnected from an ostensibly "centered" creative agent.

By calling into question a personal, emotional, or spiritual investment in artistic creation, if not repudiating it altogether, Strauss and Goethe searched for a more plausible and indeed more ethical form of truth. (Goethe's evasiveness in discussing *Wilhelm Meister* with Schiller can be read in this sense as a reluctance to steer his friend down an authoritative but ultimately false interpretive path.)[76] These figures both realized quite clearly that they were living in a post-Kantian world. Rejecting the expression of a coherent subjectivity, and thereby giving up claims of special access to truth, allowed the works to become more real, which is to say less false. Irony became the highest form of aesthetic honesty. This choice is already apparent in the quintessentially romantic works, which simultaneously laid the grounds for a critique of romanticism. *Werther*, a world-altering phenomenon, was already a deliberate and meticulous dissection of the style that it invented—it both created the Sturm und Drang and exposed its weaknesses. The fact that so many readers missed this level of the book (whether they committed suicide or not) irritated Goethe endlessly. Ultimately he attempted to remedy the misunderstanding through direct parody, producing one version that ended with a man relieving himself on Werther's grave and another in which Werther and Lotte are married (the suicide attempt having resulted only in a lost eye and singed eyebrows).[77] Strauss too became famous for works in which the apparent adoption of a style actually undermined it, and he likewise first applied this approach in works created through an apparently sincere neo-romanticism. We have seen that the stylistic plurality of *Guntram*, created by juxtaposing distinct Wagnerian models, produced a potpourri effect audible even to some among the work's first listeners (see pp. 38–39). All of the early tone poems have endings that raise questions about the seriousness of what precedes them: *Macbeth* with its original conclusion celebrating the triumph of Macduff (an ending that Bülow attacked precisely because it undermined the tragedy), *Don Juan* with a literal execution of the spirit of the rest of the piece, and *Tod und Verklärung* with a transfiguration in mundane C major, a key that for the remainder of Strauss's career would be a sign of the physical sphere.

In view of the role assumed by both Strauss and Goethe as champions of German art (despite their obvious interest in the international), one might reasonably ask why they did not fight harder on behalf of romanticism, an aesthetic that markedly enhanced the broader importance of art. The answer is that they both recognized romanticism as one side of a dialectic: the antithesis of unreflective classicism. Goethe abhorred Kant's aesthetic system because he knew that it was purely theoretical, with a shockingly limited basis in practical artistic experience. Yet at the same time, he did not believe that strengthening the connection between art and the "epidemic of philosophizing" that swept Germany in the early nineteenth century would help matters.[78] Strauss too had considerable experience of both sides; he was raised on something like a formalist perspective, and his philosophical study during the Ritter period acquainted him thoroughly with the basis of Wagnerian neo-romanticism— so thoroughly that he could not help but conclude that it was a sham. The challenge for both of them, then, was to move beyond a debate between two weak positions and on to the synthesis that would revitalize art in purely artistic terms.

The kind of post-romantic conception of art that evolved here did not completely separate art from religion and philosophy, but it conceived the relationship in a new way. Art would serve not as a better form of religion, but instead it would act as a substitute, answering that need in a new way. This was the "religion of the classics" that Strauss said he would practice "until the end." Art could not be a religion, because it was not true, but it could improve upon religion, because it was closer to the truth. As Nietzsche would point out, fragmentation, such as we find in *Faust* or Strauss's *Also sprach Zarathustra*, pushed art closer to truth precisely because art now admitted its limitations. Fragmentation meant perspectivism: the conscious disavowal of attempts to grasp a totality and a simultaneous acknowledgment that arguing on behalf of any version of a comprehensive unity, artistic or otherwise, is philosophically dishonest. What, then, were the premises of philosophical honesty? Absolute knowledge is not possible; meaning changes according to perspective; and human fulfillment, if possible, will only be attained by accepting these realities. The crucial feature of *Wilhelm Meister* for Goethe was that it could not be reduced to a single idea. Ambiguity, the one strain of romanticism with which Goethe always remained in sympathy, became the basis of a worldview as well as a theory of art.

Making sense of this new and in some ways more modest conception of art was perhaps the most difficult challenge faced by Schiller and Mahler, the two great contemporaries, who had the joy of recognizing, as only fellow geniuses could, their colleagues' greatness but who also suffered the misfortune of believing that that greatness was to some extent being squandered. Schiller and Mahler were both interested in philosophy for its own sake, and at bottom they were more romantically minded—which even in the misanthrope Mahler's case placed him more squarely in the contemporary artistic mainstream (at least among musicians) than Strauss. This devotion to the abstract was a stumbling block but also a fertile stimulus of discussion. If Goethe was clearly bothered by Schiller's philosophical bent ("it is distressing when one sees such an exceptionally gifted man tormenting himself with philosophical modes of thought that cannot be of any help to him"), Strauss was no less irritated by Mahler's metaphysical preoccupations.[79] But the differences held the relationships together or at least ensured that they would be renewed.

Perhaps it was the need for relief from such concerns that required devotion to an oddball wife, a partner as essential as she was peculiar. Neither Goethe's nor Strauss's wife contributed directly to her husband's creative work, and yet the protection from intrusions and, more important, the provision of simple pleasures created the atmosphere in which that work could take place. Domestic contentment was a condition of creative production. Given the unapologetic incorporation of the physical into their art, it is not surprising that their personal lives would be firmly rooted in the ordinary. Nevertheless, in eras that looked with suspicion (to say the least) on the connection of bourgeois domesticity to high artistic achievement, this relationship between life and art proved difficult to understand.

In the end, being understood or accepted by contemporaries was of little concern to two artists who could see easily enough that their works were entering the canon. Sustained success permitted, even justified, an autocratic approach to artistic decisions and to relations with the public. Strauss and Goethe remained strongly antidemocratic throughout their lives, and if they exhibited a certain exaggerated deference in their brief personal contact with the infamous political leaders whose rise and fall they witnessed, the core of their personalities still reflected the over-whelming confidence of a genius. The only force significant enough to influence their aesthetic convictions in a lasting way was tradition—a force the revitalization of which was their own responsibility, as they well knew.

In 1903, as his activities as tone poet and his engagement with the related intellectual issues were winding down, Strauss offered what may be his definitive statement on the place of music in human life. His editor's preface to the series of illustrated monographs *Die Musik*, al-though brief, traces the outlines of the broad theory of culture within which he situated himself and his art. The task of music, and indeed of all art, was according to Strauss a function of its nature: music was a product of culture, and thus its duty was to bear witness to a culture. Just as individual works existed as particularizations of a collective unity, so engagement with these works had as its highest goal the perception of that unity.

In its emphasis on the comprehensive and in its implicit recognition of the possibility of comparative cultural study, this characterization of art reflects the influence of Goethe. Just how important that perspective was to Strauss is shown by his elaboration of it at the head of a series of books on *music*; he lent his name to the series not to promote under-standing of particular musical issues but to address the growing separa-tion of music from culture—a separation that was a function of music's "special" status in the nineteenth century. The formalists, against whom Strauss polemicized ferociously here, earned Strauss's contempt because their arguments consigned the art to a ghetto. Wagner, on the other hand, whose works had consummated the centuries-long development of music's expressive power, deserved praise first of all because he had dem-onstrated music's "immediate connection with life and culture." In other words, Wagner had shown how music fit into a Goethean scheme of German intellectual culture.

Goethe himself had not been able to manage that feat, perhaps be-cause music always remained somehow foreign to him. He believed in it, he honored it, but he did not understand it. Wagner had supplied what Goethe had lacked, and through that vision of music's larger role he had likewise provided the aesthetic motivation for Strauss's critical musical explorations during his maturation. It was for this reason that Strauss remained, in his view, a faithful Wagnerian, notwithstanding his rejection of the metaphysical dimension of music. What German music would need above all in the twentieth century was a way past the disputes of the nineteenth century, a new unity of aesthetic conception that connected music fully to the Goethean conception of culture. By reading Wagner through Goethe's eyes, Strauss hoped to create the conditions of a productive artistic future.

II. Orchestral Composition as Philosophical Critique

5

The First Cycle of Tone Poems
Genesis of a Critical Musical Technique

*T*he detailed account of Strauss's intellectual development laid out in part 1 indicates that the relationship of the early tone poems to that development has been widely misunderstood. The separate chronologies of his musical and intellectual maturation tell a more complicated story than one of conversion, discipleship, and gradually rising independence. By turning to an overtly partisan genre in which he had not previously worked (the tone poem) and by producing several masterpieces in just a few years, Strauss cast himself as a Siegfried of New German instrumental music—a predestined champion who accomplished mighty feats after having discovered his true calling. But the completion of these three works coincided with the *beginning* of his philosophical crisis, not the end. This music was not the *result* of a career-defining intellectual shift, but an important contributing factor to a shift that came later than has been recognized.

However powerfully Strauss's music suggests the birth of a modernist movement around 1889 (the date offered by Dahlhaus as the beginning of early modernism), at that time the movement had no clear agenda in the composer's own mind.[1] Only during the final work on *Guntram* would Strauss's philosophical preparation and facility catch up to his musical skills; in the late 1880s his intellectual attitudes vis-à-vis musical idealism were characterized mostly by confusion and by questions he had not yet had time to address. His compositional activity during this period did have a critical dimension of a specifically musical sort, however, one that, when later informed by his mature worldview, would take on specific philosophical implications. At the early stage, the young Strauss's musical critique was still aimed in all directions—at artistic precedents from all sides of the musical spectrum—a feature that ultimately would be crucial in finding an adequate means for communicating a rejection of musical metaphysics.

At the time when Strauss took up the tone poem, the most basic questions regarding music remained open, at least in his own mind. The fact that in 1887 he worked simultaneously on *Macbeth* and the Violin Sonata demonstrates that however powerful the influence of Ritter, Brahmsian concerns had by no means been eclipsed by Wagnerian and Lisztian ones.[2] The subsequent choice to limit himself to programmatic music, which apparently simplified matters, soon complicated them significantly, as a new range of questions and competing viewpoints entered his awareness. Although the tone poem was fundamentally a Lisztian genre, in Strauss's hands it would have at least as much to do with Wagner, whose technique was by far the more interesting to the young composer and whose own principal genre was Strauss's ultimate goal.[3] The distinctions between Lisztian and Wagnerian methods were substantial, particularly in the area of thematic development and organization, and sorting them out required considerable effort.[4] Similarly, the issue of programmaticism raised unexpected difficulties. Ritter's devotion to Hauseggerian *Ausdruck* appealed to Strauss no more than the illustrative, quasi-cinematic possibilities offered by extramusical content.[5] This personal tendency put him at odds not only with Ritter but with a central justification of programmatic music, first articulated by Beethoven with regard to his Sixth Symphony. Working out this conflict would focus Strauss's attention ever more sharply on the distinction between the metaphysical and physical worlds, and on what those separate realms might have to do with music in the first place. Strauss was eager to create a new art for the twentieth century—an art that would draw on all nineteenth-century traditions but would deploy that influence in ways characteristic of the new age.[6] That goal entailed the dissection of any received wisdom, no matter who was offended by the process.

Choosing to focus his compositional efforts on the tone poem thus opened more questions than it settled for Strauss. If superficially it was an alignment, in the real world of artistic decision making it presented a new spectrum of conflicting ideas through which he could define his independence. It is thus no surprise that Strauss produced works marked by a peculiar, enigmatic heterogeneity. Although they are the shortest

and most tradition-based of Strauss's nine tone poems, *Macbeth*, *Don Juan*, and *Tod und Verklärung* remain to this day the subject of ongoing debates as to form and musico-programmatic signification, to the point that the predominant view holds that the very insolubility of these conflicts is itself the works' essential aesthetic substance.[7]

I would suggest, however, that the difficulties we find in these works were not originally a goal but a function, a natural outcome of a creative urge that was sizing up the alternatives and pushing forward in spite of the composer's state of intellectual uncertainty. In the mid-1890s these experiments would have productive implications that Strauss had not envisioned, leading to a more self-consciously critical approach in the later tone poems. To take an important example: when Strauss argued to Cosima that multiple kinds of programmaticism could coexist—that is, that musical expression of a program's spiritual core would not be disturbed by pervasive tone painting—he was of course rationalizing, inventing an explanation on the fly in order to placate Cosima while preserving his own artistic freedom.[8] Yet that rationalization, conceived as a balancing act, would later grow into a theory of interpretive perspectivism central to both his worldview and his artistic practice. Faced with a dilemma, Strauss used his brilliant instincts, and his unfailing trust in them, to produce not only a way out but an idea the depth of which he would not appreciate for years. This process was repeated in a myriad of other ways in the first cycle of tone poems, with Strauss's instinctive critical attitudes toward musical models producing artistic results that at the time he did not anticipate, understand, or know how to situate in a coherent aesthetic system.

Cosima seems to have recognized more quickly than Strauss the broader implications of his experimentation. Moreover, she was by no means the only person to hear him as attacking his own material in these first tone poems. In an early review of *Macbeth*, Rudolf Louis accused Strauss of trying to "expand the principle of program music *ad absurdum*," with a wealth of narrative detail that overwhelmed what Louis saw as the music's expressive and innately musical responsibilities.[9] The practice may not have been entirely unwitting, then. But whether Strauss intended to undermine the approaches he used is less important than the fact that he obviously meant to discover for himself the limits of everything he tried. This tendency led him in three main critical directions in this first cycle: exploration of (1) the limits of genre (in particular, how far an orchestral work could be pushed toward the music drama before it broke down), (2) the limits of programmaticism, and (3) the limits of sonata form. Once he had surveyed the full range of possibilities in these areas, he seems to have considered this stage of his artistic maturation process successfully concluded.[10] That at least two of the three works were masterpieces, more or less instantly entering the standard repertory, should not obscure for us their function as a kind of laboratory for Strauss. The one requirement that he unequivocally imposed on them was that they should resist the simplistic and the complacent. That determination led the composer to ideas that were far more radical than what his contemporaries, even those who thought of themselves as avant-garde, were able to imagine.

Tone Poem, Music Drama, and the Future of Musical Genre

Genre was obviously a topic of some concern to Strauss when he began writing "tone poems" (*Tondichtungen*), for he took the trouble to devise a name that would distinguish them from Liszt's "symphonic poems" (*symphonische Dichtungen*).[11] More than once he asserted that the distinction had meaning, though he gave only vague indications of what that meaning might be or how his practice differed from Liszt's. Writing to his uncle Carl Hörburger, he called *Macbeth* "a sort of symphonic poem, but not after Liszt," while to Thuille he praised the "dramatic action" of the third movement of the *Faust Symphony* as more worthy of emulation than the "character-piece" approach of the first two movements.[12] As a definition of the tone poem this explanation is problematic, for it does not adequately explain how Liszt's third movement differs in a significant formal (and therefore dramatic) way from the first movement, of which it is a more or less straightforward parody.[13] But in any case, there is no doubt that with respect to Liszt, Strauss unequivocally announced his separation from the model, however he may have conceived of the differences.

Strauss's eagerness to clarify this distinction is consonant with his ultimate career goal, which even at this stage was Wagnerian rather than Lisztian, operatic (or "music dramatic") rather than orchestral. In 1887, Strauss knew that whatever kind of music he chose to create in the next few years and whatever he called these works, the activity would serve above all as a preparatory exercise for a budding composer of music dramas. (It is easy to forget that Strauss began work on the libretto of *Guntram* before completing the first version of *Macbeth*.)[14] Just as he used lieder to experiment with novel harmonic techniques and contrasting modes of vocal delivery, so in the tone poems Strauss explored, on a more modest scale, methods and approaches (orchestrational, thematic, formal) that would be applicable in opera.[15] The analytical tradition of describing these pieces in terms of previously existing orchestral forms and genres (or deformations of them) is thus insufficient and perhaps one-sided. An instinctive awareness of this problem is apparent in the long-standing tradition of conceiving of *Salome* and *Elektra* as tone poems for the stage.[16] That overlap actually began much earlier, in orchestral works conceived as test cases in operatic composition: unstaged music dramas, as it were.[17] In the tone poems, as in Strauss's first operas, orchestral ("symphonic") and operatic procedures coexisted, regardless of the question of staging and the presence or absence of a libretto.[18] Wagner himself is of course recognized to have employed this kind of hybridization, and in his wake any sophisticated composer of German opera would naturally have attempted to transcend the number-opera tradition by means of formal and thematic innovations rooted in instrumental music.[19] But Strauss was unique among leading composers (with the possible exception of Mahler) in having applied it wholeheartedly to the sacralized domain of orchestral music.

Evaluating the tone poems from the standpoint of their tendencies toward the music drama is a useful complement to approaches focusing on how the works problematize the norms of orchestral composition. In particular it places an increased emphasis on thematic material (on individual themes and on relationships among themes), treating it as significant in its own right rather than as a collection of signposts marking deeper harmonic and formal processes. It was precisely in this area, the handling of thematic material, that Strauss made his clearest attempt to distance himself from Liszt in favor of Wagner. The fact that this shift occurred within an instrumental genre has no bearing on the reality that it did occur or on the importance that it had as a process of critical reception in Strauss's creative maturation.

Whereas the operatic tendencies of the tone poems enhanced the importance of thematic material in the overall conception, they drastically undermined the role of musical autonomy and its philosophical implications.[20] Sometime around 1887 Strauss reached a firm conclusion against the absolute necessity of tonal/formal unity in music. Turning his back on a central tenet of his training, he now considered the aesthetic of coherence utterly discredited both as a musical ideal and as a bearer of romantic metaphysical claims.[21] This position found ironic expression in the footnote to "Wenn" (mocking the old-fashioned nineteenth-century attitudes of those appalled that the song began in E-flat and ended in E). But the point was made more directly in the well-known letter to Bülow on 24 August 1888, in which Strauss laid out with deadly seriousness his contempt for the belief that music, to be great, had to be self-sufficient in a strict sense, without reference to extramusical factors.[22] The fact is, then, that the kind of formal integration that since Beethoven had been central to nineteenth-century music—and, in particular, to orchestral composition—was not a goal of the tone poems. In analyzing them it is imperative to bear this fact in mind. The determining aesthetic view in these works was that of a rising composer of music dramas, concerned not to sustain the past but to appeal to his listeners in sophisticated and exciting ways. He accomplished that goal, and in the process became famous as an orchestral composer. Nevertheless, if *Guntram* (1893) had found the success of *Salome* (1905), Strauss's abandonment of the tone poem for the music drama would likely have come twelve years earlier.

Internal evidence confirms that one basic implication of the term "tone poem" was a shift of organizational emphasis from sonata form to thematic processes more typical of the music drama. That is not to say that sonata form disappears, but that it is more vestigial than functional. In *Macbeth*, the outlines of sonata form are easy to discern: principal (m. 6) and secondary (m. 64) thematic material, a developmental space divided into two distinct episodes (m. 123 and m. 260), and a modified recapitulation that simultaneously continues the developmental process (m. 324).[23] The clarity of these outlines is in fact the best demonstration that sonata form does relatively little to advance the musico-programmatic narrative (see below, pp. 176–78, for further discussion of sonata-form operations in *Macbeth*). That responsibility is carried mostly by the handling of thematic material, which falls into two discrete practices, one Lisztian and the other Wagnerian. It is the interaction of these two, more than any formal/harmonic procedure, that drives the musical drama.

The most prominent features of the drama—Macbeth's inner conflict, his apparent triumph, and his subsequent downfall—are communicated with the relatively straightforward technique of thematic transformation. By this term, I mean Liszt's manner of adjusting a theme to diverse affective contexts without disrupting the listener's sense that all versions come from the same source.[24] The technique is easy to comprehend, even for the inexperienced listener, and thus it is well suited for communicating programmatic headlines. The motto first stated at mm. 3–4, for example, which (as James Hepokoski has noted) seems to represent the vision of regal power for which Macbeth strives, is reworked as a procession at mm. 260–61 for the coronation of the new king (ex. 5.1).[25] Shortly after this second example, Macbeth's growing doubt manifests itself in the recapitulation, where lowered dynamics, staccato articulation, and scaled-back orchestration tell us that the hero has become sneaky (ex. 5.2). Immediately prior to this section, Strauss introduced a new theme in eighth notes as an epilogue to the evil couple's moment of triumph (m. 308). At m. 516, however, a modal alteration of that idea becomes an epilogue of a different kind, marking the immediate aftermath of Macbeth's death (subsequently in combination with the second, sinister Macbeth theme, which first appears at m. 20) (ex. 5.3).

It is hardly surprising that Strauss used this straightforward, even crude method so extensively in his first full-scale programmatic work (*Aus Italien* having been conceived as a "bridge").[26] What makes it worth noting is that even as he laid out these various unmistakable markers of the progressing narrative, Strauss used a far more sophisticated procedure to communicate the drama's subtler psychological nuances. A striking

Example 5.1a. *Macbeth*, mm. 3–4

Example 5.1b. *Macbeth*, mm. 260–61

Example 5.2a. *Macbeth*, mm. 6–9

Example 5.2b. *Macbeth*, mm. 324–27

example of this contrasting approach comes in the apparently new theme at m. 123. The most plausible programmatic explanation of this theme is that it represents Macbeth's public attitude toward Duncan; at this point in the tone poem, after offering portraits of the two principal characters, it is logical for Strauss to have presented Macbeth's devotion to his lord, the most powerful force preventing him from giving in to his base inclinations.[27] The theme at m. 123 is not altogether new, however; it is foreshadowed, at pitch (with one chromatic alteration), through motives embedded in the second Macbeth theme (ex. 5.4). (Motive b likewise moves by step and then by descending fourth from the upper note of the rising minor-sixth leap, the B-flat in m. 125 being an ornament.)[28] With its syncopations and chromaticism, the theme at m. 20 creates an obvious contrast with the decisive, powerful, straightforwardly aggressive first Macbeth theme (m. 6), and thereby communicates a dualism in Macbeth's nature. Beneath the surface, however, it also harbors violent impulses toward Duncan, and these can inform our hearing of the material

Example 5.3a. *Macbeth*, mm. 308–9

Example 5.3b. *Macbeth*, mm. 516–17

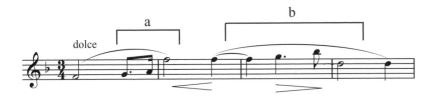

Example 5.4a. *Macbeth*, mm. 123–26

Example 5.4b. *Macbeth*, mm. 20–24

at m. 123. In musical terms, the latter theme emerges not by thematic transformation but by a leitmotivic process akin to that by which the Valhalla motif grows from the Ring motif at the beginning of scene 2 of *Das Rheingold*. The themes are distinct, in musical character and extramusical meaning; one is derived from the other, while at the same time amounting to more than a version of its source.

The subsequent conflict between these two themes—which begins at m. 145, intensifies beginning at m. 173, and reaches its climax in Duncan's murder (m. 242)—reflects the crisis produced when Macbeth's animosity becomes action. Here too Wagner's example is evident in the interaction between themes that have been patiently charged with extra-musical meaning in a manner that could never have happened in Liszt. If, then, the piece organizes itself superficially after the manner of the symphonic poem, it nevertheless also begins to show on a deeper and more significant level a mastery of the substantially more sophisticated Wagnerian method. Strauss's facility in this regard is not surprising, for he had begun studying *Oper und Drama* soon after meeting Ritter and thus was well acquainted with the technique and dramatic purposes of leitmotivic counterpoint.[29] Through that reading, and through his growing knowledge of the *Ring* operas, Strauss made steady strides in the compositional method that he believed would ground his own soon-to-begin activity as operatic composer.

Strauss's Wagnerian self-education taught him another crucial lesson that had immediate results in *Macbeth*. In order to function in an authentically Wagnerian sense, leitmotifs must act not only as dramatic signposts but as material for the weaving of a "symphonic" tapestry.[30] The requirement that the texture be permeated by material that was "thematic" (in the strong sense) is the underlying motivation of the subtle familial relationships of many themes in *Macbeth*. The listener's impression that musical ideas are cut from the same cloth is not coincidental but a consequence of the same approach to thematic invention that caused Robert Donington to posit a set of motivic "archetypes" in the *Ring*: a small group of simple, generic ideas to which all the leitmotifs can be traced.[31] Without the underlying relationships engendered by such a system of derivation, the creation of a web of thematically significant material would have been far more difficult for Strauss and indeed for Wagner.

The most important means of relating distinct themes in *Macbeth* (though not the only one) is the dotted figure that opens the motto. Not only does this first melodic idea identify the controlling programmatic idea of the tone poem—the ambition that drives Macbeth to ruin—but it simultaneously introduces a melodic figure that marks all of the thematic material dealing with Macbeth: a sixteenth note, usually accented, proceeding to a longer note that is typically on the beat and approached

Example 5.5a. *Macbeth*, MB1, mm. 6–9

Example 5.5b. *Macbeth*, MB2, mm. 20–24

by leap. Ex. 5.5 lays out the occurrences of this figure in the principal themes of *Macbeth*. In the first Macbeth theme (MB1, m. 6, ex. 5.5a), it appears no fewer than four times, first as counterpoint to the rising quarter-note line, then at the conclusion of that line, then on the fourth beat of the violins' reformulation of the quarter-note idea, and finally as the last two notes in m. 9. The liquidation of this first phrase beginning at m. 14 increases the figure's concentration, its prominence, and thus its status as a motivic element, so that the sixteenth notes in the sinewy second Macbeth theme (MB2, m. 20, ex. 5.5b), though left by conjunct motion, are heard as related. The remainder of this section then places the three themes (the Macbeth themes and the opening motto) in various contrapuntal combinations, highlighting their interrelationship by blurring the distinctions (for example at mm. 44–49, where the dotted figure as it appears in MB2 is followed by quarter notes drawn from MB1). The subtlety of these connections creates a sense of integration that is more powerful than the Lisztian technique because it operates on the level of intuition; it fosters a sense in the listener that the themes grow from one another and (perhaps more important) that the first version of a theme is not necessarily the definitive one. This impression then continues to operate throughout the piece, as shown in ex. 5-5c–e.

Because the sixteenth-note figure is used so extensively during the presentation of Macbeth's material, it can be incorporated into Lady Macbeth's themes in ways even more delicate without losing its recog-

Example 5.5c. *Macbeth*, mm. 123–26

Example 5.5d. *Macbeth*, mm. 260–64

nizability (ex. 5-5f–h). Beginning on the last eighth note of m. 75 it appears three times successively, albeit in augmentation. The "goading" grace notes in m. 81 (*pace* Hepokoski) also occur three times, before the violins take up the figure in a more direct form. Even the first theme of Lady Macbeth (m. 67) seems to participate in the process, through its connection to mm. 75–76. The only theme in the entire piece without an easily perceptible relationship to the figure is the *molto espressivo* celebration of Macbeth's attainment of the throne (mm. 308ff.)—and there the musical difference obviously marks the pure joy of triumph, an emotion that Macbeth experiences briefly and only once.

The advanced and subtle technique of melodic integration that Strauss used in this piece allowed him to Wagnerize the work in multiple ways. Besides lending the music a recognizable melodic stamp (such as one finds in *Die Meistersinger*, for example), it enabled themes to metamorphose into new themes, and it facilitated the overtly Wagnerian thematic polyphony that we hear in the recapitulation, where developmental procedures predominate. Without basic constructional similarities, the numerous themes in this work could not have been woven together in a texture both referential and symphonic. The idea of a developmental recapitulation also has its Wagnerian motivations (or Beethovenian, mediated by Wagner), simply by its combination of presentation with on-

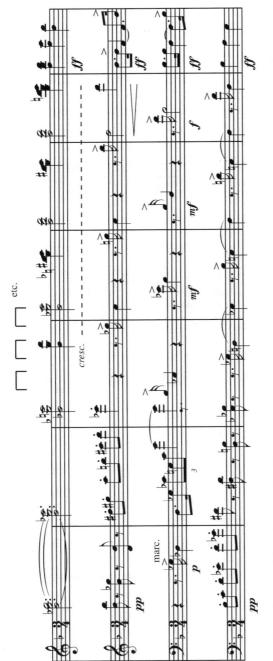

Example 5.5e. *Macbeth*, mm. 280–86

Example 5.5f. *Macbeth*, mm. 75–77

Example 5.5g. *Macbeth*, m. 83

Example 5.5h. *Macbeth*, mm. 84–85

going transformation.[32] And yet, notwithstanding the rapid pace of Strauss's process of assimilation, *Macbeth* was only a first step in the coming-to-grips with Wagner and a rudimentary one, even in comparison to *Don Juan* and *Tod und Verklärung*. It was perhaps to be expected, then, that he abandoned the work to its fate by 1892, claiming that it represented a stage of development that he had already transcended.[33]

Compared with *Macbeth*, *Don Juan* offers relatively little in the way of straightforward Lisztian thematic transformation. Examples do exist: the *Heldenthema* in particular (m. 315) is put through a variety of guises, ranging from tonal distress during conflict with the other Don Juan themes (mm. 343ff.) to glittering costume-party charm (mm. 358ff., in the glockenspiel) (ex. 5-6). The nostalgic contemplation of past loves (beginning at m. 431) also brings clever affective modifications of recognizable thematic material. These cases are of secondary importance to the unfolding drama, however, as is, to raise another fascinating but superficial example, the emotional relaxation of the G-minor love theme at m. 197 into the G-major accompanimental figure at m. 232. As arresting as

Example 5.6a. *Don Juan*, mm. 314–19

Example 5.6b. *Don Juan*, mm. 343–47

Example 5.6c. *Don Juan*, mm. 357–60

such a gesture may sound, the practice does not play a significant role in the structural or communicative processes of the piece, nor does it mark the major way-stations of the program (as it does in *Macbeth*).

Wagnerian thematic organization, on the other hand, exerts a great deal of control—more, I would hold, than any allusions to classical instrumental forms. The frequently encountered description of this work as a rondo, for example, ignores the fact that the only rondo feature is the occasional brief return of the first theme, which usually does not happen in the tonic key, rarely approximates the proportionally appropriate size of even an abbreviated refrain, and occurs infrequently given the size of the work as a whole. Ritornello would be a more accurate label (as noted by Hepokoski), but in that case the historical distance involved shows only too clearly that such designations do little to clarify the piece.[34] Rather than a rondo or a rondo-related form, *Don Juan* is (like *Macbeth*) more productively heard as loosely based on sonata form but shaped predominantly by a network of interrelated themes, one of which represents a protagonist who, not surprisingly, participates regularly in the action

As in *Macbeth*, these themes retain their distinct identities while sharing motivic connections, in a Wagnerian technique that serves musical as well as dramatic ends. The *Heldenthema* (see ex. 5.7a) is not only the most important case (for programmatic reasons and for its breakthrough character) but also the most interesting, for its multiple sources. The opening octave clearly refers to the feminine theme at m. 235 and leads to an inversion of her subsequent scalar ascent (ex. 5.7b). But the second phrase also draws on the B-major seduction theme in multiple ways: through pitch (m. 91) and rhythm (m. 94, ex. 5.7c).[35] The most important moment in the tone poem, then, the moment at which a brilliant and overpowering new theme changes the course of the entire work, is also a Wagnerian moment, with an ostensibly revolutionary musical idea growing programmatically and thematically from others. Given the weight of that event, it is natural that from here until the end the work's story is told more by thematic interaction—the symphonic web—than by the remnants of sonata form. The points made in crude fashion by the dysfunctional recapitulation (principally that neither of Don Juan's identities is able to sustain itself; see below for a discussion of sonata-related issues) are communicated with much more force and immediacy by leitmotivic counterpoint. For the target listener, evolution and interaction of thematic material is unquestionably the central focus of the drama.

If, as Strauss claimed, *Don Juan* rendered *Macbeth* obsolete, it did so largely by tightening the connections among the group of tendencies that moved the tone poem toward the music drama. As the program gained more control over structure, sonata form weakened and thematic processes took up the slack.[36] Strauss's consistent use of material that is easily

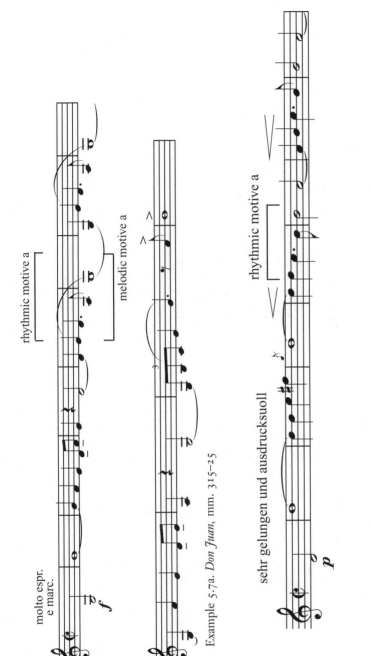

Example 5.7a. *Don Juan*, mm. 315–25

Example 5.7b. *Don Juan*, mm. 236–44

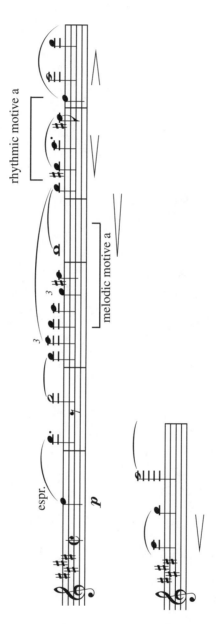

Example 5.7c. *Don Juan*, mm. 92–97

sequenced suggests that from the outset he wanted developmental techniques to remain a possibility, if not an actuality, throughout the piece. There are strikingly few moments of tonal closure in *Don Juan*—the only two significant perfect authentic cadences are in E major at m. 40 and in G major at m. 296—but there are many situations in which a section that initially seems intended to reach tonal closure is instead pushed to the breaking point, through sequences and chromatic modulation, and then simply abandoned with the beginning of a new formal/tonal section. (The B-major seduction theme [m. 90], the C-major return of the Don Juan theme [m. 169], the *Heldenthema* [m. 314], and the recapitulation of the *Heldenthema* [m. 510] all lead to such moments.) The programmatic motivation for this choice is obvious (Don Juan's premature exits), but whatever the reason, the result is increased responsibility placed on thematic material for creating shape. Strauss must have recognized that only the most sophisticated listeners would be able to make sense, or would even attempt to make sense, of tonal procedures in a work as complex as this. But those listeners held little interest for him compared to the vast majority, whose only hope at comprehension would be to hear the work as though it were accompanying stage action.

With *Tod und Verklärung* Strauss took his strongest and most self-conscious step toward a theme-based method of organization, thereby pushing the genre even more aggressively toward Wagner. Here the evolutionary formation of the principal theme is unquestionably the center of the formal process; musical progress is measured by the stages of the theme's completion, and when the entire theme finally makes its appearance, the piece is over. In this context, it is understandable that Strauss relegated thematic transformation to dramatization of the protagonist's growth from child through adolescence to adulthood. The two themes involved in this process (heard for the first time at m. 17 and m. 31, respectively) are in the typical Lisztian manner placed into new contexts (rhythmic, orchestrational, and so on) in order to suggest the moods of these different stages of life.[37] These events comprise a kind of subplot, however, with little bearing on the principal concern of the drama and at best a tangential relationship to the musical processes.

The formal role played by the Ideal theme's genesis gains strength from the further weakening of sonata form in *Tod und Verklärung*. Although once again the outlines of the sonata survive, the sections that participate most directly in the thematic genesis are the introduction, the development section, and the coda, that is, the sections least involved with the fundamental business of sonata form. The exposition and recapitulation, on the other hand, have relatively limited roles; the exposition presents only a fragment of the Ideal theme (as second theme) at the very end of the section, and the recapitulation is left entirely out of the action. It is no coincidence that the sections most important from a sonata perspective are the ones wholly given over to disease—the programmatic obstacle, the force that must be overcome—for just as Strauss meant to portray an artist overcoming the challenges separating him from the Ideal, so he wished to identify himself unequivocally as a composer who discarded obsolete formal and generic assumptions.[38] But in any case, the work's overt implementation of a new thematic process is ultimately more important than its critique of sonata form; by fully exploiting a productive new approach to musical organization, Strauss identified a way to the future instead of simply criticizing the past. For this reason, closure and culmination are given over to the non–sonata-based process, in a section far more significant than is indicated by the traditionally applied label "coda."

Because the Ideal theme's various stages of formation are so prominent, the actual roots of the theme are easy to overlook. In fact, they lie in material heard long before the tortured fragments that fight through to the surface at mm. 163ff. The first sign comes as early as m. 8, with the anacrusis/sigh that becomes the sticking point in the first direct attempts to present the theme (ex. 5-8a; compare mm. 163–64 and 320–22). A second element, and the first genuinely melodic step in the creation of its identity, comes with the entrance of the second childhood theme (m. 31), which reproduces the anacrusis and connects it to the processual quarter notes integral to the Ideal theme's character (ex. 5.8b–c).[39] Strauss clarified the relationship between these two latter themes in the coda, by using the second childhood theme as a buildup to the cli-

Example 5.8a. *Tod und Verklärung,* mm. 8–9

Example 5.8b. *Tod und Verklärung*, mm. 31–32

Example 5.8c. *Tod und Verklärung*, mm. 430–32

Example 5.9a. *Tod und Verklärung*, m. 1

mactic presentation of the Ideal. The connection to the sigh is perhaps more immediately perceptible on a musical level but therefore all the more striking programmatically, because it links a physical symptom with the transcendent vision. This example represents one of the most striking applications of Wagnerian leitmotivic derivation in Strauss's first three tone poems, a fact that may be reflected in the emphasis on Wagner in the work's sensational early reception.[40]

The sort of kinship that relates these three diverse themes also exists among themes identified with disease and struggle. The syncopation and triplets of the hesitant respiration in the opening measures are quickly taken up by the first childhood theme (see ex. 5.9b, m. 17), and then differently but in an obviously related way in the theme announcing the first violent battle with illness (ex. 5.9c). The beat-centered quality of the theme representing the struggle (m. 96) seems to break the mold (although the theme does make use of syncopation, with an accented second beat followed by a rest on the third beat), but that feature creates the

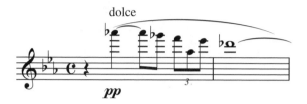

Example 5.9b. *Tod und Verklärung*, mm. 17–18

possibility of rhythmic counterpoint between members of the thematic family (e.g., at m. 147) and thus does not significantly undermine the listener's sense of a relationship. That sense is crucial during the development (m. 186), when musico-dramatic momentum is accelerated by a confrontation between the two distinct families. Each of the successive stages of the protagonist's growth (m. 186, m. 206, m. 235, and m. 256) ratchets up the directness with which material associated with the struggle antagonizes the second childhood theme. This process culminates at m. 256, when that theme, *appassionato* in the upper register of the celli, is forced into counterpoint with a chromatic line obviously derived from the suffering motive of m. 1. And it is during this clash of incompatible leitmotivic worlds that the dream is broken by the return of suffering. When the second childhood theme next returns, during the coda, it derives a new power from the utter absence of disruptive syncopation and triplets, which as signs of the physical world have no role to play in the afterlife.

Strauss himself explicitly claimed that the most remarkable feature of *Tod und Verklärung* was that the main theme did not arrive in its entirety until the end of the piece.[41] The emergence of new thematic material well into the piece also figured centrally in the other two tone poems, of course, and in this respect all three works show the influence of the *Siegfried-Idyll*, a model that shaped Strauss's practice far more strongly than any music by Liszt. In each of Strauss's first three tone poems, making sense of the new thematic material vis-à-vis the ongoing musico-programmatic action is the listener's principal interpretive task. That task is also central in the *Siegfried-Idyll*, where the A-flat "Siegfried, Hope of the World" theme enters during the developmental space and then is worked into the recapitulation, completing the picture of domestic bliss. *Macbeth* and *Don Juan* imitate this feature more or less directly but with one crucial difference: the process of incorporation fails. In both cases, this failure is motivated by the program, however, so that they represent

Example 5.9c. *Tod und Verklärung*, mm. 71–73

not a critique of the model but a tweaking of it, an appropriation that pushes it to a different end. The *Heldenthema* in *Don Juan* functions almost precisely as the A-flat theme does in the *Idyll*: it enters at the same moment in the form, a major third away from the tonic, and is recapitulated in the tonic.[42] But the six-four position of both of its presentations (mm. 315 and 510) identifies it as utopian, a fact that is confirmed by both the final reprise of the Don Juan theme (m. 564) and the tragic coda. *Macbeth*, on the other hand, presents several new themes in the development, all of them later subject to an explicit downfall in the developmental recapitulation. (Indeed, the recapitulation uses developmental techniques precisely in order to weave the themes in a way suggesting musico-programmatic destruction.)

After these two experiments, Strauss took the model a step further in *Tod und Verklärung*. Instead of entering fully formed in the middle of the piece and integrating itself into a larger process, the new theme itself becomes the process, gradually superseding the ongoing sonata form and ultimately controlling the work so comprehensively that at the culmination there is nothing left but the presentation and repetition of this one glorious melody. Both the centrality of the thematic process and the critical implications vis-à-vis sonata form mark this work as an advance toward the music drama. Likewise, the overtly antagonistic interactions among the themes, a dispute that is highlighted by the fact that they end in a purge, sharpen our sense that the themes in *Tod und Verklärung* are really leitmotifs. That said, Werbeck's recent suggestion that thematic "histories" are relatively overlooked in analyses of the tone poems seems useful but incomplete.[43] Certainly the alterations of a given theme over the course of the work represent one of Strauss's most powerful tools for communicating programmatic ideas, not least because they are relatively understandable even to modestly skilled listeners. The process is inclusive, inviting all of the audience to interpret the music actively, through a kind of listening that does not require specialized knowledge or training. But the same can be said of interactions among themes; these encounters have their own histories, and they bear at least as much of the communicative responsibility in the tone poems as any other single mechanism. Early *Erläuterungen* focused heavily on this approach, on the reasonable assumption that listeners followed the action by taking note of what themes were present at particular moments and how they affected one another.[44] Given that some of these guidebooks were sanctioned by the composer himself, we must accept that the treatment of themes was his most important means of communication with the vast majority of his audience, regardless of what other formal processes might also be involved.

Sophisticated examples of meaningful interactions among themes—or interactions that produce a continuum of meaning—can be found already in *Macbeth*. By the end of the first theme group, thematic interactions have explored, in detail, Macbeth's inner conflict. The first step is to define the participants: the motto (mm. 3–4), which comes to represent Macbeth's thirst for power (or the power that creates the thirst), is followed by two contrasting sides of Macbeth's personality, one forceful and decisive (m. 6), the other dark, slippery, and unpredictable (m. 20; note the low strings, nervous syncopation, and jerky contour). Only after this miniature exposition does the real action of the "Macbeth" section begin. We are first shown, by the repeated interruptions of the motto beginning at m. 28, that it is the latter facet of Macbeth's character that falls victim to base inclinations. His head soon swims with sinister plans, and when his own reason tries to intervene, in the guise of the first Macbeth theme at m. 37, it fragments against the continued influence of the motto. The disintegration of his better side then accelerates until the first theme is humiliatingly made to serve as a lead-in to the climactic presentation of the second (m. 49), in a moment of sick triumph celebrated together with the motto at the cadence in m. 56.

There is a great deal of dramatic content in these first sixty-three measures, much more than is contained by the observation that together they are labeled "Macbeth" and count as the principal thematic material in a sonata-form movement. Similar examples permeate all three tone poems, and I would suggest that they bear a large share of the responsibility for the works' success with the public. In all of them, the wealth of dramatic nuance in the themes challenges the importance, if not the relevance, of the work's connections with traditional formal categories. This trend obviously held significance for the early critics who heard the tone poems as importing Wagnerian techniques into an orchestral genre. A similar Wagnerization of orchestral genres would be implemented by Mahler, in much the same way and with much the same results for musical form, though his own aspirations did not extend to opera. Whatever the genre and whatever the composers' personal goals, Strauss and Mahler shared the objective of making music more inherently dramatic and programmatically communicative (i.e., more "expressive"), at the expense of the controlling power of classical forms.

Competing Modes of Programmaticism
in Strauss's First Three Tone Poems

Understanding the programmatic dimension of the first three tone poems requires coming to terms with Strauss's theory (outlined to Cosima Wagner) that music could sustain simultaneous, distinct levels of extramusical signification. As explained in chapter 1, Strauss claimed that a work's use of tone painting (imitation or representation of physical phenomena) did not prevent it from achieving the kind of "ideal" dramatic expression praised by Wagner in the letter on Liszt's symphonic poems. Few authors have noticed this theory, and none has taken it seriously, but its implications for the interpretation of Strauss's tone poems are far-reaching. On a political level, his willingness to stand up to Cosima at this early stage of his career (the letter is from 1890) and implicitly to reject Wagner's conclusions on the subject is nothing less than astounding. Yet he held fast in the face of Cosima's complaints, until both parties recognized that they had reached a stalemate. That he would have mounted such an energetic and dangerous defense is well-nigh unimaginable if *Tonmalerei* had been nothing more to him than an innocuous embellishment. Somehow it was necessary, if in a way that he had not yet fully conceptualized. Only later, after the critique of Schopenhauer, would musical illustration become active in a purposeful critique of the aesthetic foundation of nineteenth-century orchestral music.

Nevertheless, Strauss's fascination with subject matter that could be imitated in music rather than simply expressed by it clearly began in the first three tone poems. In choosing the programs for these works, Strauss avoided abstract ideas in favor of concrete human experience. Each of the three takes an individual as protagonist (as do all of the tone poems of the second cycle), and each also explores a realm of experience basic to being human: psychological distress (*Macbeth*), love and sex (*Don Juan*), illness and death (*Tod und Verklärung*). These choices show the influence of Ritter, who had problematized the phenomenal world for Strauss by characterizing everyday experience as a state of suffering that could be transcended only through the agency of music.[45] Consistent with Ritter's view, all three programs point out the tragedy of the conditions and realities of human life. In *Macbeth*, desire for physical control over a political realm leads to psychological disaster; the work begins with character portraits so that we can witness their distortion and destruction, the results of an unbridled preoccupation with the *diesseits*. *Don Juan* deals with the most basic physical drive, which is shown to be all the more powerful, but also destructive, the more purely physical it is allowed to be. Finally, *Tod und Verklärung* presents a character in combat with the physical world, with death treated as a moment of philosophical awakening impossible in the physical world. The conclusion of this tone poem, and of the cycle, thus arrives at the assumption that Ritter most wanted Strauss to accept: that the phenomenal world, the world of suffering and destruction, had a noumenal counterpart that ought to be the focus of all human endeavor.

So far, so good, from Ritter's perspective. Whatever the works' conclusions about the real and the ideal, however, it was the real that stimulated Strauss artistically. The only music in these first three tone poems that has no programmatic connection to either the physical or a psychological obsession with the physical comes in the last few minutes of the final composition. What happens in the remainder of *Tod und Verklärung* and in the previous two works is the very opposite of *weltfremd*, and that fact suggests at least an instinctively critical attitude with respect to Wagner. Strauss unquestionably recognized that for Wagner, dramatic subjects only became useful material for musical composition when they were wiped clean of narrative details and distilled into something universal. One may argue for the presence of that distillation process in the tone poems, as Strauss did to Cosima, but it is clearly not predominant, and it is prevented from taking hold precisely because of Strauss's continuing use of the kind of programmaticism that Wagner attacked in Berlioz—programmaticism that followed the "red thread" of the dramatic narrative.[46]

Strauss's early programs, then, while consistent with the Wagnerian spirit (as Ritter saw it), invited the inclusion of a kind of music that violated that spirit. Strauss responded artistically to both possibilities, and the result was a juxtaposition of divergent kinds of programmaticism in a type of competitive process not at all unexpected in a young composer still unsure of his creative direction. It is interesting in this context that the tone poem most likely to satisfy Cosima's demands, *Macbeth*, was the only one of the three that Strauss did not discuss with her. Programmatically it shows a kind of focus and concision very much in the Lisztian tradition, with a clearly identifiable and concentrated programmatic theme—a hero's ruin through ambition—translated into music in which harmonic and thematic processes create a sort of expressive analogue of that downfall. That is not all that happens in the work, however. This by-now traditional New German approach is overlaid with the musical dramatization of particular events in the plot, much as if the action was being seen onstage. These include the four landmark moments in the drama—Duncan's murder (m. 242), Macbeth's coronation (m. 260), the death of Macbeth (m. 514), and the arrival of Macduff (m. 538)—along with others in which the difficulty of pinning down the precise action intended does not dull the impression that Strauss had some particular event in mind (for example, the slinking stealth at the recapitulation, m. 324). The abundance of these moments and their importance both in the musical structure and in their connection with the drama leaves no doubt that Strauss was trying to do something very different from Liszt, however consistently the mood of his music reflected the emotional content of his program. In terms of narrative specificity Strauss moved far beyond even Berlioz, with a daring either wittingly or unwittingly critical.[47]

The musical balance shifted toward narrativity in *Don Juan*, a remarkable and unexpected choice given that the work is based on a quintessentially Schopenhauerian program. The philosophical roots of this programmatic idea are simple and straightforward, but they have never been properly spelled out.[48] From Schopenhauer's perspective, the basic condition of human nature (and indeed the basic condition of all nature) was ever-renewing desire that turns into languor immediately upon being satisfied.[49] The only genuine release is denial of the will; although death stops the cycle for the individual, it has no lasting effect on the will. The ending of the tone poem is thus both tragic (because Don Juan dies without achieving denial) and philosophically meaningful (because it traces an individual's dawning consciousness of the cycle of desire/satisfaction/languor). What starts as willing indulgence, deliberate reinforcement, becomes a determined "heroic" attempt to break free and finally a collapse when heroism proves an ineffective means of reaching the goal.

This Schopenhauerian orientation explains why the notoriously prudish Ritter did not protest against a subject so overladen with sexuality. Strauss's implementation of the topic, however, leaves little to the imagination. A setting aimed at the Lisztian features praised by Wagner would most likely have yielded music focusing on the emotional experience of increasing self-awareness—music that captured the struggle to break free from human nature. Yet Strauss treated the process of enlightenment as a plot, with music that is not inexpressive but clearly delineates the successive stages of awakening knowledge. The musical sections are obviously scenes, with various characters entering and leaving, a graphic sexual encounter traced cinematically from beginning to end, and finally a one-by-one contemplation of past loves. This structure, in which the principal musical events cannot be heard apart from the plot events that they depict, reinforces the listener's sense of narrative rather than blurring it. The details do not evaporate into an ideal "formal motive"; rather, the basic idea of the drama is used as a stimulus for the invention of details.

Strauss's claim that Cosima would be reassured by *Tod und Verklärung* seems difficult to understand and perhaps even disingenuous, given that the work is by far the most vivid of the first three tone poems in graphic extramusical allusion. The illustrative qualities of this music were overpoweringly obvious to early audiences; many found them downright offensive, such as James Henderson, who was appalled that Strauss would "prod the dying man to more gasps and record them with a phonograph and metronome for future reproduction on trombones in syncopated rhythms."[50] This groundbreaking specificity is announced from the opening, where the halting respiration of the sufferer is heard on its own for two measures. The entrance of the bassoon (followed by low winds and a horn), which contextualizes this first motive tonally (E-flat and G become scale degrees 3 and 5 of C minor) and sets the mood (by darkening it), also tells us that there will be more to the piece than tone painting. But exploring the distinction between illustrative and non-illustrative music soon becomes the main business of the introduction, which moves alternately between the sickbed and fleeting dreams of the past. Transitions between these states are always marked by the heavy sighs first heard in mm. 7–9, deep breaths that tell graphically of failing lungs. The dreamlike passages, on the other hand (mm. 16–20 and 30–45), introduce nonrepresentational thematic material, and that fact, along with the scoring for harp, initiates us into a different reality. Each time, however, the spell of these non-illustratively programmatic sections is broken by sounds of suffering, which drag us back to the physical present.

When the two types finally overlap (mm. 47ff.), the motivic connections begin to break down the distinction between reality and the other world. The connection between the protagonist's labored breathing and the first childhood theme seems to imply that the protagonist is subconsciously aware of his own suffering, even as he slips momentarily into a dream. The incorporation of the sighs into the Ideal theme (discussed above) is a prominent motivic connection and thus a striking instance in which the physical penetrates and even defines music, ostensibly representing the absolute removal from the physical. Strauss himself may not have had a clear notion of what he intended to communicate here, but the fact that he used a moment of illustration to generate programmatic music of the sort sanctioned by Wagner constitutes a significant challenge to the latter type. The attentive listener to this work is not permitted to hear any of the music without reminders of its phenomenal origins. And for those with knowledge of Wagnerian aesthetics, that practice carried the implication that one type of programmaticism infected the other and thereby undermined it.

Cosima of course did perceive *Tod und Verklärung* as a deepening threat, most of all because Strauss now seemed to have uncovered the critical potential of *Tonmalerei*.[51] Whether he consciously recognized that potential at this early stage is an open question. He may well have wanted simply to create a visual spectacle with strictly musical means, testing the limits of musical dramatization before turning to the music drama, a genre in which visual elements would finally be at his disposal. Certainly he believed that after *Tod und Verklärung* he was ready to tackle a music drama and to take up the role of Wagner's successor. If a critical reception of Wagner was involved, it was not yet coherently formulated; the study of Schopenhauer that would lead Strauss to reject the concept of Schopenhauerian music still lay in the future. But however focused or unfocused his motivations, Strauss's treatment of the tone poem in this first cycle led him in precisely the opposite direction of Wagner's recommendations for composers of programmatic music. In his confident pursuit of that direction, Strauss developed a distinctive, personal style of orchestral composition that would be amenable to critical use once his intellectual development had progressed to the point that it required that kind of artistic means.

Form, Formlessness, and
Their Implications for Musical Idealism

In the prologue, I presented evidence that programmatic music and absolute music were both regarded in late-nineteenth-century Germany and Austria as aspiring to metaphysical significance. However bitter the competition between these two approaches, they shared the basic goal of providing access to a spiritual level of reality, a realm outside normal human experience and otherwise unknowable. Ironically, the conflict's very prominence seems to have obscured its underlying motivation: to determine how music might best achieve what everyone agreed it ought to achieve, or how it might be most faithful to its true nature. The intensity of the debate corresponded to the power of the common belief, with each side claiming that the works produced by the antagonists did not deserve even to be called music.

In the end, programmatic music would lose that debate, largely because the addition of a program all too easily reduced attempts at musico-philosophical profundity to kitsch. *Tod und Verklärung* is particularly vulnerable in this respect, for spelling out aspirations almost as grandiose as those of a symphony dramatizing *Auferstehung*. In the technologically modern era around 1900, musical metaphysics necessarily shifted toward absolute music, for the sake of believability (if for no other reason).[52] That fact must be borne in mind as we try to understand the familiar complaint that Strauss's works lacked a fundamental, controlling musical logic. Even today scholars continue to fight that perception; one of the principal themes of Walter Werbeck's magnificent 1996 book on the tone poems is that Strauss frequently altered his programs during the compositional process in order to accommodate his musical choices.[53] Werbeck's systematic proof of this point is impressive, but the argument retains a defensive quality that will persist in all such projects until we ask why things would be better for Strauss if his music, not his programs, determined the final shape of his works. The answer may be that even our own generation has barely begun to question the belief that a great musical work must ultimately be a world of its own: coherent, integrated, and autonomous. The fear that a program would raise doubts about a work's musical coherence undoubtedly played into Mahler's retreat from programmaticism after the Fourth Symphony and Schoenberg's after *Verklärte Nacht*, even though both figures continued to use programs privately in their creative work. But why should musical coherence have been such an overpowering concern in the first place? What does autonomy stand for? In the historical context in which Strauss composed his tone poems, autonomy came to stand for metaphysical truth.

Rather than attempting to defend Strauss against charges that his music lacks a self-sufficient musical logic, we might respond more productively by contextualizing that lack, musically and aesthetically. The fact of the matter is that Strauss flouted autonomy, in every way that occurred to him. He attacked it programmatically, and he attacked it musically. To defend him in this arena is to falsify him. Even in the early tone poems, when his grasp of music's connections to philosophy was only partially developed at best, he showed a strong antipathy toward the conception of music as an independent art. With his pluralistic theory of programmaticism, he undermined Wagner's Schopenhauerian demand that the program be used as the emotional stimulus of a nonnarrative integrated musical form. And in strictly musical terms he found other means of assault, most importantly by dismantling sonata form through the targeting of its most prominent functional elements.

Sonata form was for composers of Strauss's generation a unique symbol of music's capacity to be independently significant. More than just a

form, it was the basic principle of classical-period composition, the foundation of the rising prestige of instrumental music, and thus an indispensable precondition of the elevated artistic status enjoyed by Beethoven
and the Austro-German masters who followed him. It was also a guiding
parameter of Strauss's own musical education, one that he had explored
and mastered with unrivaled precocious fastidiousness. By the time he
reached his early twenties, Strauss knew the form through and through—
he had studied the examples produced by earlier masters, he had created
many of his own, and he had fully absorbed the classical view, which
survived in Brahms and many others, that music reached its highest
artistic potential through application of what seemed a kind of universal
principle. To a significant extent, absolute music became absolute
through the agency of sonata form.

That said, Strauss's approach to the form in his first three tone poems
shows an aggressively critical bent, the implications of which are not
limited to the strictly musical. The distinguishing feature of Strauss's
handling of sonata form in these first three pieces is a curious combination of clarity and dysfunctionality. All three pieces are obviously
meant to be heard as sonata-form movements: the broad sectional outlines are strongly in evidence, and in particular, the course of events at
the beginning of each work matches the basic expectations of a moderately experienced listener. Yet in each case, the works fail to complete
the actions required of a successful sonata, and they fail in ways no less
obvious and prominent than those in which the works invoke sonata form
in the first place. This point may seem rudimentary, but it is worth
considering given Strauss's often-expressed frustration that listeners did
not understand him. If he expected the central points of his music to be
understood by the majority of the concert-going public, this is precisely
the musical level on which he would have expressed himself.

There is no question that each of these tone poems begins with a
sonata exposition. This fact is explicit in *Macbeth*, despite the complete
absence of a transition; indeed, the use of labels for the principal characters makes the plan almost insipidly unproblematic. The exposition is
no less obvious in *Don Juan*, notwithstanding the returns of the first Don
Juan theme (mm. 37, 50, 62), which all too often have elicited discussion
of rondo form. Superficially that theme does make numerous appear-
ances, but those returns are in non-tonic keys, and they have far less
structural importance than the perfect authentic cadence at m. 40, which
rounds off the principal theme-group, and the lengthy V/V at mm. 71–
89, which brings the (programmatically episodic) transition to a close
prior to the entrance of the secondary thematic material. Only *Tod und*

Verklärung challenges the norm, with an overly long principal theme-group that leaves doubt about the identity of the secondary theme-group. By the time we confront that difficulty, however, two recognizable formal gestures, the slow introduction and the fast principal theme, have confirmed the relevance of sonata form, with a collective weight that allows Strauss to disrupt the form earlier than in the other two works.

Even more clear than the expositions are the beginnings of the recapitulations. It is of crucial significance that Strauss satisfies, without exception and beyond all doubt, this central listener-expectation of sonata form. The use of a clear reprise rules out the possibility of hearing the music as utterly formless or as following a form dictated wholly by the program. However lost or confused one may become, at the moment of recapitulation he or she is reminded once again, and forcefully, to listen in sonata-related terms. This reminder actually becomes stronger in *Don Juan* and *Tod und Verklärung*, works that use literal citations of the principal theme instead of the subdued dynamics and modified articulation of *Macbeth*. Furthermore, the moment of recapitulation reinforces the listener's sense that a previous formal juncture marked the beginning of a developmental space, even though it may not have led immediately to traditional developmental writing. (These moments occur at m. 123 in *Macbeth*, m. 169 in *Don Juan*, and m. 186 in *Tod und Verklärung*.) Of course, the recapitulations themselves do not follow through with anything like typical recapitulatory practice. But they are still recognizable as recapitulations, and by that fact they ask the listener to evaluate the music according to how it does or does not conform to traditional expectations.

The conspicuous and unproblematic character of these sonata-form features can leave the impression that Strauss simply laid the trappings of formal organization over an essentially narrative formal scheme. The ways in which other aspects of sonata form are handled, however, suggests that he invoked the form in order to make it fail, believing that the clarity with which he announced the paradigm would make its collapse easier to perceive. This level of signification is created primarily by Strauss's treatment of the secondary theme group, which of course is the center of action in sonata form and the primary agent in the creation of both drama and musical closure. However inappropriate it may be to identify the "sonata principle" as a defining feature of every example of the form, it did operate in the vast majority of examples to which the young Strauss was exposed, and he clearly believed that to disrupt it was to undermine the form itself.[54]

None of the secondary theme-groups in Strauss's first three tone poems establishes the contrasting key with a perfect authentic cadence.[55] For someone with Strauss's intimate knowledge of the practice of Mozart and Haydn, this consistent absence cannot have been an oversight; it is a glaring formal deficiency, establishing that the exposition has misfired. Two of the three works do have clear contrasting keys, and the very ones prescribed by tradition, but they are weakened significantly. *Macbeth* arrives at the relative major by way of the Neapolitan and as an afterthought eight measures from the end of the section, and the second key of *Don Juan* is announced forcefully at the beginning of the secondary material, only to dissolve in chromatic counterpoint (the E-minor climax at m. 149 being heard as a subdominant that is subsequently reinterpreted as iii in the key of C). In *Tod und Verklärung* the challenge to the second group is even more intense, for the second key, E-flat major, is present only in various forms of its dominant (mm. 161–78), so that the premature fragment of the Ideal theme that attempts to serve as secondary material is also in harmonic terms a mere suggestion of what it attempts to be.

To highlight the consequences of failing to establish a contrasting key, Strauss composed recapitulations that are thematically as well as harmonically dysfunctional. None of the secondary thematic material in the first two tone poems is "recapitulated" in the strict sense, that is, by being brought back in the tonic key after the moment of reprise. In *Macbeth* that material does return at roughly the appropriate moment, but the treatment that it receives is developmental rather than recapitulatory, and necessarily so, because there is no structural dissonance the resolution of which it could mark. The second theme of *Don Juan*, on the other hand, utterly disappears, supplanted by the *Heldenthema*, to which it is motivically related. From the relationship between the two themes and the return of the latter theme in E major during the recapitulation, we know to hear the first entrance of the *Heldenthema* (m. 314) as a fresh attempt at a second theme. But as noted above (see p. 160), both of its presentations are over dominant pedals, so that the return in the tonic is heard as an unsupported attempt to resolve a conflict that never really existed in the first place. In sonata-form terms, *Don Juan* thus renders its failure all the more perceptible by making it twice, the second time in a high-profile attempt to rectify the error.

Tod und Verklärung pursues the implications of the two previous works in a way that yields a positive alternative to sonata procedure while deepening the criticism of the old form. The point being made with the abortive first appearance of the Ideal theme is that musical form in general must now be progressive rather than corrective ("corrective" meaning "centered around the resolution of a structural dissonance"). What drives the piece is not the necessity of resolving finished thematic material that has been presented in the wrong key, but the fragmentary presentation of unfinished thematic material that cannot complete itself melodically until it reaches the tonic key. The roots of this idea in sonata process are evident (the piece concludes when a theme that has not been in the tonic reaches it), but the idea is nevertheless new, growing from the earlier form as the Ideal theme grows from what precedes it. In that sense it is both critical and productive, just as is all three tone poems' scrambling of responsibilities held by sonata-form sections. Expositions that do not perform their function, developments that present new material in tonally stable contexts, recapitulations that incorporate traditional developmental procedures—all of these act in a dual fashion to criticize former sonata practice and to create a new, forward-directed approach to form.

Even though the three pieces show similar concerns and deal with them similarly, there is clearly a progression in the sophistication and the radical nature of Strauss's solutions. The immediate goal of this progression was of course the music drama, a genre in which the formal innovations that he explored in the tone poems would be welcome for dramatic reasons no less than for musical ones. A thoroughgoing criticism of sonata form offered, among other things, justification for the view of the music drama as the most important musical genre; the symphony's rise to predominant intellectual significance went hand-in-hand with sonata form. In the process of composing *Guntram*, however, Strauss would confront philosophical questions that would force him to reassess not only the position of the music drama but the very role of music in human existence. Because they were not specifically formulated until the early 1890s, those questions cannot have had a direct impact on the composition of the first tone poems. But Strauss's naturally critical disposition, which would lead him to study Schopenhauer for himself rather than accepting the word of another, was also at work in a musical sense during the very earliest part of his activity as a program musician. When after *Guntram* he faced the necessity of beginning over again both intellectually and musically, he returned to the forum of those early experiments with a new awareness of the implications that they had for music's philosophical significance. In the second cycle of tone poems, the musically critical side of his personality would meet the philosophically critical, the former energized by the latter and deployed with a force that would forever change the face of German musical aesthetics.

6

Eulenspiegel, Zarathustra, Quixote, Strauss
Crystallization of a Persona

*A*lthough Strauss's second cycle of tone poems seemingly returns to familiar territory, *Till Eulenspiegels lustige Streiche* (1895), *Also sprach Zarathustra* (1896), *Don Quixote* (1897), and *Ein Heldenleben* (1898) require a substantially new interpretive approach. Outwardly, the differences from previous efforts are obvious: the works are bigger (with the exception of *Till*, an overgrown miniature), they are formally more radical, and they focus with greater precision on an entrenched antagonism between individual protagonist (subjectivity) and outside world (objectivity).[1] But more important, these works came after *Guntram*, and therefore after the break with Ritter, after the rejection of Schopenhauer, after the distancing from Bayreuth, and after Strauss had begun reflecting seriously on Nietzsche's theories of a post-metaphysical age. The debacle of his first opera obviously kindled a longing for previous success, but the intellectual development that Strauss had undergone in the meantime ensured that his compositional practice would be not just different but meaningfully different.

In the aftermath of *Guntram*, Strauss found himself isolated in virtually every respect. The chances that even his closest colleagues could follow his philosophical reflections were by now almost nonexistent; none of them had fully grasped the Schopenhauerian premises of his Wagner critique, and so his subsequent rejection of Schopenhauer—which formed the initial context of Strauss's reading of Nietzsche—made little sense to them. Politically, Strauss's return to Munich in 1894 quickly resumed the old path, so that by 1896 the intendant of the Court Theater, Ernst von Possart, could call himself Strauss's "only friend"—a fact that explains why Strauss went to the trouble of composing *Enoch Arden* and serving numerous times as accompanist in a work that he considered "occasional-music rubbish" (*Gelegenheitsschund*).² And in musical terms he had long ago declared his self-sufficiency, by characterizing his first tone poems as distinct from both New German programmaticism and the sonata-form tradition of the Brahmsian school. In every respect that defined him as a musician, then, the thirty-year-old Strauss found himself a misanthrope, just at the moment when the public would decide whether to confirm his greatness or abandon him as a flash in the pan.

One important layer of meaning in the second cycle of tone poems is the process by which a renegade learned to use isolation to his advantage. As much as Strauss protested that none of his compositions was wholly autobiographical (not even *Heldenleben*), we err by ignoring the autobiographical elements or downplaying them because they communicate only fragments of truth about the music or the author.³ As Strauss came to terms with his own alienation, he wrote music about heroes coming to terms with alienation. His skill, energy, and intelligence allowed him to market those exercises, so that the very fact of his outsider status figured centrally in his continued success. But he never lost sight of the dangers inherent in going it alone, and this cognizance manifested itself in practical and intellectual respects. The practical form of this apprehension lay behind his obsession with earning money; amassing capital—by composing, by conducting, by protecting his intellectual property—was in the long run the only sure way for Strauss to protect himself from the possibility that his public appeal would wear off.⁴ On the intellectual side, the recurring Nietzschean "doubt" and "disgust" described in chapter 3 complemented that professional insecurity, reflecting persistent questions about the validity of his antimetaphysical views and the advisability of destroying a musical aesthetic so widely held by his peers. These doubts remained interior—only Strauss fully understood the relationship of the practical and the intellectual in his mind and in his art—but they were real.

Once this multileveled insecurity is made an object of study, the considerable extent to which it informed the musical processes of the tone poems becomes apparent. With each work in the second cycle of tone poems Strauss reexamined his critique of deeply rooted aesthetic traditions, asking again whether his vision of a radically new aesthetic of music was justifiable. Even for the quintessential iconoclast, the typically German integration of music with basic questions of life and worldview made the conscious reworking of musical aesthetics a philosophically and psychologically terrifying task. It is not surprising, then, that the body of work composed during this crisis shows cyclical characteristics, as Strauss continually reevaluated his questions and his solutions. This process had important relationships to Nietzsche, but it was more than Nietzschean. In its involvement with diverse intellectual sources, its intertwining of artistic and intellectual disciplines, and its willingness to entertain and indeed thematize its own self-doubts, the process was distinctively Straussian.

The works of the second cycle are of two basic types. The first, exemplified by *Till Eulenspiegel* and *Don Quixote*, is parodistic/critical. *Till* engages explicitly in critical dialogue with previous works (especially *Tristan*, *Guntram*, and *Don Juan*), as though Strauss were taking stock of his prior musical and intellectual path before moving on to a fully individual agenda. *Don Quixote*, on the other hand, takes an affectionate, understanding, but distinctly skeptical look at the effects of stubborn metaphysical convictions on a single individual—a passionate, learned, aging, misguided "Ritter." The second type of tone poem invokes a critical dilemma but uses it as context for a protagonist's dramatic struggle to imagine a different future. In *Zarathustra* the goal, a Nietzschean vision of optimism, is identified in the first bars—the most famous that Strauss ever composed—with the remainder of the work given over to the hero's valiant but unsuccessful struggle to duplicate it. Victory, of sorts, only comes at the end of *Heldenleben*, in a form tinged with resignation: *Weltflucht* (withdrawal), a retreat into the self that leaves the rest of humanity to work out its own problems. Yet the final attainment of a kind of peace, which parallels the closing gesture of the first cycle in *Tod und Verklärung*, does on the other hand reaffirm Strauss's commitment to the personal aesthetic conclusions that determined his isolation.

The fundamentally critical nature of *Don Quixote* suggests a reason why Strauss completed that work nearly a year before *Heldenleben*, even though he began sketching the latter piece first, worked for a time on both simultaneously, and recorded his early progress with the words "symphonic poem *Held und Welt* begins to take shape; as satyr play to accompany it—*Don Quichote*."[5] Because *Heldenleben* would be another attempt at a final statement, which responded to problems identified (or reidentified) by means of comedy and parody in *Don Quixote*, it had to come second, creatively and in performance.[6] That two-step process duplicated the relationship between *Till* and *Zarathustra*, although for the earlier works there is no evidence of a simultaneous conception. (Discovery of such evidence would not be surprising, however, given that Strauss's most active period of Nietzsche reading came just before and during the composition of *Till*.) On a grand scale, then, Strauss repeated himself, as he struggled to break free from a remarkably stubborn intellectual dilemma. Neither pair would fully succeed; we know that much from *Feuersnot*, a "non-opera" that returned to the comic irony of *Till* and *Don Quixote*.[7] Yet the mere act of reiteration was itself therapeutic and laid the groundwork for a more thoroughgoing independence.

Eulenspiegel and Zarathustra as Alter Egos

Till Eulenspiegels lustige Streiche was an instant and immense public success, the likes of which Strauss had never experienced and would not again until *Salome*.[8] Even in Munich, where the *Guntram* debacle on 16 November 1895 galvanized the opposition, critics applauded the work's humorous spirit and technical mastery.[9] This remarkable level of unanimity was grounded in a perception that Strauss had remained more comprehensively true to himself in this work than in any other; as Ernest Newman put it, "all the components of his nature are still held in an approximate balance."[10] No early writer seems to have commented explicitly on the irony of that judgment, however: namely, that the work through which people believed they came to know the real Strauss was a work about masks, deception, and satire. Apparently Strauss revealed the most about himself when he admitted that he might be lying.

Critics also praised the work's comic tendencies, with a palpable sense of relief akin to what Wilhelm Mauke apparently felt when declaring, in an *Erläuterung* produced with Strauss's assistance, that "this turn to humor is delightful and welcome."[11] Nevertheless, despite its slapstick moments, *Till* is not so much a comedy as a series of parodies, and the distinction is vital to effective interpretation (musical and otherwise). Every instance of the comic has a satirical or critical target, usually not far beneath the surface. And the serious elements are by no means moderately so: according to Strauss's annotations in the score, Till "swears revenge on the whole human race," he is "gripped by an inner dread of the end [of his life]," and he finally is hanged, in a violent denouement added by Strauss in a revision of the traditional tale.[12] (The legendary

Till dies in his sleep.) Certainly comic elements play a role here, but the subject matter is no lighter than any he had used previously.[13] And with respect to the intellectual dilemmas occupying him privately, the work is more directly engaged than any, as is shown not least by the fact that he dedicated it to Arthur Seidl.[14]

If, as I have suggested previously, *Till* acted as a kind of manifesto, it did so partly because Strauss for the first time used a method of ironic disguise that he would retain even after he moved on to opera.[15] This same basic method would find a place in *Don Quixote, Feuersnot, Symphonia domestica, Der Rosenkavalier,* and *Ariadne auf Naxos,* all works in which a kind of dramatic buoyancy facilitates the communication of ideas about a subject of profound personal import. In each of these cases, no matter how wild or thoroughgoing the comic impulse, the conclusion of the work is preceded by a brief parting of the veil, a moment of reflection employing a more straightforward mode of signification than has previously been available to the listener. Structurally and in musical character these moments behave as epilogues, but they also protect the music's complexity, inviting the listener to wonder whether he or she has heard all that was available to hear.

The epilogue in *Till* raises several issues that are crucial to competent interpretation of the parody. First, the focal point is a quotation—of the *Siegfried-Idyll,* the love scene in act 3 of *Siegfried,* or both.[16] The meaning of this citation is enigmatic, if not impenetrable, but at the very least it brings out into the open a practice much more widespread in the tone poem than writers have noticed. In various musical and nonmusical ways, most of them easily perceptible, *Till* invokes *Tristan, Don Juan,* and *Guntram,* along with *Siegfried,* so that Strauss shapes his protagonist's identity largely through distortion of others' identities (much as another trickster, Liszt's Mephistopheles, is created in the third movement of the *Faust-Sinfonie*). Second, the concluding evocation of a mythical hero, one whose responsibility it is to save the world, throws into relief Till's status as antihero and his antagonistic relationship with a world that he has no interest in saving. Given the sources with which *Till* is in citational dialogue, there is clearly a sense in which the tone poem wishes to overturn the concept of heroism. These interrelated concerns have a perceptible impact on the musical means used by Strauss, structurally and in the aural foreground.

In the version heard at m. 1, the first Till theme is a looking-glass view of the protagonist, befitting its function as curtain-raiser and conduit to the diegesis. Strauss's private annotation of this moment, "once upon a time there was a knavish fool" ("'es war einmal' ein Schalksnarr"), led Specht to suggest that the melody was a simply a *völkisch* syllabic rendering of that text (though he had to substitute "Schelm" for "Schalksnarr" to come up with the correct number of syllables).[17] But the real point of this particular casting of the theme is to capture the affectionate fairy-tale perception of Till, so that the entrance of the character himself (m. 46), in all his irritating D-clarinet cheek, will seem as real as possible. Strauss marked this second manifestation "lustig" (alluding to the title) because it takes a decisive step toward accuracy of characterization; the "portrait in tones" ("Konterfei in Tönen") is now more photograph than painting.[18] Yet while the thematic manipulation creates a sense of realism, it is also a parody, achieving its effect through distortion, if not defacement, of the more attractive and "normal" initial presentation.

The way one reads this instance of parody determines one's interpretation of the tone poem. From a programmatic standpoint, the music that we initially perceive as a distortion actually conveys the truth more accurately than the apparently unproblematic "original." Once again drawing on a tried-and-true Wagnerian leitmotivic technique, Strauss's first presentation of a theme takes a guise that is not definitive but rather a disguise: Till as legend, seen through the eyes of the adoring, modern, fairy-tale–reading public. This image is no less a fabrication than the passage in which Till dresses up as a parson—a theme that famously shares the same initial rhythmic profile (ex. 6.1). The real Till in fact differs more dramatically from the first of these than from the second,

Example 6.1a. *Till Eulenspiegels lustige Streiche*, mm. 1–2

Example 6.1b. *Till Eulenspiegels lustige Streiche*, mm. 179–80

for at least in the latter a small part of him (his big toe) peaks out. The idealistic fog of the opening is so thick that it can only be dispersed with a gesture too ugly to be false.

The broader implications of this opening are highlighted by the fact that precisely at the unpleasant moment when we meet Till in the flesh, we hear the Tristan chord, transposed but (as in the opening of the music drama) scored for woodwinds and complete with sforzando and decrescendo (ex. 6.2). This too acts as parody (now intertextual in nature), even though nothing about the technical treatment of the chord seems distortive. What marks it as parody is rather the context: in conjunction with the shift from romanticism to realism in our perception of Till, the chord loses its dignity and its metaphysical power—a frightening spectacle indeed for anyone familiar, as any good listener would be, with the sheer profundity symbolized by this one sonority. The moment of judgment ("death" ["Der Tod"], mm. 613–14) applies the same method to the Death motive in *Tristan* (in spite of the difference in interval), emptying it of symbolic weight by sharpening it as a gesture of realism (it sets an absent text, and it stands purely for the fear of physical destruction) (ex. 6.3).

One of the ways in which Till is defined for us, then, is through a kind of demystification that treats parody as *more* faithful to reality, not less. On the level of the program, the character's relationship to Guntram functions similarly. Both are medieval wanderers, completely without personal attachments, who seek brief associations with people in order to change them. Till hates the human race while Guntram loves it, but both aim to exert control over it. (Naturally they are represented by the same key, F major.)[19] But which of the figures is the buffoon? From Strauss's contemporaneous perspective, Till's "pranks," which seem to mock Guntram's mission, have a level of critical truth that could not be communicated straightforwardly without sounding overblown. They undermine religion, exalt earthly love over spiritual love, and reveal current philosophy as sophistry. These were the main critical concerns of Strauss's intellectual life in the mid-1890s, and we may assume that by hypothesizing their consequences for Till—death—he was anticipating a negative outcome for himself. Nevertheless, Till's final and most insidious prank is a musical one, in a definitively Straussian spirit: he translates his attack on society into a "street-ditty," a spiritually blank music-for-its-own-sake.

The relationship between *Till* and *Don Juan* plays out on more directly musical grounds (diagram 6.1). Both use a pair of returning themes

lustig

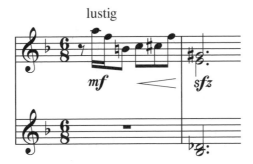

Example 6.2a. *Till Eulenspiegels lustige Streiche*, mm. 46–47

Example 6.2b. *Tristan und Isolde*, act 1, prelude, mm. 1–2 (transposed)

Example 6.3a. *Till Eulenspiegels lustige Streiche*, mm. 613–14

Example 6.3b. *Tristan und Isolde*, act I, prelude, mm. 28–29

	Entrance of protagonist (2 themes)	Encounters	Life-altering experience (G minor/major)	A single further exchange with the outside world	Reprise (hollow triumph)	Death at the hands of an antagonist; epilogue
Don Juan	m. 1	mm. 44, 90	m. 197	m. 351	m. 464	m. 586
Till Eulenspiegel	m. 1	mm. 113, 135, 158, 179, 209	m. 229	m. 293	m. 429	m. 615

Diagram 6.1. Programmatic and formal parallels in *Don Juan* and *Till Eulenspiegel*.

symbolizing the protagonist, and these take part in a series of episodes, the penultimate of which, the split between G minor and G major, has life-altering implications. After one further episode this epiphany leads through a retransition to a reprise that then drives toward a moment of hollow triumph. Finally, musico-programmatic gestures of an irresistible antagonist undermine this ecstatic display, and the piece collapses into a coda residing outside the action.

The formal parallelism between the works is obvious and extensive, but in one important respect it does breaks down. Even as *Till* casts itself as a return to the structural and programmatic model of *Don Juan*, it leaves behind the central dilemma of the earlier composition, the critique of sonata form. In *Till*, for the first time in Strauss's tone poems, there is no clearly defined exposition; the only plausible second key area is the Pastor scene, where the use of the subdominant rules out a sonata-form interpretation. Likewise, there is no explicitly marked beginning of the developmental space, and no section in which developmental procedures predominate (as in the "masked ball" section of *Don Juan*). The recapitulation focuses exclusively on one theme, the second Till theme, which appears in two different versions; like the absence of a structural second key, this feature confirms that the work has abandoned the basic dualism of sonata procedure in favor of greater attention to the development of the principal idea. And that choice also manifests itself in the work's general preoccupation with the tonic, as well as in the nearly complete saturation of the texture with motives from the two Till themes—a considerable advance on the motivic integration that pushed the first three tone poems increasingly toward opera.

The absence of a strong engagement with sonata form in *Till*, even one overtly critical in nature, means that the entire burden of structural organization falls to the series of programmatic encounters. That is essentially to say that Strauss abandoned traditional demands of large-scale orchestral structure entirely, leaving the program to shape the music in a manner very much like what was to come in *Don Quixote*. No doubt Strauss felt a kind of apprehension, if not horror, at that step, for his music was behaving much as Till did: criticizing ruthlessly while providing little in the way of a positive alternative. The work's self-centeredness is a by-product of this absolute dissociation from the safe haven of tradition, in the same way that Strauss's critical philosophical speculations of 1893–94 necessitated a withdrawal into himself. The critique was so radical and the way forward so unsure that no one but he had any hope of solving the dilemma.

When the theme known to Wagnerians as "Siegfried, Hope of the World" makes its entrance in the *Siegfried-Idyll* during the development section, it redirects the work toward a future that would have been unimaginable without the redeeming child.[20] The character of that future is unclear; however promising it sounds, it is unrealized and unfocused. The leitmotif performs essentially the same function in the music drama, calling Brünnhilde to a new life as unknown as it is hopeful. That combination of optimism and ignorance had a role to play in *Till* as well, through the suggestion that the critical process preceding it paved the way to something new, notwithstanding the death of the protagonist. The various returns of the Tristan chord—which by virtue of repetition has become the Till chord, functioning much as the augmented triad does in the *Idyll*—accomplish something different, confirming that the critique was real, whatever the other results of the drama. But the Siegfried theme suggests that a future remains to be discovered, or invented. Mapping out that post-Wagnerian landscape would be Strauss's responsibility alone, for only he had imagined it, and in important respects only he wanted it.

Strauss's choice to title the work "Till Eulenspiegel's Merry Pranks" rather than "Till Eulenspiegel" betrays an awareness that Till's actions are much easier to recognize and describe than any defining features of his character. Aside from his pranks, he really *has* no character; as a discrete individual he cannot be grasped and indeed he cannot grasp himself, a problem that Strauss captured in two themes that disguise their meter until they are nearly gone (the first [ex. 6.4a] by metric displacement, the second [ex. 6.4b] by $<^7_8>$ music embedded in a $<^6_8>$ meter). That concluding clarification may express his own desire to know himself as well as the desire of others to know him, but the fact remains that Till would not be Till if one could pin him down. He is purely reactive—which is perfectly fine for a character, but would only bring Strauss so

Example 6.4a. *Till Eulenspiegels lustige Streiche*, mm. 1–3

Example 6.4b. *Till Eulenspiegels lustige Streiche*, mm. 6–12

far. Herein lies the explanation of Strauss's move in his next tone poem to the deepest philosophizing of his career. Few would have expected that the composer of *Till* would immediately plunge himself into what is perhaps the most profound example of self-reflection in the German language. (At that stage his propensity for following a work with its aesthetic opposite had not yet been established.) But Strauss did it, because it was an absolute necessity that he accomplish what *Till* could not—that he formulate an authentic, positive personal identity.

Although *Till* and *Zarathustra* were not initially conceived as a pair, by the time Strauss began work on the latter tone poem the idea may well have occurred to him, for in many respects *Zarathustra* responds directly to ideas raised in *Till*. In particular, Till's metaphysical angst presages Zarathustra's "disgust" (*Ekel*), programmatically and musically. Strauss's experience of a related kind of dread after his rejection of Schopenhauer undoubtedly figured in his decision to emphasize an element that had little importance in the folk sources of *Till*.[21] But in *Zarathustra* that fear, now cast as "disgust at mankind"—that is, disgust at mankind's irrepressible metaphysical urge—became a central, recurring problem with which every other element in the work had to contend. The universal human quality of this fear may explain why Strauss chose, for the musical theme representing *Ekel* in *Zarathustra*, a motive embedded in Till's first theme (ex. 6.5). In the Till theme the F-major tonal orientation ameliorates the queasiness of a tritone drop followed by a chromatic

Example 6.5a. *Also sprach Zarathustra*, mm. 150–53

Example 6.5b. *Till Eulenspiegels lustige Streiche*, mm. 1–2

ascent, but the correspondence between the motives is unmistakable, especially because *Zarathustra* appropriates the motive at pitch. In the latter work the motive's increased length suggests intensification of the psychological nausea and perhaps a deeper preoccupation.

A larger-scale connection obtains in the character and ordering of episodes in *Zarathustra*. Anette Unger has demonstrated at length that after the introduction, these episodes proceed in motivically linked pairs, according to the following scheme: "Von den Hinterweltlern" / "Von der grossen Sehnsucht," "Von den Freuden- und Leidenschaften" / "Das Grablied," "Von der Wissenschaft" / "Der Genesende."[22] The first member of each of these pairs matches in content the three non-tonic episodes in *Till*: the imitation of the parson, the wooing of the "pretty girl," and the baffling of the Philistines. Likewise, each version of this series of encounters leads to a light-music allusion specifically associated with the protagonist: Till's "street-ditty" and Zarathustra's waltz. That this final section is not just large but actually an expansion of an intertextual allusion adds a layer of significance; the growth between works itself demands interpretation. Other connections between the works deepen the need for an account of why in the end they differ. Till and Zarathustra both face moments of judgment—moments in which they are condemned on the basis of how they are perceived—cast musically as enormous fortissimo explosions that bring the music to a grinding halt (mm. 577ff. in *Till*, mm. 329ff. in *Zarathustra*). The optimistic spirit of both characters is captured in a theme built around three repetitions of a melodic movement from the raised scale degree 2 to scale degree 3 (ex. 6.6). And *Zarathustra*, like *Till*, ends with a Wagner quotation, of the culminating retrogression in the *Tristan* "Liebestod" (ex. 6.7).

What, then, is the programmatic import of the waltz, given that in a sense it marks the culmination of not one but two tone poems? How does it respond to the issues raised first in *Till* and then retraced in the first half of *Zarathustra*? Answering that question must begin with the observation that Strauss's claim that he "did not intend to write philosophical music" cannot be taken seriously.[23] Certainly he did not intend the tone poem to be perceived philosophically by every listener, but he

Example 6.6a. *Till Eulenspiegels lustige Streiche*, mm. 6–9

Example 6.6b. *Also sprach Zarathustra*, m. 386

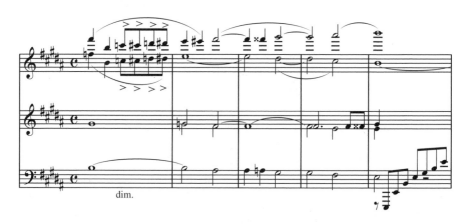

Example 6.7a. *Also sprach Zarathustra*, mm. 961–65 B: V⁷ IV

Example 6.7b. *Tristan und Isolde*, act 3, conclusion

himself wrote to Friedrich von Hausegger, at the very period during which he began work on *Zarathustra*, that while composing he sometimes attempted to "cut Nietzschean paradoxes down to size."[24] Early critics of the work agreed. Max Marschalk concluded that whether Strauss's *Zarathustra* embodied "the development of the higher man into the *Übermensch*" or "the composer's subjective observations and thoughts concerning Nietzsche and his work," the topic was philosophical rather than poetic.[25] (This assertion responded to a claim by Arthur Hahn in the guidebook sanctioned by Strauss that the composer had read Nietzsche's book as poetry, not philosophy.) Max Loewengard stated flatly that Strauss had written "philosophical music"; claims to the contrary were disingenuous, he argued, and assertions of the music's formal self-sufficiency "completely untenable."[26] Even Hahn avoided claiming that evidence of Nietzsche's philosophy was absent from the music, instead stating that one did not need to consider that evidence in order to make sense of the piece in a meaningful way.[27] Arthur Seidl, in any case, found Hahn's work crudely off the point, and he said so to Strauss.[28]

The tonal structure and the handling of themes in *Zarathustra* both show Strauss working his way through existential anxieties in order to embrace fully a post-metaphysical worldview. As he struggled privately to mediate between strong antimetaphysical convictions and recurring doubts, his music not surprisingly became a way of thinking about, if not thinking through, the philosophical dilemma. Thematically as well as tonally, each of the elements in this debate—pure physicality, human doubt, and an imagined state of reconciliation—finds a musical analogue. The solution itself is by no means final, however; in fact, it thematizes the impossibility of finding a solution, thereby clarifying and highlighting one of the central points of Nietzsche's philosophy. It is as a reflection of this private coming-to-terms with Nietzsche that the basic musical operations of the work make sense.

The confrontation between C and B, which Strauss identified as the work's motivating conflict, juxtaposes the physical and the human, objectivity and subjectivity. Strauss characterized the beginning alternately as "nature," "the sun theme," and "sunrise"—straightforward signs of pure, immutable physicality. His B-minor "Longing" motive, on the other hand, casts humanity as puny, and from Nietzsche's standpoint that impression is reinforced when the shimmering final entrance in B major (m. 954), redolent of the end of *Tristan*, links human nature with undying metaphysical hope. The terms of the B–C encounter are those of Nietzsche's prologue, in which Zarathustra declares his intention to "become like" the sun, to purge himself of the limiting characteristics of human nature. That struggle plays out in the harmonic shape of the piece, with C major standing for Zarathustra's goal and keys that lean ever closer toward C major representing his progressive but ultimately futile efforts to transcend his humanity. With a typically sure sense of pacing and direction, Strauss set a course from A-flat (an ersatz C minor) in "Von den Hinterweltlern" through C minor in "Von den Freuden- und Leidenschaften" to a thirdless C major in "Von der Wissenschaft." Following a reprise of the introduction at m. 329 and a lengthy transition that settles on the dominant of C, the "Tanzlied" seems to achieve the composition's musico-programmatic goal, with a closed section authentically in C major (mm. 409–527; the form is ternary, with a middle section in A major). The key proves unsustainable, however; through a kind of backtracking the music leads to a lengthy pedal on E (mm. 876–945) that disrupts an attempted climax on C. The E is then reinterpreted as IV/ B, and the music moves to its inescapably human coda.

While the course of the tone poem bears little resemblance to that of the philosophical text, it does highlight a "Nietzschean paradox"— Zarathustra's revolt, as human, against his own human qualities—and it does "cut it down to size" by replaying the process in stepwise, "evolutionary" terms. From this perspective the famous polytonal conclusion embraces the tragic necessity that for Nietzsche defined the human condition: Zarathustra (standing for humanity) is regularly reminded that freedom from metaphysics can be imagined but not achieved. (Similar reminders punctuate each of the early attempts at reaching C major; that is a crucial programmatic function of the sections "Von der grossen Sehnsucht," "Das Grablied," and "Der Genesende.") Yet Hans Merian and Max Steinitzer both pointed toward a sense in which the work retains a hope in the potential that it could not realize—much as Nietzsche's book points toward the arrival of the *Übermensch*, who of course never actually makes an appearance. Steinitzer, responding to the critique of Eduard Hanslick, explained the apparent bitonality as a simple alternation of subdominant (with added sixth) and dominant triads in E minor— in other words, as signs of an absent tonic.[29] This view is undoubtedly a rhetorical oversimplification of a chord that has a long and complicated history in the tone poem, but the basic validity of the idea was supported by Merian, who read Steinitzer's first chord as an "incomplete supertonic seventh chord in E minor" (the missing note being the third).[30] Even more interestingly, Merian believed that this chord functioned as a "mediator" between B and C (an explanation that has been echoed by Walter

Werbeck in considering the E pedal preceding the coda).[31] Figuratively speaking, such a mediation is the goal of the *Übermensch*, who will transcend humanity by learning to rejoice at the unbridgeable gap between subjectivity and objectivity.

In that light, it is certainly of interest that Stauss at one stage planned to end the work in E major: at the end of one of the prose plans for the work we find the phrase "dann ins Edur ganz füzuletzt."[32] That he gave up this idea is entirely consistent with an informed interpretation of Nietzsche (the *Übermensch* is only a prophecy, not a reality), as is the repeated occurrence in the tone poem of gestures that identify E as a goal not yet attainable. The C-major harmony above the E pedal, for example, can be construed in this way, as an attempted *Leittonwechsel* that refuses to take the pedal as root. Hahn took note of the near climax on E (in second inversion) in "Von den Hinterweltlern" but did not know what to make of it or its nearly verbatim return in "Von der grossen Sehnsucht."[33] The fugue, in its first, *stile antico* incarnation in "Von der Wissenschaft," breaks down at the entrance on E; when it resumes in "Der Genesende" it does so as a caricature in the manner of Berlioz, grotesquely forcing the matter. In fact, the only successful E-centered event in the piece arrives in a roundabout way during the coda, when an E triad enters unexpectedly as the goal of the *Tristan* allusion (m. 965). Of course, this momentary vision of redemption is not real; it is a glimpse of the future, powerful but fleeting.

Thematic processes in *Zarathustra* reinforce the programmatic implications of the tonal structure. The Nature motive acts as both a reminder of the C-major goal and an indicator that the goal has not been reached; thus its entrances are confined to sections that lie between attempts to reach C ("Von der grossen Sehnsucht," m. 82, and "Das Grablied," m. 178) until it is incorporated into the fugue subject in "Von der Wissenschaft." That attempt is closer than any, but it too fails, precipitating the terrifying recapitulation at m. 329. The "Tanzlied" also incorporates the motto but no more successfully, for whatever its lightness and optimism it evaporates rather than bringing about a triumphant climax in C major. The return of the motto at the very end, then, tells us directly that the goal is no closer than it ever was.

A similar trajectory toward but then away from C is at the heart of the transformations of the Longing theme (ex. 6.8). The overall contour of this thematic "history" moves from B to C and back to B, with the latter key in the meantime shifting mode from minor to major. As the theme changes, its arch-like shape is clarified one step at a time, so that

Example 6.8a. *Also sprach Zarathustra,* mm. 26–27

Example 6.8b. *Also sprach Zarathustra,* mm. 30–32

Example 6.8c. *Also sprach Zarathustra,* mm. 75–78

Example 6.8d. *Also sprach Zarathustra,* mm. 239–41

Example 6.8e. *Also sprach Zarathustra,* mm. 249–52

Example 6.8f. *Also sprach Zarathustra,* mm. 381–82

Example 6.8g. *Also sprach Zarathustra,* mm. 686–91

Example 6.8h. *Also sprach Zarathustra,* mm. 738–46

Example 6.8i. *Also sprach Zarathustra,* mm. 850–57

Example 6.8j. *Also sprach Zarathustra,* mm. 954–60

only with the final appearance is the descent to the tonic completed. That melodic motion echoes the theme's tonal evolution, both arches telling us that the existential quandary of humanity is inescapable but can be viewed from a new perspective. The Longing theme is also programmatically related to the Disgust theme, which contains in its initial F–B leap the keys of Longing's first two presentations. The particular kind of disgust at issue here is of course an initial reaction to the awareness with which the other theme reconciles itself over the long term; being human allows no hope of permanent release from human fears. But that terror can be softened, which is precisely what happens during the concluding portion of the "Nachtwandlerlied," when disgust relaxes into acceptance over the mysterious E pedal (mm. 857–945).

The programmatic idea contained in the references to E is likewise that of the Dance theme, a melody that establishes its momentum by repeatedly pointing toward E from a half step below. Even as it imagines a superhuman future, this theme promises nothing permanent; it represents the closest human approximation to C major in the piece, but it does so in an open-ended way, without a convincing melodic conclusion and without a strong final cadence, which could only be a false promise. Its very lack of closure, however, offers the hope that it will come again, and in that sense it points the listener toward another fundamental Nietzschean claim. To know the eternal recurrence, to embrace it, is the only path to redemption. The only hope for humans is recognition and self-awareness. To paraphrase Nietzsche, the same cycle that produced this theme must repeat itself endlessly, ever renewing the same terrors and joys. That is the knowledge that could not be provided by religion, or human passion, or advanced thought; it is the knowledge sought by both Till and Zarathustra, and the knowledge that must undergird one's existence in a post-metaphysical age.

Of course, none of the tonal or thematic processes that I have described has anything to do with sonata form or with the four-movement symphonic cycle. And yet, these ad hoc features are the controlling musical mechanisms of the work, notwithstanding Strauss's assertion that *Zarathustra* is "constructed according to the laws of purely musical logic," in C major, with "the dualism of a male and female main theme" and a quasi–four-movement structure.[34] Allusions to tradition are indeed present, but they operate in a forthrightly critical way, through disruptions and jumblings that any attentive amateur can perceive. "Von den Freuden- und Leidenschaften" and "Von den Hinterweltlern" assume the character of primary and secondary themes in almost stereotypical fashion, but they appear in reverse order; whereas *Till* simply abandons the sonata exposition, *Zarathustra* actually inverts it, citing the form while overtly revoking its functional power. And at the moment in the second half of the piece when one might expect the recapitulation of the secondary thematic material in the tonic, Strauss instead presents the primary material in the second key (A-flat major, mm. 629ff.), again explicitly alluding to the form in order to clarify its subversion. Paradoxically, then, *Zarathustra* incorporates sonata form as clearly as any of the tone poems to that date but also refutes it more powerfully than any. In that sense the piece follows battle lines laid out by Strauss already in 1888, when he declared to Johann Leopold Bella that he had "completely abolished" sonata form.[35] In 1896, audiences had still not gotten the point, and so Strauss tried yet again, more insistently than ever, to announce that it was time for instrumental music to move on.

The out-and-out rejection of sonata form should tell us all the more clearly that leitmotivic interaction, the structure and ordering of "episodes," and novel tonal procedures have unprecedented formal responsibilities—in combination with the program—even if they do not produce the kind of closure or cohesion that one associates with music of the classical tradition. We would expect nothing less of an authentically Nietzschean composer in the 1890s than that he would "revalue musical values," even values that many continue to hold dear even today. And yet, that said, *Zarathustra* is not primarily critical. Merian's "concealed symmetry," for example, exerts a great deal of organizational force, if one is able to let go of traditional expectations sufficiently to hear it (diagram 6.2).[36] The notion that the second half of this piece repeats the first half, but with a different approach and different results, has strong musical and programmatic appeal. And more than that, it offers another example of the large-scale repetition manifested in the relationship between *Till* and *Zarathustra*. The process might well reflect an interest in the eternal recurrence, but it definitely tells us that in his tone poems Strauss was returning repeatedly to the same musical and philosophical (or by now, psychological) issues. Until he settled this problem to his satisfaction, these cycles would continue.

Other and Self: Don Quixote and Ein Heldenleben

In several important respects, *Don Quixote* marked a turning point in Strauss's career as orchestral composer. It was the first tone poem conceived and written after the death of Alexander Ritter. It was the first

Inroduction	Von den Hinterweltlern	Von Den grossen Sehnsucht		Von den Fraeuden und Leidenschaften	Das Grablied	Von der Wissenschaft	Der Genesende	
closed	open	closed	open	closed	open	open (fugue 1)	open (fugue 2)	"Wandlung": Natur; retransition
C (PAC m. 19)	(f) (b)	A flat (PAC m. 66)	b C:V	c (PAC m. 157)	b F sharp: V	C B	(e)	C C:V

Das Tanzlied							Das Nachtwandlerlied	
closed	open	closed (themes: Freuden und Leidenschaften)				open (Steigerung 1)	(Steigerung 2)	open
C (PAC m. 527)	C G (PAC m. 613)	A flat (PAC m. 681)				C (B) (F) C	(F) (modulation) (D) C (6/3)	B (V-IV m. 965)

Diagram 6.2. Hans Merian's "Concealed Symmetry" in *Also sprach Zarathustra*.

work to make Strauss's attack on idealism explicit, which it did by relying on a literary work much more straightforward in its critical aims than Nietzsche's text. And *Don Quixote* was Strauss's first large-scale orchestral work to forego any allusion to sonata form; *Till* lacked an exposition but not a reprise, and even *Zarathustra* had maintained a connection, albeit a scrambled one. These features of *Don Quixote* do not of course rule out all possibility of connection to Strauss's past, however, particularly to *Till*, the only other predominantly comic tone poem and the prototype for unfettered indulgence in *Tonmalerei*. (Del Mar considered *Till* and *Don Quixote* Strauss's masterpieces, reviving the claim that Strauss was more true to himself when giving free rein to his comedic and illustrative impulses.)[37] But while the special brilliance of these two pieces is undeniable, in the latter instance it took on a radical intensity symptomatic of both a deepening confidence in his creative direction and a new freedom from responsibility to those who had helped him along the way.

When in August 1897 Strauss leaked the news that he was working on a tone poem based on *Don Quixote*, he knew that the serial, pictographic nature of the text would soon have the public beside itself trying to determine which of the many episodes he had chosen to treat. The prospect of hearing Strauss's virtuosic technical imagination applied to a literary source stupefyingly rich in narrative detail raised expectations—calculatedly—of unprecedented feats of musical illustration. And Strauss did not disappoint. More than any work before it, *Don Quixote* communicates through ongoing, meticulous analogy to dramatic action. Even mental experiences, such as inane proverbs or the descent into insanity, are made physical through musical analogues that render them understandable. Although Strauss identified many of these pictorial details in a guide written by the ever-reliable Arthur Hahn, the listener is always made to feel that new discoveries remain possible for those who know their Cervantes or who simply have a good imagination. In the introduction, for example, which is perfectly recognizable on a general level as a representation of a weak mind being overwhelmed by a profusion of knight stories, Strauss actually had particular individuals and events in mind for virtually every distinctive melodic idea. Yet neither Strauss's heavily annotated autograph nor the pocket score that he annotated for Clemens Krauss makes any mention of the knight (m. 45) who encounters a woman (m. 46), gives in to lower impulses (m. 51), and loses his strength (m. 56); this material is only to be found in the sketches.[38] Such cases, and the implication that others exist about which we have no evidence, tell us that the presence of a "program" in the idealized Wagnerian sense has now given way entirely to spectacular and elaborate illustration.

No less radical than the work's absorption in the illustrative mode of programmaticism is its total repudiation of an independent musical structure. The designation of variation form in the title says little about the actual practice of the music. Variation in the traditional sense of progressive alteration of a theme does not happen; what changes is not so much the melodies but their environment. Where variation in the usual sense does apply is in the formal notion of a series of discrete sections that are related by common material but do not share an overarching organic relationship on a structural level. Strauss may well have used the term for precisely this reason—to suggest that the inherent formlessness of the theme-and-variations form would here be brought forward and celebrated—for the music presents itself overtly as a loose conglomeration of scenes whose strongest connections are not musical but programmatic. Nothing could demonstrate this looseness more clearly than the fact that Strauss actually considered several different orderings of the variations; his decisions as he composed individual variations were thus demonstrably not made with a view to the place of each moment in an overarching formal plan.[39]

On the level of form, *Don Quixote* completes a progression begun with *Macbeth* and advanced with steady steps in every intervening work. To review: *Macbeth* clearly retained sonata form but included new themes in the development and shifted developmental procedures to the recapitulation. *Don Juan* began with a clear exposition then abandoned its second theme, turning in the recapitulation to a theme introduced during the development, but undermining this attempted novelty by recapitulating it in six-four position. In *Tod und Verklärung* the second theme exists only in elemental, fragmentary form during the exposition and is not heard in its entirety until the coda; the exposition is never completed, then, and the category of recapitulation is wholly discarded in favor of a process of thematic formation. Because the exposition had now been rendered obsolete, Strauss abandoned it entirely in *Till* and allowed his allusions to sonata form (principally the moment of recapitulation) to relinquish even the appearance of a structural function. Finally, *Zarathustra* presented the components of the form—first theme, second theme, developmental procedures, reprise—but left them in disarray, the ruins of former glory.

In *Don Quixote*, Strauss for the first time completely abandoned this dialogue and in so doing cut his ties not just with a particular classical form but with the very idea of purely musical large-scale formal coherence. Yes, one might still listen to the music and enjoy it on its own terms, but the choices that produced that music and the shape that music took were inextricably bound up with the program. To deny that fact or to suggest that musical choices were primary because the program was revised during the compositional process is to impose a rehabilitation that the work itself repudiates. Whatever Strauss said with words, with his music he announced a categorical rejection of autonomy in favor of the structural model provided by opera. He may also have conceived of it as a shift toward the Berliozian programmatic approach censured by Wagner (signaled by the loaded adjective "fantastische" in the title). But he clearly meant to move far beyond what Berlioz had dared—to make the continuous linkage with a program a principle of composition and, for those willing to engage the work on its own terms, a principle of listening.

Cervantes's text provided incomparably suitable material through which to pursue such a project, so that one can understand Strauss's determination to use the subject notwithstanding the existence of several earlier settings by German composers (Mendelssohn, Rubinstein, Kienzl).[40] Yet his reasons extended beyond the opportunities for illustrative composition. *Don Quixote* also offered a unique possibility for bringing the intellectual background of his orchestral project to concrete and personal expression. Although he never discussed his reasons for choosing this topic, Strauss cannot have failed to recognize the striking parallels between the tragic delusions of Cervantes's *Ritter* and the unhappy idealism of Alexander Ritter, the don's coincidental namesake, whose own battles continued until his death. Indeed, so thoroughgoing is this connection that one can recount the salient features of both figures' biographies simultaneously. Like the character, Ritter was obsessed with an outdated mode of idealism, and he lived in semiretirement, buried in his books. Ever willing to share his views through grandiose, self-important oration, his efforts intensified with his frustration at others' inability to understand. That anger, combined with extensive reading and a tendency to interpret his sources simplistically, produced a pathetic confusion and a hardening of his misguided convictions. By the end he saw enemies everywhere, even in his closest friends, who continued to look after him no matter how flagrantly he mistreated them. (Bülow, for example, responded to Ritter's public castigations by secretly arranging for a percentage of his posthumous royalties to be paid to Ritter.) Generally regarded as an annoying but harmless screwball, he dealt with his nostalgia by wandering in search of a place untainted by the modern. At the end, not having found an appropriate objectification of his concept of "sacred love" (a notion privately parodied by Strauss and Thuille), he projected it onto the best available candidate (Aldonza/Sonja von Schéhafzoff), who for her part appreciated the attention but had limited patience with life on a pedestal. Some measure of peace accompanied his final days, when a friend, whom he regarded as an enemy, helped him by humoring him. (Strauss continued to program Ritter's works after their estrangement, for example performing *Sursum corda!* in a concert only a week before its composer's death.) But the end was characterized more by exhaustion than enlightenment, and among those who knew him it aroused only pity.

The challenge that Strauss faced in composing music for this subject was to produce both incisive criticism and affectionate understanding. He met it in part by giving the don music both undeniably beautiful and recognizably misguided. In its effervescent lyricism, the F-sharp-major vision of "paradise" (mm. 332–69) rivals the Presentation of Rose, which also captures, in the same key, a radiant moment of unimagined joy. But here, the experience is marked in multiple ways as a delusion. The F-sharp tonic recalls our first encounter with Dulcinea, when her original G major dropped curiously to F-sharp as Don Quixote sank deeper into confusion (mm. 24ff.). With its amplification into a full-blown set piece, that dream receives the full Straussian expressive treatment, complete with a luminous concluding chord as convincing as a final cadence. (Such chords were a special interest of Strauss, growing from his fascination with the final moment of *Tristan*.) The character of that gesture is not Strauss's only means of telling us to listen to this music from the outside: after it is over, Sancho immediately spoils the mood (m. 381), and in fact during the rhapsodic vision he makes interjections (mm. 369–71) that go unnoticed by his master but not by us. We are on Sancho's side, then, or at least we hear things as he does, because we are sane.

As if sincerity were not undermined sufficiently by the association with insanity, Strauss also caricatures it. Don Quixote's "enraptured dec-lamations," which many listeners have found the most convincing mo-ments of the piece, are actually to be played "sentimentally" (m. 432), the excessive, grotesque quality of the emotion deliberately brought for-ward by the performer. (The inflated religiosity in *Zarathustra*'s "Von den Hinterweltlern" is similarly deceptive.) As at the end of the vision of paradise, the outside world rudely interrupts, now through a natural phenomenon rather than a person (the breeze, at m. 452); this is not illustration for its own sake, but illustration as an antidote to attractive nonsense. Other times, emotional overstatement is written into the music itself, as at mm. 359–62, where the melody's absurd repetition of the third scale degree is clearly a self-parody (ex. 6.9). If it is musical "ba-nality" that raises the don's "fiercest ire" (Strauss's label for Don Quix-ote's response to the "Banalitäten" at m. 320), one wonders how he is able to bear his own utterances, which are always just ambitious and weak enough to identify themselves undeniably as kitsch. In *Tod und Verklä-rung*, a work with which *Don Quixote* shares a fair amount of common ground (the piece traces the search for an ideal, paints a graphic moment of death, and concludes with a heartfelt, ostensibly profound elegy), the music of spirituality may be banal, but it is not deliberately so. Here a conclusion that it was intentional is not only easy but necessary.

Aside from Don Quixote's soliloquies, the few moments of unequiv-ocal musical abstraction in this piece express confusion, most palpably during the reading of the *Ritterromane*, but also in opening bars, where the move from D major to A-flat major and back again lets us know that the protagonist is at the very least a strange bird. The pictorial moments, conversely, remain eminently understandable, no matter how many are piled on top of one another—even the sheep, with dissonances perhaps more piercing than any other in the nineteenth century, are crystal clear in musico-programmatic terms. Only once in the piece, at the very end, does Strauss write music that eschews moment-by-moment illustration without overtly caricaturing itself. Perhaps by then the point had been

Example 6.9. *Don Quixote*, mm. 358–63

made, and he felt free to pay a final homage to his friend, not without humor, and free of excessive pathos. Strauss knew what Ritter would have thought of the work as a whole; by casting the Knight of the Blank Moon in the guise of Brahms's First Symphony he gave a spot-on representation of how Ritter would have regarded what was being done to him (mm. 640–59). But the final episode of lyricism gives the don one last chance to speak for himself, as though Strauss were composing, on behalf of his friend, an imagined rebuttal. Here, finally, sincerity is not made to seem repulsive; beneath all his flaws, Ritter did what he did out of belief in an ideal that, had it been real, would have been beautiful.

However old the controversy, the central issue in reading *Ein Heldenleben* remains whether the work is meaningfully autobiographical. For better or worse, the most important pieces of evidence leave every possibility open. One could reasonably argue, for example, that the use of his own music for the "Hero's Works of Peace" was partly a matter of convenience and partly a way of setting off the knee-jerk critical response so important to Strauss's notoriety.[41] Strauss himself equivocated, as usual, obliquely affirming the tone poem's autobiographical character while hinting that there was more to the story.[42] Yet he also explicitly stated to Romain Rolland that the music for the "Hero's Companion" represented his wife, in all her feminine "complexity." This admission tightens the connection between music and personal experience, suggesting that the other main programmatic themes, the hero's "resignation" and his struggle against adversaries, could have a similarly detailed personal resonance beyond their general applicability to the life of any controversial artist.

Weltflucht, construed superficially as retirement from full-time conducting, was always a primary goal for the mature Strauss, but by 1898 the word also held a deeper meaning for him, given the isolation he imposed on himself by developing a post-Schopenhauerian aesthetic of music. Withdrawal was in fact a natural outcome of his *Vollendung;* his radical aesthetic independence ensured not only that he would have enemies, but indeed that every composer and critic would be disposed against him for one reason or another. The fact that *Heldenleben* surveys and summarizes the career of its hero, then, is itself evidence of an autobiographical agenda; such a summary was Strauss's personal goal for the work, as he attempted once again to close out the orchestral phase of his career and move on to opera. His only previous work with a newly invented program, *Tod und Verklärung*, was built around a similar goal, but now Strauss proceeded more methodically, bringing his subject sharply into focus before beginning composition. (Strauss remarked that the program had been entirely finished before he began composing; Werbeck refuted this notion but did find that the program was largely complete at the pre-compositional stage, and much more so than is the case in any other tone poem.)[43] The work actually has dual autobiographical connotations, then, as an ending and as a struggle against outside forces.

Surprisingly, a sustained reading of *Heldenleben* as an explicitly autobiographical work has never been published, perhaps because Strauss's comfortable bourgeois life has seemed not sufficiently eventful for the idea to hold water. But could he have been sincere when remarking that he found himself quite as interesting a musical subject as Alexander or Napoleon?[44] And what new perspectives on the work might be revealed by taking at face value a possibility implied in so many ways? The most important effect would be to revise our understanding of the antagonists, which figure prominently throughout the piece—not just in one or two sections—but which are too often reductively understood as caricatures of critics. Judging by the whole of Strauss's career up to 1898, the idea that critics significantly impeded his progress is untenable, especially given the parallel case of Mahler, who experienced the true measure of public rejection. Strauss managed to climb to the pinnacle of the Austro-German musical world in less than a decade, making a name for himself as a musical leader in cities from Chicago to St. Petersburg. The only case in which he experienced a reaction at all resembling the unanimous revulsion that we hear in *Heldenleben* came after the single Munich performance of *Guntram*, and not only was that reaction expected by Strauss (he had been prepared by the lukewarm reception of the four Weimar performances in 1894, and he had adjusted his compositional approach in the meantime, in *Till*), but in a sense it mirrored the private upheaval that had accompanied the work's revision. From an informed perspective, it is difficult to imagine that an autobiographical representation of Strauss's obstacles would concentrate predominantly on critics, even if it used signs of musical pedantry to delineate the character of the resistance.

As discussed in chapter 3, Strauss's most extensive prose sketch of the *Heldenleben* program describes the antagonists as "inner enemies and outer enemies."[45] The music makes no distinction between the two, but that choice is entirely consistent with biographical fact, given that both forms of opposition boiled over during the *Guntram* period. The first phase of Strauss's career (mm. 1–117?) had built confidently and inexorably toward a single moment of personal creative triumph, an ultimate goal served by all of the composer's creative activities: the completion of *Guntram* (perfect authentic cadence at m. 94). Reaching that goal brought a moment of private exhilaration but also, more or less immediately, a barrage of criticism not only from the public but from private quarters (most especially Ritter, but also Strauss's father, Rösch, Thuille, the Wagner family, and so on). And most important, it unleashed the philosophical doubts that sent Strauss into the philosophy of Nietzsche and began the subsequent period of intellectual doubt and unrest. What initially seemed to be an end, then—a culmination—instead became a beginning, whether Strauss liked it or not.

The heterogeneously motivated unease generated by the *Guntram* experience of course became a self-renewing fact of Strauss's inner life. Not surprisingly, the disposition of conflicts in *Heldenleben* replays the

moments when this struggle became most intense. After the initial erup-
tion of the inner and outer critics undermined the long-anticipated moment of triumph (m. 118), Strauss immersed himself in a period of
thoughtful private regrouping (G minor, m. 137). Courtship and marriage then followed, after which he felt prepared to confront the problem
directly (in *Till* and *Zarathustra*). This choice obviously bore fruit, as he
confirmed his place at the forefront of his generation of composers. But
public success was a product of thematizing rather than vanquishing his
inner doubts—the ones marked as unresolvable at the end of *Zarathustra*—so that he naturally made another turn inward and renewed his
efforts to grasp the unifying dilemma at work in all of his creations. The
"Hero's Works of Peace" can in this sense be heard as a representation
of *Heldenleben* itself—a moment of autobiographical reflection on what
he had tried to achieve in the tone poems and on the extent to which he
had succeeded. The work's failure to vanquish the doubts was by now a
foregone conclusion, like the "Ekel" that returns in an even more powerful guise than any it had assumed in *Zarathustra* (mm. 780–871). Two
facts remained, and Strauss's future existence would be defined by his
ability to negotiate their coexistence: the private joy of a creator whose
activities are nurtured by domestic stability, and the periodic moments
of anxiety produced by radical philosophical choices that he could neither
avoid nor comprehensively justify.

It is not surprising that in a work with the audacity to quote the
composer's previous music, the key to interpretation should be the relationship between the present composition and the others. Turning to
a comparison with *Don Quixote*, then, the first observation to be made is
that as in *Till* and *Zarathustra* Strauss here again used a basic programmatic and formal skeleton to construct two very different works. Although *Heldenleben* obviously places the trappings of sonata form in the
foreground—a male first group, a female second group, a development
built around battle imagery, a clear recapitulation that synthesizes the
male and female themes, and an epilogic coda—it does so with an artless
lack of ambiguity that stamps it as ironic. And indeed, the separate sections are just as easily heard, and more productively so, as reviving the
episodic technique of *Don Quixote*, in which each succeeding installment
of the story provides a new environment to be entered and investigated
by the themes of the hero. There is no section of this work in which the
protagonist does not appear; even when we do not immediately hear him,
he is clearly observing, for he soon enters and offers his reaction (most

notably in the "Adversaries" and "Companion" sections). Traditional sonata form has no stronger impact on the workings of this piece, then, than traditional variation form does on *Don Quixote*.

A further intertextual and formal issue relevant here is the connection between *Heldenleben* and Beethoven's *Eroica*. Strauss openly acknowledged the relationship but limited his discussion to the common key, the importance of the horns, and his decision to leave out the funeral march. Certainly he recognized, however, that the culmination of Beethoven's model played out in a fourth movement that combines features of the theme and variations and sonata form. There, as in Strauss's work, this combination allows the hero's reactions to vicissitudes and conquests to be monitored on an ongoing basis rather than distilled so as to fit into a generalized expressive paradigm. Sonata form could supply the kind of sweep that Strauss required in an orchestral work of "grand" character, but the variation set offered better opportunities for the continual narrative illustration that had now become an indispensable feature of his compositional style. Once again, Beethoven pointed the way toward the future or at least provided a model through which Strauss could imagine the future on his own terms.

The parallels between *Heldenleben* and *Don Quixote* at significant moments suggest further that Strauss is somehow offering us different versions of the same story. In *Heldenleben*, we come to know the protagonist through a swirling polyphonic mélange of leitmotifs, a representational technique that communicates not just heroism but psychological complexity. The same textural procedure introduces us to the "Knight of the Sorrowful Countenance"—the real protagonist of *Don Quixote*—by putting us inside his head during his slide into insanity. Strauss also chose a single method for handling the issues of companionship and femininity in the two works, although the common ground here is more difficult to spot because two characters in *Don Quixote* are folded into one in *Heldenleben*. The events involving companions follow the same pattern in both works: a conversation, sometimes contentious, with a partner who is obviously physically present leads to an F-sharp/G-flat section illustrating the redemptive power of the feminine.[46] One of the principal differences between the tone poems is of course that in *Heldenleben* feminine power is successfully integrated into the hero's personality. (Her impact is conveyed not just by the incorporation of her themes in the reprise but by the normalization at m. 627 of the chromatic anomaly from m. 7 [ex. 6.10].) He is able to succeed where Don Quixote is not precisely because the feminine ideal is for him not just an ideal, but one

Example 6.10a. *Ein Heldenleben*, mm. 7–10

Example 6.10b. *Ein Heldenleben*, mm. 627–30

side of an individual who also manifests the real-world qualities represented by Sancho, Don Quixote's only earthly companion.

With regard to the endings of *Don Quixote* and *Heldenleben*, the central musico-programmatic point cannot be grasped without reference to the earlier pair within this cycle. All four of the tone poems in the second cycle end with epilogues. *Till* and *Don Quixote* both retreat from the comically critical to the sentimental with happy endings of a playful sort, as if not wanting to leave an aftertaste of the serious matters considered within. But *Zarathustra* and *Heldenleben* thematize the continuing problem. The intrusion of the antagonists (mm. 857ff.) into the "idyll" replays, through ugliness rather than repetition, the effect of the Cs at the end of *Zarathustra*; it tells us is that such disturbances can never be eliminated. And if we miss the point, the none-too-subtle quotation of the *Zarathustra* Nature motive (m. 910) announces the obvious. Yet at the same time, the end of *Heldenleben* projects a level of acceptance, if not optimism, that is not found in *Zarathustra*, and that confirms the character's *Vollendung*. The emphasis is no longer on irreconcilability but on a mature method of dealing with irreconcilability. Creative activity and domestic security reinforce one another, in this music and in Strauss's adult life, insulating him from the catastrophic psychological consequences that otherwise might have attended his philosophical conclusions. From the time of the revision of *Guntram* Strauss had wondered how he could make a life for himself as a composer without being philosophically dishonest. His answer, the conclusion of the *Vollendete*, was by devoting himself to work and to family.

If Strauss found *Heldenleben* more acceptable than *Tod und Verklärung* as a farewell to the tone poem, it was not because the opera that followed it was substantially more successful than *Guntram*. Although initially received with greater politeness, *Feuersnot* quickly fell into a neglect almost as comprehensive as that of its predecessor. But this time Strauss saw no need to return to the drawing board. Here again the confidence he felt in his new maturity was grounded in the work's relationship to Beethoven. The letters to Bülow show that Beethoven was as strong a factor as any in Strauss's initial move to programmatic music.[47] Predictably, both attempts by Strauss to bring his orchestral period to an end returned to Beethoven and indeed to the two great symphonies of personal triumph. In the second example, the relationship between the two seems to have been much on his mind, as though they presented two alternate forms of victory—one now discredited but still possessing enough force to stimulate insecurity and thus dialogue.

Strauss's contemplation of these alternatives plays out in *Heldenleben* through interactions between the tonics of the two pieces, C and E-flat.[48] At the beginning of *Tod und Verklärung* he had already experimented, briefly, with the ambiguities inherent in the keys' close relationship—picking up, of course, on Beethoven's similar game at the beginning of the Fifth. Now, however, he exploited C as a disruptive force rather than a clarification, and he did so systematically, across the work, with the protagonist's E-flat heroic vision constantly subject to doubts associated with the obsolete redemptive vision marked by C. In the opening theme, Cs take an unusually prominent role, as though probing to determine whether a redirection might be possible (in m. 2, m. 6, and the fourth beat of m. 3, where the C seems to have replaced an E-flat); they do not elicit any indication of C minor, but by m. 7 the chromatic alterations confirm that E-flat has been problematized. C goes on to assume a more important structural role in this opening section, supporting versions of the main theme at mm. 45 and 98 and thereby signaling its growing power. From here to the end, C consistently makes itself felt at moments of tension. The high point of the G-minor section after the first appearance of the antagonists is in C minor (m. 161). The battle begins in C minor, and the trumpet's highest note is C^{111}. The transition from abject disgust to the *Vollendung* moves from C major to E-flat major, but traces of the struggle remain in the new melody's prominent C (m. 845), which on its return at m. 857 triggers renewed strife. Finally, the last allusion to C, at mm. 910–12, omits the actual note but makes a strong gesture simply by virtue of the Nature motive's associations.

The tone C is one of the few cases with regard to which Strauss's music shows strong but conflicting extramusical associations: it was the key of his most carefully constructed metaphysical vision but also of his unsurpassably brilliant image of absolute objectivity. Neither one nor the other of these allusive precedents seems to have dominated in *Heldenleben*. Instead, the note now stood for a debate that he wished to leave behind. Like the triumph of the *Eroica*, the triumph of *Heldenleben* is thoroughly human: it is not a struggle against fate or against anything larger than life, but a struggle to achieve the best that is available to humans. In the end, Strauss wished to live his life equally distant from the chimeras—metaphysics and the complete absence of metaphysics— that he had tried to conceive through C-related music. His success at achieving this goal can be measured in one way by the fact that his last two programmatic orchestral works would be "symphonies" and thus another kind of return to Beethovenian roots, but one focused on the great model's alter ego: the Beethoven of the *Pastoral*, the "characteristic" Beethoven. If he had not convinced himself that other, more contentious matters had been settled, that choice would not have been possible.

7

Absolute Music, Twentieth-Century Aesthetics, and the Symphonies of Richard Strauss

$\mathcal{T}$here is no shortage of work-immanent explanations for the failure of Strauss's final two large-scale orchestral pieces.[1] As examples of the calculatedly overblown, *Symphonia domestica* (1903) and *Eine Alpensinfonie* (1915) may be unsurpassed in the history of Western music. Beneath it all, however, the works' problems reflect a change in the composer, a new ambivalence, as though whatever irresistible imperative had driven the first seven tone poems no longer existed. From early in the genesis of these works, Strauss questioned whether he had anything further to say in the orchestral medium. In a 1902 interview with the *Neue freie Presse*, after confirming that his current projects included two "symphonic poems," he admitted that thus far he had developed only their subject matter (*Stoff*), and that he could not tell which of the two, if either, would ever be realized. Furthermore, he revealed that an earlier post-*Heldenleben* project, provisionally titled "Spring" (*Frühling*), had progressed much further—well into the musical stages—only to stall. (A particell of several hundred measures survives.)[2] As disappointing as such cases could be, Strauss concluded whimsically, one was powerless to prevent them: "we conscious humans have no control over the creative principle in us."[3]

The anonymous reporter wisely took Strauss's rationalization with a grain of salt, avoiding a direct challenge but noting that certain parts of the composer's face appeared to contradict others, "as with all ironists." This suspicion might have been explored further, for inhibitors of Strauss's creativity at that time are not difficult to imagine. After adding four substantial masterpieces to the two that had made his reputation, he found himself firmly ensconced in the standard repertoire, no longer required to battle for survival. His conducting career had peaked at the same time (in the city where only a short time before he had been a qualified failure), giving him all the security and prestige that an artist could hope to enjoy.[4] But for a composer who thrived on confrontation, success could be an enemy—at least in the orchestral realm where the great struggle had been fought. The five years between *Heldenleben* and *Domestica* represented a greater length of time than he had required to produce all of the works of the second cycle. And although some of that period was taken up with *Feuersnot*, that comic "non-opera" (*Nichto-perchen*) was hardly comparable to *Guntram* in proportions or intentions.[5] For the first time in some fifteen years, Strauss found himself without a clear direction as an orchestral composer, and by 1902 the public and critics such as Erich Urban were beginning to notice that he had reached some kind of an impasse.[6]

But why not move on, once and for all, to opera, now that the di-lemmas of his youth no longer obtained? Why insist on continued labor in a genre that no longer stimulated him? The sixteen-year composi-tional history of the *Alpensinfonie* testifies to a deep and continuing inner conflict. Over a length of time longer than that from *Macbeth* to *Do-mestica*, Strauss stubbornly refused to let this piece go unfinished, giving new meaning to his creed that he would produce "not what I can, but what I must." Yet more than once he claimed to be fed up with the project; he may not have touched it at all from 1903 until 1911, and much of the subsequent activity came while he was waiting for Hof-mannsthal to supply him with a new libretto. *Domestica* likewise filled up the hours until his operatic impulses found an outlet, and yet he con-tinued to work on it even after he had begun *Salome*, no doubt because it dealt in a uniquely straightforward way with subject matter nearer to his heart than any other. Like the *Alpensinfonie*, it reached completion because its personal significance outweighed all artistic challenges and misgivings.

As problematic as the creative process obviously was, once he had finished these pieces, Strauss's attitude toward them changed entirely. He cannot help but have noticed that public acclaim did not rescue the works from an unprecedentedly harsh critical reaction, which ranged from distaste to revulsion.[7] Yet for whatever reason, Strauss abandoned all his doubts. The Carnegie Hall premiere of *Domestica*, which produced a minor scandal, left him convinced that the work was "brilliant" in every respect.[8] Shortly after conducting the first performance of the *Alpensinfonie* in Dresden in October 1915 (and famously commenting "I have finally learned to orchestrate"), Strauss declared to Hofmannsthal that "it really is good!"[9] These expressions of confidence were not meant for public consumption and thus had nothing to do with shaping reception. In both compositions, a difficult genesis gave way to true fondness, which remained with him to the end of his life (manifested in continued performances, for example on the 1948 London tour).

Strauss's reasons for finishing these works and for remaining partial to them in the face of opposition from antagonists and friends alike are crucial for understanding what the mature composer took away from the intellectual dilemmas of his youth. I would suggest that two were paramount, both of them highly personal but easy to uncover when the surviving sources are placed in context. First, *Domestica* and the *Alpensinfonie* together lay out the components of the worldview that Strauss evolved in response to his philosophical crisis of the 1890s. In a variety of documents, most of them produced solely for his own use, Strauss described his personal and artistic devotion to a complex of mutually reinforcing ideals: work, family, and nature. These components were valuable not just in their own right but because they cooperatively insulated him from the fruitless metaphysical dilemmas that had plagued him for so long. Second, the return to the symphony, in works that had nothing but the name in common with the nineteenth-century symphonic tradition, had the dual benefit of closing out his orchestral career as he had begun it— with two symphonies—and highlighting Strauss's conscious disengagement of his art from an ostensible metaphysical capacity. This latter effect raises important questions about Strauss's relationship with Schoenberg, whose modernism diverged from Strauss's not only in its single-minded pursuit of atonality but also in its increasing preoccupation with "absolute" genres (in the case of Schoenberg's instrumental music). Considered from this perspective, Schoenberg's and Strauss's modernisms grew as mirror images of one another, the former devoting new means to an older aesthetic, the latter using existing materials to promote an entirely new conception of the art.

Symphonia domestica and Eine Alpensinfonie as Documents of the Mature Straussian Worldview

The precedent of *Till Eulenspiegel* was obviously not far from Strauss's mind when he settled down to compose *Symphonia domestica:* superficially jocular, in F major, and relying extensively on moment-by-moment illustration, both works ended a hiatus during which the major creative product was an opera. Together with *Don Quixote* these three pieces comprise a type, by virtue of the controlling authority of tone painting, although in this latest example Strauss somehow managed to outdo himself yet again (as noted in 1910 by Theo Schäfer).[10] The step by which he upped the ante—and earned the consternation of critics not yet able to decide about Strauss, such as Romain Rolland and Rudolf Louis—was the incorporation of the explicitly autobiographical approach of *Heldenleben*, which had been disconcerting enough in a composition that kept its distance from *Tonmalerei.* One innovation of the new work was thus to bridge a gap between the two kinds of tone poem in the second cycle and perhaps, by extension, between the critical mission of the one and the forward-looking philosophical hypothesizing of the other.

To most listeners, none of this altered the perception that Strauss had reached a new low. Beneath Franz Strauss's caveat about the household-service implications of the word "domestic" lay an insinuation that his son was not only unconcerned with distinctions between high and low but blind to them—which is to say that he had bad taste.[11] Rolland, one of the most cultured champions that Strauss ever had, flatly stated that *Domestica*, or more precisely, the program of *Domestica*, "verges, and sometimes a bit more than that, on bad taste."[12] Louis similarly believed that the "ludicrous and tasteless" program had spoiled music that might otherwise be considered among Strauss's finest.[13] The recommended path, from each of these advisors, was that taken by Mahler (though none of them mentioned him by name): suppression, a reconceptualization of the program as scaffolding rather than as an aid to interpretation.[14]

The desperation behind this suggestion should be obvious. With *Domestica*, suppression was a completely unworkable option. Withholding the program of a non-illustrative programmatic work raises no questions with the audience, who has no reason to suspect its existence. (The discovery of a program for Schoenberg's First String Quartet, for example, came as a complete surprise.)[15] *Domestica*, on the other hand, is filled with moments that are obviously connected to particular extramusical events, whether one knows precisely what those events are or not. For a composer to deny them would at best be flirtation—it would be to tell the audience that there is something he is not telling them. Moreover, while Strauss did enjoy playing that game with his audience occasionally, his friends actually had in mind something more serious and more strange: to safeguard the peace of mind of that spectacularly self-deceiving listener who would endeavor to pass the entire forty minutes without once noticing a moment of pictorialism. Such an experience would of course hardly count as engagement with the work on its own terms.

Fear may be the most reasonable explanation of how such an argument could be advanced by sophisticated cultural observers. Those who admired Strauss and felt a personal concern for his reputation sensed an unprecedented danger in his new combination of rampant illustration and unconcealed autobiography. These two tendencies, now united and brought unapologetically into the open, synthesized the most controversial aspects of *Don Quixote* and *Heldenleben*. In so doing they pushed Strauss's orchestral project, apparently by design, much further in a direction that to some had already signaled the beginnings of a decline. Ernest Newman described this "unfortunate" progression explicitly. In *Heldenleben*, which he considered to be in some respects Strauss's finest composition, he nevertheless heard moments of "laborious stupidity, unworthy of a man of Strauss's genius." And he declined to write them off as accidents: "there must be a flaw, one thinks, in the mind of a man who can deliberately spoil a great and beautiful artistic conception by inserting such monstrosities as these in it." Subsequently, *Domestica* "did not dispel these fears" but deepened them, with "realistic effects in the score . . . at once so atrociously ugly and so pitiably foolish that one listens to them with regret that a composer of genius should ever have fallen so low."[16] Focusing on himself as programmatic subject had caused Strauss, in Newman's view, to lose all sense of "balance as an orchestral writer," and no signs were yet available in 1908 that the development could be reversed.

Divergent cultural perspectives thus did not prevent Rolland, Louis, and Newman from reaching the same conclusions about *Domestica*. And these were not knee-jerk reactions; each writer couched the critique in explicitly constructive terms: they wanted Strauss to succeed, and they believed that they could help by separating the wheat from the chaff. Strangely, none of them addressed the likelihood that Strauss had anticipated a negative reception. It is at least conceivable that this possibility figured in his decision to hold the premiere in New York, where a scandal was virtually assured but could be written off as American incomprehension (thus tainting future attacks made on similar grounds). Whether or not that advantage occurred to him, there can be no doubt that he intended *Domestica* at least in part as a provocation. The sort of prank played by Till in a comfortably removed folkish setting Strauss now perpetrated in the "real world," at the risk of earning, on the artistic level, the same fate as his character. Indeed, the features that horrified even his friends strike one as a kind of death wish, not only because they dwell on material resistant to sacralization (e.g., childcare, into which the idealized vision of the child deflates) but because they undo the sublimation of art and love. One hardly knows which would be more difficult for a critic in 1904 to accept: the reduction of artistic creation to an evening's labor in a kind of workshop; the suggestion that excessively profound thought leads to confusion; or the transformation of redemption-through-love into the routine of the marital bed. What is certain is that in the process of describing his domestic paradise he took aim at the principal themes of romanticism.

The *Alpensinfonie* is of course another work built around illustration, but it did not start that way. Indeed, the story of its genesis is that of a program undergoing marked transformations as the composer simultaneously honed a philosophical message and searched for the best musical means to convey it. That genesis has been described by Rainer Bayreuther and Walter Werbeck, but without sustained reference to the personal concerns that prevented the work from going the way of *Frühling*.[17] In contrast to these writers I would suggest that the work's connection to Nietzsche, which became explicit with the diary entry of 19 May 1911 in which Strauss declared that he would use the title "Der Antichrist," must have been conscious and determined from the beginning. The connection is not proved by a single factor, however, but by the simultaneous presence of three features whose confluence points toward Nietzsche. First, as is well known, the biography of the painter Karl Stauffer, which was to have been the programmatic subject of the "Künstlertragödie" (the *Alpensinfonie*'s first incarnation), had obvious parallels with Nietzsche's: the descent into insanity, the seeking of wisdom through contemplation at mountain retreats, rejection by a woman he loved (cf. Lou Andreas-Salomé). Second, Strauss's fragmentary descriptions of Stauffer, which served as mnemonic devices, relied on the jargon of his own Nietzsche reception from the early 1890s: Stauffer is a "consciously working artist" ("bewußt arbeitenden Künstler"), plagued by "doubt" ("Zweifel") but given to moments of relief in the presence of nature. Finally, the image of the sunrise, which figured in the program from the beginning and was apparently the first music that Strauss composed for the work, not only recalled Nietzsche but harked back to the central image of Strauss's previous Nietzsche-related work.

When Strauss declared "I will name my Alpensinfonie: the Antichrist," he was deciding to publicize a feature of the work that had been intentional all along but that he had meant to keep to himself. Even though he eventually reversed his decision about the title, the outburst confirms the obvious: that his efforts in this piece had been directed against the same musical, religious, and philosophical complex that had preoccupied him since the mid-1890s. Two of Nietzsche's principal enemies, Schopenhauer and Christianity, were to be held responsible for trapping Wagner and misdirecting his artistic genius. But the finished composition would also offer a solution, through "work . . . and worship of glorious eternal nature." Nature would replace metaphysics, by stimulating creativity, giving one energy for work, and freeing music from its ill-conceived association with religion.[18] That solution had not been available to Mahler, whose pantheism had exacerbated the problem of religion rather than solved it. In a diary entry from 22 November 1915, after praising "the Jew Carl Becker" for being one of the few to recognize that the *Alpensinfonie* "overcomes . . . the temptation of the unknowable," Strauss blamed both Jews and Christians for the insidious workings of metaphysics on artists such as Mahler. "It was an unproductive race such as that of the Jews that could devise this Christian, Jewish metaphysics, that could replace production with speculation."[19] The future of music lay with nature because nature knew nothing of this history.

The initial plans for "Die Alpen," which supplanted the "Künstlertragödie" program, followed an artist's evolving perception of nature to the stage at which it could be used as a liberation from metaphysics. This first version of the symphony fell into a four-movement scheme moving from a mountain climb (as first movement; this is the first mention of an *Aufstieg* in any of the sketches) through "rustic joy" (second movement), "dreams and ghosts" (third movement), and finally "freedom through work: artistic creation" (final movement). This plan retained its basic outline over the long hiatus, with the principal alteration in 1911 coming in the final movement's re-titling as "freedom through nature." But as Strauss became more involved in the piece, he collapsed the four-movement plan into two movements, the first once again representing the climb, the second meditating on mankind's predilection for error as a seeker of God and metaphysical truth. This plan too was abandoned, of course, with the result that in the final product only one movement, representing a climb up and down a mountain, survived.

Given the precedents of *Till*, *Don Quixote*, and *Domestica*, this shift toward illustration clearly intensified the work's critical impact vis-à-vis metaphysics, although that fact has been universally overlooked. Likewise, in this final one-movement plan Strauss followed the example of *Domestica* by folding into the piece a significant component of his personal, post-metaphysical worldview: the belief that a healthy intellectual future could be built on the relationship between nature and artistic creation. This step was intended to respond to the Nietzschean issues with which he had dealt in his private reflections and particularly in *Zarathustra*, issues that were still on his mind after the end of the second cycle. The continuing presence of this piece of unfinished business is indicated by the several important ways in which the *Alpensinfonie* engages with *Zarathustra*, ways that simultaneously recapitulate the prior discussion and push things forward.

The use of a program in which an individual climbs to physical heights in order to think high thoughts is already a straightforward evocation of Nietzsche, the philosopher "from high mountains" (as he calls himself in the "epode" of *Jenseits von Gut und Böse*). Thus the return of the "Nature" motive on the summit (first in F, m. 566, then in C, m. 597) clinches the obvious, reminding us of Zarathustra's experience of the mountain sunrise and drawing a parallel between this climb and Zarathustra's own return to the mountain. The characters' experiences also parallel one another at the base of the mountain. Strauss's musical setting of the "Entry into the Forest" strongly evokes, in its final section, Zarathustra's encounter with the forest hermit in "Hinterweltlern" (it is important to recall Nietzsche's pun on "Hinterwäldlern" here). In both instances Strauss cast the forest in A-flat, with the key serving as a potential second key area of the sonata form. Likewise, A-flat moves both times to G after an initial eight-bar period (G major in *Zarathustra*, G minor in the *Alpensinfonie* [m. 237]), then winds its way back to a well-prepared perfect authentic cadence (m. 261 in the *Alpensinfonie*). A lyrical cadential extension follows, in the *Alpensinfonie* strengthening the allusion by quoting the distinctive and saccharine raised supertonic moving to the major mediant (mm. 263–64) (ex. 7.1).

The recollection of Zarathustra's experience in the woods tells us something else that ought to be obvious, namely that the need for mountain air is motivated by the same factors in the two pieces. The encounter

Example 7.1. *Eine Alpensinfonie*, mm. 263–64

with Nature at the midpoint produces another parallelism, this time in response, with a culminating but open-ended section in C major that both celebrates the recognition of a higher truth and rules out its capacity for finality. In *Zarathustra*, the return of "Nature" leads, after a period of tonal uncertainty, to the arrival of the waltz (in C major), the musico-programmatic goal of the work. Likewise, in the *Alpensinfonie* the appearance of "Nature" in C major initiates a climactic section in that key, now highlighted by a meaningful interweaving of the three principal leit-motifs. The confluence of "Nature," the "Mountain" theme (so labeled by Strauss), and a theme meant to represent "Worship" (*Anbetung*) of the natural world marks an important difference between the *Alpensinfonie* and *Zarathustra:* nature now represents not unfathomable objectivity but a healthy focus for religious impulses (ex. 7.2). But as in *Zarathustra*, the attainment of the programmatic goal can only be temporary, given the Nietzschean reality that any redemption must eternally renew itself by starting from scratch. For philosophical reasons, C major cannot last, even though its programmatic significance far outweighs that of the tonic.

The philosophical problem that Strauss faced in his Nietzschean com-positions—how to move beyond pure criticism to the creation of a pos-itively defined worldview—was the same problem that Nietzsche himself faced and failed to solve. I would argue that Strauss found more success than Nietzsche, at least insofar as he found ways to conceptualize a life radically purged of metaphysics. Nevertheless, the formal structure of these last two symphonies indicates that Strauss concluded, in a perfectly reasonable interpretation of the philosopher, that a positive Nietzschean worldview could not be separated from criticism, that is, from an ongoing repetition of the thought processes that led to the critique in the first place. This conclusion would explain why Strauss returned in the *Alpen-*

Example 7.2. *Eine Alpensinfonie*, mm. 597–606

sinfonie and *Domestica* to the formal approach applied in the tone poems up to and including *Zarathustra*: a species of sonata form that emphasized its functional inadequacies. Now the revaluation of musical values was animated by a deeper purpose, however; it reinforced a personal philosophy that would replace the one he had rejected.

The inversion of sonata procedure in the *Alpensinfonie* follows the lines laid out in *Zarathustra*. Both works collapse onto a defective recapitulation whose inadequacy plays out in relatively straightforward tonal and thematic gestures. As discussed in chapter 6, the recapitulation in *Zarathustra* proceeds in a direct reversal of normal procedure, with the first subject ("Of Joys and Passions") returning in a weakened guise and in the sonata form's second key (A-flat). In the *Alpensinfonie*, the entire recapitulatory space ("Tempest and Storm. Descent") is controlled by the dominant, B-flat minor. That the work as a whole is in E-flat major seems beyond question; the opening B-flat material ("Nacht") gradually clarifies into the dominant of E-flat, in which key the first subject appears ("Der Aufstieg"). (The move to E-flat is further prepared by a diversion to A major, the tritone equivalent of E-flat, for the "Sonnenaufgang.")[20]

The tritone-related keys of A-flat and D serve as a second-key complex, with D marked as the authentic second key by the entrance of the second subject (m. 325). The mirroring of this exposition and ascent by a B-flat-controlled descent does not suggest B-flat as tonic, however. The subsequent entrance of the "Ausklang," in E-flat and supporting a transmuted version of the earlier C-major climax, clearly identifies B-flat as the dominant. The "Abstieg," then, which recalls the themes of the exposition in reverse order, presents the strange phenomenon of a dominant-based recapitulation, a recapitulation gone wrong.

The ending of the work deepens the problem by intensifying the functional ambiguity of B-flat and E-flat, in an epilogic "Ausklang" in E-flat and a return to the B-flat framing device of "Nacht." As its name suggests, the character of "Ausklang" as conclusion is resigned, not triumphant, and certainly not heroically corrective. In particular, the entrance of the organ (a fatalistic allusion to *Zarathustra*) and the perplexing absence of strings during the initial presentation of the melody (mm. 1047ff.) confirm that this music has no capacity for closure. The "soft ecstasy" in the performance direction responds to the perception of truth, not of eternity. The passage does act as an abbreviated second recapitulation by presenting the second subject in the tonic, but it does so too late and too briefly. Its purpose then is not to remedy the basic defect of the first recapitulation but to offer a nostalgic vision of what should have happened. And it does so with a clear humility and a sense of its own limitations, finally sinking onto the dominant for the return of "Nacht."

The same sort of tonally inverted recapitulation is found in *Domestica*, a work in F with a second key of D that forms the basis of important recapitulatory events. But here the troublesome recapitulation is prepared by formal operations that are in conflict with themselves from the beginning of the work. Notwithstanding his justification of formal freedoms in programmatic music, Strauss seems in *Domestica* to be less concerned with finding a design uniquely adequate to the programmatic idea than with responding negatively to the symphonic expectations that he sets up. The stated four-part plan of thematic exposition, scherzo, adagio, and finale would be more credible if the formal divisions of the music actually coincided with the labels. Diagram 7.1 shows, however, that formal divisions before and after the beginning of the scherzo have far more musical weight than those to which Strauss's labels draw our attention. Indeed, the first two of the three labeled themes comprise a fully integrated and orthodox sonata-form movement, complete with restatement of the second-key material in the tonic. The most credible second-key

I. Thema. (mm. 1-40)	II. Thema. (mm. 41-156)	III. Thema. (mm. 157-217)	Scherzo. (mm. 218-598)

miniature sonata form

1st subject	2nd subject (3 motives)	Dev. 2nd subject (3 motives)	
F	B B flat F sharp	F	F: PAC
m. 1	41 47 55	99 110 115	152

large-scale sonata form

1st subject	(bridge?)		2nd subject	baby's screams; aunts and uncles		
F		F: PAC	d D		D PAC	extension
		152	157 182	192-217	218 363	-393
m. 1					quotation from Guntram, Act III, finale	end of scherzo/ exposition?

episodes (as dev.?):	transition to Wiegenlied	Wiegenlied	Mässig langsam
return to F		g	G
393-467	468-516	517-558	559-98
"Heimweg," m. 436-67			

Diagram 7.1. Conflicting formal divisions in the first two sections of *Symphonia domestica*.

area of the large-scale sonata form, on the other hand, concludes with a strong cadence 145 measures into the scherzo, far from any of the labeled divisions. And this move too is revoked, by an immediate return to F major and a curious epilogue concluding on a cadence that emphasizes its finality with a Mozartian triple suspension (m. 465).

Domestica differs from the *Alpensinfonie*, then, in that it never really gets off the ground as a sonata, even though it twice makes an attempt. The unexpected reappearances of the tonic key (at m. 152 and m. 436) revoke the large-scale sonata form, and the piece enters a series of episodes (standing in for development, as in the earlier sonata-based tone poems) without having had a functional exposition. Given this voluntary deficiency, the finale comes across less as a recapitulation than as what it says it is: a double fugue serving as fourth movement. As at the beginning, the themes of the father and mother appear in F major and B minor, and a reappearance of Bubi's theme in its original D major brings the fight to an end (m. 1060). As if to reinforce the fact that, tonally speaking, nothing has changed, that theme returns once more in the coda, this time in majestic culmination scored for horns. Such is the power of this moment that even Papa's original theme, the first significant motive of the work, is drawn into D, triple forte in the trombones (m. 1343). The music does not reach a final cadence in D, of course, instead lurching back to F for the coda. But the message is clear: the tonal rules of this work are profoundly different from those of the sonata.

By its belated introduction of F major, then, and by driving the piece to an end that is not justified in terms of tonal structure, the coda draws attention to the work's formal anomalies. This tendency of *Domestica* to question itself also plays out in situations less closely related to structure. On the first page of the score we hear a supertonic rapture, labeled "Papa composes" in a sketch, that is introduced by the prosaic sounds of Papa's good mood and broken off by his annoyance when his inspiration runs out (ex. 7.3). By framing a moment of creation with "nonmusical" music,

Example 7.3. *Symphonia domestica*, mm. 1–16

Strauss holds the act of expression at a remove, while we observe an individual slipping into and out of a creative reverie. (Fittingly, his performance direction here is "träumerisch.") The implication is that all such moments could be viewed in this way, from the outside, with a clear sense that what is going on is not real. Another prominent instance of putting quotation marks around a moment of ostensible musical profundity comes when we first hear the moving and expressive theme of the son. Once again the ideal and the real are juxtaposed, at the expense of the former, when the theme's quiet denouement gives way to the child's piercing screams (m. 192). Strauss's technique is not impartial here; he wants us to retain our perspective, to recognize that this is an indulgence in sentimentality.

Along the same lines, the prominent examples of intertextuality in *Domestica* ask us to listen from the outside and not to get caught up in music's powers of seduction. The Mendelssohn allusion (ex. 7.4), widely recognized since the work's premiere, allows various interpretive possibilities, but all of them bring the music down to earth. It is of course a lullaby, which in the domestic setting qualifies it as a species of *Hausmusik*. If the allusion is actually a quotation, which is not unthinkable, Strauss's purpose may have been to borrow not just Mendelssohn's mel-

Example 7.4a. *Symphonia domestica*, mm. 519–24

Example 7.4b. Mendelssohn, "Venetianisches Gondellied," *Lieder ohne Worte*, op. 19b, nr. 6, mm. 8–11

ody but also the subtle banality associated with the *Lieder ohne Worte.* Either way, the music's hint of ordinariness combines with its familiarity to ensure that we will not be fully taken in—we are watching a scene of musical expression but not participating in it. The use of a Mozart allusion at the crucial moment of resolution (m. 1119) similarly prevents us from hearing that music with absolute immediacy. (A similar moment in *Der Rosenkavalier* has been discussed by Lewis Lockwood.)[21] A number of reasons moved Strauss to eschew at this moment the powerful nineteenth-century musical technique through which he had become famous: among them, an eagerness finally to please his father (now in his eighties) and a desire to emphasize the modesty and simplicity of the domestic life that had become the center of his existence. But Strauss also apparently concluded that the bliss associated with domestic life was unreachable, or uncommunicable, by "modern" music. In citing music from a past that could never be recovered, Strauss knew that he was being sentimental and furthermore that his listeners would have no choice but to recognize their own experience of this music as sentimental. The effect is not to undercut its power, though, but to undercut the potential exaggeration of that power.

Citation plays an even more important role in the *Alpensinfonie*, with many of the work's most important moments drawing on intertextual associations. The fact that Strauss borrowed (unconsciously or otherwise) a passage from the second movement of the Bruch Violin Concerto, for example, is all the more striking because of the fame of the source and the prominence of its location in the new work: at the very culmination (mm. 602ff.). Strauss's playful acknowledgment of the connection in rehearsal—"once again from the Bruch concerto, gentlemen"—apparently produced no confusion whatsoever.[22] But he might just as easily have said "once again from *Zarathustra,*" or "once again from the Grail," or "once again from my Second Symphony" (ex. 7.5). None of these allusions is any less recognizable than the Bruch, and they all mark important formal events. Indeed, the example from *Parsifal* simultaneously refers to the "Streiter der Liebe" leitmotif from *Guntram,* which itself refers to the Grail: it acts as an allusion to an allusion, highlighting the process of allusion itself.

For listeners who noticed these references—and any reasonably experienced listener in 1915 would have recognized them—the work could not support the kind of emotional or spiritual immediacy for which late-nineteenth-century Austro-German composers of all persuasions strived. Using the manner of *Heldenleben* but with a greater range of source

Example 7.5a. *Eine Alpensinfonie*, mm. 1–8

Example 7.5b. Strauss, Symphony No. 2 in F Minor, first movement, op. 12, mm. 1–4

and formal placement, the *Alpensinfonie* fashions itself as a commentary on music. In a sense it keeps its distance from the art, then, and the listener has no choice but to do likewise, maintaining perspective not only on the citations but on the composition that delivers them. Furthermore, the music funnels that sense of externality specifically at the issue of Strauss's artistic development, which is highlighted through the allusions' progression: from the first large orchestral work that received an opus number (the Second Symphony), through *Guntram*, to the intellectually decisive *Zarathustra*. On this level, the *Alpensinfonie* sets itself up as a conclusion, a final statement on a formative process begun with the composer's first engagement with the orchestral medium.

The goal of that process is deeply connected to the goal of *Domestica*, however differently the two are treated artistically. In his first thoughts for *Domestica*, Strauss had already drawn a connection between everyday family life and the ideas raised on the opening pages of *Zarathustra*: a poetic treatment of the work's subject begins, "My wife, my child and my music / Nature and sun, these are my happiness."[23] This complex of themes, which defined the only redemption Strauss sought or could understand, also governed the "Künstlertragödie," which initially dealt primarily with Stauffer's domestic situation (not just his romantic attachment but the couple's life together) and his struggle to succeed as an artist. Nature, which was to serve in that work as a backdrop, eventually took center stage, while in *Domestica* it dropped fully from view. Art remained central to both of them, however, so that in their final versions the two symphonies comprised a pair, one member of which considered the relationship between art and the family, and the other, the parallels between natural and artistic experience. Only together, then, did they communicate the complete picture of how Strauss meant to ground his post-metaphysical artistic practice.

The Symphonic Ideal in Strauss's Early and Late Works for Orchestra

Along with their programmatic and structural similarities, *Domestica* and the *Alpensinfonie* share the strange paradoxical claim (expressed in their titles) to be materially oriented symphonies. There may have been an element of retrospection in this choice; a century earlier their "characteristic" tendencies would not have seemed unusual.[24] But the history of the symphony in the second half of the nineteenth century had long since closed off that option. The genre's reemergence in the 1870s, after disappearing for a quarter-century, depended on the mutually reinforcing traits of autonomy and grandeur. (Brahms and Bruckner both understood this, despite their differences; Mahler initially did not.) As separation from phenomenal reality increased, so did the once-lost prestige of the genre. Nietzsche described the origins of this crucial development in 1878, the year of Brahms's First Symphony, reflecting on the most influential symphony of the century: "At a certain place in Beethoven's Ninth Symphony . . . [one] might feel that he is floating above the earth in a starry dome, with the dream of *immortality* in his heart; all the stars seem to glimmer around him, and the earth seems to sink ever deeper downwards."[25] This attitude about the Ninth would persist well into the twentieth century, for example in Georg Gräner's 1924 biography of Bruckner, issued in the *Die Musik* series edited by Strauss. "Movement by movement," Gräner held, the Ninth rose above the "human/earthly" to the "spiritual/super-earthly," until it reached a call for human unity that sprang from Beethoven's "cosmic experience of feeling."[26]

For the late Nietzsche, of course, this musical direction, which he had supported enthusiastically in his youth, was unhealthy and even sinister. In construing metaphysics as a symbolic rejection of the earth, his critique of the musical autonomy associated with the symphony thus merged with his opposition to Wagner. The evil perpetrated by this collective musical idealism was at bottom just another manifestation of the general problem—as is demonstrated by his other uses of the symbol. Zarathustra, who in his first speech admonishes his listeners "to remain

true to the earth . . . and not to believe those who speak to you of su-
perterrestrial hopes," later rails against "the sick and dying who despised
the body and the earth and invented the things of heaven and the redeeming drops of blood."[27] In *Beyond Good and Evil*, the critical counterpart of *Zarathustra*, Nietzsche traced the process by which the Christian
church "reverse[d] the whole love of the earthly and of dominion over
the earth into hatred of the earth and the earthly."[28] The substance of
Nietzsche's comment on the Ninth, then, is that Beethoven gave this
worldview artistic form (whether he meant to or not), communicating it
through the uniquely powerful medium of the symphony. Nietzsche's
choice of Beethoven rather than Wagner to illustrate this point is telling;
the problem was bigger than Wagner and became most dangerous in a
work that predated and in a sense overshadowed Wagner's achievement.

This message would have been clear to Strauss, who knew *Human,
All Too Human* (see chapter 3 on its connection to *Zarathustra*) and in
any case could easily have pieced together the argument from other
works. Because music, by its very nature, was implicated in the human
tendency to metaphysics, autonomy was not a way out but rather the
deepest, most dangerous manifestation of the problem. At the same time,
however, when properly understood, autonomy was also a prominent and
accessible target. In the 1902 interview with the *Neue freie Presse*, Strauss
confirmed his grasp of the status quo but kept his critical intentions to
himself: "Why should music not have the capacity to be philosophical?
Indeed, metaphysics and music are two sisters. One can express one's
worldview even in music, and if one wishes to begin to grasp the riddles
of the universe, it may be that one can do so only with the help of music."
This remark establishes beyond any doubt that the relationship between
music and metaphysics was on Strauss's mind during the conception of
these symphonies. The works' realization, however, could not have announced more clearly that the composer's views on the matter were outside the mainstream and decisively critical.

From a musical standpoint, Strauss understood the mainstream from
the inside, although his tone poems obscure this fact. His first two major
works for orchestra, like his last two, were symphonies, but while the
latter flouted tradition, the former seem determined to fit in. This fact
is particularly important because neither of the early symphonies was
purely a student work, however great the differences between them and
the tone poems. In the case of the Second Symphony in F Minor (op.
12), the public's acceptance of it as the work of a master is evident from
the locations where it was performed within a year of its premiere: New

York, Cologne, Meiningen, Munich, and Berlin. The First Symphony in D Minor, which Strauss withdrew, nevertheless impressed Hermann Levi (and his superiors) enough to be included on a regular subscription concert, after initially being accepted only for rehearsal. Steinitzer described the premiere as a triumph, celebrated by eighteen hundred enthusiastic listeners and culminating in a politically significant public congratulation from Levi.[29] Both pieces thus represented attempts by a mature if young composer (Strauss had completed his studies of form and counterpoint with Friedrich Wilhelm Meyer before composing the First) who wanted to contribute as soon as possible to the collective project of making the symphony great again. In the early 1880s, before Strauss met Ritter, he undoubtedly considered that effort the highest calling of a composer. In the early 1900s, at the conclusion of everything that Ritter had brought about, he cannot have forgotten his first steps along the road.

The failure of the early symphonies to attract scholarly attention, and particularly to elicit commentary on whether they had any relationship to his future artistic choices, is largely a function of their style. The features of these works most remarked on by listeners have been their obvious debts to great composers of the past and their astonishing formal control and correctness. Both of these supported a consensus that despite obvious technical polish the symphonies lacked originality. This assessment did not come in the form of an attack, however, such as Mahler would have to face on the grounds of insufficient thematic novelty but excessive formal and orchestrational innovations. By apparently playing it safe all the way around, Strauss at least ensured that he would not be hissed.

Yet if he was playing it safe, these tendencies nevertheless provide an important lens on his later works. His scrupulous formal clarity tells us, for example, that however formless his mature music may seem, it is deliberately so. More important is what we learn from the predilection for intentional and unintentional references. This propensity does not diminish between the First and Second Symphonies, nor does it evolve chronologically, for example from a work based on Haydn, Mozart, and Beethoven to one drawing on Mendelssohn, Schumann, and Brahms. In both of these works a wide variety of chronologically and stylistically distinct influences interact in ways that prefigure Strauss's future practice—even if at that early date he had no idea what that future practice would entail. I would hold that by the time Strauss reached his late teens, the proposition that he was working his way through the previous century of Austro-German music does not stand up to scrutiny. By 1880, the now fully trained composer had a repertory of musical knowledge from which he drew in a nonlinear manner, blending influences experimentally without regard for anachronism. Clearly, as he got older his interest in citation and stylistic inconsistency only increased. There is every reason to assume that the early examples, unwitting or otherwise, had a role in that development.

If we consider the First Symphony as a whole, there are at least three distinct layers of influence, each of which manifests itself through technical predilections as well as allusions to specific works. At the beginning of the symphony, Haydn predominates. The slow introduction clearly draws on this model, with a carefully paced establishment of the dominant and a presentation of motives that return transformed later in the work. These features are contradicted by the relatively wide harmonic range, but that inconsistency in no way obscures the Haydnesque proportions and function of this section. The tonal plan of the exposition, with the minor dominant tonicized (perfect authentic cadence, A minor, m. 94) but then abandoned immediately for the authentic second key (F major), recalls the three-key plan of the *Farewell Symphony*'s first movement, in which a proposed second key is immediately revoked in favor of the other option.[30] Strauss followed Haydn's typical practice by excising a large portion of this digression in the reprise, though he adds a characteristic moment of wit by briefly diverting the recapitulation to a different non-tonic key (B-flat, with a perfect authentic cadence at m. 421). Other, less structurally oriented reminiscences of Haydn can also be found in the symphony, for example in the second movement's recapitulation, where a running violin countermelody employs a typical Haydnesque variation technique.

The strikingly clear-cut formal junctures in this work point more toward Mozart than Haydn, but overall, Beethoven emerges as the most important competing influence. This tendency manifests itself in the last movement as triumphant bombast imitating the Fifth Symphony—in the character of the principal theme group, the overly large coda, and the excessive repetitions of the concluding chord. The massive but directionless development sections in the outer movements likewise attempt, unsuccessfully, to reproduce a powerful feature of Beethoven's style; in particular the fugal section in the last movement pushes things a step too far, with its superimposed triplets and eighths. In the first movement, several moments point toward specific Beethovenian precedents: the deceptive cadence that begins the coda (m. 451) uses dynamics and texture to recall the transition between the final two movements of the Fifth,

Example 7.6a. Strauss, Symphony No. 1 in D Minor, first movement, mm. 447–52

Example 7.6b. Strauss, Symphony No. 1 in D Minor, first movement, mm. 289–93

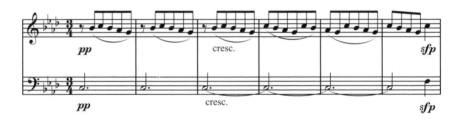

Example 7.6c. Beethoven, *Egmont* Overture, mm. 157–62

and the stringing together of motives at mm. 289–92 evokes the retransition of the *Egmont Overture* (ex. 7.6). More generally, the tendency of the principal theme to liquidate (first at mm. 59–66) clearly reflects Beethoven's practice.

Although the impact of classical precedents is widespread, later influences figure prominently as well and have a particularly conspicuous effect given the otherwise antiquated context. The Mendelssohnian flavor of the first movement's principal theme offers perhaps the most arresting example; its scherzo-like articulation and orchestration are not prepared in the slightest by the introduction (ex. 7.7). The broad registral sweep

Example 7.7. Strauss, Symphony No. 1 in D Minor, first movement, mm. 51–58

of some of the work's melodic material (first movement, mm. 178–81; second movement, mm. 21–25) and the hemiola found in the third movement (mm. 76ff.) suggest that Brahms had made more of an impact on Strauss in 1880 than he was yet willing to admit. And in the Andante, a traditionally lyrical slow movement in the manner of Haydn's late symphonies, Schubertian dominant ninth chords (mm. 22–23), and a hesitant attempt at developing variation (compare mm. 10–17 with mm. 1–9) introduce elements of the new that do not easily blend with the old.

Steinitzer also heard the influence of Schumann in this symphony, not least in its "intensive seriousness, opposing all triviality."[31] That composer would figure much more prominently in the Second Symphony, but not at the expense of continued reliance on techniques of Haydn and Mozart. Indeed, in some respects this classical element became stronger in the Second, because Strauss understood it better. The possibility that melodic material can become accompanimental, or vice versa, is explored much more thoroughly here and right from the beginning. The opening motive, a descending scale that reveals itself at the last minute as B-flat minor rather than F minor, becomes the accompaniment to the principal theme at m. 9. An additional accompanimental figure, introduced at m. 18, also serves that function in the second group (m. 89) but then emerges as a theme in its own right during the coda (mm. 318ff.). The resulting thematic integration is also fostered by the movement's flirtation with monothematicism; the second theme is not a quotation of the first, but it clearly shares the same motivic root (ex. 7.8). And formally, the work is no less clear than the previous symphony, with cadences and textural changes marking the expected junctures as unmistakably as in any work of Mozart.

Again as in the First, Beethoven plays a role distinct from his relationship to Haydn and Mozart. These instances are especially noteworthy in developmental material, in which Strauss uses both reminiscences and Beethovenian techniques. As before, the model is Beethoven's middle period; the most obvious sources are the slow movement of the Seventh Symphony (in the chromatically inflected stepwise descent at mm. 139–43 of the first movement), the development of the *Eroica*, first movement (repeated tutti pounding of a single dissonance, in movement one, mm. 193–99), and the *Egmont Overture*, this time in the same key (intensification through repetition of rising motive over dominant harmony, in movement four, mm. 346–49). The developmental coda in the first movement clearly emulates the first movements of the *Eroica* and the Fifth and succeeds in building momentum that carries over into the succeeding movements. In the last movement, on the other hand, the model is the *Pastoral*, with single triads extended into blocks of sound spread over a number of measures (mm. 184–219).

Example 7.8a. Strauss, Symphony No. 2 in F Minor, first movement, mm. 9–16

Example 7.8b. Strauss, Symphony No. 2 in F Minor, first movement, mm. 67–70

Surveying these two layers of allusion provides a context for hearing the later influences, which are undeniable but do not create a homogeneous late-nineteenth-century character any more than classical influences produce homogeneity in the First Symphony. The tonal plan of the first movement—F-minor tonic and D-flat-major/-minor second key area—harks back to Schubert's *Unfinished,* though Beethoven and Brahms are other possible sources.[32] The fourth movement of Brahms's Third obviously affected the mood and character of Strauss's finale and finds a specific reference at mm. 237–55 of the fourth movement and similar passages. The metric displacement in the first movement (mm. 152ff.), imposed with accents and cut off with startling abruptness, also recalls Brahms (and by extension, Schumann). One might hear in the remarkably thick orchestration of the second movement's trio an unfortunate reminder of Schumann; this example is one of many. Perhaps the most striking reference of all comes with the main theme of the fourth movement, an agitated low-string melody rising beneath tremolo and sounding very much like Bruckner. The overblown recapitulation of themes from all three previous movements in the coda of the fourth seems to point to this source as well, rather than to Beethoven's Ninth, because it functions as a culminating gesture.

While allusion and pastiche can hardly have been fully intentional in these works, the variety and prominence of the influences does seem at odds with the works' technical accomplishment—that is, one feels that a composer of Strauss's obvious accomplishments ought to have known better. Erich Urban suggested that Strauss's persistent use of allusion in early maturity may have been a strategy for concealing his own identity: "for my part, I know of no other composer who as a beginner showed so little of his own face as Strauss."[33] In any case, naïveté and carelessness do not provide credible explanations, unless carelessness was itself a choice, a more or less calculated determination to let such things stand uncorrected. It is vital here to recognize that the symphonies exist on a historical continuum reaching from student works produced by studied imitation to mature works that borrowed music explicitly and for the purpose of parody. Allusion and stylistic juxtaposition obviously came at the cost of the composer's and the music's autonomy: they undermined stylistic independence; they directed the listener's attention outside the work; and they disallowed the assumption that the work followed as the logical next step in a linear evolution of the artistic material. But when did Strauss realize this? In 1885, when he conceived the *Burleske,* a work that combined overt parodistic allusions to Wagner and Brahms? Or perhaps two years earlier, when his finale of the Second Symphony simultaneously engaged with Brahms, Bruckner, and Beethoven? In any case, answering the question of when the practice became witting is less important, in my view, than recognizing the relatedness between the student practice and the mature technique. Somewhere in that development, Strauss decided that a method that was familiar to him could be used for more sophisticated ends.

One of the more interesting features of the *Burleske* is that its combination of allusions to Brahms and Wagner anticipates a basic contention of Schoenberg's argument in "Brahms the Progressive": that for the generation after Brahms, the influence of these two figures would not be mutually exclusive.[34] Whereas Schoenberg treated his two great predecessors as divergent paths ultimately unified in his own achievement, Strauss treated them as objects of parody, confirming in his own way that in the long run the differences once so passionately debated would not matter. The sense in which the *Burleske* acts as a burlesque has never been entirely clear, however, and that problem has to be solved before the implications for late-nineteenth-century masters can be fully understood. For all its pyrotechnics and its allusive qualities, the work presents relatively few direct parodies of specific musical passages. Instead, the burlesque seems to depend on the tension between the peculiar qualities of the concerto as a genre and the musical assumptions that Strauss associated with his stylistic sources.

The defining musical feature of the *Burleske* is excess. The piece is self-consciously too long (by five minutes, according to Del Mar), too concerned with technical display (Bülow called it "unplayable"), too slavishly normal in its form, and too large in conception for the ordinariness of its principal thematic idea. Absurd repetition, such as at mm. 53–60, suggests caricature, not of a particular composer but of a large-scale genre that allows itself be taken hostage at any moment by a single performer; the explosion of fortissimo octaves in m. 61 corroborates this impression, once again requiring that the orchestra wait for the soloist to finish. The overgrown coda, with its dramatic struggles and misplaced cadenza (which comes after the sonata form has been closed off by the cadence at m. 812), likewise assumes a shape dictated by the whims of the player. In all of its manifestations in this work, overindulgence is qualitatively typical of the concerto but pushed beyond the normal limits, as though to expose a flaw in the genre's conception.

At the same time, the overall flavor of the work is Brahmsian; engagement with Wagner comes at specific moments, while Brahms, as virtually every commentator has noted, stamps the work as a whole. Brahms had of course attempted in his own concertos to push the genre toward the symphony and away from itself—to redeem it, in a sense, from its unhealthy tendencies, so that it might become fully "musical" in the strong sense of the late nineteenth century. As he burlesqued the concerto, then, Strauss seems also to have burlesqued the idea of a Brahmsian concerto or to have imagined what might have happened had Brahms embraced the showman-like qualities of a genuine virtuoso concerto. That is certainly the effect of the pianist's virtuosically enhanced quotation of the D-minor Ballade (noted by Edward Newman and R. Larry Todd), which gives way immediately to pure, empty passagework (ex. 7.9). Whatever the success of Brahms's concertos, there is no chance that this work will approach the character of the symphony. And in that sense the commentary deals not only with Brahms but with a tendency of many great concertos from the nineteenth century, which in one way or another strive to transcend their concerto status.

By using a caricature of the concerto to counteract the aesthetically loaded synthesis of concerto and symphony, Strauss celebrated, in a roundabout way, the contentless technical display that he seemed to be mocking. It was this feature of the piece, its combination of brilliance, superficiality, and ease, that impressed the listeners who had an opportunity to hear it. Specht found the music's very banality a sign of "health and strength," qualities so appealing that they obviated any need for originality in the traditional sense.[35] Moving beyond originality and writing a concerto that emphasized its hackneyed concerto-like aspects acted as first steps in a demystification of the symphonic medium—that is, of the high seriousness associated with the symphony and exploited to the full by both Brahms and Wagner. In its precocious way, the *Burleske* thus began to clear the path that would be followed by Strauss's orchestral music.

Unlike Strauss's other concertos, the *Burleske* confronted a historical problem with which he would need to come to terms before fully embracing the orchestral medium. Its use of virtuosity to question a certain kind of orchestral seriousness or substance located it particularly close to issues confronted by Liszt in the first two stages of his career: the period of the traveling virtuoso and the Weimar period during which he composed the symphonic poems. It is important to recognize that in this work, at least, Strauss came down on the side of earlier, virtuosic, ostensibly empty Liszt, the Liszt who treated the *Symphonie fantastique* as a

Example 7.9a. Brahms, Ballade in D Minor, op. 10, no. 1, "Edward," mm. 1–9

Example 7.9b. Strauss, *Burleske*, mm. 21–29

showpiece. In the *Burleske* Strauss celebrated precisely the musical approach that the symphonic poems seem designed to transcend. Although the initial motivation for the piece may well have been the influence of Ritter, as the music took shape its independent qualities came increasingly to the fore, demonstrating that even at this early stage Strauss would not be pigeonholed.

Aus Italien followed much the same course. Strauss considered the work a bridge, and in many respects it did combine elements of his past and his future: it is both programmatic and multi-movement (the only such example in his output), and the movements generally correspond in character to those of the symphony (with the first two movements exchanged), but with considerable formal modifications in three cases. The dedication to Bülow seems fitting for music with this kind of varied ancestry, and the range of musicians who approved of it, which included figures as diverse as Ritter and Meyer, confirms that it had something to please virtually any persuasion. But even as it facilitated a transition it also served a higher purpose, as a kind of testing ground for various ideas and approaches, and in this capacity it did not show prejudice toward any view advocated by a particular Straussian mentor. Indeed, by the end it gave clear signs of an independent future that would leave no one fully satisfied.

If there is a tension in *Aus Italien* it is less between the demands of absolute and programmatic music than between kinds of programmaticism. Seidl pointed out that the work deals extensively with both, but he emphasized the type geared toward "expression," in which a program defined a "Stimmung" that could be translated into music.[36] That approach does indeed predominate in the first two movements, with the first in particular offering novelties of harmonic progression (famously so in the introduction) and form that mimic the originality of Liszt and Wagner. The second movement, however, typifies the problems of this approach more than its strengths: listeners rightly complained that the character of the music seemed to have little to do with the program (however strongly the visit to Rome had stimulated Strauss's musical imagination) and the program had little effect on the straightforward sonata form.[37] The third movement, on the other hand, seems to have been the one that interested Strauss most, and it is clearly meant to intensify the programmatic dimension by focusing on brilliance of illustration, which is laid over and overshadows a continuing suggestion of mood. His specific intent, as he told it, was to explore the "interplay" of natural sounds and human experience, the latter being "expressed by the melodic elements."[38] Any union between the two would only be "partial," presumably because the distinction itself brought something of interest to the artwork.

Already at this stage, then, Strauss was reflecting on a basic dichotomy within programmatic music that the course of German music since Beethoven had not resolved. Mendelssohn, whose influence can still be felt in *Aus Italien* (especially in the second and third movements), had pointed the way in his overtures toward a synthesis of illustration and programmatic expression, but Strauss seemed here more interested in undoing it than appropriating it. To find him thinking in these terms three years before discussing the issue in detail with Cosima Wagner (see pp. 54–56) is to recognize that his stubborn resolve in that debate was not a momentary whim but a settled conviction that predated the tone poems. In certain technical respects *Aus Italien* similarly foretells Strauss's future: important melodic tendencies find their first examples here (ex. 7.10), and the Lisztian direct major-third relationships particularly common in the early tone poems are foreshadowed in the first and second movements. (In the first movement, a G-major introduction gives way to an E-flat-major main theme; the second movement explores a C-major/E-major relationship within the harmonically closed principal theme group, while in the recapitulation the return of the secondary material begins in E before moving to C.) The intimations of maturity in this conception

Example 7.10a. *Aus Italien*, first movement, "Auf der Campagna," mm. 65–70

Example 7.10b. *Aus Italien*, first movement, "Auf der Campagna," mm. 114–15

Example 7.10c. *Aus Italien*, third movement, "Am Strand vom Sorrent," mm. 190–91

of programmaticism are more significant, however, because they point toward an element of style that is more definitively personal.

The most strikingly original movement of the piece is however the fourth, which made early audiences particularly mad (it transformed a lukewarm reception at the Munich premiere into a full-scale hissing controversy) and made Strauss particularly happy (the fact that people thought he was crazy showed that he was on the right path, he told his father). Given those facts, the borrowing of "Funiculi, funicula" ought to be regarded as cheek rather than oversight (which is hardly a credible explanation) or mere bad taste (a tendency that Strauss freely embraced in a variety of contexts).[39] Clearly he found something exciting about a tune written to celebrate an advance in technology, and he enjoyed the enormous and excessive development of that musical idea into a musical structure of proportions obviously incommensurate with the mundane nature of the subject. He would take precisely that approach in the fugue in *Domestica*, a work just as closely related to this first programmatic attempt as is the *Alpensinfonie*. In their self-consciously overblown qualities, all three of these works invert the romantic concept of the miniature: they say little with enormous means, but in the process compensate the listener with unprecedented feats of sheer technical brilliance.

For his last programmatic orchestral work, on the other hand, Strauss took the opposite approach. *Metamorphosen* uses a limited scale, limited orchestra, and limited musical material to deal with the most substantial and personal program of his career: the unforeseen consequences of human choice. As I argued in chapter 4, the *Metamorphosen* shows Strauss reflecting, with Goethe's help, on the moral ramifications of the decentered self. From a panicked, newly pessimistic standpoint, the choices of his orchestral period seemed not only questionable but perhaps exactly wrong. Particularly his sense of the heroic nature of his endeavor suffered, which may explain why he returned to the section of the *Eroica* that he had purposefully omitted from *Heldenleben*, the funeral march. Now an entire work would grow from what he had overlooked, or ignored, in the inexperienced confidence of his youth.

The metamorphosis to which the title alludes is of course thematic in nature; harmonic processes are largely coloristic, especially in the foreground, where the peculiar successions operate by the same principle as the beginning of *Aus Italien*. There is, however, a large-scale formal/harmonic structure of a remarkably straightforward, perceptible sort that belies the sophistication of the thematic processes. This formal plan (see diagram 7.2) projects a naïveté that collapses when the apparently im-

Principal section	Episode 1	Episode 2	Development	Preparation of CM climax (substitute for recapitulation, as in *Tod und Verklärung*)	Retransition	Recapitulation (with double return)
Cm	GM	EM	modulatory	CM	C: V	Cm
m. 1	m. 82	m. 145	m. 197	m. 345		m. 390

Diagram 7.2. The form of *Metamorphosen*.

minent culmination in C major (m. 345) gives way instead to an emphatically pessimistic recapitulation in C minor (m. 390). At this moment an underlying, inexorable process toward doom is brought fully to consciousness and confirmed, destroying a level of experience (represented by the form) whose ease had discouraged the listener from probing further. Dark reality, which had been recognizable all along but not difficult to ignore, undermines its superficial, optimistic alternative.

In its biographical context, this structural tension has self-critical implications, with sonata form standing for an obliviousness of which the elderly Strauss feared he was guilty. The sanguine carelessness with which he had discarded musical tradition—including sonata form—now found expression through the very form that had embodied that tradition, while the unforeseen implications, moral and artistic, were intensified without resistance in the symphonic web of motives that had been Strauss's ideal of compositional technique throughout both his orchestral and operatic careers. There is an admission of error here, then—a recognition that his technical choices, and above all his determination to separate technique from aesthetics, had initiated a process leading to destruction. In the end he feared, if not decided, that his own view of life had been as misguided and narrow-minded as sonata form. Only intuition might have saved him, but as with his motivic metamorphosis, by the time he detected the problem, the process had gone too far.

Notes

Intellectual History and Artistic Production

1. The italics are Schoenberg's. Arnold Schoenberg, "New Music" (1923), in *Style and Idea*, ed. Leonard Stein, trans. Leo Black (New York: St. Martin's Press, 1975), 137.

2. Although Strauss took definite steps to help Schoenberg's career early on, the relationship went sour, particularly when Alma Mahler related Strauss's comment that the younger composer would "do better to shovel snow instead of scribbling on manuscript paper." Erwin Stein, ed., *Arnold Schoenberg: Letters*, trans. Eithne Wilkins and Ernst Kaiser (New York: St. Martin's Press, 1965), 50–51. Günter Brosche, on the other hand, has demonstrated that Strauss continued to offer professional encouragement and financial support to Schoenberg as late as 1918. Günter Brosche, "Richard Strauss und Arnold Schoenberg," *Richard Strauss-Blätter*, n.s., 2 (December 1979): 21–28.

3. This theme has recently been explored in Bernd Edelmann, Birgit Lodes, and Reinhold Schlötterer, eds., *Richard Strauss und die Moderne* (Berlin: Henschel, 2001).

4. The term "modernism" was first used to describe music of the 1890s by Hermann Bahr. Carl Dahlhaus, *Nineteenth-Century Music*, trans. J. Bradford Robinson (Berkeley and Los Angeles: University of California Press, 1989), 334–35. See also idem, "Musikalische Moderne und Neue Musik," *Melos/Neue Zeitschrift für Musik* 2 (1976): 90.

5. The classic discussion of this preconception is Carl Dahlhaus, "Neoromanticism," in *Between Romanticism and Modernism: Four Studies in the Music of the Later Nineteenth Century*, trans. Mary Whittall (Berkeley and Los Angeles: University of California Press, 1980), 1–18, esp. 4–8. Neo-romantic interpretive approaches remain alive and well today, for example, in the recent work of Scott Burnham on Mozart. See Scott Burnham, "On the Beautiful in Mozart," in *Music and the Aesthetics of Modernity*, ed. Karol Berger and Anthony Newcomb (Berkeley and Los Angeles: University of California Press, forthcoming).

6. Gustav Brecher, who was certainly no antagonist of Strauss, articulated this view as early as 1900. Gustav Brecher, *Richard Strauß: Eine monographische Skizze* (Leipzig: Hermann Seemann Nachfolger, [1900]), 12, 17–19, 22–23.

7. The widespread notion that Strauss represented an "end of music" is discussed in Morten Kristiansen, "Richard Strauss's *Feuersnot* in Its Aesthetic and Cultural Context: A Modernist Critique of Musical Idealism" (PhD diss., Yale University, 2000), 8.

8. For example, Arnold Whittall's coverage of Strauss in his recent book

concentrates on the "expressionistic music drama," drawing a general principle from the observation that "the music for the troubled, troubling character of Kly-temnestra in *Elektra* begins to approach the expressionistically febrile mood of Schoenberg's deranged protagonist in his atonal monodrama *Erwartung*." Arnold Whittall, *Musical Composition in the Twentieth Century* (Oxford: Oxford University Press, 1999).

9. Theodor Adorno, "Richard Strauss. Born June 11, 1864," trans. Samuel Weber and Shierry Weber, *Perspectives of New Music* 4 (1965): 17.

10. Ernst Otto Nodnagel, *Jenseits von Wagner und Liszt* (Königsberg: Ost-preußischen Druckerei und Verlagsanstalt, 1902), 185–86.

11. Theodor Adorno, "Richard Strauss at Sixty," trans. Susan Gillespie, in *Richard Strauss and His World*, ed. Bryan Gilliam (Princeton: Princeton University Press, 1992), 408.

12. James Hepokoski, "Fiery-Pulsed Libertine or Domestic Hero? Strauss's *Don Juan* Reinvestigated," in *Richard Strauss: New Perspectives on the Composer and His Work*, ed. Bryan Gilliam (Durham, N.C.: Duke University Press, 1992), 164–65.

13. Arnold Schoenberg, "Brahms the Progressive," in *Style and Idea*, 398–441. Walter Frisch's account of this essay concentrates, like the essay itself, on the unique subtlety of Brahmsian developing variation, but Frisch ultimately points out that Schoenberg was concerned fundamentally with integrating Brahms into that group of late-nineteenth-century composers whose works determined what Adorno would call the "state of the material." Walter Frisch, *Brahms and the Principle of Developing Variation* (Berkeley and Los Angeles: University of California Press, 1984), 163.

14. Carl Dahlhaus, *The Idea of Absolute Music*, trans. Roger Lustig (Chicago: University of Chicago Press, 1989), 10.

15. Anette Unger, *Welt, Leben und Kunst als Themen der "Zarathustra-Kompositionen" von Richard Strauss und Gustav Mahler* (Frankfurt am Main: Peter Lang, 1992), 80.

16. Felix M. Gatz, *Musik-Ästhetik in ihren Hauptrichtungen: Ein Quellenbuch der deutschen Musik-Ästhetik von Kant und der Frühromantik bis zur Gegenwart mit Einführung und Erläuterungen* (Stuttgart: Ferdinand Enke, 1929). Gatz (1892–1942), a performer as well as an academic, studied at the Universities of Berlin, Erlangen, and Heidelberg and was a protégé of Nikisch and Paul Scheinpflug. From 1925–34 he served as lecturer (*Dozent*) on musical aesthetics at the Akademie für Musik und darstellende Kunst in Vienna. After immigrating to the United States, he taught at Duquesne University and New York University before becoming the head of the music department at the University of Scranton.

17. Ibid., 21–50.

18. For example, Gatz obviously intended to consider various attitudes toward music's character as a "romantic" art in the specifically Hegelian sense, and to arrange those attitudes in an evolutionary historical account. His project was thus in this sense doubly influenced by Hegel, and in its treatment of musical autonomy it exemplifies what Nietzsche would call the "generalization" of German romanticism. See Stephen Houlgate, *Hegel, Nietzsche and the Criticism of Metaphysics* (Cambridge: Cambridge University Press, 1986), 35.

19. Gatz, *Musik-Ästhetik in ihren Hauptrichtungen*, 22. My discussion of Gatz's ideas is a summation of his entire thirty-page introduction; I will cite only quoted material.

20. Ibid., 36, 32.

21. Ibid., 39.

22. Ibid., 42.

23. Ibid., 43.

24. Ibid., 44.

25. Ibid., 45.

26. Ibid., 48–49.

27. Richard Strauss, "Aus meinen Jugend- und Lehrjahren," in *Betrachtungen und Erinnerungen*, 2d ed., ed. Willi Schuh (Zurich: Atlantis, 1957), 210.

28. This point has been made by Ernst-Joachim Danz, who faults Gatz for misclassifying Hausegger but notes the more important fact that Hausegger's views are fully consistent with Gatz's *Incarnationsaesthetik*. Ernst-Joachim Danz, *Die objektlose Kunst: Euntersuchungen zur Musikästhetik Friedrich von Hauseggers* (Regensburg: Gustav Bosse, 1981), 207–10.

29. These translations from Hausegger's *Die Musik als Ausdruck* are by Martin Cooper and taken from Bojan Bujic, ed., *Music in European Thought, 1851–1912* (Cambridge: Cambridge University Press, 1988), 108–13.

30. On the history of formalism after Hanslick and especially on the ability of formalism-as-autonomy to encompass apparently antithetical aesthetic views, see Edward Lippman, *A History of Western Musical Aesthetics* (Lincoln: University of Nebraska Press, 1992), 301–19.

31. Eduard Hanslick, *Vom Musikalisch-Schönen*, ed. Dietmar Strauß, vol. 1, *Historisch-kritische Ausgabe* (Mainz: Schott, 1990), 22.

32. Ibid., 78.

33. Ibid., 22.

34. Ibid., 165.

35. Ibid., 170.

36. Ibid., 171.

37. Ibid.

38. August Wilhelm Ambros, *The Boundaries of Music and Poetry. A Study in Musical Aesthetics*, trans. J. H. Cornell (New York: G. Schirmer, 1893), 9–12; quoted in Bujic, *Music in European Thought, 1851–1912*, 76–78.

39. Constantin Floros, for example, argues for a programmatic link between the ostensibly "absolute" Fifth Symphony and the First and Second Symphonies. Constantin Floros, *Gustav Mahler: The Symphonies*, trans. Vernon Wicker and Jutta Wicker (Portland, Ore.: Amadeus Press, 1993), 141.

40. Mahler to Arthur Seidl, 17 February 1897. Herta Blaukopf, ed., *Gustav Mahler Briefe* (Vienna: Paul Zolnay, 1982), no. 216. This letter is discussed in Stephen Hefling, "Miners Digging from Opposite Sides: Mahler, Strauss, and the Problem of Program Music," in *Richard Strauss: New Perspectives*, 41–53.

41. Kristiansen, "Richard Strauss's *Feuersnot*," 113–15, 126–28.

42. Dieter Borchmeyer, *Richard Wagner: Theory and Theater*, trans. Stewart Spencer (Oxford: Clarendon Press, 1991), 103.

43. In the words of Borchmeyer: "in spite of their common appeal to *Die Welt*

als Wille und Vorstellung, neither Wagner's nor Nietzsche's theory of music and musical drama can be reconciled with Schopenhauer's *magnum opus*." Ibid., 172.

44. Richard Specht, for example, held that Strauss's celebrity persona—what Hermann Bahr called his "sportliche Leistung"—was just as responsible as his music for his popularity. One of the goals of Specht's biography was to raise the public's understanding of the music to the level of its enthusiasm for the composer. Richard Specht, *Richard Strauss und sein Werk*, vol. 1, *Der Künstler und sein Weg; Der Instrumentalkomponist* (Leipzig: E. P. Tal & Co., 1921), 17.

45. Adorno compared Strauss's technical facility with the purchasing power of a "big industrialist": "He does not need to check his books: production goes on without a care." Adorno, "Richard Strauss. Born June 11, 1864," 14.

46. This philosophy found creative expression in an early sketch for *Eine Alpensinfonie*, with a planned fourth movement the theme of which was to be "liberation [*Befreiung*] through work." Franz Trenner, *Die Skizzenbücher von Richard Strauss* (Tutzing: Hans Schneider, 1977), 18.

47. An early (and fleeting) glimpse into this private world was provided by Strauss's friend Wilhelm Klatte in "Aus Richard Strauss' Werkstatt," *Die Musik* 16 (1923–24): 636–41.

48. Strauss, "Aus meinen Jugend-und Lehrjahren," 203–18.

49. This statement was reported by Ritter in an article for the *Allgemeine Musikzeitung*. Siegmund von Hausegger, *Alexander Ritter: Ein Bild seines Charakters und Schaffens* (Berlin: Marquardt & Co., [1907]), 79–80.

50. The best attempt to deal with the complexity of these relationships in the late Bülow is Frithjof Haas, *Hans von Bülow. Leben und Wirken: Wegbereiter für Wagner, Liszt und Brahms* (Wilhelmshaven: F. Noetzel, Heinrichshofen Bücher, 2002).

51. On 7 April 1886, as Strauss concluded his engagement at Meiningen, he wrote to Bülow that he had conducted the *Tristan* Prelude and conclusion "so far as possible, naturally, according to *your* intentions." Gabriele Strauss, ed., *Lieber Collega!: Richard Strauss in Briefwechsel mit zeitgenössischen Komponisten und Dirigenten* (Berlin: Henschel, 1996), 36.

52. Willi Schuh, *Richard Strauss. Jugend und frühe Meisterjahre. Lebenschronik 1864–1898* (Zurich: Atlantis, 1976), 387.

53. See Theodor Pfeiffer, *Studien bei Hans von Bülow* (Berlin: Friedrich Luckhardt, 1894), and José Vianna da Motta, *Nachtrag zu Studien bei Hans von Bülow* (Berlin: Friedrich Luckhardt, 1896); these sources have been edited and translated by Richard Zimdars as *The Piano Master Classes of Hans von Bülow* (Bloomington: Indiana University Press, 1993).

54. Erich Urban, for example, called him the "Eckart of the New Germans," comparing him to Dietrich Eckart, the right-wing Munich political activist who would later found the German Workers' Party and participate in Hitler's Beer Hall Putsch. Erich Urban, *Strauss contra Wagner* (Berlin: Schuster & Loeffler, 1902), 59.

55. Scott Warfield, "Friedrich Wilhelm Meyer (1818–1893): Some Biographical Notes on Strauss' Composition Teacher," *Richard-Strauss-Blätter*, n.s., 37 (June 1997): 54–74.

56. Scott Warfield, "'Reveal nothing to him of his market value': The Pub-

lication of Strauss's First Three Tone Poems," unpublished manuscript. On Strauss's early dealings with publishers see also Barbara A. Petersen, "*Die Händler und die Kunst:* Richard Strauss as Composer's Advocate," in *Richard Strauss: New Perspectives,* 115–18.

57. Peter Jelavich, *Munich and Theatrical Modernism: Politics, Playwriting, and Performance, 1890–1914* (Cambridge: Harvard University Press, 1985), 23–32.

58. Strauss was always conscious of the deniability inherent in his art. When discussing the deplorable limitations imposed by censorship in Berlin around 1900, he observed that "fortunately, in music you can say everything; no one understands you." Michael Kennedy, *Richard Strauss: Man, Musician, Enigma* (Cambridge: Cambridge University Press, 1999), 128.

59. Alma Mahler, *Gustav Mahler: Memories and Letters,* ed. Donald Mitchell, trans. Basil Creighton (New York: Viking Press, 1969), 50–51.

60. Franz Strauss and Alice Strauss, eds., *The Correspondence between Richard Strauss and Hugo von Hofmannsthal,* trans. Hanns Hammelmann and Ewald Osers (Cambridge: Cambridge University Press, 1980), 302, 354, 396.

61. "He was at home in German literature like no other musician." Karl Böhm, *Ich erinnere mich ganz genau,* ed. Hans Weigel (Zurich: Biogees, 1968), 101. Strauss's friendship with Romain Rolland testifies eloquently to this quality.

62. Strauss, "Aus meinen Jugend- und Lehrjahren," 207.

63. Strauss, "Brief über das humanistische Gymnasium," in *Betrachtungen und Erinnerungen,* 133.

64. Thus the complaints that the elderly Strauss would voice about his grandsons' education. Kurt Wilhelm, *Richard Strauss: An Intimate Portrait,* trans. Mary Whittall (New York: Rizzoli, 1989), 197–98.

65. Strauss, "Brief über das humanistische Gymnasium," 128–33.

66. The topics of his coursework are given by Max Steinitzer, *Richard Strauss,* 4th–8th eds. (Berlin: Schuster & Loeffler, 1914), 39. Strauss's comment comes from "Meine Freunde und Förderer meines Werkes," an unpublished manuscript in the Richard-Strauss-Archiv (RSA).

67. See William J. McGrath, *Dionysian Art and Populist Politics in Austria* (New Haven: Yale University Press, 1974).

68. Arthur Seidl, "Richard Strauss: Eine Charakter-Skizze," in *Straussiana: Aufsätze zur Richard Strauß-Frage aus drei Jahrzehnten* (Regensburg: Gustave Bosse, [1913]), 11–66. A biographical sketch of Seidl can be found in Ludwig Frankenstein, *Arthur Seidl: Ein Lebensabriß* (Regensburg: Gustav Bosse, [1913]).

69. Seidl to Strauss, 22 December 1896. RSA. For a more extended discussion of this letter see below, pp. 100.

70. Arthur Seidl, "Also sang Zarathustra," in *Moderner Geist in der deutschen Tonkunst: Gedanken eines Kulturpsychologen zur Wende des Jahrhunderts* (Regensburg: Gustave Bosse, [1913]), 108–10.

71. The "braunes Tagebuch," as it has come to be known, is held in the RSA.

72. Schuh, *Richard Strauss. Jugend und frühe Meisterjahre,* 312–20, 322–27.

73. Ibid., 315.

74. The correspondence with Cosima Wagner has been published in Franz Trenner, ed., with assistance of Gabriele Strauss, *Cosima Wagner / Richard Strauss: Ein Briefwechsel* (Tutzing: Hans Schneider, 1978). Letters from Rösch to Strauss

and from Seidl to Strauss are held at the RSA. Letters from Strauss to these two figures have been lost.

75. Strauss's growing publicity machine in the 1890s is described in Walter Werbeck, *Die Tondichtungen von Richard Strauss* (Tutzing: Hans Schneider, 1996), 281–289.

1. The "Conversion"

1. This "Nachempfindungsbacillus" was detected by the anonymous reviewer of the Munich premiere of *Guntram* (1893). *Bayerische Kurier*, 19 November 1895.

2. Derrick Puffett, "*Salome* as Music Drama," in *Richard Strauss: "Salome,"* ed. Derrick Puffett (Cambridge: Cambridge University Press, 1989), 58–87.

3. Walter Frisch's forthcoming essay on Wagnerian allusion in *Ariadne auf Naxos* is the most extensive project of this kind yet undertaken. See "Dancing in Chains: Reflections on *Ariadne auf Naxos*," in *Richard Strauss Studies*, ed. Timothy L. Jackson and Graham Phipps (Cambridge: Cambridge University Press, forthcoming).

4. Leon Botstein, "The Enigmas of Richard Strauss: A Revisionist View," in *Richard Strauss and His World*, ed. Bryan Gilliam (Princeton: Princeton University Press, 1992), 16–21.

5. Looking back on this period Strauss wrote that "the decisive factor in my future development" was the "spiritual stimulus" he received from Alexander Ritter, whose principal contribution, according to Strauss, was to introduce him to Wagner's writings and to Schopenhauer. Richard Strauss, "Aus meinen Jugend- und Lehrjahren," in *Betrachtungen und Erinnerungen*, 2d ed., ed. Willi Schuh (Zurich: Atlantis, 1957), 209.

6. Strauss to Cosima Wagner, 28 January 1889 (the earliest known letter in the correspondence). Franz Trenner, ed., with assistance of Gabriele Strauss, *Cosima Wagner / Richard Strauss: Ein Briefwechsel* (Tutzing: Hans Schneider, 1978), 3.

7. See the preface of Gilliam, *Richard Strauss and His World*, viii.

8. One important attempt to deal with this enormous field is David C. Large and William Weber, eds., *Wagnerism in European Culture and Politics* (Cornell, N.Y.: Cornell University Press, 1984).

9. The complex infighting at Bayreuth in the 1880s is described in Winfried Schüler, *Der Bayreuther Kreis von seiner Entstehung bis zum Ausgang der wilhelminischen Ära* (Münster: Aschendorrf, 1971). See also David C. Large, "Wagner's Bayreuth Disciples," in *Wagnerism in European Culture and Politics*, 72–125.

10. Steinitzer's word is "Umschwung." Max Steinitzer, *Richard Strauss* (Berlin: Schuster & Loeffler, 1911), 11. The metaphor of the conversion maintains its currency today, for example in Michael Kennedy's description of the fracture that developed between Strauss and his father "when Richard became a converted Wagnerian." Michael Kennedy, *Richard Strauss: Man, Musician, Enigma* (Cambridge: Cambridge University Press, 1999), 10.

11. Steinitzer, *Richard Strauss*, 24; Willi Schuh, *Richard Strauss. Jugend und frühe Meisterjahre. Lebenschronik 1864–1898* (Zurich: Atlantis, 1976), 35, 36 (quote).

12. Franz Strauss's specialty was challenging the conductor's authority during rehearsal. Richard Strauss described one such scene during which Wagner became so furious that he could not speak and "ran away." The elder Strauss's response: "I have put him to flight." Richard Strauss, "Erinnerungen an meinen Vater," in *Betrachtungen*, 195. To protect himself from accusations that his horn parts were unplayable, Wagner had Hans Richter try them out before rehearsal. Steinitzer, *Richard Strauss*, 22.

13. Ibid., 24.

14. Ibid., 25–26.

15. Strauss, *Betrachtungen*, 196.

16. Strauss to Thuille, undated (spring 1878). Franz Trenner, ed., *Richard Strauss / Ludwig Thuille: Ein Briefwechsel* (Tutzing: Hans Schneider, 1980), 46–47; a selection from these letters, translated by Susan Gillespie, appears in Gilliam, *Richard Strauss and His World*, 193–236.

17. Thuille is best known as the coauthor with Rudolf Louis of the *Grundriss der Harmonielehre* (Stuttgart: C. Grüninger, 1907), a well-respected text. A useful early source on Thuille is Friedrich Munter, *Ludwig Thuille: Ein erster Versuch* (Munich: Drei Masken, 1923). More recently an excellent collection of essays has appeared: Alexander L. Suder, ed., *Ludwig Thuille* (Tutzing: Hans Schneider, 1993).

18. Veit Veltzke, *Vom Patron zum Paladin: Wagnervereinigungen im Kaiserreich von der Reichsgründung bis zur Jahrhundertwende* (Bochum: Brockmeyer, 1987), 324–27.

19. The only biographical treatment of Seidl is Ludwig Frankenstein, *Arthur Seidl: Ein Lebensabriß* (Regensburg: Gustav Bosse, 1913). A *festschrift* appeared the same year: Bruno Schuhmann, ed., *Musik und Kultur: Festschrift zum 50. Geburtstag Arthur Seidl's* (Regensburg: Gustav Bosse: 1913).

20. Seidl became a frequent contributor to the *Bayreuther Blätter*, making his debut with a review of Paul Deussen's *Elemente der Metaphysik*, *Bayreuther Blätter* 9 (1886): 91–97. Subsequently he published six full-scale articles in the journal: "Richard Wagner's 'Parsifal' und Schopenhauer's 'Nirwana,' "Bayreuther Blätter* 11 (1888): 277–306; "Jesus der Arier—Christentum oder Buddhismus?" *Bayreuther Blätter* 13 (1890): 45–65; "Dramaturg und Drama," *Bayreuther Blätter* 13 (1890): 121–42; "Ueber musikalische Erziehung," *Bayreuther Blätter* 16 (1893): 2–10, 55–66; "Die Kunstlehre der Meistersinger. Ein Vortrag," *Bayreuther Blätter* 16 (1893): 362–92; and "Das Jenseits der Künstlers. Eine Besprechung," *Bayreuther Blätter* 18 (1895): 137–53. He also reviewed Heinrich von Stein's *Helden und Welt*, *Bayreuther Blätter* 11 (1888): 198–200, and contributed an obituary of Richard Pohl, *Bayreuther Blätter* 20 (1897): 116–21. Significantly, Seidl's dissertation was reviewed in the journal, positively, by Friedrich von Hausegger (*Bayreuther Blätter* 11 [1888]: 198–200).

21. On the dispute over performing rights see Frederic Spotts, *Bayreuth: A History of the Wagner Festival* (New Haven: Yale University Press, 1994), 100–1.

22. He maintained a particular fondness for *Tristan* and *Meistersinger* but felt "antipathy" for the last two *Ring* operas and *Parsifal*. Letter to Eugen Spitzweg, 12 August 1882. Marie von Bülow, ed., *Hans von Bülows Leben, dargestellt aus seinen*

Briefen, 2d ed. (Leipzig: Breitkopf & Härtel, 1921), 382–83. Bülow's Wagner repertory is listed in Hans-Joachim Hinrichsen, *Musikalische Interpretation: Hans von Bülow* (Stuttgart: Franz Steiner, 1999), 509.

23. Strauss, *Betrachtungen*, 183, 186.

24. George Marek, *Cosima Wagner* (New York: Harper & Row, 1981), 211. See also Spotts, *Bayreuth: A History of the Wagner Festival*, 91.

25. Julia Liebscher, "Richard Strauss und Friedrich Nietzsche," *Richard Strauss-Blätter*, n.s., 27 (June 1992): 11–12. Bülow may have liked *Die Geburt der Tragödie*, but he hated Nietzsche's music. After perusing the latter's *Manfred Meditation* in 1872, Bülow described it in a letter to Nietzsche as "the most unpleasant and anti-musical of writings on music-sheets that has come before my eyes in a long time." Quoted in Curt Paul Janz, "The Form-Content Problem in Friedrich Nietzsche's Conception of Music," in *Nietzsche's New Seas: Explorations in Philosophy, Aesthetics, and Politics*, ed. Michael Allen Gillespie and Tracy B. Strong (Chicago: University of Chicago Press, 1988), 106–7.

26. See pp. 40–42 for a biographical sketch of Ritter.

27. See Schuh, *Richard Strauss. Jugend und frühe Meisterjahre*, 133–34.

28. The most thorough survey of Strauss's conducting activities at Weimer can be found in Kenneth Birkin, "Richard Strauss in Weimar. Part 1: The Concert Hall," *Richard Strauss-Blätter*, n.s., 33 (June 1995): 3–36; and "Richard Strauss in Weimar. Part 2: The Opera House," *Richard Strauss-Blätter*, n.s., 34 (December 1995): 3–56.

29. Hans von Wolzogen detailed his career as a Wagnerian in a strikingly brief autobiography, the *Lebensbilder* (Regensburg: Gustav Bosse, 1923). On Ernst von Wolzogen's relationship with the Bayreuth circle see Morten Kristiansen, "Richard Strauss's *Feuersnot* in Its Aesthetic and Cultural Context: A Modernist Critique of Musical Idealism" (PhD diss., Yale University, 2000), 190–98.

30. Wolzogen, *Lebensbilder*, 71, 82.

31. Richard Strauss, "Brief eines deutschen Kapellmeisters über das Bayreuther Orchester," *Bayreuther Blätter* 15 (1892): 126–32.

32. Schuh, *Richard Strauss. Jugend und frühe Meisterjahre*, 425.

33. Schüler, *Der Bayreuther Kreis*, 131.

34. Cosima herself suggested to Chamberlain in 1892 that Ritter might serve as composer of a musical setting of the former's "Antigone." Chamberlain declined, citing Wagner's assertion that in opera the poet should be older than the composer. Cosima Wagner to Chamberlain, 27 March 1892. Paul Pretzsch, ed., *Cosima Wagner und Houston Stewart Chamberlain im Briefwechsel 1888–1908* (Leipzig: Philipp Reclam jun., 1934), 281.

35. Bronsart to Strauss, 8 July 1890. Gabriele Strauss, ed., *Lieber Collega!: Richard Strauss im Briefwechsel mit zeitgenössischen Komponisten und Dirigenten* (Berlin: Henschel, 1996), 171.

36. Ibid., 172–73, 175, 178.

37. *Neue Musik-Zeitung* 15 (1894): 142.

38. *Münchener Bote*, 19 November 1895.

39. *Bayerische Kurier*, 19 November 1895.

40. The *Zukunftsmusiker* remark comes from the autobiographical sketch Strauss gave to James Huneker in 1898, which has now been published in Walter

Werbeck, *Die Tondichtungen von Richard Strauss* (Tutzing: Hans Schneider, 1996), 527–30. Other published writings by Strauss about Ritter's influence include "Aus meinen Jugend- und Lehrjahren" and "Erinnerungen an die ersten Aufführungen meiner Opern," both in *Betrachtungen und Erinnerungen;* the unpublished memoir "Meine Freunde und Förderer" (housed in the Richard-Strauss-Archiv [RSA]), excerpts from which appear in Schuh, *Richard Strauss. Jugend und frühe Meisterjahre,* 137; and notes for an unwritten article on Ritter's operas (also at RSA), partly reproduced in Schuh's biography, 200–4. The Wihan letter also appears in Schuh, *Richard Strauss. Jugend und frühe Meisterjahre,* 170–73.

41. The earliest secondary literature on Ritter is a twelve-part biography by Friedrich Rösch that appeared in the *Musikalisches Wochenblatt* from 30 December 1897–14 April 1898. A decade later Siegmund von Hausegger published *Alexander Ritter: Ein Bild seines Charakters und Schaffens* (Berlin: Marquardt & Co., [1907]) as volumes 26–27 of the monograph series edited by Strauss, *Die Musik.* Other works include Max von Schillings, "Alexander Ritter," *Redende Kunst* 2 (1896); Josef Hofmiller, "Alexander Ritter, der Dichter und Komponist," *Die Gesellschaft* 4 (1894) and 8 (1898); Hermann Teibler, "Alexander Ritter," *Die Musik* 1, no. 4 (1902); Hans Joachim Moser, *Geschichte der deutschen Musik,* vol. 3 (Stuttgart: J. G. Cotta, 1928), 222ff.; and idem, *Das deutsche Lied seit Mozart* (Tutzing, 1968), 2:180ff. Most recently, Roswitha Schlötterer has reexamined the Ritter-Strauss friendship in "Richard Strauss uns sein Münchner Kreis," in *Jugendstilmusik?: Münchner Musikleben 1890–1918,* ed. Robert Münster and Hellmut Hell (Wiesbaden: Dr. Ludwig Reichert, 1987), 13–24. A pamphlet published for the 1897 meeting of the Allgemeiner Deutscher Musikverein and entitled *Zum Andenken Alexander Ritters. Festgabe der "Neuen Musikalischen Rundschau" zur Mannheimer Tonkünstler-Versammlung* contains contributions by Strauss, Hermann Bischoff, Rudolf Louis, Friedrich von Hausegger, Arthur Seidl, Hans von Wolzogen, Heinrich Porges, August Stradal, and Engelbert Humperdinck.

42. The notes are held at the RSA. Strauss eventually offered the article to Hans von Wolzogen for publication in the *Bayreuther Blätter,* but Wolzogen did not accept it. Strauss to Wolzogen, 9 August 1890, Bayerische Staatsbibliothek, Ana 330, I, Wolzogen.

43. Alexander Ritter, "Vom Spanisch-Schönen," *Allgemeine Musikzeitung* 18, no. 10 (1891): 128–29.

44. In any case, those who would promote the Bayreuth cause now recognized a need to keep anti-Semitism "unter uns," for the financial good of the festivals. Veltzke, *Vom Patron zum Paladin,* 332.

45. Strauss to Thuille, 19 November 1890. Trenner, *Richard Strauss / Ludwig Thuille,* 115.

46. Strauss to Bülow, 24 August 1888. Gabriele Strauss, *Lieber Collega!,* 81–83.

47. Schuh, *Richard Strauss. Jugend und frühe Meisterjahre,* 303.

48. Ritter to Strauss, 17 January 1893. Charles Youmans, ed., "Ten Letters from Alexander Ritter to Richard Strauss, 1887–1894," *Richard Strauss-Blätter,* n.s., 35 (June 1996): 10–16.

49. Schuh, *Richard Strauss. Jugend und frühe Meisterjahre,* 290–91.

50. Alexander Ritter, "Drei Kapitel: von Franz Liszt, von der 'heiligen Eliz-

abeth' in Karlsruhe, und von unserm ethischen Defekt," *Bayreuther Blätter* 13 (1890): 380–88.

51. Ibid., 381.

52. Idem, "Was lehrt uns das Festspieljahr 1891?" *Bayreuther Blätter* 15 (1892): 1–20, esp. 2–3.

53. According to chapter reports published in the *Bayreuther Blätter* Seidl gave lectures for the society on 13 February 1891 (topic unspecified), 16 February 1891 (on Glasenapp's *Wagner-Lexikon*), 16 December 1891 ("Die Sage von 'Tristan und Isolde'"), 12 February 1892 (topic unspecified), 9 December 1892 (on Robert Franz), and 7 March 1893 ("Das Richard Wagner-Museum und seine Bedeutung für Weimar"). Not every meeting was reported, so this is only a partial list. The meetings also included musical performances, usually of piano/vocal arrangements of excerpts from Wagner's operas and music dramas, with Strauss at the keyboard. *Bayreuther Blätter* 14 (1891): 96, 200; *Bayreuther Blätter* 15 (1892): 294; *Bayreuther Blätter* 16 (1893): 198.

54. Strauss to Franz Strauss, 1 July 1889, 12 July 1889. Willi Schuh, ed., *Richard Strauss: Briefe an die Eltern, 1882–1906* (Zurich: Atlantis, 1954), 107, 110.

55. Ritter to Strauss, 27 July 1889. Youmans, "Ten Letters from Alexander Ritter to Richard Strauss," 7.

56. Strauss to Franz Strauss, 4 July 1889. Schuh, *Briefe an die Eltern,* 110.

57. Pretzsch, ed., *Cosima Wagner und Houston Stewart Chamberlain,* 213, 230.

58. In 1896, Seidl described that plan as a narrowly averted disaster. Seidl to Strauss, 15 January 1896. RSA.

59. In 1894, the Munich Hoftheater planned a production of *Lohengrin* in the style of the tenth century, thus distinguishing itself from "inaccurate" competing productions that used the twelfth century as model. Thus a brief report in the *Allgemeine Musik-Zeitung* 21, no. 18 (1894): 255.

60. Strauss to Cosima Wagner, 3 March 1890. Trenner, *Cosima Wagner / Richard Strauss,* 30.

61. Cosima's Herculean efforts in preparing for the first Bayreuth production of *Tannhäuser* seem designed to compensate for that lack of direct experience. Spotts, *A History of the Wagner Festival,* 107–8.

62. Strauss to his parents, 3 July 1891. Schuh, *Briefe an die Eltern,* 138–39.

63. Strauss to Cosima Wagner, 28 March 1892. Trenner, *Cosima Wagner / Richard Strauss,* 122–23.

64. Cosima Wagner to Strauss, 25 February 1890. Ibid., 26.

65. Strauss to Cosima Wagner, 26 November 1889. Cosima Wagner to Strauss, 26 March 1890. Ibid., 11, 39.

66. Strauss to Cosima Wagner, 3 March 1890. Ibid., 29.

67. Cosima Wagner to Strauss, 6 March 1890. Ibid., 31–32.

68. Richard Wagner, "Über Franz Liszt's symphonische Dichtungen: Brief an M. W.," in *Gesammelte Schriften und Dichtungen von Richard Wagner* (Leipzig: C.F.W. Siegel, [1907]), 5:193–94.

69. Cosima Wagner to Strauss, undated (winter 1891). Trenner, *Cosima Wagner / Richard Strauss,* 79. Arthur Seidl, "Richard Strauss: Eine Charakter-Skizze" (1896), in *Straussiana: Aufsätze zur Richard Strauß-Frage aus drei Jahrzehnten* (Regensburg: Gustav Bosse, [1913]), 51.

70. In the week prior to the Munich premiere of *Guntram* (16 November 1895) it was reported that Cosima was in Munich, possibly to attend rehearsals of Strauss's new work. Whatever her reasons for being in Munich, she was gone by the day of the performance. *Bayerischer Kurier und Münchner Fremdenblatt*, 12 November 1895.

71. Richard Strauss, *Lieder: Gesamtausgabe*, ed. Franz Trenner, vol. 1, *Lieder für eine Singstimme und Klavier, Opus 10–Opus 41* (London: Boosey & Hawkes, 1964), 166.

72. Hofmannsthal to Strauss, 1 August 1918. Franz Strauss and Alice Strauss, eds., *The Correspondence between Richard Strauss and Hugo von Hofmannsthal*, trans. Hanns Hammelmann and Ewald Osers (Cambridge: Cambridge University Press, 1980), 309.

73. Cosima Wagner to Houston Stewart Chamberlain, 26 April 1896. Pretzsch, *Cosima Wagner und Houston Stewart Chamberlain*, 463.

2. Music and the "Denial of the Will"

1. A single article has been devoted to this topic: Bernhard Adamy, "Schopenhauer bei Richard Strauss," *Jahrbuch der Schopenhauer Gesellschaft* 61 (1980): 195–98.

2. Richard Strauss, *Betrachtungen und Erinnerungen*, 2d ed., ed. Willi Schuh (Zurich: Atlantis, 1957), 210.

3. Arthur Hübscher, *Denker gegen den Strom. Schopenhauer: Gestern-Heute-Morgen* (Bonn: Bouvier Verlag Herbert Grundmann, 1973), 242, 246–47, 271–72.

4. Both Latin and Greek were central to the curriculum at the Ludwigs-Gymnasium. In 1882 an instructor wrote that in spite of his considerable musical activities Strauss had shown, thanks to "great industry," a "mature understanding in the interpretation [*Erklärung*] of the classics." His grades in classical languages were higher than those in French and German. Franz Trenner, *Richard Strauss: Dokumente seines Lebens und Schaffens* (Munich: C. H. Beck, 1954), 20.

5. Hofmannsthal and Strauss regularly exchanged recommendations of historical texts. Franz Strauss and Alice Strauss, eds., *The Correspondence between Richard Strauss and Hugo von Hofmannsthal*, trans. Hanns Hammelmann and Ewald Osers (Cambridge: Cambridge University Press, 1980), 302, 354, 396. Alma Mahler also noted that Strauss and Mahler shared a passion for history. Alma Mahler, *Gustav Mahler: Memories and Letters*, ed. Donald Mitchell, trans. Basil Creighton (New York: Viking Press, 1969), 51.

6. Max Steinitzer, *Richard Strauss*, 5th–8th edition (Berlin: Schuster & Loeffler, 1914), 39. For discussion of these academic figures and their milieu, see Klaus Christian Köhnke, *The Rise of Neo-Kantianism*, trans. R. J. Hollingdale (Cambridge: Cambridge University Press, 1991).

7. Ibid., 79.

8. Steinitzer, *Richard Strauss*, 39–40.

9. The basic principles of this movement, and their foundation in a critique of metaphysics, are discussed in Michael Benedikt, "Friedrich Jodls *Kritik des Idealismus*," in *Wilhelm Bolin und Friedrich Jodl im Kampf um die Aufklärung: Festschrift*

für Juha Manninen, ed. Georg Gimpl (Frankfurt am Main: Peter Lang, 1996), 271–86.

10. Bryan Magee, *The Philosophy of Schopenhauer* (Oxford: Clarendon Press, 1997), 428.

11. Steinitzer, *Richard Strauss*, 39–40.

12. Erich Urban, *Strauss contra Wagner* (Berlin: Schuster & Loeffler, 1902), 60–61.

13. Willi Schuh, *Richard Strauss: Jugend und frühe Meisterjahre. Lebenschronik 1864–1898* (Zurich: Atlantis, 1976), 138. Although many of Strauss's books from this era have been lost, this edition (*Arthur Schopenhauer's sämmtliche Werke*, 5 vols., ed. Julius Frauenstädt [Leipzig: F. A. Brockhaus, 1888]) survives at the RSA.

14. Rüdiger Safranski, *Schopenhauer and the Wild Years of Philosophy*, trans. Ewald Osers (Cambridge: Harvard University Press, 1990), 334.

15. Letter to Johanna Strauss, 8 June 1892. Bayerische Staatsbibliothek, Ana 330, I, Strauss.

16. Siegmund von Hausegger, *Alexander Ritter: Ein Bild seines Charakters und Schaffens* (Berlin: Marquardt & Co., [1907]), 57.

17. Ritter to Strauss, 17 January 1893. RSA.

18. On Ritter's Socratic relationship with young contemporaries, see August Richard, "Alexander Ritter und seine Tafelrunde," *Zeitschrift für Musik* 100 (1933): 817–18.

19. Arthur Schopenhauer, *Die Welt als Wille und Vorstellung* (Stuttgart: Philipp Reclam Jun., 1987), 1:536. Translations of Schopenhauer are adapted from *The World as Will and Representation*, trans. E. G. J. Payne (Indian Hills, Colo.: Falcon's Wing Press, 1958; reprint, New York: Dover, 1969). The page of this excerpt is 383; subsequent page references will include the page numbers in both editions, e.g., 536/383.

20. Magee, *The Philosophy of Schopenhauer*, 428.

21. Schopenhauer, *Die Welt als Wille*, 1:535/383.

22. The complexities of inferring Schopenhauer's atheism are described in David Berman, "Schopenhauer and Nietzsche: Honest Atheism, Dishonest Pessimism," in *Willing and Nothingness: Schopenhauer as Nietzsche's Educator*, ed. Christopher Janaway (Oxford: Clarendon Press, 1998), 178–80.

23. After Ritter's death Hans von Wolzogen would praise the passion that he brought to this mission, in particular his "flammende Natur" that heaped "Zorn" on "das Unechte." Hans von Wolzogen, "Gedenkwort," in *Zum Andenken Alexander Ritters* (Mannheim: Neue Musikalische Rundschau, 1897), 19.

24. Ritter to Strauss, 17 January 1893. RSA.

25. Ibid.

26. Excerpts from the correspondence related to *Guntram* are gathered into a "'Guntram'-Chronik" in Schuh, *Richard Strauss. Jugend und frühe Meisterjahre*, 274–300. The longer (and most important) of these letters are abridged, however, limiting their usefulness. Accounts of the revision abound; the most interesting is Arthur Seidl, "Richard Strauss: Eine Charakter-Skizze," in *Straussiana: Aufsätze zur Richard Strauß-Frage aus drei Jahrzehnten* (Regensburg: Gustav Bosse, [1913]), 44–51.

27. Ritter to Strauss, 17 January 1893. RSA.

28. Strauss to Ritter, 3–4 February 1893. Schuh, *Richard Strauss. Jugend und frühe Meisterjahre*, 289–92. Strauss to Thuille, 13 February 1893. Franz Trenner, ed., *Richard Strauss / Ludwig Thuille: Ein Briefwechsel* (Tutzing: Hans Schneider, 1980), 127–29.

29. Strauss to Ritter, 3–4 February 1893. Schuh, *Richard Strauss. Jugend und frühe Meisterjahre*, 290.

30. Seidl, *Richard Strauss*, 37–38.

31. Strauss to Ritter, 3–4 February 1893. Schuh, *Richard Strauss. Jugend und frühe Meisterjahre*, 290.

32. Schopenhauer, *Die Welt als Wille*, 1:383–84/267.

33. Ibid., 364/252–53.

34. Strauss to Thuille, 13 February 1893. Trenner, *Richard Strauss / Ludwig Thuille*, 128.

35. Rösch to Strauss, 15 March 1893. RSA.

36. Schuh, *Richard Strauss. Jugend und frühe Meisterjahre*, 292.

37. Schopenhauer, *Die Welt als Wille*, 1:362/252.

38. Ibid., 364/253.

39. Ibid.

40. Ibid., 364–65/253.

41. Ibid., 298–99/203.

42. Ibid., 301/205.

43. Ibid., 535–36/382–83.

44. Ibid., 535/382.

45. Strauss to Ritter, 3–4 February 1893. Schuh, *Richard Strauss. Jugend und frühe Meisterjahre*, 291.

46. Seidl, *Richard Strauss*, 50–51.

47. Seidl to Strauss, 15 January 1896. RSA.

48. Strauss to Thuille, 13 February 1893. Trenner, *Richard Strauss / Ludwig Thuille*, 128.

49. Hans Vaihinger, *The Philosophy of "As If"* (London: K. Paul, Trench, Truber, and Co., 1924), xxix.

50. In her diaries Cosima reported only one, relatively insubstantial, conversation about Schopenhauer during this period. Martin Gregor-Dellin and Dietrich Mack, eds., *Cosima Wagner's Diaries*, trans. Geoffrey Skelton, *Volume 1, 1869–1877* (New York: Harcourt Brace, 1976), 272.

51. Cosima Wagner to Strauss, 15 March 1893. Franz Trenner, ed., with assistance of Gabriele Strauss, *Cosima Wagner / Richard Strauss: Ein Briefwechsel* (Tutzing: Hans Schneider, 1978), 150.

52. Strauss to Cosima Wagner, 1 March 1893. Ibid., 148.

53. Schopenhauer, *Die Welt als Wille*, 1:278/188.

54. Ibid., 287–88/195–96.

55. Strauss to Cosima Wagner, 1 March 1893. Trenner, *Cosima Wagner / Richard Strauss*, 148.

56. Ibid.

57. Ibid.

58. Schopenhauer, *Die Welt als Wille*, 1:286/194.

59. Ibid., 451/319. Strauss's annotation reads "Trifft alles auf künstlerisches Produktion nicht zu!" RSA.

60. Strauss to Cosima Wagner, 1 March 1893. Trenner, *Cosima Wagner / Richard Strauss*, 148.

61. Rösch to Strauss, 15 March 1893. RSA.

62. Ibid.

63. Strauss to Cosima Wagner, 15 March 1893. Trenner, *Cosima Wagner / Richard Strauss*, 150.

64. Some of this material appears in Schuh, *Richard Strauss. Jugend und frühe Meisterjahre*, 316–20.

65. Schopenhauer, *Die Welt als Wille*, 1:433/306.

66. Strauss to Ritter, 3–4 February 1893. Strauss to Franz Strauss, 1 February 1893. Schuh, *Richard Strauss. Jugend und frühe Meisterjahre*, 289–90.

67. Schopenhauer, *Die Welt als Wille*, 1:404/283–84.

3. Strauss's Nietzsche

1. Theodor Adorno, "Richard Strauss. Born June 11, 1864," trans. Samuel Weber and Shierry Weber, *Perspectives of New Music* 4 (1965): 22.

2. John Daverio, "Richard Strauss's *Also sprach Zarathustra* and the 'Union' of Poetry and Philosophy," in *Nineteenth-Century Music and the German Romantic Ideology* (New York: Schirmer, 1993), 214–15, 221.

3. John Williamson, *Strauss: "Also sprach Zarathustra"* (Cambridge: Cambridge University Press, 1993), 29.

4. Hefling introduces this quotation as follows: "But Strauss, from the point at which he 'joined the Lizstians,' as he put it, tended to interpret the Schopenhauer-Wagner position on program music rather freely and simply—to the extent that he actually understood it." Stephen E. Hefling, "Miners Digging from Opposite Sides: Mahler, Strauss, and the Problem of Program Music," in *Richard Strauss: New Perspectives on the Composer and His Work*, ed. Bryan Gilliam (Durham, N.C.: Duke University Press, 1992), 44.

5. Reimann (1850–1906), an organist and critic in Berlin, had earlier published an explanatory essay in the program of the premiere of the revised version of *Macbeth* (29 February 1892). See Scott Warfield, "The Genesis of Richard Strauss's *Macbeth*" (PhD diss., University of North Carolina at Chapel Hill, 1995), 241, 521–23.

6. "Will es mir scheinen, als ob das Problem, dessen Lösung versucht wird, ein vorwiegend philosophisches und nicht ein vorwiegend dichterisches ist." Max Marschalk, "Frei nach Nietzsche," *Die Zukunft* 17 (1896): 617; quoted in Julia Liebscher, *Richard Strauss, Also sprach Zarathustra. Tondichtung (frei nach Friedr. Nietzsche) für grosses Orchester op. 30* (Munich: W. Fink, 1994), 105.

7. *Hamburger Nachrichten*, 3 December 1896; quoted in Walter Werbeck, *Die Tondichtungen von Richard Strauss* (Tutzing: Hans Schneider, 1996), 254.

8. *Berliner Tageblatt*, 18 November 1896, 589; quoted in Werbeck, *Tondichtungen*, 257.

9. Strauss to Thuille, 13 February 1893. Franz Trenner, ed., *Richard Strauss / Ludwig Thuille; Ein Briefwechsel* (Tutzing: Hans Schneider, 1980), 128. Strauss to Cosima Wagner, 10 April 1893. Franz Trenner, ed., with assistance of Gabriele Strauss, *Cosima Wagner / Richard Strauss: Ein Briefwechsel* (Tutzing: Hans Schneider, 1978), 155.

10. Arthur Seidl, "Richard Strauss: Eine Charakter-Skizze," in *Straussiana: Aufsätze zur Richard Strauß-Frage aus drei Jahrzehnten* (Regensburg: Gustave Bosse, [1913]), 46.

11. Herman Bischoff, "Guntram," *Allgemeine Musik-Zeitung* 23 (1896): 268.

12. Gustav Brecher, *Richard Strauss: Eine monographische Skizze* (Leipzig: Hermann Seemann Nachfolger, [1900]), 23–24.

13. Ernst Otto Nodnagel, *Jenseits von Wagner und Liszt* (Königsberg: Ostpreußische Druckerei und Verlagsanstalt, 1902), 80.

14. Otto Lessmann, "Die XXX. Tonkünstler-Versammlung des Allgemeinen Musikvereins. Weimar 31. Mai–6. Juni," *Allgemeine Musik-Zeitung* 24 (1894): 336.

15. Reinhard Gerlach, "Richard Strauss: Prinzipien seiner Kompositionstechnik," *Archiv für Musikwissenschaft* 23 (1966): 285.

16. Ritter to Strauss, 17 January 1893. RSA.

17. Rösch to Strauss, 27 December 1892. RSA. Three months later Rösch would continue to maintain that because Guntram was going to do penance, his "individualistic" language was inappropriate. Rösch to Strauss, 15 March 1893. RSA.

18. Rösch to Strauss, 15 March 1893. RSA.

19. Friedrich Nietzsche, *Zur Genealogie der Moral*, pt. 6, vol. 2, *Nietzsche Werke*, ed. Giorgio Colli and Mazzino Montinari (Berlin: de Gruyter, 1968), 428. Translation from Friedrich Nietzsche, *The Genealogy of Morals*, trans. Francis Golffing (Garden City, N.Y.: Doubleday Anchor, 1956), 297. Page references to Nietzsche's works will include the page numbers in both editions, e.g., 428/297.

20. Ibid., 309/191.

21. Friedrich Nietzsche, *Jenseits von Gut und Böse*, pt. 6, vol. 2, *Nietzsche Werke*, ed. Giorgio Colli and Mazzino Montinari (Berlin: de Gruyter, 1968), 92. Translation from Friedrich Nietzsche, *Beyond Good and Evil*, trans. R. J. Hollingdale (London: Penguin, 1990), 96. Friedrich Nietzsche, *Menschliches, Allzumenschliches*, pt. 6, vol. 1, *Nietzsche Werke*, ed. Giorgio Colli and Mazzino Montinari (Berlin: de Gruyter, 1968), 44. Translation from Friedrich Nietzsche, *Human, All Too Human*, trans. Marion Faber (Lincoln: University of Nebraska Press, 1984), 32.

22. Friedrich Nietzsche, *Götzen-Dämmerung*, pt. 6, vol. 3, *Nietzsche Werke*, ed. Giorgio Colli and Mazzino Montinari (Berlin: de Gruyter, 1968), 77. Translation from Friedrich Nietzsche, *The Twilight of the Idols*, trans. R. J. Hollingdale (London: Penguin, 1990), 52. Nietzsche, *Zur Genealogie der Moral*, 368/241.

23. Nietzsche, *Jenseits von Gut und Böse*, 65/76.

24. Willi Schuh, *Richard Strauss: Jugend und frühe Meisterjahre. Lebenschronik 1864–1898* (Zurich: Atlantis, 1976), 292.

25. Nietzsche, *Zur Genealogie der Moral*, 419/288–89.

26. Ibid., 420/290.

27. Nietzsche, *Götzen-Dämmerung*, 93/66.

28. A useful survey of Seidl's life and thought appears in Morten Kristiansen,

"Richard Strauss's *Feuersnot* in Its Aesthetic and Cultural Context: A Modernist Critique of Musical Idealism" (PhD diss., Yale University, 2000), 80–94. Flickers of a renewed interested in Seidl can be found in Leon Botstein, "An Unpublished Piece of Mahleriana," *The Musical Quarterly* 86 (2002): 3–5.

29. See chapter 1, n. 53, for reports of Seidl's activities with the Weimar Wagner Society.

30. Arthur Seidl, *Hat Richard Wagner eine Schule hinterlassen?* (Kiel: Lipsius & Tischer, 1892), 56; quoted in Kristiansen, "Richard Strauss's *Feuersnot*," 82. See chapter 1, n. 20, for a list of Seidl's essays for the *Bayreuther Blätter*.

31. Arthur Seidl, *Die Wagner-Nachfolge im Musikdrama*, *Wagneriana* (Berlin: Schuster, 1901), 3:389; quoted in Kristiansen, "Richard Strauss's *Feuersnot*," 85.

32. Seidl, *Die Wagner-Nachfolge*, 521, 524; quoted in Kristiansen, "Richard Strauss's *Feuersnot*," 92–93

33. Seidl assisted with the preparation of the first Nietzsche edition during the years 1898–99, working alongside Franz Overbeck.

34. Seidl, "Richard Strauss," 46.

35. Ibid., 33–34.

36. Schuh, *Richard Strauss. Jugend und frühe Meisterjahre*, 290.

37. Seidl, "Richard Strauss," 62.

38. Transcribed in Schuh, *Richard Strauss. Jugend und frühe Meisterjahre*, 262–66.

39. Richard Strauss to Franz Strauss, 7 April 1892. Bayerische Staatsbibliothek, Ana 330, I, Strauss.

40. Friedbert Streller, "Der junge Strauss und die Renaissance der Stirnerschen Anarchismus," in *Richard Strauss: Leben, Werk, Interpretation, Rezeption. Internationales Gewandhaus-Symposium 1989* (Leipzig: C. F. Peters, 1991), 63.

41. Rösch to Strauss, 9 April 1893. RSA.

42. "War er ja doch früher 'Wagnerianer'!" Ibid.

43. Rösch to Strauss, 15 March 1893. RSA.

44. Ibid. Strauss's letters to Rösch are lost, but Rösch frequently quoted Strauss verbatim in his remarkably fastidious responses. (This letter extends beyond thirty pages.)

45. Strauss to Cosima Wagner, 1 March 1893. Trenner, *Cosima Wagner / Richard Strauss*, 148.

46. Nietzsche, *Jenseits von Gut und Böse*, 80/89.

47. Rösch to Strauss, 9 April 1893. RSA.

48. Trenner sketchbook 3. RSA.

49. Strauss to Cosima Wagner, 10 April 1893. Trenner, *Cosima Wagner / Richard Strauss*, 155.

50. Nietzsche, *Jenseits von Gut und Böse*, 126–29/125–28.

51. Strauss to Cosima Wagner, 10 April 1893. Trenner, *Cosima Wagner / Richard Strauss*, 155.

52. Nietzsche, *Jenseits von Gut und Böse*, 196, 187/177, 170.

53. Ibid., 209/188.

54. Rösch to Strauss, 15 March 1893. RSA. Strauss to Cosima Wagner, 1 March 1893. Trenner, *Cosima Wagner / Richard Strauss*, 148.

55. Nietzsche, *Jenseits von Gut und Böse*, 25/47. Strauss was to conclude that

the origin of good musical ideas could not be traced: "whence they come, no one knows." Richard Strauss, "Vom melodischen Einfall," in *Betrachtungen und Erinnerungen*, 2d ed., ed. Willi Schuh (Zurich: Atlantis, 1957), 161.

56. Nietzsche, *Jenseits von Gut und Böse*, 110/111.

57. Strauss to Cosima Wagner, 10 April 1893. Trenner, *Cosima Wagner / Richard Strauss*, 155.

58. Schuh, *Richard Strauss. Jugend und frühe Meisterjahre*, 316–20.

59. Arthur Schopenhauer, *Die Welt als Wille und Vorstellung, Arthur Schopenhauer's sämmtliche Werke*, vol. 2 (Leipzig: Brockhaus, 1888), 376, 385, 358–59. RSA.

60. Both passages appear in section 54. Ibid., 334, 330. Translation from Arthur Schopenhauer, *The World as Will and Representation*, trans. E. F. J. Payne (New York: Dover, 1969), 283–84.

61. "Sein im Werden/Endziel dieses ewigen Werdens das Bewüßtsein davon!" Schopenhauer, *Die Welt als Wille*, 333.

62. "Ich verrate euch ein Geheimnis: auch *Strauss* begrüßte die *aufgehende* Sonne als 'einsame Mensch.'" Arthur Seidl, "Also sang Zarathustra" (1900), in *Moderner Geist in der deutschen Tonkunst: Gedanken eines Kulturpsychologen zur Wende des Jahrhunderts* (Regensburg: Gustav Bosse, [1913]), 108.

63. Strauss is quoted by Seidl in a letter to Strauss of 22 December 1896. RSA.

64. Ibid.

65. Seidl to Strauss, 14 March 1897. RSA.

66. Seidl to Strauss, 22 December 1896. RSA.

67. Werbeck, *Tondichtungen*, 255–56. Werbeck is right to conclude that the Hahn guide was based on information provided by Strauss himself, but he overextends the argument by holding that the guide therefore "corresponds precisely to his ideas (*Vorstellungen*) about the content of the work." Such one-dimensionality is not credible, particularly in this complicated context.

68. Trenner, *Cosima Wagner / Richard Strauss*, 26–37. On multiple layers of interpretation, see pp. 54–56.

69. Robert Gooding-Williams, *Zarathustra's Dionysian Modernism* (Stanford, Calif.: Stanford University Press, 2001), 46.

70. "Du sollst mich helfen—nicht mich *belehren* über Dinge die ich schon weiß." Quoted by Rösch in his letter to Strauss of 9 April 1893. RSA.

71. "Ich komme wieder zu diesem gleichen und selbigen Leben, im Grössten und auch im Kleinsten." Friedrich Nietzsche, *Also sprach Zarathustra: Ein Buch für Alle und Keinen*, pt. 6, vol. 1, *Nietzsche Werke*, ed. Giorgio Colli and Mazzino Montinari (Berlin: de Gruyter, 1968), 272. Translation from Friedrich Nietzsche, *Thus Spoke Zarathustra*, trans. R. J. Hollingdale (London: Penguin, 1969), 237–38.

72. The sketches of *Zarathustra* are discussed in Werbeck, *Tondichtungen*, 132–47.

73. Ibid., 165.

74. Ibid., 158.

75. Stephan Kohler, "Richard Strauss: *Eine Alpensinfonie*, op. 64," *Neue Zeitschrift für Musik* 143, no. 11 (November 1982): 42–46.

76. Werbeck, *Tondichtungen*, 165.

77. The connection between the parson disguise and the afterworldsmen is

noticed by Bryan Gilliam in "Richard Strauss," in *The Nineteenth-Century Symphony*, ed. D. Kern Holoman (New York: Schirmer, 1997), 356. Strauss's annotations of the *Till* score in this section read "Als Pastor verkleidet trieft er von Salbung u. Moral!" (m. 179) and "Fasst ihn ob des Spottes mit der Religion doch ein heimliches Grauen an vor dem Ende" (m. 196). Werbeck, *Tondichtungen*, 540.

78. Tim Ashley, *Richard Strauss* (London: Phaidon, 1999), 116–17.

79. The first evidence of the work comes in a poem headed "Mein Heim," beginning as follows: "Mein Weib, mein Kind und meine Musik / Natur und Sonne, die sind mein Glück." A more thorough treatment of this issue as it relates to *Domestica* and *Eine Alpensinfonie* appears in Charles Youmans, "The Twentieth-Century Symphonies of Richard Strauss," *The Musical Quarterly* 84 (2000): 238–58.

80. Werbeck, *Tondichtungen*, 182.

81. "Wäre nicht hier (im Zustande des empfangenden Weibes) der Weg zur Erlösung des Willens zu suchen! Nicht in der Verneinung des Willens, sondern in dem 'Bewußtsein' der Bejahung?" Schuh, *Richard Strauss. Jugend und frühe Meisterjahre*, 316.

82. Werbeck has shown that Strauss advanced considerably in the sketching of both tone poems before breaking off work on *Heldenleben*. Werbeck, *Tondichtungen*, 160.

4. Goethe and the Development of Strauss's Mature Worldview

1. Michael Kennedy, *Richard Strauss: Man, Musician, Enigma* (Cambridge: Cambridge University Press, 1999), 357.

2. Michael Kater, *Composers of the Nazi Era* (New York: Oxford University Press, 2000), 257.

3. Strauss to Willi Schuh, 6 December 1945. Willi Schuh, ed., *Richard Strauss: Briefwechsel mit Willi Schuh* (Zurich: Atlantis, 1969), 87.

4. The tradition is alive and well today, for example in the work of Maria Publig, who cites the late Strauss's immersion in Goethe while arguing that the composer lost not only his hope for but his interest in the future of postwar Germany. Maria Publig, *Richard Strauss: Bürger, Künstler, Rebell. Eine historische Annäherung* (Graz: Styria, 1999), 238, 244–45.

5. Lewis Lockwood, "The Element of Time in *Der Rosenkavalier*," in *Richard Strauss: New Perspectives on the Composer and His Work*, ed. Bryan Gilliam (Durham, N.C.: Duke University Press, 1992), 248–55; Leon Botstein, "The Enigmas of Richard Strauss: A Revisionist View," in *Richard Strauss and His World*, ed. Bryan Gilliam (Princeton: Princeton University Press, 1992), 12–13, 17–19; Bryan Gilliam, *The Life of Richard Strauss* (Cambridge: Cambridge University Press, 1999), 89–91.

6. In his "Brief über das humanistische Gymnasium" (1945) Strauss called Goethe the "last peak" in a group of Western cultural figures who had given humanity a set of "eternal spiritual values" (*ewige Geisteswerte*). Richard Strauss, *Betrachtungen und Erinnerungen*, 2d ed., ed. Willi Schuh (Zurich: Atlantis, 1957), 129.

7. Personal communication, Richard Strauss (the composer's grandson), Garmisch-Partenkirchen, 24 June 1994.

8. Richard Strauss, "Tagebuch der Griechenland- und Ägyptenreise (1892)," in *Richard Strauss Jahrbuch 1854*, ed. Willi Schuh (Bonn: Boosey & Hawkes, 1954), 89.

9. Franz Strauss and Alice Strauss, eds., *The Correspondence between Richard Strauss and Hugo von Hofmannsthal*, trans. Hanns Hammelmann and Ewald Osers (Cambridge: Cambridge University Press, 1980), 340.

10. Hofmannsthal to Strauss, 8 March 1912. Franz Strauss and Alice Strauss, *Richard Strauss and Hugo von Hofmannsthal*, 121.

11. Timothy L. Jackson, "The Metamorphosis of the *Metamorphosen:* New Analytical and Source-Critical Discoveries," in *Richard Strauss: New Perspectives*, 193–241.

12. The most extended treatment of this brief period is R. Larry Todd, "Strauss before Liszt and Wagner: Some Observations," in *Richard Strauss: New Perspectives*, 3–40.

13. Richard Strauss, *Richard Strauss: Briefe an die Eltern, 1882–1906*, ed. Willi Schuh (Zurich: Atlantis, 1954), 56–58, 60–67; idem, "Erinnerungen an Hans von Bülow," in *Betrachtungen und Erinnerungen*, 188–91; idem, "Aus meinen Jugend- und Lehrjahren," in *Betrachtungen und Erinnerungen*, 207–9.

14. Strauss, "Erinnerungen an Hans von Bülow," 190.

15. Strauss to Josephine Strauss, 28 October 1885. Strauss, *Briefe an die Eltern*, 66–67.

16. Strauss to Franz Strauss, 24 October 1885. Ibid., 63.

17. A discussion of influences on the early orchestral works of Strauss can be found in Scott Warfield, "The Genesis of Richard Strauss's *Macbeth*" (PhD diss., University of North Carolina at Chapel Hill, 1995), 36–82.

18. Mahler's and Strauss's differing perspectives on "music about music" are treated in Anette Unger, *Welt, Leben, und Kunst als Themen der "Zarathustra-Kompositionen" von Richard Strauss und Gustav Mahler* (Frankfurt am Main: Peter Lang, 1992), 133–34.

19. Eduard Hanslick, "'Wanderers Sturmlied' von Richard Strauss" [1892], in *Fünf Jahre Musik* (Berlin: Allgemeiner Verein für Deutsche Litteratur, 1896; reprint, Farborough: Gregg, 1971), 204.

20. Todd, "Strauss before Liszt and Wagner," 16–25.

21. The methods by which Wagner used the half-diminished seventh chord (or minor triad with added sixth) to control local and structural instability have been outlined in Robert Bailey, *Wagner: Prelude and Transfiguration from "Tristan and Isolde"* (New York: Norton, 1985), 122–24.

22. Derrick Puffett discussed pitch-specific allusions in Strauss in "'Lass Er die Musi, wo sie ist': Pitch Specificity in Strauss," in *Richard Strauss and His World*, ed. Gilliam, 138–63.

23. Carl Dahlhaus described some of the challenges that faced composers trying to mediate between the Wagnerian and Brahmsian legacies in "Issues in Composition," in *Between Romanticism and Modernism: Four Studies in the Music of the Later Nineteenth Century*, trans. Mary Whittall (Berkeley and Los Angeles: University of California Press, 1980), 40–78.

24. In the view of Rudolf Brandmeyer, the spirit described in the poem found its way into the language itself, through the repudiation of metrical organization and through other Pindaric *"Kühnheiten."* Rudolf Brandmeyer, *Die Gedichte des jungen Goethe* (Göttingen: Vandenhoeck & Ruprecht, 1998), 122.

25. Del Mar called the piece a "broad Maestoso Sonata movement." Norman Del Mar, *Richard Strauss: A Critical Commentary on His Life and Works* (London: Barrie and Rockliff, 1962), 1:33.

26. James Hepokoski, "Fiery-Pulsed Libertine or Domestic Hero? Strauss's *Don Juan* Reinvestigated," in *Richard Strauss: New Perspectives*, 135–41.

27. Strauss to Humperdinck, 27 March 1885. Gabriele Strauss, ed., *Lieber Collega!: Richard Strauss im Briefwechsel mit zeitgenössischen Komponisten und Dirigenten* (Berlin: Henschel, 1996), 203.

28. *Münchener Bote*, 19 November 1895.

29. Strauss's first work on *Lila* took place in 1878. Franz Trenner, *Richard Strauss Werkverzeichnis*, 2d ed. (Vienna: Verlag Dr. Richard Strauss, 1999), 42. The psychological topic of *Lila* has brought it more critical attention than other libretti from this era of Goethe's output, but to a limited extent. John R. Williams, *The Life of Goethe: A Critical Biography* (Oxford: Blackwell, 2001), 147.

30. Strauss to Cosima Wagner, 30 September 1895. Franz Trenner, ed., with assistance of Gabriele Strauss, *Cosima Wagner / Richard Strauss: Ein Briefwechsel* (Tutzing: Hans Schneider, 1978), 215–16.

31. The specific conception of insanity applied by Goethe in *Lila* is described in Gottfried Diener, *Goethes "Lila": Heilung eines "Wahnsinns" durch "psychische Kur"* (Frankfurt am Main: Athenäum, 1971), 147–49.

32. In response to Strauss's query about how to deal with the fourth act, Cosima provided a set of revisions for all four acts. These were apparently conceived in a general sense by her but worked out in detail by a young female author who wrote under the name of "Günther von Freiberg." The revised text was sent to Strauss and is now held in the RSA. Trenner, *Cosima Wagner / Richard Strauss*, 211–14.

33. Strauss to Cosima Wagner, 12 April 1896. Ibid., 222.

34. Ibid., 221.

35. Bryan Gilliam, *The Life of Richard Strauss* (Cambridge: Cambridge University Press, 1999), 107. Strauss had suggested to Hofmannsthal during composition of this opera to "make up our minds that *Frau ohne Schatten* shall be the last romantic opera." Franz Strauss and Alice Strauss, *Richard Strauss and Hugo von Hofmannsthal*, 259.

36. On the difficulties of the immediate postwar situation in Berlin see Alexandra Richie, *Faust's Metropolis: A History of Berlin* (New York: Carroll & Graf, 1998), 284–324.

37. See Bryan Gilliam, "Strauss's *Intermezzo*: Innovation and Tradition," in *Richard Strauss: New Perspectives*, 259–83.

38. Michael Kennedy gives a full account of this episode in *Richard Strauss*, 200–1. See also Kurt Wilhelm, *Richard Strauss: An Intimate Portrait*, trans. Mary Whittall (New York: Rizzoli, 1989), 150–52.

39. A reading of these songs as further rebellion against Bote and Bock is offered by Barbara A. Petersen in "Die Händler und die Kunst: Richard Strauss

as Composers' Advocate," in *Richard Strauss: New Perspectives*, 115–32, esp. 121–23.

40. Typically this hubris plays out against a backdrop of irony and humor. See Manfred Eickhölter, *Die Lehre vom Dichter in Goethes Divan* (Hamburg: Helmut Buske, 1984), 117–22.

41. The translations, by Pamela Marwood, are taken from *The Songs of Richard Strauss*, EMI SLS 792, LP, 1971.

42. At mm. 22ff. the personal quality of the diatonic material is intensified with a quotation of the "Aufstieg" theme from the *Alpensinfonie*, at pitch (E-flat), marking the text's mention of nature.

43. Theodor Adorno, "Richard Strauss. Born June 11, 1864," trans. Samuel Weber and Shierry Weber, *Perspectives of New Music* 4 (1965): 14–32, and *Perspectives of New Music* 5 (1966): 113–29. Richard Strauss, "Letzte Aufzeichnung," in *Betrachtungen und Erinnerungen*, 182.

44. Looking back on *Tod und Verklärung* in 1931 Strauss held that the motivating factor of the composition was a "musical need . . . to write a piece that begins in C minor and ends in C major." Willi Schuh, *Richard Strauss: Jugend und frühe Meisterjahre. Lebenschronik 1864–1898* (Zurich: Atlantic, 1976), 187–88.

45. Gilliam, *The Life of Richard Strauss*, 173.

46. Strauss changed this ending at the behest of Bülow, who said that "an Egmont overture can certainly end with a triumphal march of Egmont, but a symphonic poem named 'Macbeth' cannot end with the triumph of Macduff." Strauss, "Aus meinen Jugend- und Lehrjahren," 211.

47. Jackson, "The Metamorphosis of the *Metamorphosen*," 195.

48. Willi Schuh, "Gruelmärchen um Richard Strauss' *Metamorphosen*," *Schweizerische Musikzeitung* 103 (1963): 438.

49. Nietzschean threads in the *Deutsche Motette* are discussed in Ulrich Konrad, "Die *Deutsche Motette* op. 62 von Richard Strauss: Entstehung, Form, Gehalt," in *Richard Strauss und die Moderne*, ed. Bernd Edelmann, Birgit Lodes, and Reinhold Schlötterer (Berlin: Henschel, 2001), 308–10.

50. Kennedy, *Richard Strauss*, 362.

51. Matthijs Vermeulen, "Een dubbel schandaal: Het Concertgebouw herdenkt Hitler," *De Groene Amsterdammer*, 11 October 1947, p. 7; the article appeared shortly thereafter in German translation as "Ein doppelter Skandal. Das Concertgebouw gedenkt Hitlers," *National Zeitung*, Basel, 25 October 1947, p. 2. See Timothy L. Jackson, "The Metamorphosis of the *Metamorphosen*: New Analytical and Source-Critical Discoveries," 201–2.

52. The most recent treatment of this period is Bryan Gilliam, "'Friede im Innern': Außenwelt und Innenwelt von Richard Strauss um 1935," in *Richard Strauss und die Moderne*, 93–111.

53. Ernst Krause, *Richard Strauss: Der letzte Romantiker* (Munich: Wilhelm Heyne, 1963), 458.

54. Translation from Gilliam, *The Life of Richard Strauss*, 174.

55. Walter Thomas Anderman, *Bis der Vorhang fiel: Berichtet nach Aufzeichnungen aus den Jahren 1940 bis 1945* (Dortmund: K. Schwalvenberg, 1947), 241; quoted in Michael Kater, *Composers of the Nazi Era* (New York: Oxford University Press, 2000), 217.

56. Wilhelm, *Richard Strauss*, 197.

57. Gilliam, *The Life of Richard Strauss*, 183.

58. Biographical information on Goethe in this section is drawn principally from three sources: Karl Otto Conrady, *Goethe: Leben und Werk*, vol. 1, *Hälfte des Lebens* (Königstein: Athenäum, 1982), and vol. 2, *Summe des Lebens* (Königstein: Athenäum, 1985); Nicholas Boyle, *Goethe: The Poet and the Age*, vol. 1, *The Poetry of Desire (1749–1790)* (Oxford: Clarendon Press, 1991), and vol. 2, *Revolution and Renunciation (1790–1803)* (Oxford: Clarendon Press, 2000); and Richard Friedenthal, *Goethe: His Life and Times* (Cleveland: World Publishing Company, 1963).

59. Adorno, "Richard Strauss. Born June 11, 1864," 25.

60. Friedrich Sengle, *Kontinuität und Wandlung: Einführung in Goethes Leben und Werk*, ed. Marianne Tilch (Heidelberg: C. Winter, 1999), 223.

61. David E. Wellbery, for example, sees Goethe's early lyric poetry as "one of Romanticism's significant beginnings," a view that he justifies not only through criticism of the poetry but with the historical observation that the 1770s was also Kant's "silent decade," in which the philosopher for the first time "elaborated the problem of transcendentality." David E. Wellbery, *The Specular Moment: Goethe's Early Lyric and the Beginnings of Romanticism* (Stanford, Calif.: Stanford University Press, 1996), 56.

62. Thomas Mann, "Goethes 'Werther,'" in *Goethes "Werther": Kritik und Forschung*, ed. Hans Peter Hermann (Darmstadt: Wissenschaftliche Buchgesellschaft, 1994), 101.

63. Hannebre Schlaffer, *Wilhelm Meister: Das Ende der Kunst und die Wiederkehr des Mythos* (Stuttgart: J. B. Metzler, 1980), 40.

64. A case study of Goethe's influence on the romantics can be found in Géza von Molnár, "'Wilhelm Meister' from a Romantic Perspective. Aspects of Novalis' Predisposition That Resulted in His Initial Preference for Goethe's Novel," in *Versuche zu Goethe: Festschrift für Erich Heller*, ed. Volker Dürr and Géza von Molnár (Heidelberg: Lothar Stiehm, 1976), 235–47.

65. Hans Henning, *Goethes "Götz von Berlichingen" in der zeitgenössischen Rezeption* (Leipzig: Zentralantiquariat der Deutschen Demokratischen Republik, 1988), 355–58.

66. Monika Lemmel, *Poetologie in Goethes west-östlichem Divan* (Heidelberg: Carl Winter, 1987), 16.

67. Some 850 drawings by Goethe survive from his journey to Italy. Their clarity and objectivity speaks to Goethe's dual tendencies as artist and scientist. Conrady, *Goethe*, 1:449.

68. Ibid., 436.

69. Friedenthal, *Goethe*, 264.

70. Gilliam, *The Life of Richard Strauss*, 179.

71. Boyle, *Goethe*, 1:640.

72. Stefan Blessin, *Goethes Romane: Aufbruch der Moderne* (Paderborn: Ferdinand Schöningh, 1996), 241.

73. Ibid., 73.

74. Friedenthal in particular emphasized Goethe's awareness that he might easily have broadened his popularity and prevented misunderstandings by avoiding such shifts. Friedenthal, *Goethe*, 270.

75. Erich Heller, "Die Zweideutigkeit von Goethe's 'Faust,'" in *Aufsätze zu Goethes Faust I*, ed. Werner Keller (Darmstadt: Wissenschaftliche Buchgesellschaft, 1974), 65.

76. Karl Schlechta, "Goethes 'Wilhelm Meister,'" in *Goethes "Wilhelm Meister": Zur Rezeptionsgeschichte der Lehr- und Wanderjahre*, ed. Klaus F. Gille (Königstein: Athenäum, 1979), 261.

77. Friedenthal, *Goethe*, 130.

78. Ibid., 339.

79. Ibid., 341.

5. The First Cycle of Tone Poems

1. Carl Dahlhaus, *Nineteenth-Century Music*, trans. J. Bradford Robinson (Berkeley and Los Angeles: University of California Press, 1989), 330.

2. Strauss to Franz Wüllner, 30 January 1888. Franz Grasberger, ed., *Der Strom der Töne trug mich fort: Die Welt um Richard Strauss in Briefen* (Tutzing: Hans Schneider, 1967), 38. He was still touching up the Andante in September of 1888 even as he finished the first draft of the *Guntram* plot. Strauss to Franz Strauss, 6 September 1888. Richard Strauss, *Richard Strauss: Briefe an die Eltern, 1882–1906*, ed. Willi Schuh (Zurich: Atlantis, 1954), 104.

3. Strauss's comments about Liszt in this period are restricted almost exclusively to the claim that Liszt applied in orchestral music a principle that Wagner applied in dramatic music: the idea that all music should have a "poetic idea" as stimulus. With regard to the technical implementation of that principle, however, Wagner's method held much more interest for Strauss than Liszt's. In other words, Strauss's belief in the "Lisztian" view that "new ideas must seek out new forms" did not prevent him from practicing it in a Wagnerian way. Richard Strauss, *Betrachtungen und Erinnerungen*, 2d ed., ed. Will Schuh (Zurich: Atlantis, 1957), 210.

4. Particularly important here would be degrees of subtlety. In thematic terms, the technique that Wagner described as his "art of the most refined, gradual transition" took on ever-increasing importance for the maturing Strauss, at the expense of the more conspicuous transformational methods employed by Liszt. On the Wagnerian technique see Carl Dahlhaus, *Richard Wagner's Music Dramas*, trans. Mary Whittall (Cambridge: Cambridge University Press, 1971), 57–61.

5. Strauss's interests here seem to reflect the influence of A. B. Marx, whose theories of programmaticism made considerable room for illustrative and narrative details. No evidence exists that Strauss ever consulted Marx's writings directly, but he might well have done so, and moreover, Marx's ideas were so widely disseminated that it is difficult to imagine Strauss not having encountered them through multiple secondhand sources. The possibility of a connection is particularly compelling given that it was Marx who first expressed the conviction that a work's form must be determined by its poetic content. Stefan Kunze, ed., *Ludwig van Beethoven. Die Werke im Spiegel seiner Zeit. Gesammelte Konzertberichte und Rezensionen bis 1830* (Laaber: Laaber-Verlag, 1987), 387. For an account of Marx's views concerning the role of external events in programmatic music, see Judith Silber

Ballan, "Marxian Programmatic Music: A Stage in Mendelssohn's Musical Development," in *Mendelssohn Studies*, ed. R. Larry Todd (Cambridge: Cambridge University Press, 1992), 149–61.

6. Strauss's eagerness to begin the new century, which is of course obvious from the subtitle of *Also sprach Zarathustra*, also found its way into informal utterances. For example, a letter to his parents on 31 December 1899, sending good wishes for the new year, also expresses relief that 1900 would be "the last year of the nineteenth century." Strauss, *Briefe an die Eltern*, 229.

7. In the words of James Hepokoski, "a more productive goal of analysis would be to uncover a 'modern' composition's ambiguities. Stressing the work's unresolved tensions, such an analysis would seek the piece's essential aesthetic moment in the pull of those tensions." James Hepokoski, "Fiery-Pulsed Libertine or Domestic Hero? Strauss's *Don Juan* Reinvestigated," in *Richard Strauss: New Perspectives on the Composer and His Work*, ed. Bryan Gilliam (Durham, N.C.: Duke University Press, 1992), 135.

8. This exchange is contained in letters of 25 February 1890, 3 March 1890, 6 March 1890, and 22 March 1890. Franz Trenner, ed., with assistance of Gabriele Strauss, *Cosima Wagner / Richard Strauss: Ein Briefwechsel* (Tutzing: Hans Schneider, 1978), 26, 29, 31–32, 35–36. See the discussion in chapter 1, pp. 54–56.

9. Rudolf Louis, review of *Macbeth*, *Blätter für Haus- und Kirchenmusik* 4 (1900): 90; quoted in Mark-Daniel Schmid, "The Tone Poems of Richard Strauss and Their Reception History from 1887–1908" (PhD diss., Northwestern University, 1997), 158.

10. The strongest evidence for this conclusion is the nearly complete halt of his compositional activity after he completed *Tod und Verklärung* (on 18 November 1889), which allowed him to concentrate on the libretto of *Guntram*.

11. John Williamson has discussed this terminological distinction in *Strauss: "Also sprach Zarathustra"* (Cambridge: Cambridge University Press, 1993), 16–19.

12. Max Steinitzer, *Richard Strauss* (Berlin: Schuster & Loeffler, 1911), 60. Franz Trenner, ed., *Richard Strauss / Ludwig Thuille: Ein Briefwechsel* (Tutzing: Hans Schneider, 1980), 15–16.

13. The third movement's coda and to a lesser extent its development section (with quotation of material from the "Gretchen" movement) are of course new, but they do not obscure the overriding formal parallels between the first and last movements, i.e., the fact that they follow essentially the same sonata-based plan.

14. The first of three versions of *Macbeth* was finished on 9 January 1888. Scott Warfield has determined through study of the sketches that work began in the spring of 1887. Scott Warfield, "The Genesis of Richard Strauss's *Macbeth*" (PhD diss., University of North Carolina at Chapel Hill, 1995), 121. The first sign of work on *Guntram* is a letter of 26 August 1887 to Marie von Bülow in which Strauss says he is "working further on the draft of an original libretto." Willi Schuh, *Richard Strauss: Jugend und frühe Meisterjahre. Lebenschronik 1864–1898* (Zurich: Atlantis, 1976), 274.

15. As suggested by Oscar Bie, Strauss learned from Ritter that lieder could serve as a testing ground for vocal techniques drawn from Wagner's music dramas. Oscar Bie, *Das deutsche Lied* (Berlin: S. Fischer, [1926]), 257. Walter Niemann also

concluded that Ritter's most successful and characteristic music was to be found in his lieder. Walter Niemann, *Die Musik der Gegenwart* (Berlin: Schuster & Loeffler, 1921), 220. August Stradal credited Ritter with producing the finest example of a new genre, the Wagnerian song cycle (in the *Liebesnächte*, for soprano and baritone). August Stradal, "Lieder," in *Zum Andenken Alexander Ritters* (Mannheim: Neue Musikalische Rundschau, 1897), 23–24.

16. See, for example, Henry T. Finck, *Richard Strauss: The Man and His Work* (Boston: Little, Brown, and Company, 1917), 243. More recently, see Joseph Kerman, *Opera as Drama*, new and revised ed. (Berkeley and Los Angeles: University of California Press, 1988), 208–9.

17. This approach to the tone poems has also been applied by Daniel Harrison, in an analysis of *Tod und Verklärung* that is ultimately less concerned with genre—operatic or symphonic—than with identifying particular moments of correspondence between music and program. See Daniel Harrison, "Imagining *Tod und Verklärung*," *Richard Strauss Blätter*, n.s., 29 (1993): 22–52. Further investigation of operatic procedures anticipated in the tone poems can be found in Reinhard Gerlach, "Die Orchesterkomposition als musikalisches Drama: Die Teil-Tonalitäten der 'Gestalten' und der bitonale Kontrapunkt in Ein Heldenleben von Richard Strauss," *MusikTheorie* 6 (1991): 55–78.

18. Bryan Gilliam, "Strauss's Preliminary Opera Sketches: Thematic Fragments and Symphonic Continuity," *Nineteenth-Century Music* 9 (1986): 176–88.

19. This cross-fertilization is the topic of Anthony Newcomb's seminal article "The Birth of Music Out of the Spirit of Drama," *Nineteenth-Century Music* 5 (1981): 38–66.

20. It is perhaps for this reason that Harrison decided not to deal with sonata-form issues in *Tod und Verklärung*. See n. 6 of Harrison, "Imagining *Tod und Verklärung*," 48.

21. A challenge of the aesthetic of coherence as applied to Wagner appears in Carolyn Abbate, "Wagner, 'On Modulation,' and *Tristan*," *Cambridge Opera Journal* 1, no. 1 (1989): 34–38.

22. Gabriele Strauss, ed., *Lieber Collega!: Richard Strauss im Briefwechsel mit zeitgenössischen Komponisten und Dirigenten* (Berlin: Henschel, 1996), 81–83.

23. The transparency of these moments has not prevented basic disagreements over the formal outlines, which are summarized in James Hepokoski, "Structure and Program in *Macbeth*: A Proposed Reading of Strauss's First Symphonic Poem," in *Richard Strauss and His World*, ed. Bryan Gilliam (Princeton: Princeton University Press, 1992), 68–71.

24. The most thorough discussion of this technique in Liszt remains László Somfai: "Die musikalischen Gestaltwandlungen der Faust-Symphonie von Liszt," *Studia musicologica Academiae scientiarum hungaricae* 2 (1962): 87–137.

25. Hepokoski, "Structure and Program in *Macbeth*," 71.

26. Strauss to (his uncle) Carl Hörburger, 11 June 1888. Grasberger, *Der Strom der Töne*, 41.

27. This choice also makes sense in terms of the play's action, the major event at this point (the end of act 1) being the arrival of Duncan at Macbeth's home. Strauss's music at m. 123 seems to capture the ceremonial character of this visit.

28. Denis Wilde has also highlighted this connection, noting the similarity of contour and the rising sixth. Denis Wilde, *The Development of Melody in the Tone Poems of Richard Strauss* (Lewiston, N.Y.: Edwin Mellen Press, 1990), 43, 47.

29. See chapter 1, p. 43.

30. Carolyn Abbate has summarized Wagner's post–*Oper und Drama* position on this issue in "Opera as Symphony, a Wagnerian Myth," in *Analyzing Opera,* ed. Carolyn Abbate and Roger Parker (Berkeley and Los Angeles: University of California Press, 1989), 100–3.

31. Robert Donington, *Wagner's "Ring" and Its Symbols* (London: Faber and Faber, 1963), 275–77.

32. In other words, this music continues Beethoven's challenge to the distinction between presentation and development, described effectively (for example) in Carl Dahlhaus, *Ludwig van Beethoven: Approaches to His Music,* trans. Mary Whittall (Oxford: Clarendon Press, 1991), 116–18.

33. Walter Werbeck, *Die Tondichtungen von Richard Strauss* (Tutzing: Hans Schneider, 1996), 244–45.

34. Hepokoski, "*Don Juan* Reinvestigated," 145.

35. These connections are also noted in ibid., 151, and Wilde, *The Development of Melody,* 91.

36. Strauss wrote to Oscar Posa, for example, that *Don Juan* included three specific female characters, "whose melodic outlines are very sharply defined." Strauss to Posa, 31 January 1900. Grasberger, *Der Strom der Töne,* 129.

37. See mm. 186ff., 206ff., 235ff., etc.

38. In 1890, Strauss told Johann Leopold Bella, for example, that he would "completely abolish" sonata form. Strauss to Bella, 3 March 1890. Franz Zagiba, *Johann L. Bella (1843–1936) und das Wiener Musikleben* (Vienna: Notringes der wissenschaftliche Verbände Österreichs, 1955), 48.

39. The most sensitive treatment of these relationships comes in Harrison, "Imagining *Tod und Verklärung,*" 34–36.

40. Gustav Brecher and Arthur Seidl both noted this work's particularly close connection to Wagner; for Brecher that tendency signaled a regression. Gustav Brecher, *Richard Strauss: Eine monographische Skizze* (Leipzig: Hermann Seemann Nachfolger, [1900]), 22. Arthur Seidl, "Richard Strauss: Eine Charakter-Skizze," in *Straussiana: Aufsätze zur Richard-Strauß-Frage aus drei Jahrzehnten* (Regensburg: Gustav Bosse, [1913]), 15. The Wagner connection is also discussed in Schmid, "The Tone Poems of Richard Strauss," 176–77.

41. The work "makes the main theme its point of culmination and does not state it until the middle." Michael Kennedy, *Richard Strauss: Man, Musician, Enigma* (Cambridge: Cambridge University Press, 1999), 110.

42. In this case the status of the theme as "new" is not affected by its derivation from earlier material; this again is a standard Wagnerian procedure.

43. Werbeck, *Die Tondichtungen von Richard Strauss,* 421.

44. The *Erläuterungen* published in Herwarth Walden, ed., *Richard Strauss: Symphonies und Tondichtungen* (Berlin: Schlesinger, 1908), are filled with this kind of discussion, with each significant thematic idea given a number so that interactions can be described conveniently by shorthand reference to the various threads of the texture.

45. Thus Ritter's claim that "striving for the greatest possible *Willensvernei-nung* remains the only demonstrable goal of our existence" ("bleibt das Streben nach möglichster Willensverneinung der einzig nachweisbare Zweck unseres Daseins"). Ritter to Strauss, 17 January 1893. RSA.

46. Richard Wagner, "Über Franz Liszt's symphonische Dichtungen," in *Sämtliche Schriften und Dichtungen* (Leipzig: Breitkopf und Härtel, [1911]), 5:193–94.

47. Strauss expressed a favorable opinion of Berlioz to Cosima Wagner from the early days of their friendship, calling him a "peculiar [*eigenartig*] genius" in a letter of 26 November 1889, but always tempering his praise with qualifications that he knew she would expect. Trenner, *Cosima Wagner / Richard Strauss*, 11, 48–49, 67.

48. Specht, for example, consciously chose not to reflect extensively on the program, as a way of acknowledging "the richness of the music beside the poverty of the poetry." Others seem to have followed his lead. Richard Specht, *Richard Strauss und sein Werk*, vol. 1, *Der Künstler und sein Weg; Der Instrumentalkomponist* (Leipzig: E. P. Tal & Co., 1921), 185.

49. Arthur Schopenhauer, *Die Welt als Wille und Vorstellung* (Stuttgart: Philipp Reclam Jun., 1987), 1:249–50.

50. This quotation, from 1897, appears in Joseph Horowitz, *Wagner Nights* (Berkeley and Los Angeles: University of California Press, 1994), 287.

51. Cosima heard the work as a further distancing from the Wagner/Liszt position and said so to Strauss. After attending a Berlin performance of *Tod und Verklärung* in February 1891, she warned Strauss not to allow "the jumble of modernity" to derail his artistic development and urged him to leave aside "Russian and French material." Trenner, *Cosima Wagner / Richard Strauss*, 194, 197.

52. See the prologue, pp. 13–15.

53. A concise statement of this view comes at the end of Werbeck's discussion of the *Don Juan* sketches; similar passages can be found in his treatments of the sketches for each of the tone poems. Werbeck, *Die Tondichtungen von Richard Strauss*, 118.

54. Notwithstanding James Hepokoski's recent expansive critique of this principle, as a basic norm it clearly affected Strauss's conception of how the form typically functioned. James Hepokoski, "Beyond the Sonata Principle," *Journal of the American Musicological Society* 55 (2002): 91–154.

55. Which is to say that none of them enacts the "Essential Expositional Closure" identified by Hepokoski and Warren Darcy as the defining moment of a sonata exposition. James Hepokoski and Warren Darcy, "The Medial Caesura and Its Role in the Eighteenth-Century Sonata Exposition," *Music Theory Spectrum* 19 (1997): 119.

6. Eulenspiegel, Zarathustra, Quixote, Strauss

1. That is to say, they focus on the conflict that Strauss identified in the "letzte Aufzeichnung" as central to his entire oeuvre. Two of the five works he mentioned in this connection belong to the second cycle of tone poems. *Tod und Verklärung*,

by contrast, thematizes the subject/object antagonism, but in order to set up a redemptive synthesis that the mature Strauss rejected. Richard Strauss, "Letzte Aufzeichnung," in *Betrachtungen und Erinnerungen*, 2d ed., ed. Willi Schuh (Zurich: Atlantis, 1957), 182.

2. Willi Schuh, *Richard Strauss: Jugend und frühe Meisterjahre. Lebenschronik 1864–1898* (Zurich: Atlantis: 1976), 433, 398.

3. By telling his father that suggestions of autobiographical content in *Heldenleben* were "only partly true," Strauss confirmed that they were at least to some extent valid. Strauss to Franz Strauss, 24 March 1899. Richard Strauss, *Richard Strauss: Briefe an die Eltern, 1882–1906*, ed. Willi Schuh (Zurich: Atlantis, 1954), 221.

4. The desire to take full advantage of his popularity is apparent in Strauss's hard-nosed negotiations prior to the Berlin appointment, in which he secured offers from America and London in order to push the Berlin offer higher. Money was not everything, however; the offers that he turned down were worth approximately twice the one that he accepted. A representative description of the negotiations can be found in the letter to Pauline of 8 April 1898. Franz Grasberger, ed., *Der Strom der Töne trug mich fort: Die Welt um Richard Strauss in Briefen* (Tutzing: Hans Schneider, 1967), 115–16.

5. The "first idea" for *Don Quixote* was noted by Strauss on 10 October 1896, but Werbeck has suggested that the first musical sketches related to either work were for *Heldenleben*, followed by activity on both simultaneously during the beginning of 1897. Walter Werbeck, *Die Tondichtungen von Richard Strauss* (Tutzing: Hans Schneider, 1996), 159–60. The diary entry, from 16 April 1897, is quoted in Schuh, *Richard Strauss*, 475.

6. One of Strauss's recommended programs of his works was *Don Quixote* followed by *Ein Heldenleben*. Richard Strauss, "Meine Werke in guter Zusammenstellung" (1941), in *Betrachtungen und Erinnerungen*, 160.

7. On the basic critical dimension of *Feuersnot* see Morten Kristiansen, "Richard Strauss's *Feuersnot* in Its Aesthetic and Cultural Context: A Modernist Critique of Musical Idealism" (PhD diss., Yale University, 2000), 13–18.

8. Mark-Daniel Schmid, "The Tone Poems of Richard Strauss and Their Reception History from 1887–1908" (PhD diss., Northwestern University, 1997), 232–45, 269–72.

9. This even in negative reviews, for example that of the *Bayerischer Kurier*, 1–2 December 1895, in which the anonymous author complained about material lifted from *Tristan* but nonetheless praised Strauss's "astounding mastery of the orchestra" and "refinement of orchestration."

10. Ernest Newman, *Richard Strauss* (London: J. Lane, 1908; reprint, Freeport, N.Y.: Books for Libraries Press, 1969), 75.

11. Wilhelm Mauke, "Till Eulenspiegels lustige Streiche," in *Richard Strauss: Symphonien und Tondichtungen*, ed. Herwarth Walden (Berlin: Schlesinger, [1908]), 92.

12. Strauss's annotations of two different *Till* scores (his own and Wilhelm Mauke's) are reproduced in Werbeck, *Die Tondichtungen von Richard Strauss*, 540–41.

13. Strauss recognized the dual importance in the work of the "lustig" and

the "Drastik," and he advised Franz Wüllner not to allow the latter element to be overwhelmed by the former. Strauss to Wüllner, 26 September 1895, in Gabriele Strauss, ed., *Lieber Collega!: Richard Strauss in Briefwechsel mit zeitgenössischen Komponisten und Dirigenten*, (Berlin: Henschel, 1996), 311.

14. Seidl responded cordially, but expressed his wish that he had been the dedicatee of a Till opera rather than a tone poem. Seidl to Strauss, 18 June 1895. RSA.

15. "Already in *Till Eulenspiegel* we find a work with the character of a manifesto." Charles Youmans, "Richard Strauss's *Guntram* and the Dismantling of Wagnerian Musical Metaphysics" (PhD diss., Duke University, 1996), 171.

16. Given Strauss's close ties to Wahnfried, it is not inconceivable that he knew that the theme dated from the "Starnberg days," i.e., that it predated both *Siegfried* and the *Siegfried-Idyll*. Werner Breig, "The Musical Works," in *Wagner Handbook*, ed. Ulrich Müller and Peter Wapnewski, trans. John Deathridge (Cambridge: Harvard University Press, 1992), 454–55.

17. Richard Specht, *Richard Strauss und sein Werk*, vol. 1, *Der Künstler und sein Weg; Der Instrumentalkomponist* (Leipzig: E. P. Tal & Co., 1921), 221.

18. Mauke, "Till Eulenspiegels lustige Streiche," 92.

19. The ambivalent heroism that Strauss associated with this key is shown by the fact that he also used it for Papa in *Symponia domestica* and Aegisthus in *Elektra*. For a concise discussion of associative tonality in Strauss see Bryan Gilliam, *Richard Strauss's "Elektra"* (Oxford: Clarendon Press, 1991), 67–69. The topic receives extended treatment in Edmund Wachten, "Das Formproblem in der sinfonischen Dichtungen von Richard Strauss" (PhD diss., University of Berlin, 1933).

20. Mark Anson-Cartwright has identified structural motivic functions of this theme's characteristic augmented triad in the *Idyll*. I would hold, nevertheless, that on the programmatic level and with its introduction of the new key of A-flat the theme's role is to push the work from the ordinary (conventional sonata form) to some higher plane of expression, which may be prefigured in other operations of the augmented triad but still is heard as new. Mark Anson-Cartwright, "Chord as Motive: The Augmented-Triad Matrix in Wagner's *Siegfried Idyll*," *Music Analysis* 15 (1996): 57–63.

21. The tradition of imposing new ideas onto this character in the retelling of the story goes back to sixteenth-century oral reception. Werner Wunderlich, *Till Eulenspiegel* (Munich: Wilhelm Fink, 1984), 97–98. The malleability of the character in this early period is also discussed in Reinhard Tenberg, *Die deutsche Till Eulenspiegel-Rezeption bis zum Ende des 16. Jahrhunderts* (Würzburg: Königshausen und Neumann, 1996), 204–8.

22. Anette Unger, *Welt, Leben und Kunst als Themen der "Zarathustra-Kompositionen" von Richard Strauss und Gustav Mahler* (Frankfurt am Main: Peter Lang, 1992), 172–209.

23. The earliest surviving source of this quotation is James Huneker's *Mezzotints in Modern Music* (New York: C. Scribner's Sons, 1899), 145. No German source has been found, despite the best efforts of Werbeck (*Die Tondichtungen von Richard Strauss*, 258, n. 663) and Unger (*Welt, Leben und Kunst*, 164), both of whom quoted from Norman Del Mar, *Richard Strauss: A Critical Commentary on His Life and Work* (London: Barrie and Rockliff, 1962), 1:134.

24. Strauss's letter to Hausegger, which is now in private possession, is reprinted in full in Werbeck, *Die Tondichtungen von Richard Strauss*, 531–39; the quotation appears on p. 536.

25. Max Marschalk, review of *Also sprach Zarathustra*, *Die Zukunft* 17 (1896): 617.

26. Max Loewengard, "Also sprach Zarathustra," *Das Magazin für Literatur* 65 (1896): 1544, 1542.

27. Hahn's guide was first published in 1896 by H. Bechhold, Frankfurt a.M., in conjunction with the premiere of the tone poem in Frankfurt on 27 November 1896. It subsequently appeared as Arthur Hahn, "Also sprach Zarathustra: Tondichtung frei nach Fr. Nietzsche: Op. 30," in *Richard Strauss: Symphonien und Tondichtungen*, ed. Herwarth Walden (Berlin: Schlesinger, [1908]). This citation is taken from pp. 109–11.

28. Seidl to Strauss, 14 March 1897. RSA.

29. Max Steinitzer, *Richard Strauss*, 5th–8th ed. (Berlin: Schuster & Loeffler, 1914), 152.

30. Hans Merian, *Richard Strauss' Tondichtung "Also sprach Zarathustra": Eine Studie über die moderne Programmsymphonie* (Leipzig: Meyers, 1899), 52–53.

31. Werbeck, *Die Tondichtung en von Richard Strauss*, 364.

32. Franz Trenner, ed., *Die Skizzenbücher von Richard Strauss* (Tutzing: Hans Schneider, 1977), 4.

33. Hahn, *"Also sprach Zarathustra,"* 115–16.

34. *Berliner Tageblatt*, Nr. 589 (18 November 1896); quoted in Werbeck, *Die Tondichtungen von Richard Strauss*, 257.

35. See chapter 5, note 38.

36. Merian, *Richard Strauss' Tondichtung "Also sprach Zarathustra,"* 45.

37. Del Mar, *Richard Strauss*, 163.

38. Werbeck, *Die Tondichtungen von Richard Strauss*, 155, 232.

39. Ibid., 154.

40. These works include Mendelssohn's singspiel *Die Hochzeit des Camacho* (1825; it was his only opera performed in public during his lifetime), Rubinstein's orchestral "character picture" *Don Quixote* (1870), and Kienzl's opera *Don Quixote* (1897).

41. Nodnagel made both of these points: the quotations facilitated an autobiographical streak that had already become a formula before *Heldenleben*, and this newly blatant approach offered a "convenient handle" to his critics. Ernst Otto Nodnagel, *Jenseits von Wagner und Liszt* (Königsberg: Ostpreußischen Druckerei und Verlagsanstalt, 1902), 93–94.

42. See n. 3 concerning Strauss's letter to his father on 24 March 1899.

43. Werbeck, *Die Tondichtungen von Richard Strauss*, 104.

44. Romain Rolland, "French Music and German Music," in *Richard Strauss and Romain Rolland: Correspondence*, ed. and trans. Rollo Meyers (London: Calder and Boyars, 1968), 211.

45. Schuh read this passage as "new enemies and former friends" ("neuen Feinden und einstigen Freunden") and included a facsimile in *Richard Strauss*, 494–95. Werbeck's alternate reading ("inneren Feinden [Zweifel, Ekel] u. äußeren

Feinde") seems preferable, however, in spite of the inconsistent plural form; see *Die Tondichtungen von Richard Strauss*, 164–65.

46. In a continuity draft for the conclusion of *Guntram*, Strauss notated music in F-sharp that appears in the opera in G-flat. The enharmonic distinction thus seems not to have made a difference to him with regard to affect. Trenner sketchbook 2, RSA.

47. This impact is clear not only in the famous letter of 24 August 1888 but in an earlier one (26 December 1887) describing in great detail the shortcomings of a performance of the Ninth Symphony conducted by Hermann Levi. The common thread in this diatribe is that the reading lacked "expression" (*Ausdruck*), a word that in Strauss's new aesthetic was more loaded than any other. Gabriele Strauss, *Lieber Collega!*, 67–68.

48. The kind of tonal pairing used here by Strauss was of course a staple of nineteenth-century harmonic technique and has been the theme of at least one extended study: William Kinderman and Harald Krebs, eds., *The Second Practice of Nineteenth-Century Tonality* (Lincoln: University of Nebraska Press, 1996).

7. Absolute Music, Twentieth-Century Aesthetics, and the Symphonies of Richard Strauss

1. The notion that these works did in fact fail has been disputed only by the staunchest Straussian partisans, such as Roland Tenschert, who claimed as late as 1944 that *Domestica* was "one of the high points in all [Strauss's] output." Roland Tenschert, "Um das Erbe Franz Liszts: Die Programmusik," in *3 x 7 Variationen über das Thema Richard Strauss* (Vienna: Wilhelm Frick, 1944), 44.

2. These sketches are described in Walter Werbeck, *Die Tondichtungen von Richard Strauss* (Tutzing: Hans Schneider, 1996), 164.

3. This article is quoted in full in ibid., 531–33.

4. Strauss's first long-term formal engagement in Berlin, as conductor of the Berlin Philharmonic for the 1894–95 season (replacing Bülow), ended unhappily after one year with his removal in favor of Nikisch.

5. Richard Strauss, "Letzte Aufzeichnung," in *Betrachtungen und Erinnerungen*, 2d ed., ed. Willi Schuh (Zurich: Atlantis, 1957), 182.

6. Urban felt that *Feuersnot* was an anomaly, a sort of pastime until the crucial next step for Strauss, a new tone poem, could be composed. Erich Urban, *Strauss contra Wagner* (Berlin: Schuster & Loeffler, 1902), 88.

7. Mark-Daniel Schmid has shown that while *Domestica* found widespread public acclaim in its first three years, it was largely panned by the critics and by 1908 had essentially fallen out of the repertoire. Mark-Daniel Schmid, "The Tone Poems of Richard Strauss and Their Reception History from 1887–1908" (PhD diss., Northwestern University, 1997), 410–49.

8. Strauss to his parents, 22 March 1904. Richard Strauss, *Richard Strauss: Briefe an die Eltern, 1882–1906*, ed. Willi Schuh (Zurich: Atlantis, 1954), 295.

9. Strauss to Hofmannsthal, 15 November 1915. Franz Strauss and Alice Strauss, eds., *The Correspondence between Richard Strauss and Hugo von Hofmannsthal,*

trans. Hanns Hammelmann and Ewald Osers (Cambridge: Cambridge University Press, 1980), 237.

10. Schäfer held that *Domestica* was basically different from all Strauss's other works in its desire to be "more objective." Theo Schäfer, "Richard Strauss als Symphoniker," in *Richard Strauss Woche Muenchen 23.–28. Juni* (Munich: F. Bruckmann, 1910), 96.

11. Franz Strauss to Richard Strauss, 23 March 1903. Strauss, *Briefe an die Eltern*, 278–79.

12. Romain Rolland, "French Music and German Music," in *Richard Strauss and Romain Rolland: Correspondence*, ed. and trans. Rollo Myers (London: Calder and Boyars, 1968), 212.

13. Rudolf Louis, *Die Deutsche Musik der Gegenwart*, rev. ed. (Munich: Georg Müller, 1912), 173; a translation by Susan Gillespie appears in Bryan Gilliam, ed., *Richard Strauss and His World* (Princeton: Princeton University Press, 1992), 307.

14. On this step in Mahler's career, see Constantin Floros, *Gustav Mahler: The Symphonies*, trans. Vernon Wicker and Jutta Wicker (Portland, Ore.: Amadeus Press, 1993), 112–13.

15. See Arnold Schoenberg, *Sämtliche Werke*, Abteilung 6, Reihe B, Band 20, *Streichquartette I, Kritischer Bericht, Skizzen Fragmente*, ed. Christian Martin Schmidt (Mainz: B. Schott's Söhne, 1986), 109–10.

16. Ernest Newman, *Richard Strauss* (London: J. Lane, 1908; reprint, Freeport, N.Y.: Books for Libraries Press, 1969), 82–83.

17. This complex genesis is considered in detail, through an extensive study of all available sketches, in Rainer Bayreuther, *Richard Strauss' "Alpensinfonie": Entstehung, Analyse und Interpretation* (Hildesheim: Georg Olms, 1997). See also Werbeck, *Die Tondichtungen von Richard Strauss*, 183–207.

18. A facsimile of this diary entry has been published in Stephan Kohler, "Richard Strauss: *Eine Alpensinfonie*, op. 64," *Neue Zeitschrift für Musik* 143, no. 11 (November 1982): 42–46. It reads, in part: "Gustav Mahler nach schwerer Krankheit am 19. [*sic*] Mai verschieden. . . . Der Jude Mahler konnte im Christentum noch Erhebung gewinnen. Der Held Rich. Wagner ist als Greis, durch den Einfluß Schopenhauers wieder zu ihm herabgestiegen. . . . Ich will meine Alpensinfonie den Antichrist nennen, als da ist: sittliche Reinigung aus eigener Kraft, Befreiung durch die Arbeit, Anbetung der ewigen herrlichen Natur."

19. These entries are found in Strauss's "braunes Tagebuch." RSA.

20. The applicability of Schoenberg's theory of tritone equivalency to the music of Strauss has been considered most recently by Graham H. Phipps and John Williamson. See Graham H. Phipps, "The Logic of Tonality in Strauss's *Don Quixote*: A Schoenbergian Evaluation," *Nineteenth-Century Music* 9 (1986): 191–93; and John Williamson, *Strauss: "Also sprach Zarathustra"* (Cambridge: Cambridge University Press, 1993), 91–92.

21. Lewis Lockwood, "The Element of Time in *Der Rosenkavalier*," in *Richard Strauss: New Perspectives on the Composer and His Work*, ed. Bryan Gilliam (Durham, N.C.: Duke University Press, 1992), 252.

22. Gabriele Strauss, ed., *Lieber Collega!: Richard Strauss im Briefwechsel mit zeitgenössischen Komponisten und Dirigenten* (Berlin: Henschel, 1996), 193.

23. Werbeck, *Die Tondichtungen von Richard Strauss*, 173.

24. Tenschert discussed the *Alpensinfonie* in these terms, citing a "naiveté of invention" and "simplicity of structure" common to that work, Beethoven's *Pastoral* Symphony, and "most other masterworks of pastoral character." Tenschert, "Um das Erbe Franz Liszts: Die Programmusik," 46.

25. Friedrich Nietzsche, *Menschliches, Allzumenschliches*, part 6, vol. 1, *Nietzsche Werke*, ed. Giorgio Colli and Mazzino Montinari (Berlin: de Gruyter, 1968), 147.

26. Georg Gräner, *Anton Bruckner, Die Musik* (Leipzig: Fr. Kistner and C.F.W.S. Siegel, [1924]), 51:12.

27. Friedrich Nietzsche, *Also sprach Zarathustra: Ein Buch für Alle und Keinen*, part 6, vol. 1, *Nietzsche Werke*, ed. Giorgio Colli and Mazzino Montinari (Berlin: de Gruyter, 1968), 9, 33.

28. Friedrich Nietzsche, *Jenseits von Gut und Böse*, part 6, vol. 2, *Nietzsche Werke*, ed. Giorgio Colli and Mazzino Montinari (Berlin: de Gruyter, 1968), 80.

29. Max Steinitzer, *Richard Strauss*, 5th–8th ed. (Berlin: Schuster & Loeffler, 1914), 38–39.

30. On the powerful destabilizing effects of this plan see James Webster, *Haydn's "Farewell" Symphony and the Idea of Classical Style* (Cambridge: Cambridge University Press, 1991), 33–37.

31. Steinitzer, *Richard Strauss*, 33.

32. Concerning this tonal relationship, Scott Warfield discusses the possible antecedents of Beethoven's String Quartet in F Minor, op. 95, and Brahms's Piano Quintet in F Minor, op. 34. Scott Warfield, "The Genesis of Richard Strauss's *Macbeth*" (PhD diss., University of North Carolina at Chapel Hill, 1995), 74.

33. Urban believed that this tendency showed no signs of weakening in any of the works up to and including *Wandrers Sturmlied*. Erich Urban, *Richard Strauss* (Berlin: Gose & Tetzlaff, 1901), 11.

34. "What in 1883 seemed an impassable gulf was in 1897 no longer a problem." Arnold Schoenberg, "Brahms the Progressive," in *Style and Idea*, ed. Leonard Stein (New York: St. Martin's Press, 1975), 399.

35. Richard Specht, *Richard Strauss und sein Werk*, vol. 1, *Der Künstler und sein Weg; Der Instrumentalkomponist* (Leipzig: E. P. Tal & Co., 1921), 33.

36. Arthur Seidl, "Richard Strauss: Eine Charakter-Skizze," in *Straussiana: Aufsätze zur Richard-Strauß-Frage aus drei Jahrzehnten* (Regensburg: Gustav Bosse, [1913]), 19–20.

37. Strauss to his parents, 11 May 1886. *Briefe an die Eltern*, 98. Strauss also commented to Bülow on the power that the Italian landscape had exercised on his musical imagination. Strauss to Bülow, 23 June 1886. Gabriele Strauss, *Lieber Collega!*, 36.

38. Norman Del Mar, *Richard Strauss: A Critical Commentary on His Life and Works* (London: Barrie and Rockliff, 1962), 1:43.

39. Schäfer, for one, implicitly contradicted the oversight explanation by referring to the "universally known 'Funiculi'." Schäfer, "Richard Strauss als Symphoniker," 86.

Works Cited

Abbate, Carolyn. "Opera as Symphony, a Wagnerian Myth." In *Analyzing Opera*, edited by Carolyn Abbate and Roger Parker, 92–124. Berkeley and Los Angeles: University of California Press, 1989.

———. "Wagner, 'On Modulation,' and *Tristan.*" *Cambridge Opera Journal* 1, no. 1 (1989): 34–38.

Adamy, Bernhard. "Schopenhauer bei Richard Strauss." *Jahrbuch der Schopenhauer Gesellschaft* 61 (1980): 195–98.

Adorno, Theodor. "Richard Strauss at Sixty." Translated by Susan Gillespie. In *Richard Strauss and His World*, edited by Bryan Gilliam, 406–15. Princeton: Princeton University Press, 1992.

———. "Richard Strauss. Born June 11, 1864." Translated by Samuel Weber and Shierry Weber. *Perspectives of New Music* 4 (1965): 14–32, and 5 (1966): 113–29.

Anderman, Walter Thomas. *Bis der Vorhang fiel: Berichtet nach Aufzeichnungen aus den Jahren 1940 bis 1945.* Dortmund: K. Schwalvenberg, 1947.

Anson-Cartwright, Mark. "Chord as Motive: The Augmented-Triad Matrix in Wagner's *Siegfried Idyll.*" *Music Analysis* 15 (1996): 57–71.

Ashley, Tim. *Richard Strauss.* London: Phaidon, 1999.

Bailey, Robert. *Wagner: Prelude and Transfiguration from "Tristan and Isolde."* New York: Norton, 1985.

Ballan, Judith Silber. "Marxian Programmatic Music: A Stage in Mendelssohn's Musical Development." In *Mendelssohn Studies*, edited by R. Larry Todd, 149–61. Cambridge: Cambridge University Press, 1992.

Bayreuther, Rainer. *Richard Strauss' "Alpensinfonie": Entstehung, Analyse und Interpretation.* Hildesheim: Georg Olms, 1997.

Benedikt, Michael. "Friedrich Jodls *Kritik des Idealismus.*" In *Wilhelm Bolin und Friedrich Jodl im Kampf um die Aufklärung: Festschrift für Juha Manninen*, edited by Georg Gimpl, 271–86. Frankfurt am Main: Peter Lang, 1996.

Berman, David. "Schopenhauer and Nietzsche: Honest Atheism, Dishonest Pessimism." In *Willing and Nothingness: Schopenhauer as Nietzsche's Educator*, edited by Christopher Janaway, 178–95. Oxford: Clarendon Press, 1998.

Bie, Oscar. *Das deutsche Lied.* Berlin: S. Fischer, [1926].

Birkin, Kenneth. "Richard Strauss in Weimar. Part 1: The Concert Hall." *Richard Strauss-Blätter*, n.s., 33 (June 1995): 3–36.

———. "Richard Strauss in Weimar. Part 2: The Opera House." *Richard Strauss-Blätter*, n.s., 34 (December 1995): 3–56.

Bischoff, Hermann. "Guntram." *Allgemeine Musik-Zeitung* 23 (1896): 193–94, 213–14, 227–29, 239–41, 253–54, 267–68.

Blaukopf, Herta, ed. *Gustav Mahler Briefe*. Vienna: Paul Zolnay, 1982.

Blessin, Stefan. *Goethes Romane: Aufbruch der Modern*. Paderborn: Ferdinand Schöningh, 1996.

Böhm, Karl. *Ich erinnere mich ganz genau*. Edited by Hans Weigel. Zurich: Biogees, 1968.

Borchmeyer, Dieter. *Richard Wagner: Theory and Theater*. Translated by Stewart Spencer. Oxford: Clarendon Press, 1991.

Botstein, Leon. "The Enigmas of Richard Strauss: A Revisionist View." In *Richard Strauss and His World*, edited by Bryan Gilliam, 3–32. Princeton: Princeton University Press, 1992.

———. "An Unpublished Piece of Mahleriana." *The Musical Quarterly* 86 (2002): 3–5.

Boyle, Nicholas. *Goethe: The Poet and the Age*. Vol. 1, *The Poetry of Desire (1749–1790)*. Oxford: Clarendon Press, 1991.

———. *Goethe: The Poet and the Age*. Vol. 2, *Revolution and Renunciation (1790–1803)*. Oxford: Clarendon Press, 2000.

Brandmeyer, Rudolf. *Die Gedichte des jungen Goethe*. Göttingen: Vandenhoeck & Ruprecht, 1998.

Brecher, Gustav. *Richard Strauß: Eine monographische Skizze*. Leipzig: Hermann Seemann Nachfolger, [1900].

Breig, Werner. "The Musical Works." In *Wagner Handbook*, edited by Ulrich Müller and Peter Wapnewski, translated by John Deathridge, 397–483. Cambridge: Harvard University Press, 1992.

Brosche, Günther. "Richard Strauss und Arnold Schoenberg." *Richard Strauss-Blätter*, n.s., 2 (December 1979): 21–28.

Bujic, Bojan, ed. *Music in European Thought, 1851–1912*. Cambridge: Cambridge University Press, 1988.

Bülow, Marie von, ed. *Hans von Bülows Leben, dargestellt aus seinen Briefen*. 2d ed. Leipzig: Breitkopf & Härtel, 1921.

Burnham, Scott. "On the Beautiful in Mozart." In *Music and the Aesthetics of Modernity*, edited by Karol Berger and Anthony Newcomb. Berkeley and Los Angeles: University of California Press, forthcoming.

Conrady, Karl Otto. *Goethe: Leben und Werk*. Vol. 1, *Hälfte des Lebens*. Königstein: Athenäum, 1982.

———. *Goethe: Leben und Werk*. Vol. 2, *Summe des Lebens*. Königstein: Athenäum, 1985.

Dahlhaus, Carl. *The Idea of Absolute Music*. Translated by Roger Lustig. Chicago: University of Chicago Press, 1989.

———. "Issues in Composition." In *Between Romanticism and Modernism: Four Studies in the Music of the Later Nineteenth Century*. Translated by Mary Whittall. Berkeley and Los Angeles: University of California Press, 1980.

———. *Ludwig van Beethoven: Approaches to His Music*. Translated by Mary Whittall. Oxford: Clarendon Press, 1991.

———. "Musikalische Moderne und Neue Musik." *Melos/Neue Zeitschrift für Musik* 2 (1976): 90.

———. "Neo-romanticism." In *Between Romanticism and Modernism: Four Studies in the Music of the Later Nineteenth Century.* Translated by Mary Whittall. Berkeley and Los Angeles: University of California Press, 1980.

———. *Nineteenth-Century Music.* Translated by J. Bradford Robinson. Berkeley and Los Angeles: University of California Press, 1989.

———. *Richard Wagner's Music Dramas.* Translated by Mary Whittall. Cambridge: Cambridge University Press, 1971.

Danz, Ernst-Joachim. *Die objektlose Kunst: Untersuchungen zur Musikästhetik Friedrich von Haulseggers.* Regensburg: Gustav Bosse, 1981.

Daverio, John. "Richard Strauss's *Also sprach Zarathustra* and the 'Union' of Poetry and Philosophy." In *Nineteenth-Century Music and the German Romantic Ideology.* New York: Schirmer, 1993.

Del Mar, Norman. *Richard Strauss: A Critical Commentary on His Life and Works.* Vol. 1. London: Barrie and Rockliff, 1962.

Diener, Gottfried. *Goethes "Lila": Heilung eines "Wahnsinns" durch "psychische Kur."* Frankfurt am Main: Athenäum, 1971.

Donington, Robert. *Wagner's "Ring" and Its Symbols.* London: Faber and Faber, 1963.

Edelmann, Bernd, Birgit Lodes, and Reinhold Schlötterer, eds. *Richard Strauss und die Moderne.* Berlin: Henschel, 2001.

Eickhölter, Manfred. *Die Lehre vom Dichter in Goethes Divan.* Hamburg: Helmut Buske, 1984.

Finck, Henry T. *Richard Strauss: The Man and His Work.* Boston: Little, Brown, and Company, 1917.

Floros, Constantin. *Gustav Mahler: The Symphonies.* Translated by Vernon Wicker and Jutta Wicker. Portland, Ore.: Amadeus Press, 1993.

Frankenstein, Ludwig. *Arthur Seidl. Ein Lebensabriß.* Regensburg: Gustav Bosse, 1913.

Friedenthal, Richard. *Goethe: His Life and Times.* Cleveland: World Publishing Company, 1963.

Frisch, Walter. *Brahms and the Principle of Developing Variation.* Berkeley and Los Angeles: University of California Press, 1984.

———. "Dancing in Chains: Reflections on *Ariadne auf Naxos.*" In *Richard Strauss Studies,* edited by Timothy L. Jackson and Graham Phipps. Cambridge: Cambridge University Press, forthcoming.

Gatz, Felix M. *Musik-Ästhetik in ihren Hauptrichtungen: Ein Quellenbuch der deutschen Musik-Ästhetik von Kant und der Frühromantik bis zur Gegenwart mit Einführung und Erläuterungen.* Stuttgart: Ferdinand Enke, 1929.

Gerlach, Reinhard. "Die Orchesterkomposition als musikalisches Drama: Die Teil-Tonalitäten der 'Gestalten' und der bitonale Kontrapunkt in Ein Heldenleben von Richard Strauss." *MusikTheorie* 6 (1991): 55–78.

———. "Richard Strauss: Prinzipien seiner Kompositionstechnik." *Archiv für Musikwissenschaft* 23 (1966): 277–88.

Gilliam, Bryan. "'Friede im Innern': Außenwelt und Innenwelt von Richard Strauss um 1935." In *Richard Strauss und die Moderne,* edited by Bernd Edelmann, Birgit Lodes, and Reinhold Schlötterer, 93–111. Berlin: Henschel, 2001.

———. *The Life of Richard Strauss.* Cambridge: Cambridge University Press, 1999.

———. "Richard Strauss." In *The Nineteenth-Century Symphony,* edited by D. Kern Holoman, 345–68. New York: Schirmer, 1997.

———, ed. *Richard Strauss: New Perspectives on the Composer and His Work.* Durham, N.C.: Duke University Press, 1992.

———, ed. *Richard Strauss and His World.* Princeton: Princeton University Press, 1992.

———. *Richard Strauss's "Elektra."* Oxford: Clarendon Press, 1991.

———. "Strauss's *Intermezzo:* Innovation and Tradition." In *Richard Strauss: New Perspectives on the Composer and His Work,* edited by Bryan Gilliam, 259–83. Durham, N.C.: Duke University Press, 1992.

———. "Strauss's Preliminary Opera Sketches: Thematic Fragments and Symphonic Continuity." *Nineteenth-Century Music* 9 (1986): 176–88.

Gimpl, Georg. *Wilhelm Bolin und Friedrich Jodl im Kampf um die Aufklärung: Festschrift für Juha Manninen.* Frankfurt am Main: Peter Lang, 1996.

Gooding-Williams, Robert. *Zarathustra's Dionysian Modernism.* Stanford, Calif.: Stanford University Press, 2001.

Gräner, Georg. *Anton Bruckner.* Leipzig: Fr. Kistner und C.F.W.S. Siegel, [1924].

Grasberger, Franz, ed. *Der Strom der Töne trug mich fort: Die Welt um Richard Strauss in Briefen.* Tutzing: Hans Schneider, 1967.

Gregor-Dellin, Martin, and Dietrich Mack, eds. *Cosima Wagner's Diaries.* 2 vols. Translated by Geoffrey Skelton. New York: Harcourt Brace, 1976.

Haas, Frithjof. *Hans von Bülow. Leben und Wirken: Wegbereiter für Wagner, Liszt und Brahms.* Wilhelmshaven: F. Noetzel, Heinrichshofen Bücher, 2002.

Hahn, Arthur. "Also sprach Zarathustra: Tondichtung frei nach Fr. Nietzsche: Op. 30." In *Richard Strauss: Symphonien und Tondichtungen,* edited by Herwarth Walden, 109–27. Berlin: Schlesinger, [1908].

Hanslick, Eduard. *Vom Musikalisch-Schönen.* Vol. 1, *Historisch-kritische Ausgabe.* Edited by Dietmar Strauß. Mainz: Schott, 1990.

———. "'Wanderers Sturmlied' von Richard Strauss" [1892]. In *Fünf Jahre Musik.* Berlin: Allgemeiner Verein für Deutsche Litteratur, 1896. Reprint, Farborough, United Kingdom: Gregg, 1971.

Harrison, Daniel. "Imagining *Tod und Verklärung.*" *Richard Strauss Blätter,* n.s., 29 (June 1993): 22–52.

Hausegger, Friedrich von. Review of "Vom Musikalisch-Erhabenen," by Arthur Seidl. *Bayreuther Blätter* 11 (1888): 198–200.

Hausegger, Siegmund von. *Alexander Ritter: Ein Bild seines Charakters und Schaffens.* Berlin: Marquardt & Co., [1907].

Hefling, Stephen. "Miners Digging from Opposite Sides: Mahler, Strauss, and the Problem of Program Music." In *Richard Strauss: New Perspectives on the Composer and His Work,* edited by Bryan Gilliam, 41–53. Durham, N.C.: Duke University Press, 1992.

Heller, Erich. "Die Zweideutigkeit von Goethe's 'Faust.'" In *Aufsätze zu Goethes Faust I,* edited by Werner Keller, 64–85. Darmstadt: Wissenschaftliche Buchgesellschaft, 1974.

Henning, Hans. *Goethes "Götz von Berlichingen" in der zeitgenössischen Rezeption.* Leipzig: Zentralantiquariat der Deutschen Demokratischen Republik, 1988.

Hepokoski, James. "Beyond the Sonata Principle." *Journal of the American Musicological Society* 55 (2002): 91–154.

———. "Fiery-Pulsed Libertine or Domestic Hero? Strauss's *Don Juan* Reinvestigated." In *Richard Strauss: New Perspectives on the Composer and His Work,* edited by Bryan Gilliam, 135–75. Durham, N.C.: Duke University Press, 1992.

———. "Structure and Program in *Macbeth:* A Proposed Reading of Strauss's First Symphonic Poem." In *Richard Strauss and His World,* edited by Bryan Gilliam, 67–89. Princeton: Princeton University Press, 1992.

Hepokoski, James, and Warren Darcy. "The Medial Caesura and Its Role in the Eighteenth-Century Sonata Exposition." *Music Theory Spectrum* 19 (1997): 115–54.

Hinrichsen, Hans-Joachim. *Musikalische Interpretation: Hans von Bülow.* Stuttgart: Franz Steiner, 1999.

Hofmiller, Josef. "Alexander Ritter, der Dichter und Komponist." *Die Gesellschaft* 4 (1894) and 8 (1898).

Horowitz, Joseph. *Wagner Nights.* Berkeley and Los Angeles: University of California Press, 1994.

Houlgate, Stephen. *Hegel, Nietzsche and the Criticism of Metaphysics.* Cambridge: Cambridge University Press, 1986.

Hübscher, Arthur. *Denker gegen den Strom. Schopenhauer: Gestern-Heute-Morgen.* Bonn: Bouvier Verlag Herbert Grundmann, 1973.

Huneker, James. *Mezzotints in Modern Music.* New York: C. Scribner's Sons, 1899.

Jackson, Timothy L. "The Metamorphosis of the *Metamorphosen:* New Analytical and Source-Critical Discoveries." In *Richard Strauss: New Perspectives on the Composer and His Work,* edited by Bryan Gilliam, 193–241. Durham, N.C.: Duke University Press, 1992.

Janz, Curt Paul. "The Form-Content Problem in Friedrich Nietzsche's Conception of Music." In *Nietzsche's New Seas: Explorations in Philosophy, Aesthetics, and Politics,* edited by Michael Allen Gillespie and Tracy B. Strong, 97–116. Chicago: University of Chicago Press, 1988.

Jelavich, Peter. *Munich and Theatrical Modernism: Politics, Playwriting, and Performance, 1890–1914.* Cambridge: Harvard University Press, 1985.

Kater, Michael. *Composers of the Nazi Era.* New York: Oxford University Press, 2000.

Kennedy, Michael. *Richard Strauss: Man, Musician, Enigma.* Cambridge: Cambridge University Press, 1999.

Kerman, Joseph. *Opera as Drama.* New and revised ed. Berkeley and Los Angeles: University of California Press, 1988.

Kinderman, William, and Harald Krebs, eds. *The Second Practice of Nineteenth-Century Tonality.* Lincoln: University of Nebraska Press, 1996.

Klatte, Wilhelm. "Aus Richard Strauss' Werkstatt." *Die Musik* 16 (1923–24): 636–41.

Kohler, Stephan. "Richard Strauss: *Eine Alpensinfonie*, op. 64." *Neue Zeitschrift für Musik* 143, no. 11 (November 1982): 42–46.

Köhnke, Klaus Christian. *The Rise of Neo-Kantianism*. Translated by R. J. Hollingdale. Cambridge: Cambridge University Press, 1991.

Konrad, Ulrich. "Die *Deutsche Motette* op. 62 von Richard Strauss: Entstehung, Form, Gehalt." In *Richard Strauss und die Moderne*, edited by Bernd Edelmann, Birgit Lodes, and Reinhold Schlötterer, 283–310. Berlin: Henschel, 2001.

Krause, Ernst. *Richard Strauss: Der letzte Romantiker*. Munich: Wilhelm Heyne, 1963.

Kristiansen, Morten. "Richard Strauss's *Feuersnot* in Its Aesthetic and Cultural Context: A Modernist Critique of Musical Idealism." PhD diss., Yale University, 2000.

Kunze, Stefan, ed. *Ludwig van Beethoven. Die Werke im Spiegel seiner Zeit. Gesammelte Konzertberichte und Rezensionen bis 1830*. Laaber: Laaber-Verlag, 1987.

Large, David C., and William Weber, eds. *Wagnerism in European Culture and Politics*. Cornell, N.Y.: Cornell University Press, 1984.

Lemmel, Monika. *Poetologie in Goethes west-östlichem Divan*. Heidelberg: Carl Winter, 1987.

Lessmann, Otto. "Die XXX. Tonkünstler-Versammlung des Allgemeinen Musikvereins. Weimar 31. Mai–6. Juni." *Allgemeine Musik-Zeitung* 24 (1894): 336.

Liebscher, Julia. *Richard Strauss, Also sprach Zarathustra. Tondichtung (frei nach Friedr. Nietzsche) für grosses Orchester op. 30*. Munich: W. Fink, 1994.

———. "Richard Strauss und Friedrich Nietzsche." *Richard Strauss-Blätter*, n.s., 27 (June 1992): 10–38.

Lippman, Edward. *A History of Western Musical Aesthetics*. Lincoln: University of Nebraska Press, 1992.

Lockwood, Lewis. "The Element of Time in *Der Rosenkavalier*." In *Richard Strauss: New Perspectives on the Composer and His Work*, edited by Bryan Gilliam, 248–55. Durham, N.C.: Duke University Press, 1992.

Loewengard, Max. "Also sprach Zarathustra." *Das Magazin für Literatur* 65 (1896): 1542–1544.

Louis, Rudolf. *Die Deutsche Musik der Gegenwart*. Rev. ed. Munich: Georg Müller, 1912.

Magee, Bryan. *The Philosophy of Schopenhauer*. Oxford: Clarendon Press, 1997.

Mahler, Alma. *Gustav Mahler: Memories and Letters*. Edited by Donald Mitchell. Translated by Basil Creighton. New York: Viking Press, 1969.

Mann, Thomas. "Goethes 'Werther.'" In *Goethes "Werther": Kritik und Forschung*, edited by Hans Peter Hermann, 88–101. Darmstadt: Wissenschaftliche Buchgesellschaft, 1994.

Marschalk, Max. Review of *Also sprach Zarathustra*. *Die Zukunft* 17 (1896): 617.

Marek, George. *Cosima Wagner*. New York: Harper & Row, 1981.

Marschalk, Max. "Frei nach Nietzsche." *Die Zukunft* 17 (1896): 617.

Mauke, Wilhelm. "Till Eulenspiegels lustige Streiche." In *Richard Strauss: Sym-*

phonien und Tondichtungen, edited by Herwarth Walden, 92–108. Berlin: Schlesinger, [1908].

McGrath, William J. *Dionysian Art and Populist Politics in Austria*. New Haven: Yale University Press, 1974.

Merian, Hans. *Richard Strauss' Tondichtung "Also sprach Zarathustra": Eine Studie über die moderne Programmsymphonie*. Leipzig: Meyers, 1899.

Molnár, Géza von. "'Wilhelm Meister' from a Romantic Perspective. Aspects of Novalis' Predisposition That Resulted in His Initial Preference for Goethe's Novel." In *Versuche zu Goethe: Festschrift für Erich Heller*, edited by Volker Dürr and Géza von Molnár, 235–47. Heidelberg: Lothar Stiehm, 1976.

Moser, Hans Joachim. *Das deutsche Lied seit Mozart*. Rev. ed. Vol. 2. Tutzing: Hans Schneider, 1968.

———. *Geschichte der deutschen Musik*. Vol. 3. Stuttgart: J. G. Cotta, 1928.

da Motta, José Vianna. *Nachtrag zu Studien bei Hans von Bülow*. Berlin: Friedrich Luckhardt, 1896.

Munter, Friedrich. *Ludwig Thuille: Ein erster Versuch*. Munich: Drei Masken, 1923.

Newcomb, Anthony. "The Birth of Music Out of the Spirit of Drama." *Nineteenth-Century Music* 5 (1981): 38–66.

Newman, Ernest. *Richard Strauss*. London: J. Lane, 1908. Reprint, Freeport, N.Y.: Books for Libraries Press, 1969.

Niemann, Walter. *Die Musik der Gegenwart*. Berlin: Schuster & Loeffler, 1921.

Nietzsche, Friedrich. *Also sprach Zarathustra: Ein Buch für Alle und Keinen*. Part 6, vol. 1, *Nietzsche Werke*. Edited by Giorgio Colli and Mazzino Montinari. Berlin: de Gruyter, 1968.

———. *Götzen-Dämmerung*. Part 6, vol. 3, *Nietzsche Werke*. Edited by Giorgio Colli and Mazzino Montinari. Berlin: de Gruyter, 1968.

———. *Jenseits von Gut und Böse*. Part 6, vol. 2, *Nietzsche Werke*. Edited by Giorgio Colli and Mazzino Montinari. Berlin: de Gruyter, 1968.

———. *Menschliches, Allzumenschliches*. Part 6, vol. 1, *Nietzsche Werke*. Edited by Giorgio Colli and Mazzino Montinari. Berlin: de Gruyter, 1968.

———. *Zur Genealogie der Moral*. Part 6, vol. 2, *Nietzsche Werke*. Edited by Giorgio Colli and Mazzino Montinari. Berlin: de Gruyter, 1968.

Nodnagel, Ernst Otto. *Jenseits von Wagner und Liszt*. Königsberg: Ostpreußischen Druckerei und Verlagsanstalt, 1902.

Petersen, Barbara A. "*Die Händler und die Kunst:* Richard Strauss as Composers' Advocate." In *Richard Strauss: New Perspectives on the Composer and His Work*, edited by Bryan Gilliam, 115–32. Durham, N.C.: Duke University Press, 1992.

Pfeiffer, Theodor. *Studien bei Hans von Bülow*. Berlin: Friedrich Luckhardt, 1894.

Phipps, Graham H. "The Logic of Tonality in Strauss's *Don Quixote*: A Schoenbergian Evaluation." *Nineteenth-Century Music* 9 (1986): 191–93.

Pretzsch, Paul, ed. *Cosima Wagner und Houston Stewart Chamberlain im Briefwechsel 1888–1908*. Leipzig: Philipp Reclam jun., 1934.

Publig, Maria. *Richard Strauss: Bürger, Künstler, Rebell. Eine historische Annäherung*. Graz: Styria, 1999.

Puffett, Derrick. "'Lass Er die Musi, wo sie ist': Pitch Specificity in Strauss." In *Richard Strauss and His World*, edited by Bryan Gilliam, 138–63. Princeton: Princeton University Press, 1992.

———. "*Salome* as Music Drama." In *Richard Strauss: "Salome,"* edited by Derrick Puffett, 58–87. Cambridge: Cambridge University Press, 1989.

Richard, August. "Alexander Ritter und seine Tafelrunde." *Zeitschrift für Musik* 100 (1933): 817–18.

Richie, Alexandra. *Faust's Metropolis: A History of Berlin.* New York: Carroll & Graf, 1998.

Ritter, Alexander. "Drei Kapitel: von Franz Liszt, von der 'heiligen Elizabeth' in Karlsruhe, und von unserm ethischen Defekt." *Bayreuther Blätter* 13 (1890): 380–88.

———. "Vom Spanisch-Schönen." *Allgemeine Musikzeitung* 18, no. 10 (1891): 128–29.

———. "Was lehrt uns das Festspieljahr 1891?" *Bayreuther Blätter* 15 (1892): 1–20.

Rolland, Romain. "French Music and German Music." In *Richard Strauss and Romain Rolland: Correspondence*, edited and translated by Rollo Myers, 197–215. London: Calder and Boyars, 1968.

Rösch, Friedrich. "Alexander Ritter" [twelve-part series] *Musikalisches Wochenblatt*, 30 December 1897–14 April 1898, 9ff.

Safranski, Rüdiger. *Schopenhauer and the Wild Years of Philosophy.* Translated by Ewald Osers. Cambridge: Harvard University Press, 1990.

Schäfer, Theo. "Richard Strauss als Symphoniker." In *Richard Strauss Woche Muenchen. 23.–28. Juni.* Munich: F. Bruckmann, 1910.

Schillings, Max von. "Alexander Ritter." *Redende Kunst* 2 (1896).

Schlaffer, Hannebre. *Wilhelm Meister: Das Ende der Kunst und die Wiederkehr des Mythos.* Stuttgart: J. B. Metzler, 1980.

Schlechta, Karl. "Goethes 'Wilhelm Meister.'" In *Goethes "Wilhelm Meister": Zur Rezeptionsgeschichte der Lehr- und Wanderjahre*, edited by Klaus F. Gille, 257–61. Königstein: Athenäum, 1979.

Schlötterer, Roswitha. "Richard Strauss uns sein Münchner Kreis." In *Jugendstilmusik?: Münchner Musikleben 1890–1918*, edited by Robert Münster and Hellmut Hell, 13–24. Wiesbaden: Dr. Ludwig Reichert, 1987.

Schmid, Mark-Daniel. "The Tone Poems of Richard Strauss and Their Reception History from 1887–1908." PhD diss., Northwestern University, 1997.

Schoenberg, Arnold. "Brahms the Progressive." In *Style and Idea.* Edited by Leonard Stein. New York: St. Martin's Press, 1975.

———. "New Music." In *Style and Idea.* Edited by Leonard Stein. Translated by Leo Black. New York: St. Martin's Press, 1975.

———. *Sämtliche Werke.* Abteilung 6, Reihe B, Band 20, *Streichquartette I, Kritischer Bericht, Skizzen Fragmente.* Edited by Christian Martin Schmidt. Mainz: B. Schott's Söhne, 1986.

Schopenhauer, Arthur. *Die Welt als Wille und Vorstellung.* Vol. 1. Stuttgart: Philipp Reclam Jun., 1987.

———. *Die Welt als Wille und Vorstellung.* Vol. 2, *Arthur Schopenhauer's sämmtliche Werke.* Leipzig: Brockhaus, 1888.

Schuh, Willi. "Gruelmärchen um Richard Strauss' *Metamorphosen*." *Schweizerische Musikzeitung* 103 (1963): 438.

———, ed. *Richard Strauss: Briefe an die Eltern, 1882–1906*. Zurich: Atlantis, 1954.

———, ed. *Richard Strauss: Briefwechsel mit Will Schuh*. Zurich: Atlantis, 1969.

Schuh, Willi. *Richard Strauss. Jugend und frühe Meisterjahre. Lebenschronik 1864–1898*. Zurich: Atlantis, 1976.

Schuhmann, Bruno, ed. *Musik und Kultur: Festschrift zum 50. Geburtstag Arthur Seidl's*. Regensburg: Gustav Bosse, 1913.

Schüler, Winfried. *Der Bayreuther Kreis von seiner Entstehung bis zum Ausgang der wilhelminischen Ära*. Münster: Aschendorrf, 1971.

Seidl, Arthur. "Also sang Zarathustra." In *Moderner Geist in der deutschen Tonkunst: Gedanken eines Kulturpsychologen zur Wende des Jahrhunderts*. Regensburg: Gustave Bosse, [1913].

———. "Dramaturg und Drama." *Bayreuther Blätter* 13 (1890): 121–42.

———. "Das Jenseits der Künstlers. Eine Besprechung." *Bayreuther Blätter* 18 (1895): 137–53.

———. "Jesus der Arier—Christentum oder Buddhismus?" *Bayreuther Blätter* 13 (1890): 45–65.

———. "Die Kuntstlehre der Meistersinger. Ein Vortrag." *Bayreuther Blätter* 16 (1893): 362–92.

———. Obituary of Richard Pohl. *Bayreuther Blätter* 20 (1897): 116–21.

———. Review of *Elemente der Metaphysik*, by Paul Deussen. *Bayreuther Blätter* 9 (1886): 91–97.

———. Review of *Helden und Welt*, by Heinrich von Stein. *Bayreuther Blätter* 11 (1888): 198–200.

———. "Richard Strauss: Eine Charakter-Skizze." In *Straussiana: Aufsätze zur Richard Strauß-Frage aus drei Jahrzehnten*. Regensburg: Gustave Bosse, [1913].

———. "Richard Wagner's 'Parsifal' und Schopenhauer's 'Nirwana.'" *Bayreuther Blätter* 11 (1888): 277–306.

———. "Ueber musikalische Erziehung." *Bayreuther Blätter* 16 (1893): 2–10, 55–66.

———. *Die Wagner-Nachfolge im Musikdrama*. Vol. 3, *Wagneriana*. Berlin: Schuster, 1901.

Sengle, Friedrich. *Kontinuität und Wandlung: Einführung in Goethes Leben und Werk*. Edited by Marianne Tilch. Heidelberg: C. Winter, 1999.

Somfai, László. "Die musikalischen Gestaltwandlungen der Faust-Symphonie von Liszt." *Studia musicologica Academiae scientiarum hungaricae* 2 (1962): 87–137.

Specht, Richard. *Richard Strauss und sein Werk*. Vol. 1, *Der Künstler und sein Weg; Der Instrumentalkomponist*. Leipzig: E. P. Tal & Co., 1921.

Spotts, Frederic. *Bayreuth: A History of the Wagner Festival*. New Haven: Yale University Press, 1994.

Stein, Erwin, ed. *Arnold Schoenberg: Letters*. Translated by Eithne Wilkins and Ernst Kaiser. New York: St. Martin's Press, 1965.

Steinitzer, Max. *Richard Strauss*. Berlin: Schuster & Loeffler, 1911.

———. *Richard Strauss*. 4th–8th eds. Berlin: Schuster & Loeffler, 1914.

Stradal, August. "Lieder." In *Zum Andenken Alexander Ritters*, 23–24. Mannheim: Neue Musikalische Rundschau, 1897.

Strauss, Franz, and Alice Strauss, eds. *The Correspondence between Richard Strauss and Hugo von Hofmannsthal*. Translated by Hanns Hammelmann and Ewald Osers. Cambridge: Cambridge University Press, 1980.

Strauss, Gabriele, ed. *Lieber Collega!: Richard Strauss im Briefwechsel mit zeitgenössischen Komponisten und Dirigenten*. Berlin: Henschel, 1996.

Strauss, Richard. "Aus meinen Jugend- und Lehrjahren." In *Betrachtungen und Erinnerungen*. 2d ed. Edited by Willi Schuh. Zurich: Atlantis, 1957.

———. "Brief eines deutschen Kapellmeisters über das Bayreuther Orchester." *Bayreuther Blätter* 15 (1892): 126–32.

———. "Brief über das humanistische Gymnasium." In *Betrachtungen und Erinnerungen*. 2d ed. Edited by Willi Schuh. Zurich: Atlantis, 1957.

———. "Erinnerungen an Hans von Bülow." In *Betrachtungen und Erinnerungen*. 2d ed. Edited by Willi Schuh. Zurich: Atlantis, 1957.

———. "Erinnerungen an meinen Vater." In *Betrachtungen und Erinnerungen*. 2d ed. Edited by Willi Schuh. Zurich: Atlantis, 1957.

———. "Letzte Aufzeichnung." In *Betrachtungen und Erinnerungen*. 2d ed. Edited by Willi Schuh. Zurich: Atlantis, 1957.

———. "Meine Werke in guter Zusammenstellung." In *Betrachtungen und Erinnerungen*. 2d ed. Edited by Willi Schuh. Zurich: Atlantis, 1957.

———. "Tagebuch der Griechenland- und Ägyptenreise (1892)." In *Richard Strauss Jahrbuch 1854*, edited by Willi Schuh, 89–96. Bonn: Boosey & Hawkes, 1954.

———. "Vom melodischen Einfall." In *Betrachtungen und Erinnerungen*. 2d ed. Edited by Willi Schuh. Zurich: Atlantis, 1957.

Streller, Friedbert. "Der junge Strauss und die Renaissance der Stirnerschen Anarchismus." In *Richard Strauss: Leben, Werk, Interpretation, Rezeption. Internationales Gewandhaus-Symposium 1989*, 62–65. Leipzig: C. F. Peters, 1991.

Suder, Alexander L., ed. *Ludwig Thuille*. Tutzing: Hans Schneider, 1993.

Teibler, Hermann. "Alexander Ritter." *Die Musik* 1, no. 4 (1902).

Tenberg, Reinhard. *Die deutsche Till Eulenspiegel-Rezeption bis zum Ende des 16. Jahrhunderts*. Würzburg: Königshausen und Neumann, 1996.

Tenschert, Roland. "Um das Erbe Franz Liszts: Die Programmusik." In *3 x 7 Variationen über das Thema Richard Strauss*. Vienna: Wilhelm Frick, 1944.

Thuille, Ludwig, and Rudolf Louis. *Grundriss der Harmonielehre*. Stuttgart: C. Grüninger, 1907.

Todd, R. Larry. "Strauss before Liszt and Wagner: Some Observations." In *Richard Strauss: New Perspectives on the Composer and His Work*, edited by Bryan Gilliam, 3–40. Durham, N.C.: Duke University Press, 1992.

Trenner, Franz. *Richard Strauss: Dokumente seines Lebens und Schaffens*. Munich: C. H. Beck, 1954.

———, ed. *Richard Strauss / Ludwig Thuille: Ein Briefwechsel*. Tutzing: Hans Schneider, 1980.

———. *Richard Strauss Werkverzeichnis*. 2d ed. Vienna: Verlag Dr. Richard Strauss, 1999.

———. *Die Skizzenbücher von Richard Strauss*. Tutzing: Hans Schneider, 1977.

———, ed., with assistance of Gabriele Strauss. *Cosima Wagner / Richard Strauss: Ein Briefwechsel*. Tutzing: Hans Schneider, 1978.

Unger, Anette. *Welt, Leben und Kunst als Themen der "Zarathustra-Kompositionen" von Richard Strauss und Gustav Mahler*. Frankfurt am Main: Peter Lang, 1992.

Urban, Erich. *Richard Strauss*. Berlin: Gose & Tetzlaff, 1901.

———. *Strauss contra Wagner*. Berlin: Schuster & Loeffler, 1902.

Vaihinger, Hans. *The Philosophy of "As If."* London: K. Paul, Trench, Truber, and Co., 1924.

Veltzke, Veit. *Vom Patron zum Paladin: Wagnervereinigungen im Kaiserreich von der Reichsgründung bis zur Jahrhundertwende*. Bochum: Brockmeyer, 1987.

Wachten, Edmund. "Das Formproblem in der sinfonischen Dichtungen von Richard Strauss." PhD diss., University of Berlin, 1933.

Wagner, Richard. "Über Franz Liszt's symphonische Dichtungen: Brief an M. W." In *Sämtliche Schriften und Dichtungen*. Vol. 5. Leipzig: Breitkopf und Härtel, [1911].

Walden, Herwarth, ed. *Richard Strauss: Symphonies und Tondichtungen*. Berlin: Schlesinger, [1908].

Warfield, Scott. "Friedrich Wilhelm Meyer (1818–1893): Some Biographical Notes on Strauss's Composition Teacher." *Richard-Strauss-Blätter*, n.s., 37 (June 1997): 54–74.

———. "The Genesis of Richard Strauss's *Macbeth*." PhD diss., University of North Carolina at Chapel Hill, 1995.

———. "'Reveal nothing to him of his market value': The Publication of Strauss's First Three Tone Poems." Unpublished manuscript.

Webster, James. *Haydn's "Farewell" Symphony and the Idea of Classical Style*. Cambridge: Cambridge University Press, 1991.

Wellbery, David E. *The Specular Moment: Goethe's Early Lyric and the Beginnings of Romanticism*. Stanford, Calif.: Stanford University Press, 1996.

Werbeck, Walter. *Die Tondichtungen von Richard Strauss*. Tutzing: Hans Schneider, 1996.

Whittall, Arnold. *Musical Composition in the Twentieth Century*. Oxford: Oxford University Press, 1999.

Wilde, Denis. *The Development of Melody in the Tone Poems of Richard Strauss*. Lewiston, N.Y.: Edwin Mellen Press, 1990.

Wilhelm, Kurt. *Richard Strauss: An Intimate Portrait*. Translated by Mary Whittall. New York: Rizzoli, 1989.

Williams, John R. *The Life of Goethe: A Critical Biography*. Oxford: Blackwell, 2001.

Williamson, John. *Strauss: "Also sprach Zarathustra."* Cambridge: Cambridge University Press, 1993.

Wolzogen, Hans von. "Gedenkwort." In *Zum Andenken Alexander Ritters*, 19. Mannheim: Neue Musikalische Rundschau, 1897.

———. *Lebensbilder*. Regensburg: Gustav Bosse, 1923.

Wunderlich, Werner. *Till Eulenspiegel*. Munich: Wilhelm Fink, 1984.

Youmans, Charles. "The Private Intellectual Context of Richard Strauss's *Also sprach Zarathustra*." *Nineteenth-Century Music* 22 (1998): 101–26.

———. "Richard Strauss's *Guntram* and the Dismantling of Wagnerian Musical Metaphysics." PhD diss., Duke University, 1996.

———, ed. "Ten Letters from Alexander Ritter to Richard Strauss, 1887–1894." *Richard Strauss Blätter*, n.s., 35 (June 1996): 3–24.

———. "The Twentieth-Century Symphonies of Richard Strauss." *The Musical Quarterly* 84 (2000): 238–58.

Zagiba, Franz. *Johann L. Bella (1843–1936) und das Wiener Musikleben*. Vienna: Notringes der wissenschaftliche Verbände Österreichs, 1955.

Zimdars, Richard. *The Piano Master Classes of Hans von Bülow*. Bloomington: Indiana University Press, 1993.

Index

Charles Youmans is Assistant Professor of Musicology at Penn State University.

DATE DUE